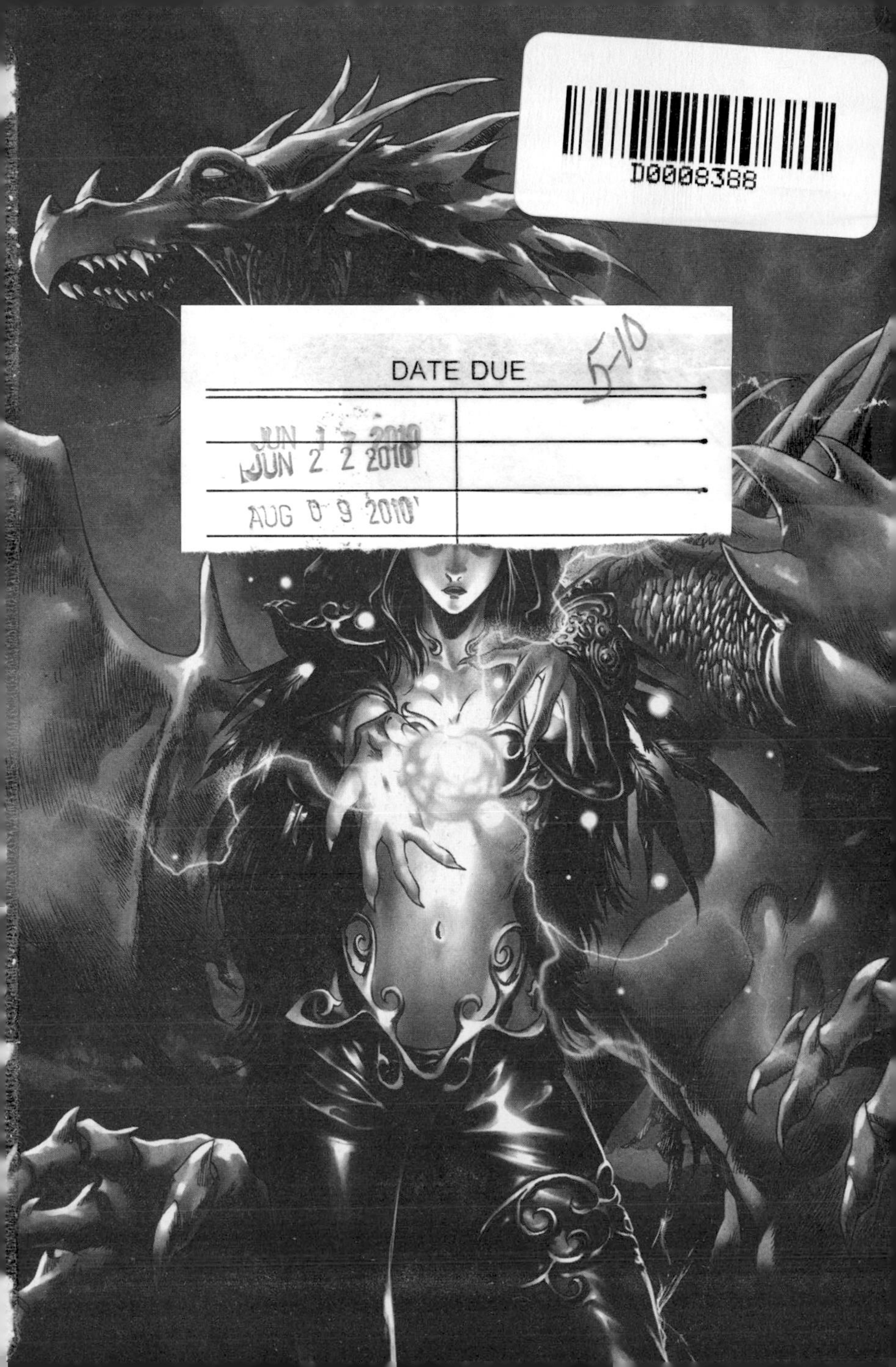

Warcraft®: The Sunwell Trilogy™ Vol. 3

Written by Richard A. Knaak

Illustrated by Jae-Hwan Kim

Lettering and Layout - Rob Steen
Production Artist - Lucas Rivera
Cover Artist - Jae-Hwan Kim
Cover Design - James Lee

Editor - Rob Tokar
Digital Imaging Manager - Chris Buford
Pre-Production Supervisor - Erika Terriquez
Art Director - Anne Marie Horne
Production Manager - Elisabeth Brizzi
Managing Editor - Vy Nguyen
Editor-in-Chief - Rob Tokar
VP of Production - Ron Klamert
Publisher - Mike Kiley
President and C.O.O. - John Parker
C.E.O. and Chief Creative Officer - Stuart Levy

A TOKYOPOP® Manga

TOKYOPOP and are trademarks or registered trademarks of TOKYOPOP Inc.

TOKYOPOP Inc.
5900 Wilshire Blvd. Suite 2000
Los Angeles, CA 90036

E-mail: info@TOKYOPOP.com
Come visit us online at www.TOKYOPOP.com

Special thanks to Chris Metzen, Lisa Pearce, Cory Jones, Brian Hsieh, Gloria Soto, and Matt Kassan.

ISBN: 978-1-4278-0780-9

First TOKYOPOP printing: May 2007

10 9 8 7 6 5 4 3 2 1

Printed in the USA

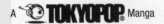

Warcraft®
The Sunwell Trilogy™

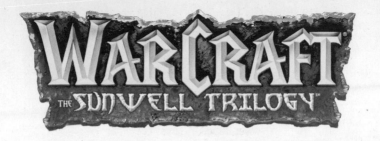

Volume 3

Ghostlands

Written by
Richard A. Knaak

Illustrated by
Jae-Hwan Kim

TOKYOPOP®

HAMBURG // LONDON // LOS ANGELES // TOKYO

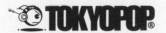

HISTORY OF THE WORLD OF

The world of Azeroth has long been plagued by the misuse of magic. Originally, only dragons and night elves were able to practice the mystic arts, though eventually even humans began to wield the unstable energy. Unfortunately, the unrestrained spell-casting eventually caught the attention of a malevolent, extra-dimensional force known as the Burning Legion.

The Burning Legion's first attempt to invade Azeroth, known as the War of the Ancients, was only thwarted after many lives were lost and the world's sole continent was shattered. With their second attempt, the Burning Legion used the orcs from the world of Draenor as their pawns.

Twisted and corrupted by the Burning Legion's influence, the orcs invaded Azeroth through the Dark Portal. After many ferocious battles, this Second War ended with the orcs' defeat and imprisonment. Still determined to conquer Azeroth, the Burning Legion created one of its most twisted servants, the Lich King, to weaken Azeroth's defenders.

The Lich King spread a plague of death and terror across Azeroth that was meant to snuff out human civilization. All those who died from the dreaded plague would arise as the undead, and their spirits would be bound to the Lich King's iron will forever.

The army of the dead swept across the land, and Quel'Thalas, the glorious homeland of the high elves which had stood for thousands of years, was no more. The undead Scourge then moved south to Dalaran, and then to Kalimdor, home of the night elves.

Though the undead Scourge was stopped at Kalimdor, they had essentially transformed Lordaeron and Quel'Thalas into toxic Plaguelands. Grieving for the loss of their homeland, most of the high elves have adopted a new name and a new mission. Calling themselves blood elves, they now seek out and siphon magic from any available source, including demons.

Meanwhile, half of the undead forces staged a coup for control over the undead empire. Eventually, the banshee Sylvanas Windrunner and her rebel undead--known as the Forsaken--claimed the ruined capital city of Lordaeron as their own and vowed to drive the Scourge from the land.

Currently the Lich King resides in Northrend; he is rumored to be rebuilding the citadel of Icecrown. His trusted lieutenant, Kel'Thuzad, commands the Scourge in the Plaguelands. Sylvanas and her rebel Forsaken hold only the Tirisfal Glades, a small portion of the war-torn kingdom, while the humans, orcs, and night elves are trying to rebuild their societies.

WarCraft®
The Sunwell Trilogy™

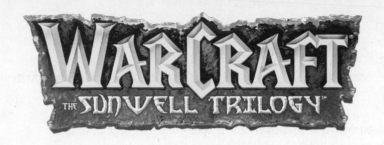

The story thus far...

The Sunwell was a pool of mystical energy that was the essence of the high elves' lives. Located in the elven city of Quel'Thalas, this source of magic was as important to the elves as eating or breathing. They used its vast power to build their cities, mold the landscape and make whatever they desired. Unfortunately, Dar'Khan was a high elf who desired much more than the rest of his brethren, leading him to an unholy pact with Arthas, the corrupted human knight who would later become the Lich King.

Dar'Khan enabled the undead Scourge to bypass Quel'Thalas' fabled defenses while he drained the Sunwell's energies. While his proud home was overrun by vicious, zombified corpses, and Dar'Khan fought his fellow elven sorcerers for control of the well, something went horribly wrong. The Sunwell's power exploded spectacularly, ravaging what little remained untouched by the Scourge. Dar'Khan was saved by the power of his dark lord, and sent across the continent in search of the Sunwell's escaped magic...though he was not alone in his quest.

MALYGOS, LORD OF THE BLUE DRAGONFLIGHT, COMMANDED
YOUNG KALECGOS TO INVESTIGATE A STRANGE SURGE OF
MAGICAL POWER. HOWEVER, BEFORE HE COULD REACH HIS
DESTINATION, KALEC WAS SHOT DOWN BY A MOTLEY BAND
OF DRAGON HUNTERS LED BY HARKYN GRYMSTONE.

ASSUMING THE FORM OF A HALF-ELF TO ESCAPE THE
HUNTERS' NETS, A WOUNDED KALEC WAS AIDED BY
ANVEENA, A KIND, INNOCENT MAIDEN WHO LIVED NEARBY.
KALEC TRIED TO WARN ANVEENA
AWAY, BUT SHE SEEMED
UNCONCERNED ABOUT THE
PURSUING HUNTERS. EVEN MORE
REMARKABLY, THE YOUNG WOMAN
SEEMED UNFAZED BY KALEC'S
TRUE NATURE, THOUGH MOST
PEOPLE'S REACTION TO MEETING A
DRAGON WOULD BE TO FLEE OR
TRY TO KILL IT.

STILL ON THE RUN FROM
GRYMSTONE'S BAND, KALEC AND
ANVEENA FOUND ANVEENA'S HOME
REDUCED TO BURNING WRECKAGE
BY DAR'KHAN, WHO PLACED PAIN-
INDUCING MYSTICAL COLLARS
AROUND THEIR NECKS TO FORCE
THEM TO REVEAL ALL THEY KNEW
ABOUT THE SUNWELL.

DAR'KHAN TRIED TORTURING
KALEC FOR INFORMATION, BUT
HE WAS INTERRUPTED BY THE
ARRIVAL OF TYRYGOSA, A
FEMALE BLUE DRAGON WHO IS

Kalecgos
A young blue dragon. Though trapped in
humanoid form by a mystical collar Dar'Khan
placed around his neck, Kalec retains many
of his magical talents, including the ability to
create a sword out of nothingness.

ALSO KALEC'S INTENDED. TOGETHER, TYRI AND KALEC
MANAGED TO WIPE OUT DAR'KHAN'S UNDEAD SERVANTS
AND DRIVE THE ELF AWAY...BUT THEY COULD NOT
REMOVE THE COLLARS HE HAD PLACED ON HIS TWO
CAPTIVES.

SIFTING THROUGH THE SHATTERED TIMBERS OF
ANVEENA'S HOME IN SEARCH OF HER PARENTS, THE TRIO
INSTEAD DISCOVERED A STRANGE EGG, WHICH HOUSED AN
EVEN STRANGER WINGED SERPENT. ANVEENA NAMED
HIM RAAE (FOR THE NOISE HE MAKES) AND KALEC AND
TYRI SUSPECTED THAT THE BIZARRE CREATURE MIGHT
HAVE SOMETHING TO DO WITH THE SUNWELL ENERGY
THAT HAD DRAWN THE ATTENTION OF THE BLUE
DRAGONFLIGHT AND DAR'KHAN.

SINCE KALEC'S COLLAR PREVENTED HIM FROM
TRANSFORMING, TYRI CARRIED HER COMPANIONS TO THE
TOWN OF TARREN MILL IN SEARCH OF BOREL, A MAN

Anveena
A caring, innocent young maiden. Anveena helped a wounded Kalecgos escape from dragon
hunters, though her home and parents were destroyed.

whom Anveena's parents had spoken of often. Though she had never met him, she believed he might be able to help them remove Dar'Khan's collars. The group attracted a lot of attention in the small town, including that of paladin Jorad Mace.

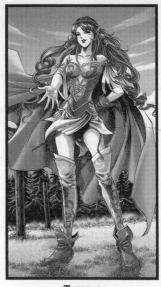

Tyrygosa
A female blue dragon and Kalec's intended. When forced to assume a humanoid shape, she refuses to look merely human. In her words, "At least elves are aesthetically pleasing."

At Tarren Mill, Grymstone had the dragons cornered when he suddenly found that he and his band were surrounded by the undead Scourge and Dar'Khan. Dar'Khan revealed that he had disguised himself as a human prince to provide the vengeful dwarf with the resources needed to kill any dragons that might be drawn to the area by the Sunwell's power. As Dar'Khan prepared to take Raac from Anveena, a surprise attack from Jorad Mace helped the dragons and dragon hunters turn the tide.

With their combined efforts, the undead were wiped out and Dar'Khan was consumed in a blast of Tyri's dragon fire. When Mace informed the others that they might find Borel on Aerie Peak, an apologetic Harkyn Grymstone advised them to seek his cousin, Loggi, who resided in the mountains near there.

Hoping that Loggi might be able to remove the magical collars, Kalec, Anveena, Tyri, Raac and Jorad Mace searched not only for the dwarf, but

Jorad Mace
A human paladin whose loyalty was sworn to Arthas...before Arthas betrayed his father, his homeland and his species. Mace is continually haunted by his terrible loss.

ALSO FOR THE MYSTERIOUS BOREL. THOUGH THEY EVENTUALLY FOUND LOGGI AT AERIE PEAK, THEY ALSO ENDED UP IN THE MIDDLE OF A WAR BETWEEN THE UNDEAD ICHOR AND THE FORSAKEN BARON MORDIS. MORDIS TRIED TO SACRIFICE ANVEENA TO DEFEAT ICHOR, ONLY TO BE DESTROYED HIMSELF ALONG WITH HIS UNDEAD OPPONENT. IN THE MIDST OF THE MELEE, KALEC WAS RESCUED FROM A POTENTIALLY FATAL FALL BY A MYSTERIOUS FORCE THAT SEEMED TO EMANATE FROM ANVEENA. THE SURPRISES ONLY MOUNTED AS THE SUPPOSEDLY DEAD DAR'KHAN SUDDENLY RE-APPEARED, KILLED LOGGI AND KIDNAPPED ANVEENA.

AND NOW--WITH ONLY THE QUESTIONABLE GUIDANCE OF RAAC TO AID THEM--KALEC, JORAD, AND TYRI MUST GIVE CHASE. THE TERRIBLE CHILL FILLING THE YOUNG BLUE'S BEING IS NOT FROM THE BATTLE IN THE SNOW, BUT RATHER BECAUSE HE FEARS HE KNOWS JUST WHERE THE MURDEROUS RENEGADE IS TAKING ANVEENA...

CHAPTER ONE
THE NIGHTMARE PLAINS

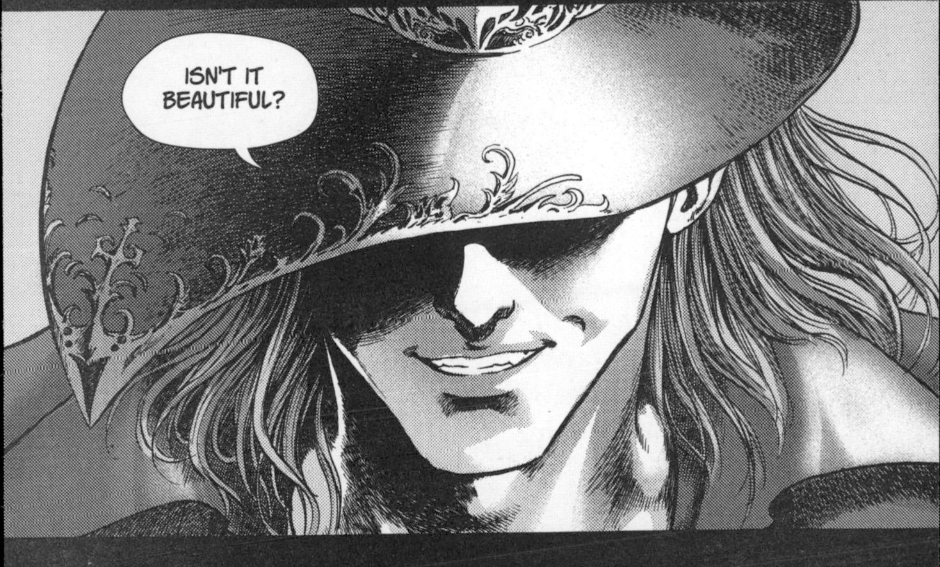
ISN'T IT BEAUTIFUL?

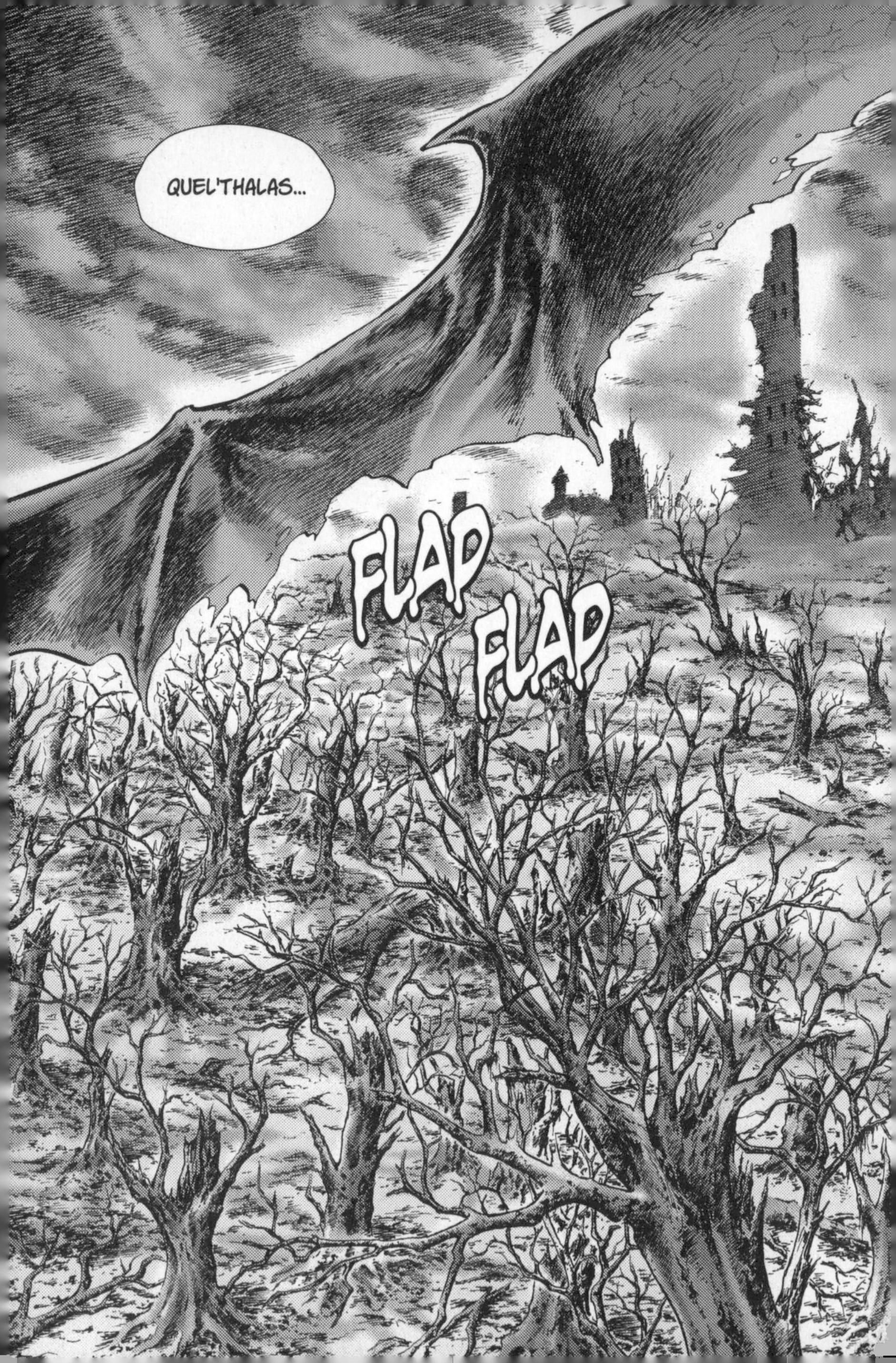
QUEL'THALAS...
FLAP
FLAP

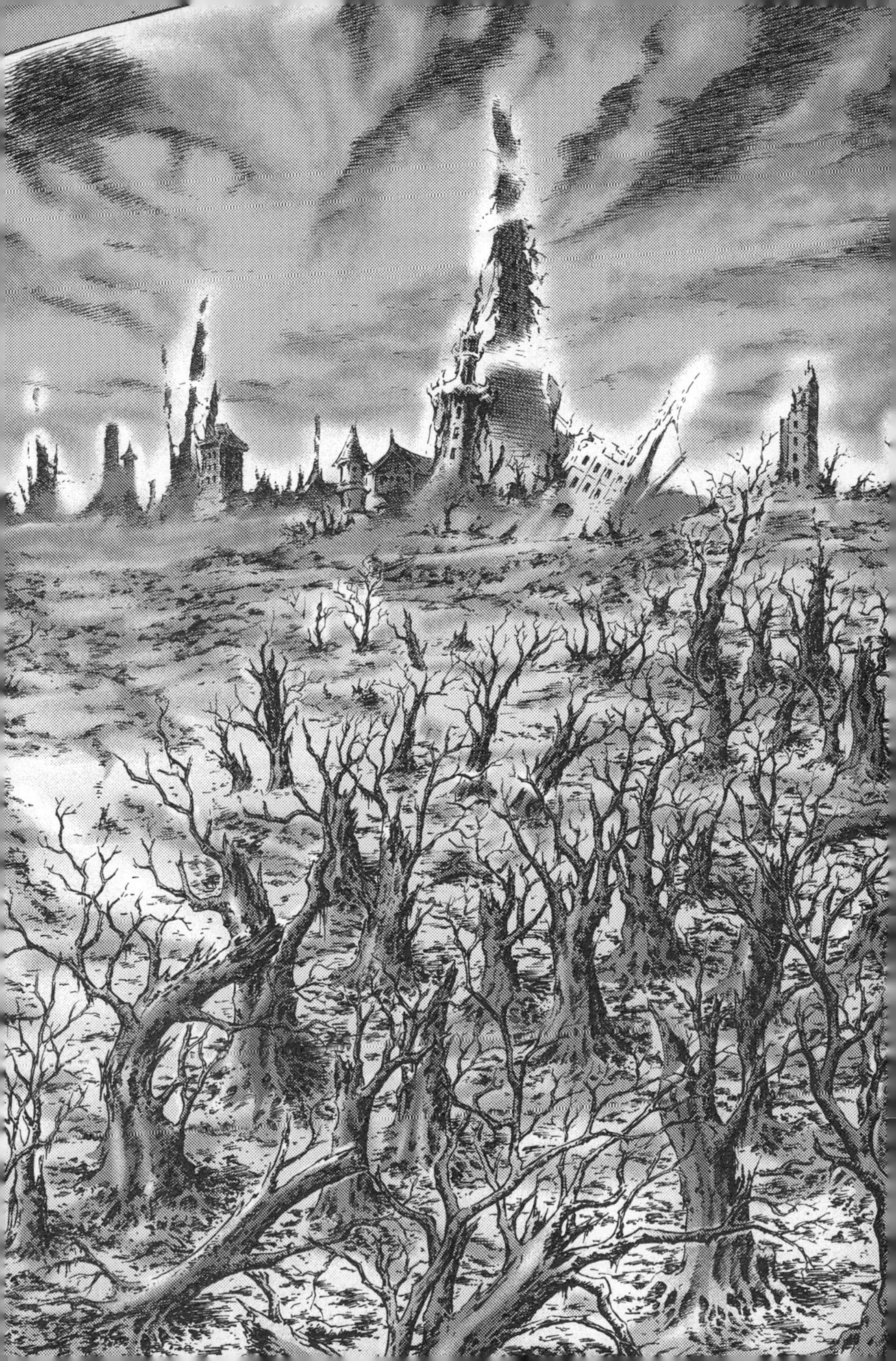

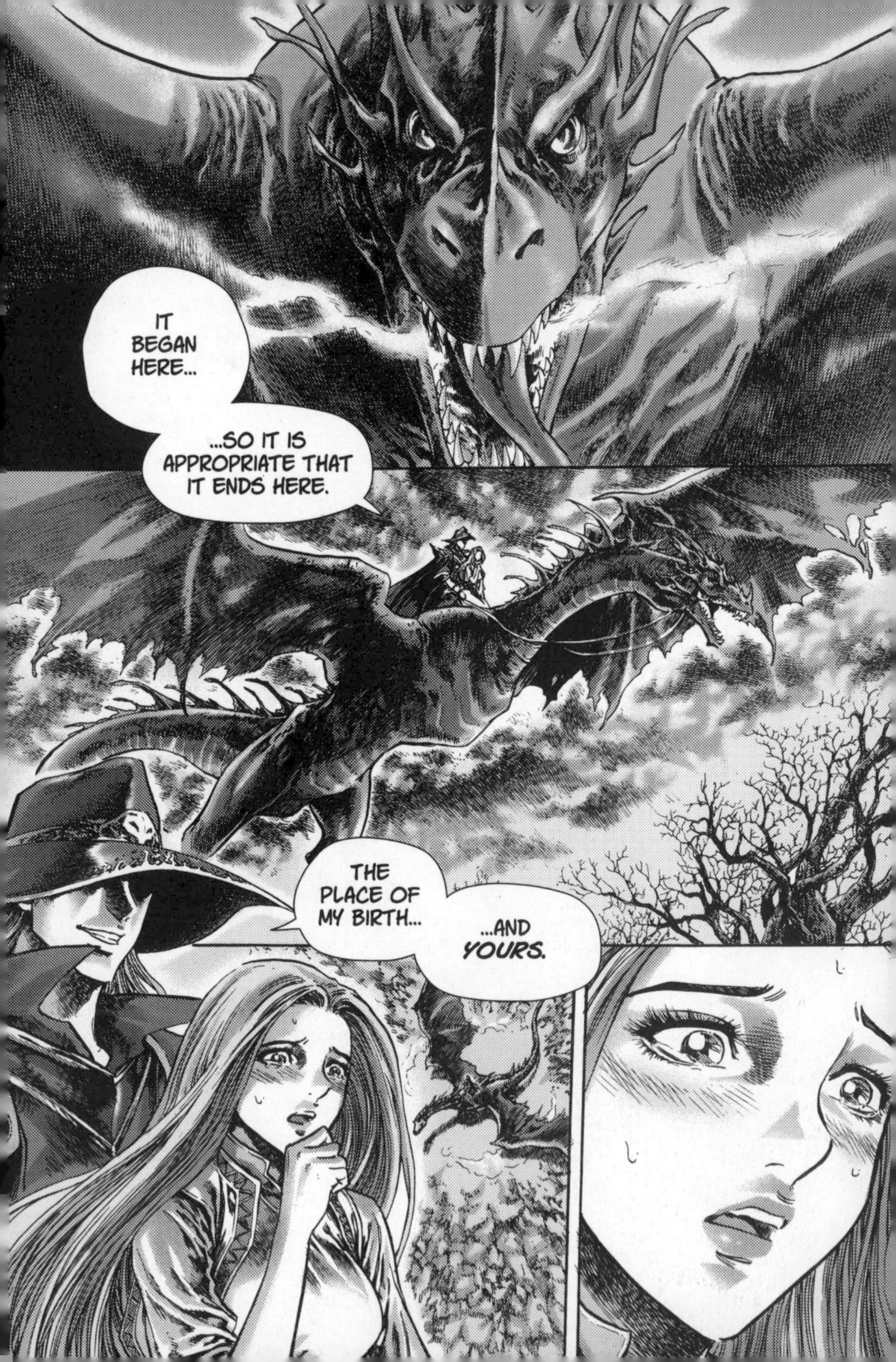
IT BEGAN HERE...
...SO IT IS APPROPRIATE THAT IT ENDS HERE.
THE PLACE OF MY BIRTH...
...AND *YOURS.*

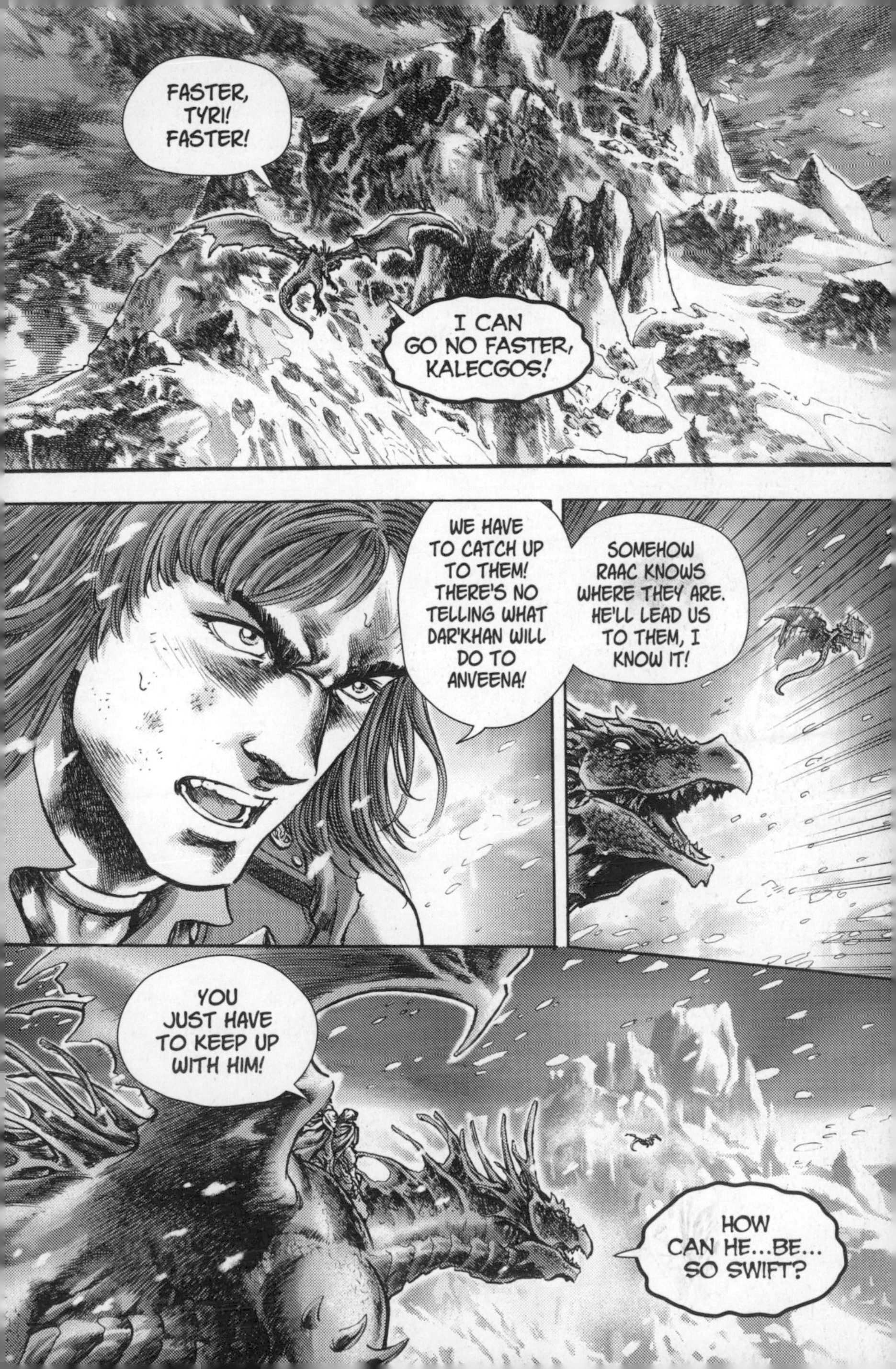
FASTER, TYRI! FASTER!
I CAN GO NO FASTER, KALECGOS!
WE HAVE TO CATCH UP TO THEM! THERE'S NO TELLING WHAT DAR'KHAN WILL DO TO ANVEENA!
SOMEHOW RAAC KNOWS WHERE THEY ARE. HE'LL LEAD US TO THEM, I KNOW IT!
YOU JUST HAVE TO KEEP UP WITH HIM!
HOW CAN HE...BE... SO SWIFT?

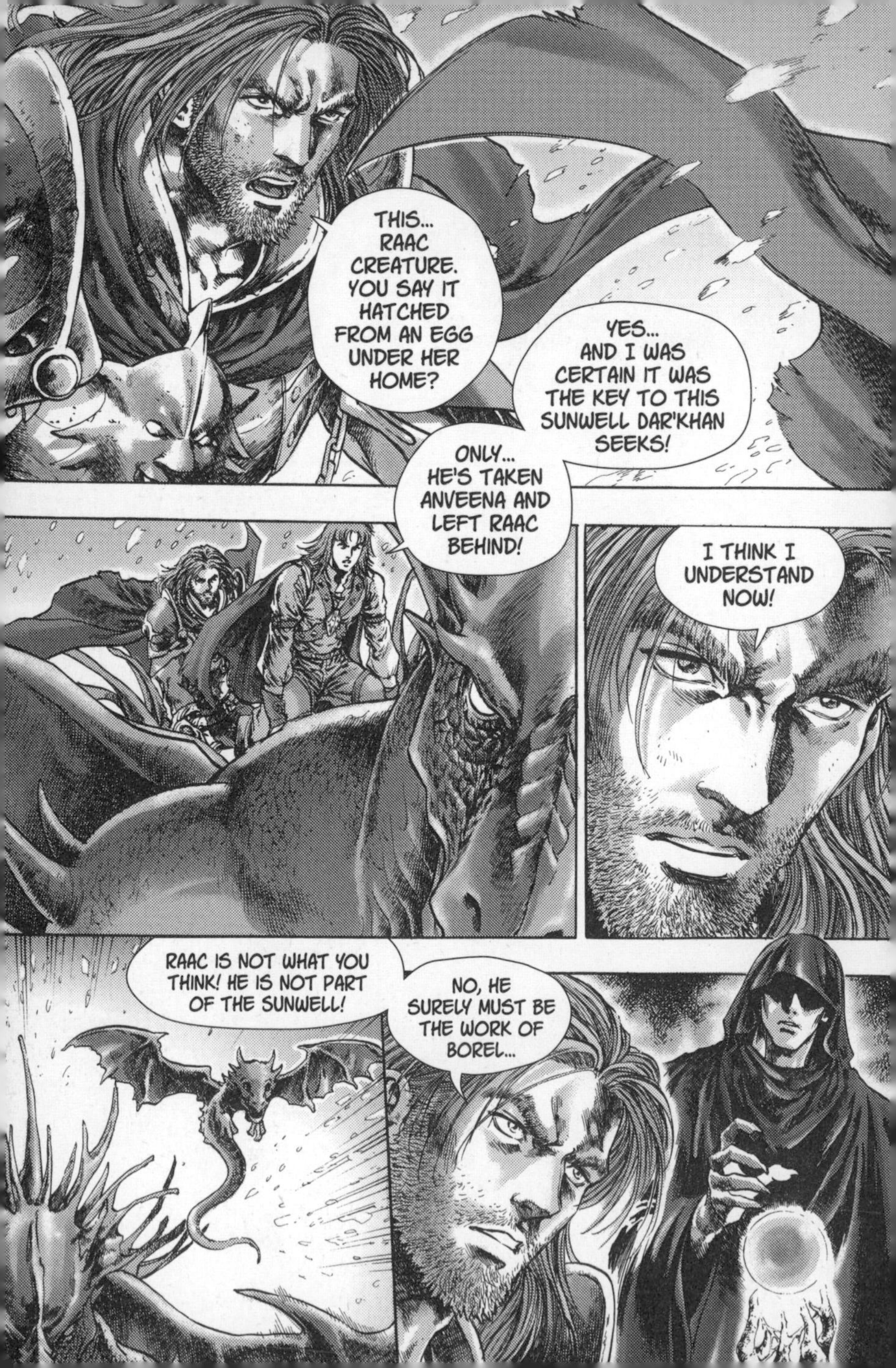
THIS... RAAC CREATURE. YOU SAY IT HATCHED FROM AN EGG UNDER HER HOME?
YES... AND I WAS CERTAIN IT WAS THE KEY TO THIS SUNWELL DAR'KHAN SEEKS!
ONLY... HE'S TAKEN ANVEENA AND LEFT RAAC BEHIND!
I THINK I UNDERSTAND NOW!
RAAC IS NOT WHAT YOU THINK! HE IS NOT PART OF THE SUNWELL!
NO, HE SURELY MUST BE THE WORK OF BOREL...

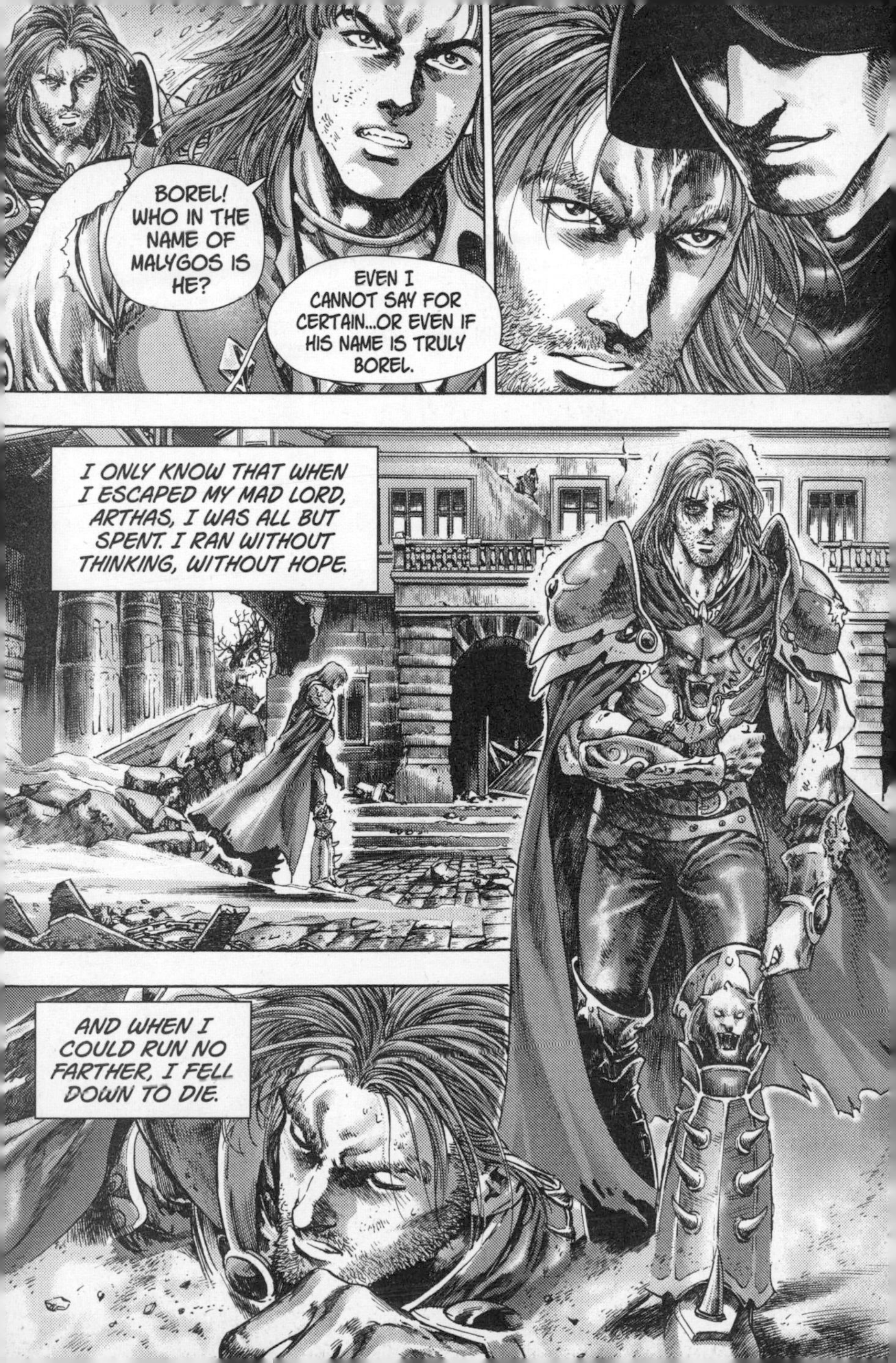
BOREL! WHO IN THE NAME OF MALYGOS IS HE?
EVEN I CANNOT SAY FOR CERTAIN...OR EVEN IF HIS NAME IS TRULY BOREL.
I ONLY KNOW THAT WHEN I ESCAPED MY MAD LORD, ARTHAS, I WAS ALL BUT SPENT. I RAN WITHOUT THINKING, WITHOUT HOPE.
AND WHEN I COULD RUN NO FARTHER, I FELL DOWN TO DIE.

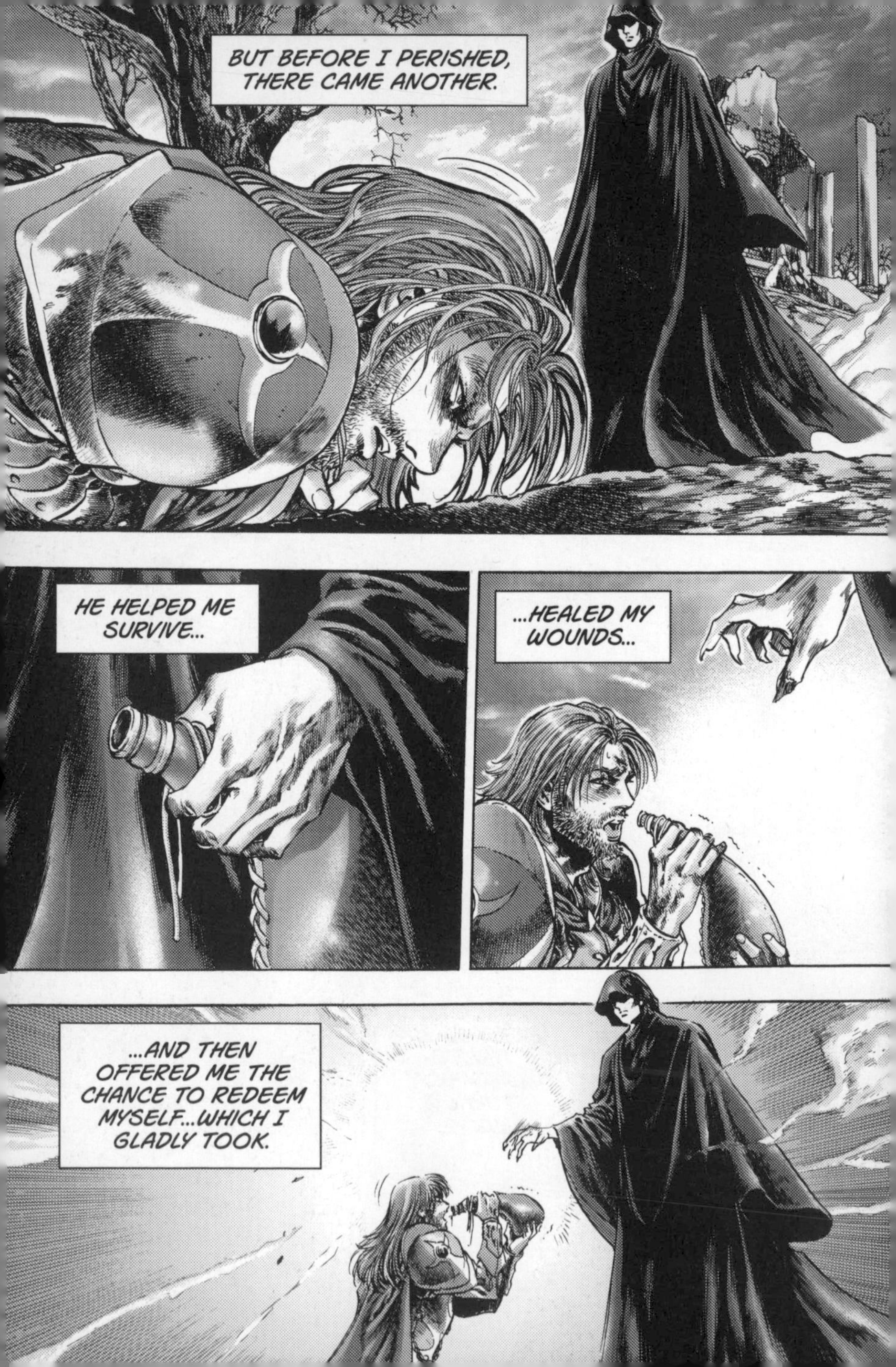
BUT BEFORE I PERISHED, THERE CAME ANOTHER.
HE HELPED ME SURVIVE...
...HEALED MY WOUNDS...
...AND THEN OFFERED ME THE CHANCE TO REDEEM MYSELF...WHICH I GLADLY TOOK.

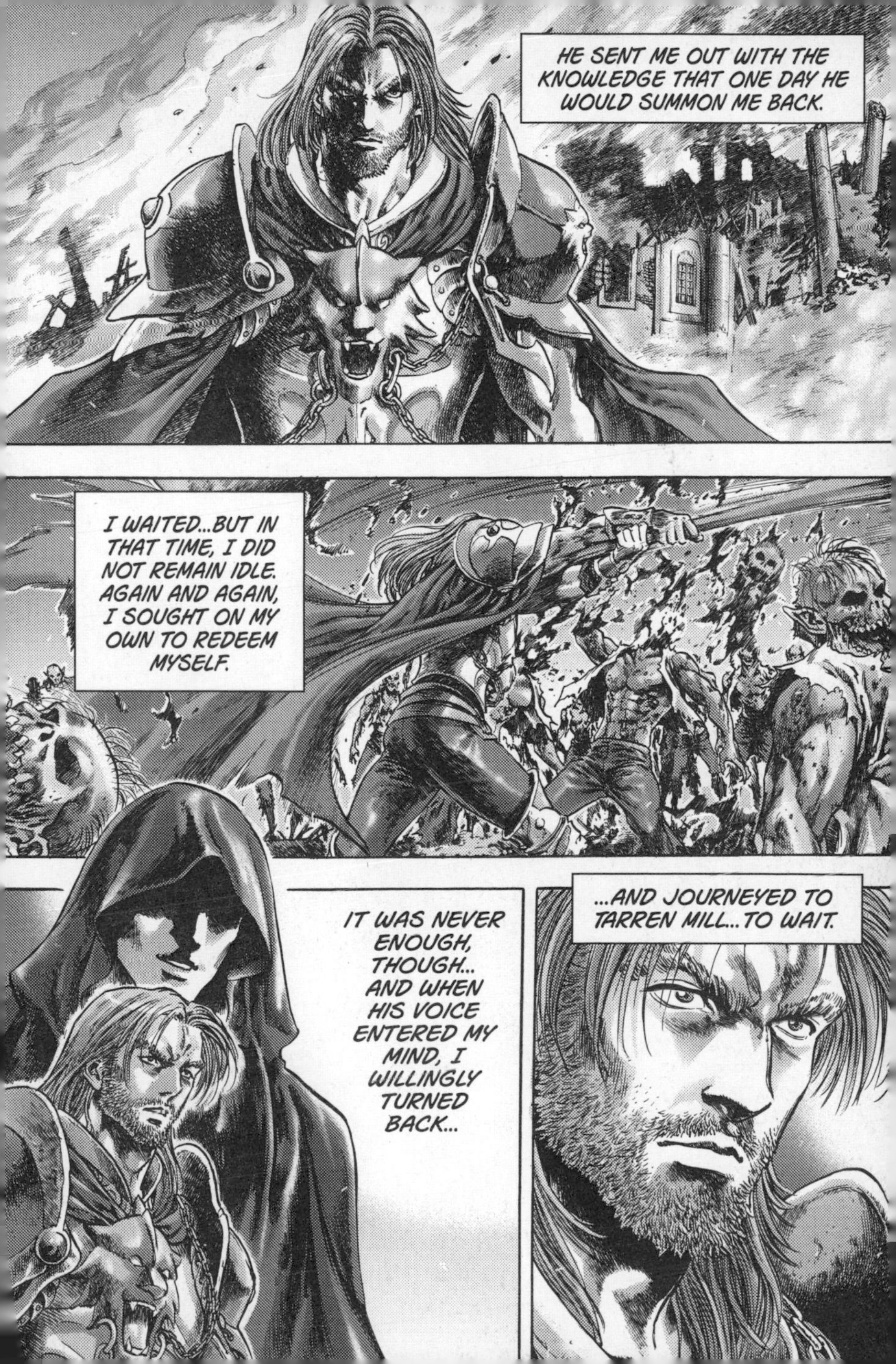
HE SENT ME OUT WITH THE KNOWLEDGE THAT ONE DAY HE WOULD SUMMON ME BACK.
I WAITED...BUT IN THAT TIME, I DID NOT REMAIN IDLE. AGAIN AND AGAIN, I SOUGHT ON MY OWN TO REDEEM MYSELF.
IT WAS NEVER ENOUGH, THOUGH... AND WHEN HIS VOICE ENTERED MY MIND, I WILLINGLY TURNED BACK...
...AND JOURNEYED TO TARREN MILL...TO WAIT.

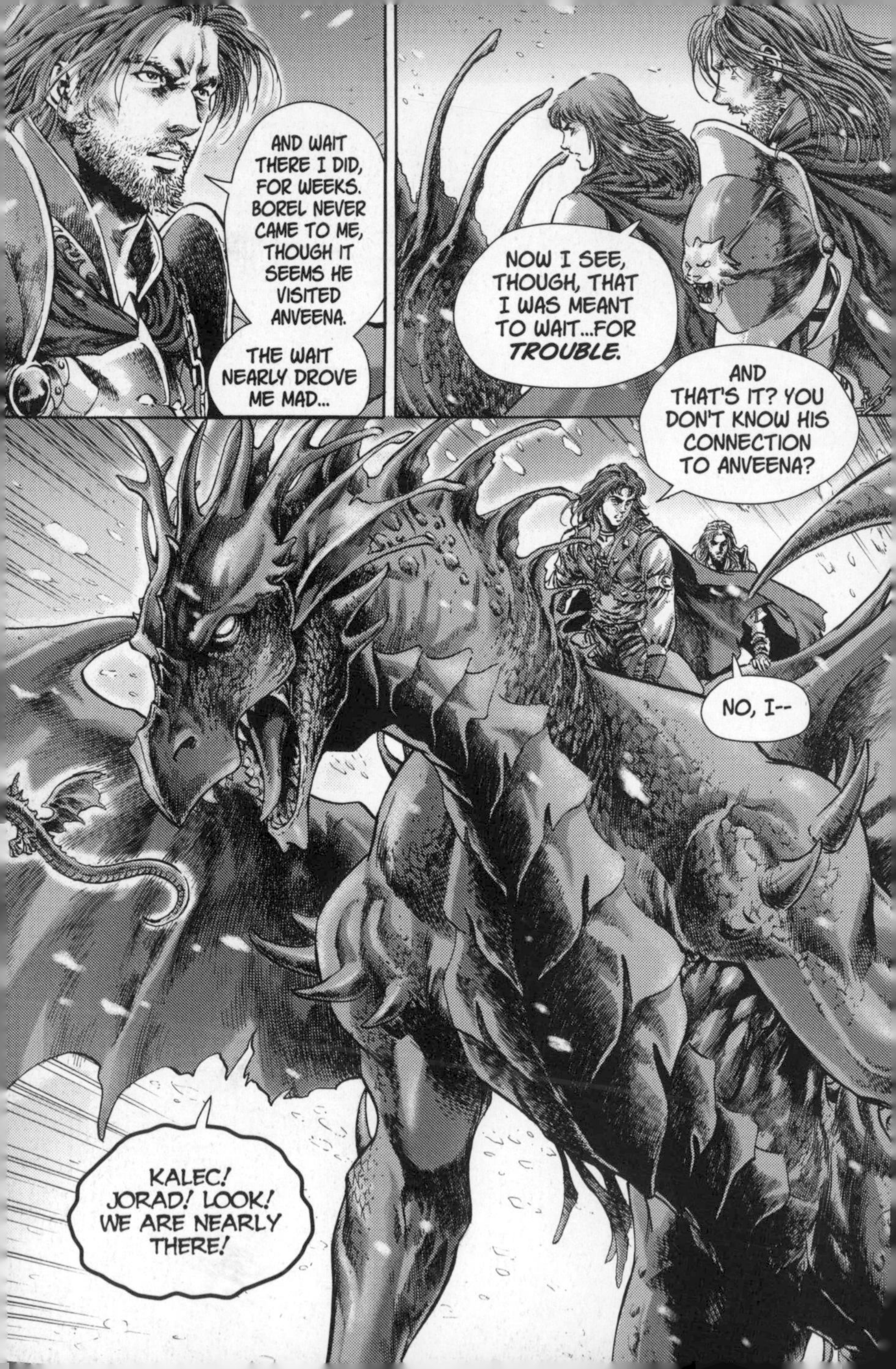
AND WAIT THERE I DID, FOR WEEKS. BOREL NEVER CAME TO ME, THOUGH IT SEEMS HE VISITED ANVEENA.
THE WAIT NEARLY DROVE ME MAD...
NOW I SEE, THOUGH, THAT I WAS MEANT TO WAIT...FOR *TROUBLE.*
AND THAT'S IT? YOU DON'T KNOW HIS CONNECTION TO ANVEENA?
NO, I--
KALEC! JORAD! LOOK! WE ARE NEARLY THERE!

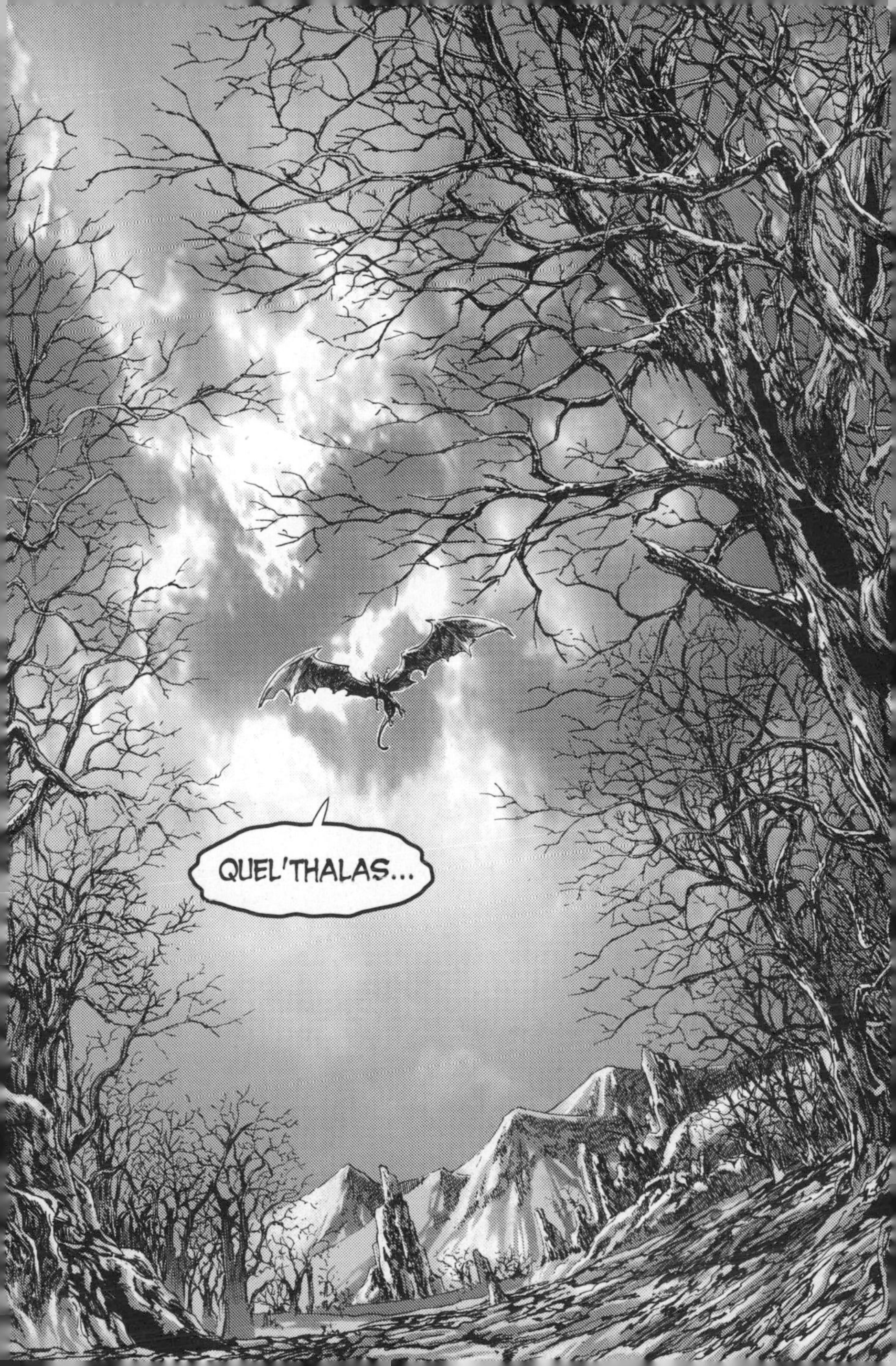
QUEL'THALAS...

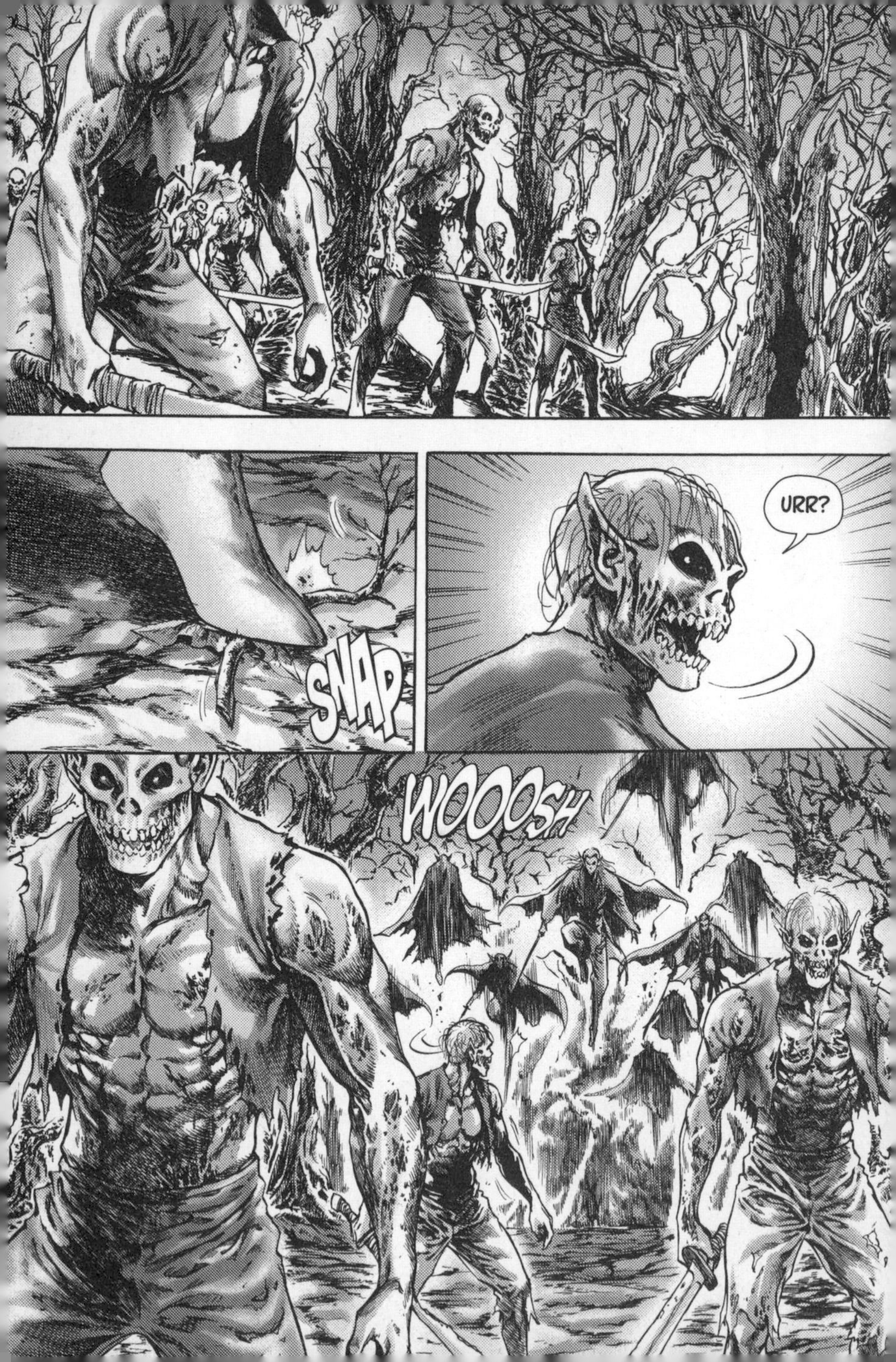
SNAP
URR?
WOOOSH

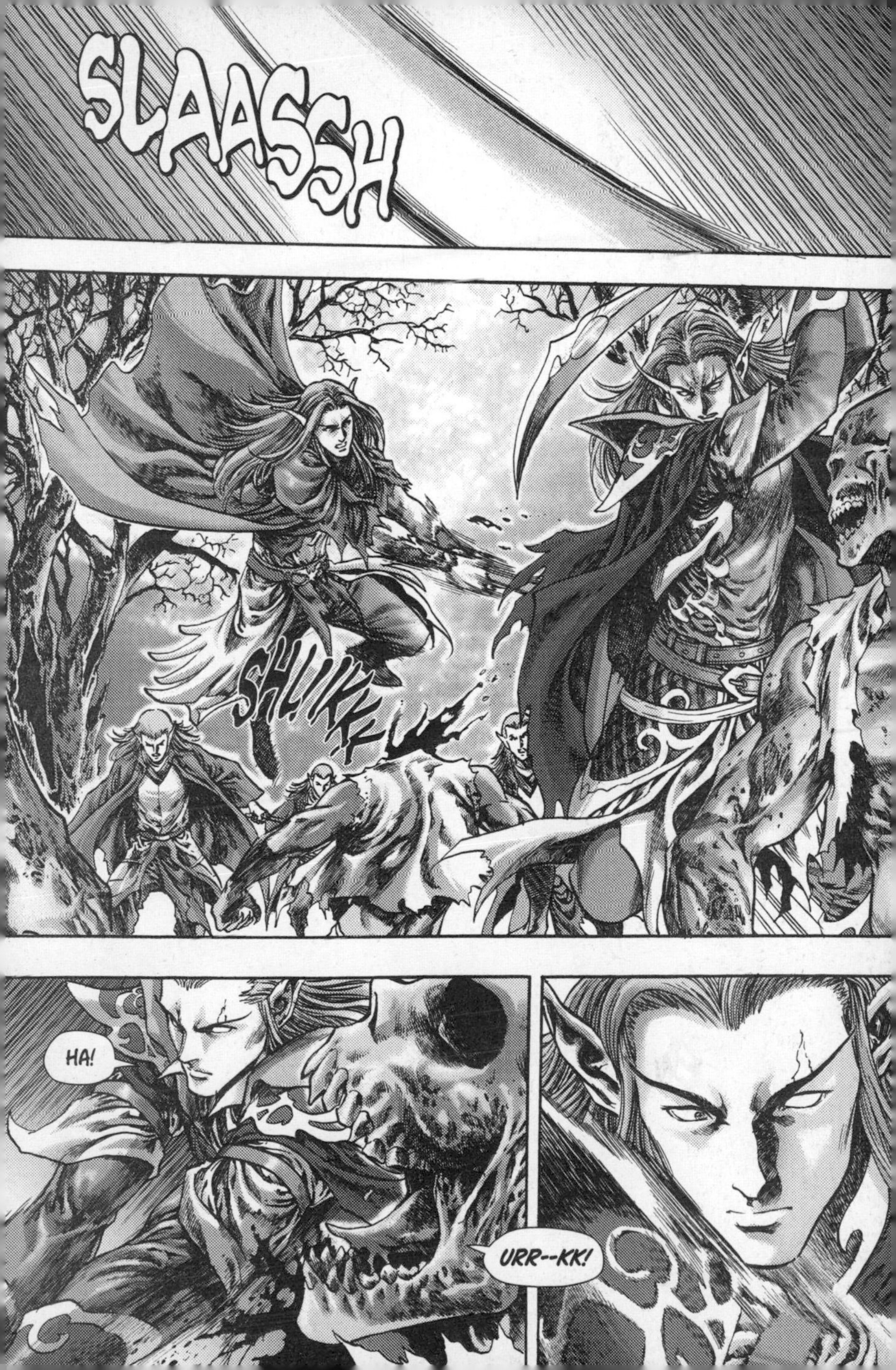
SLAASSH
SHUKKK
HA!
URR--KK!

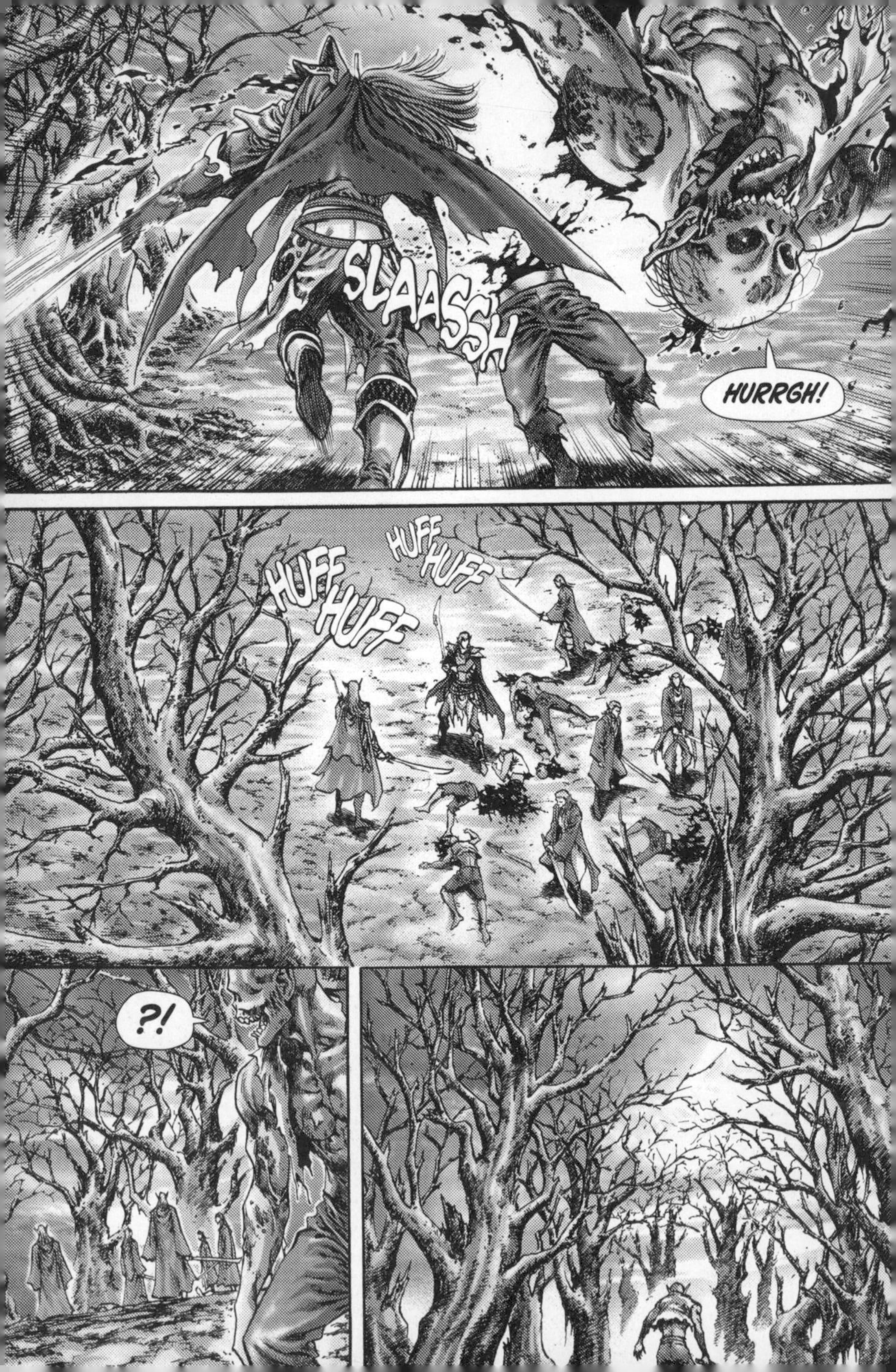
SLAASSH
HURRGH!
HUFF HUFF
HUFF HUFF
?!

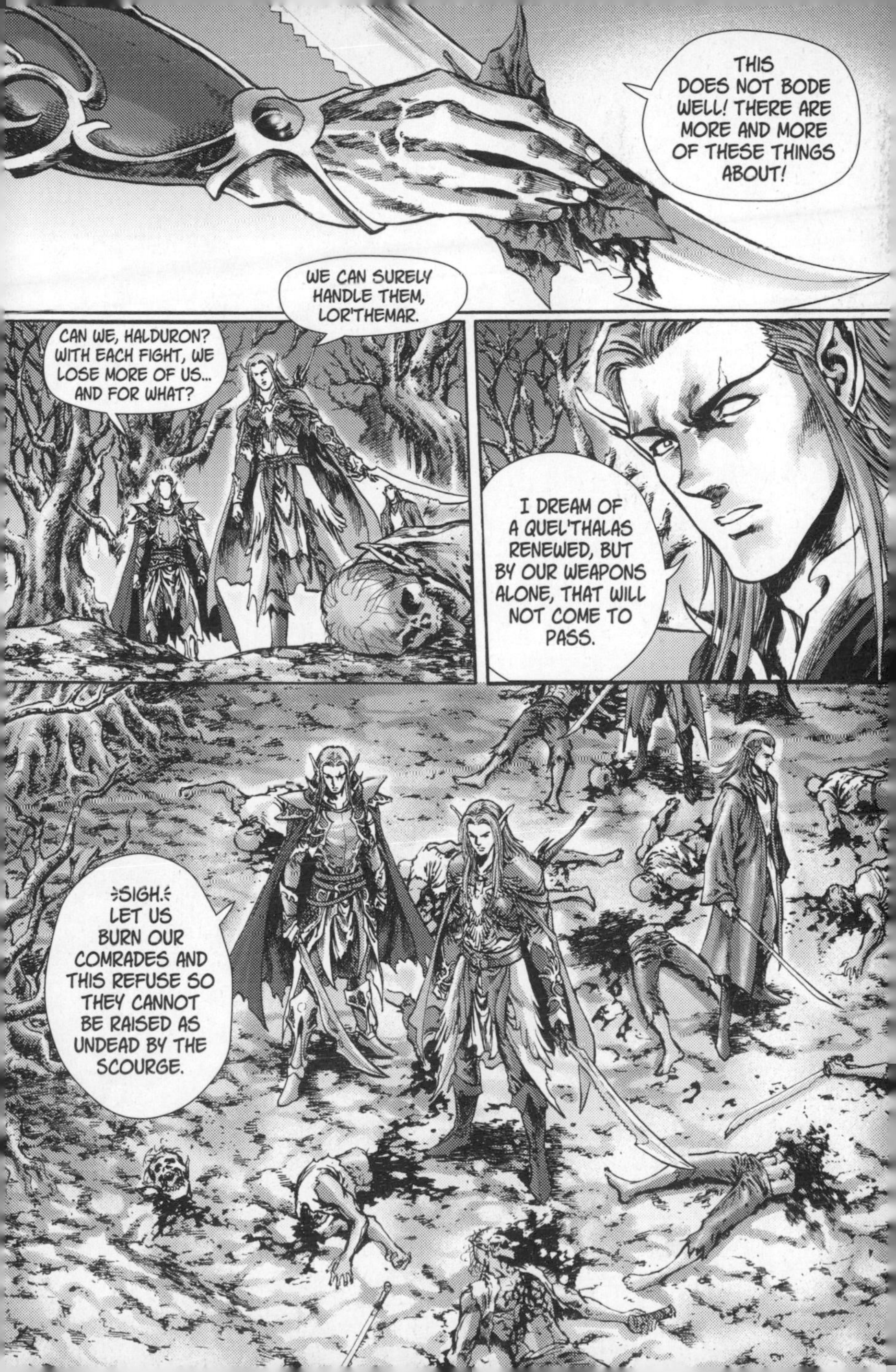
THIS DOES NOT BODE WELL! THERE ARE MORE AND MORE OF THESE THINGS ABOUT!
WE CAN SURELY HANDLE THEM, LOR'THEMAR.
CAN WE, HALDURON? WITH EACH FIGHT, WE LOSE MORE OF US... AND FOR WHAT?
I DREAM OF A QUEL'THALAS RENEWED, BUT BY OUR WEAPONS ALONE, THAT WILL NOT COME TO PASS.
SIGH. LET US BURN OUR COMRADES AND THIS REFUSE SO THEY CANNOT BE RAISED AS UNDEAD BY THE SCOURGE.

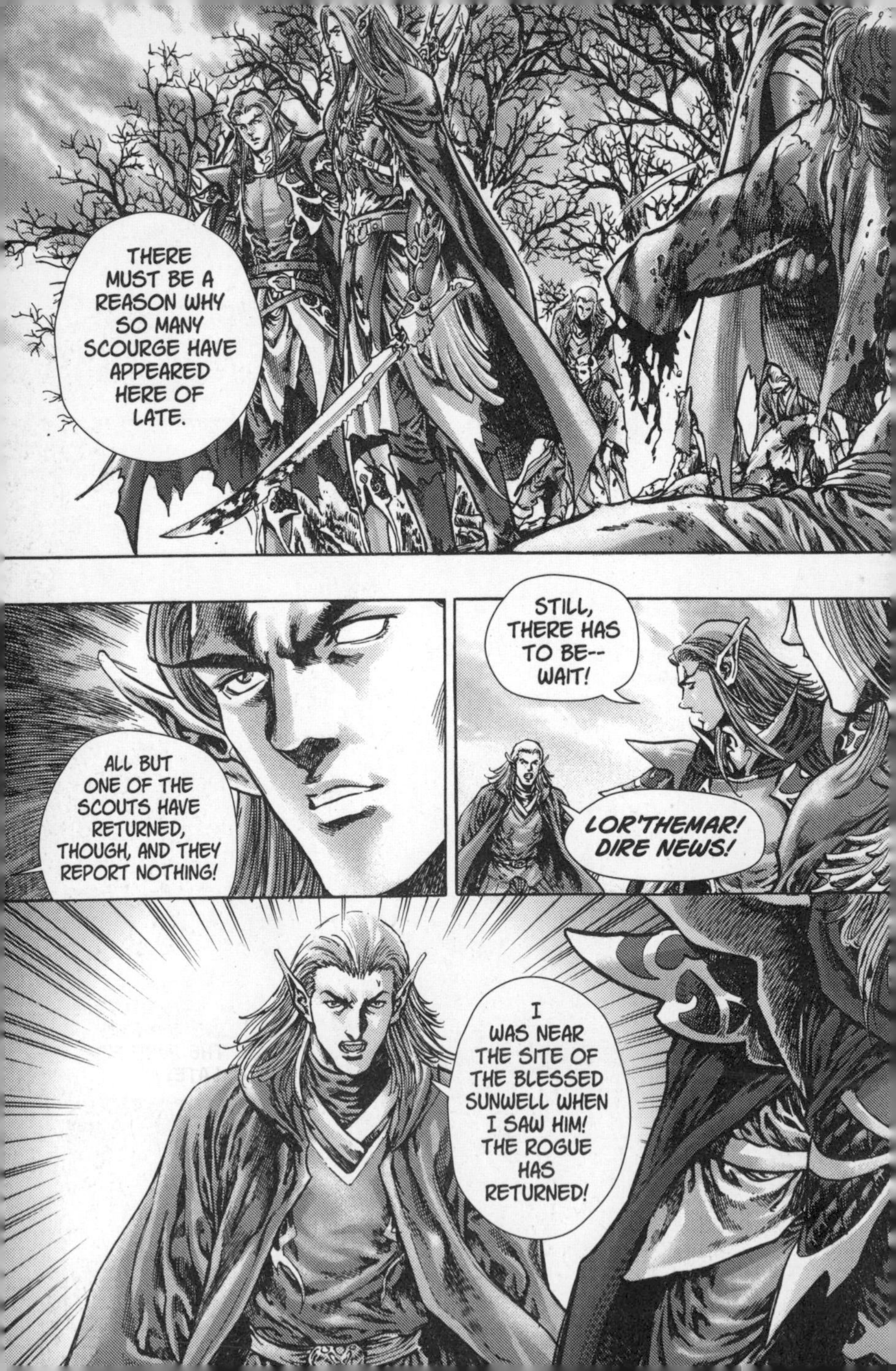
THERE MUST BE A REASON WHY SO MANY SCOURGE HAVE APPEARED HERE OF LATE.
ALL BUT ONE OF THE SCOUTS HAVE RETURNED, THOUGH, AND THEY REPORT NOTHING!
STILL, THERE HAS TO BE-- WAIT!
LOR'THEMAR! DIRE NEWS!
I WAS NEAR THE SITE OF THE BLESSED SUNWELL WHEN I SAW HIM! THE ROGUE HAS RETURNED!

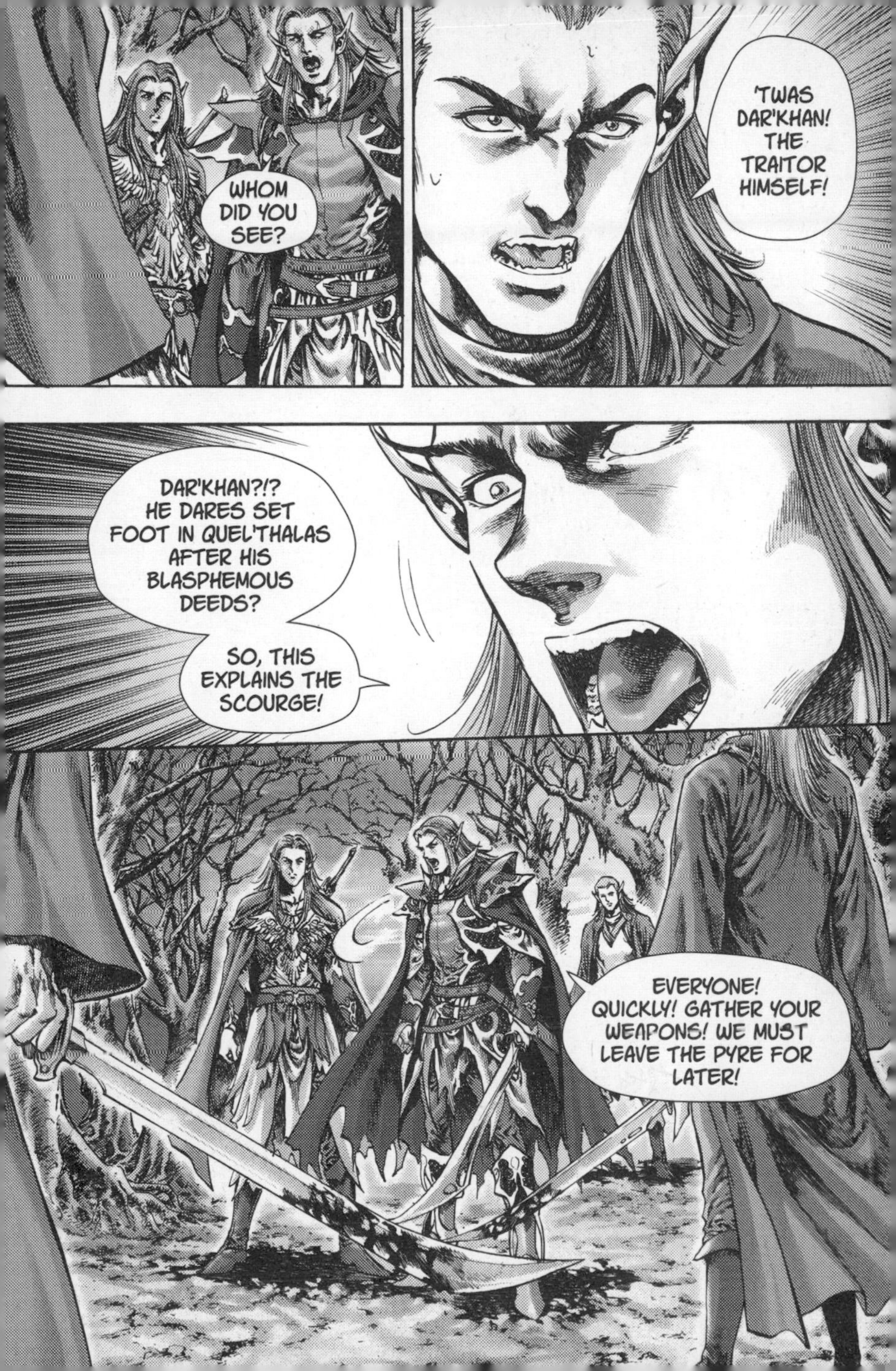
WHOM DID YOU SEE?
'TWAS DAR'KHAN! THE TRAITOR HIMSELF!
DAR'KHAN?!? HE DARES SET FOOT IN QUEL'THALAS AFTER HIS BLASPHEMOUS DEEDS?
SO, THIS EXPLAINS THE SCOURGE!
EVERYONE! QUICKLY! GATHER YOUR WEAPONS! WE MUST LEAVE THE PYRE FOR LATER!

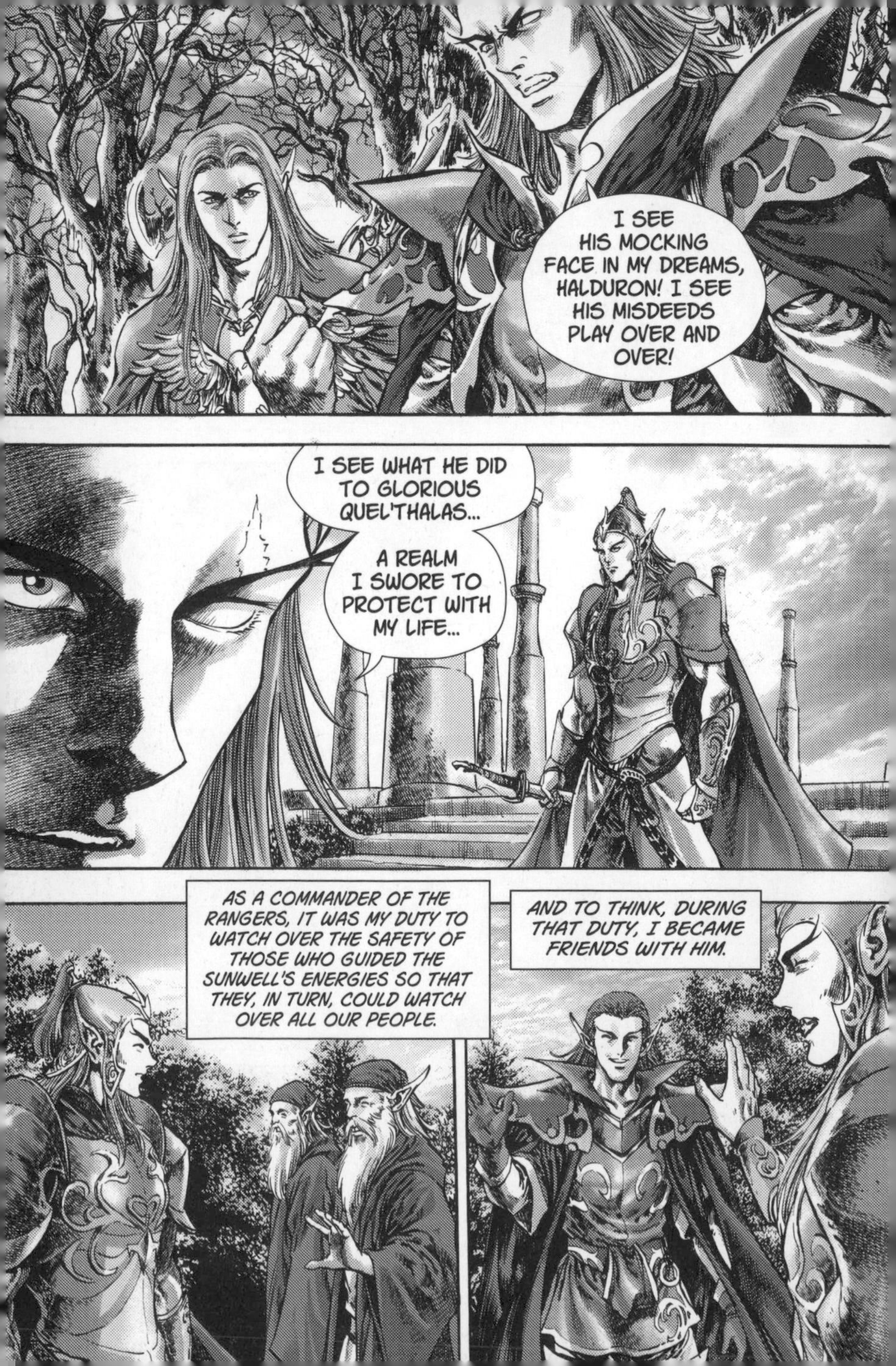
I SEE HIS MOCKING FACE IN MY DREAMS, HALDURON! I SEE HIS MISDEEDS PLAY OVER AND OVER!
I SEE WHAT HE DID TO GLORIOUS QUEL'THALAS...
A REALM I SWORE TO PROTECT WITH MY LIFE...
AS A COMMANDER OF THE RANGERS, IT WAS MY DUTY TO WATCH OVER THE SAFETY OF THOSE WHO GUIDED THE SUNWELL'S ENERGIES SO THAT THEY, IN TURN, COULD WATCH OVER ALL OUR PEOPLE.
AND TO THINK, DURING THAT DUTY, I BECAME FRIENDS WITH HIM.

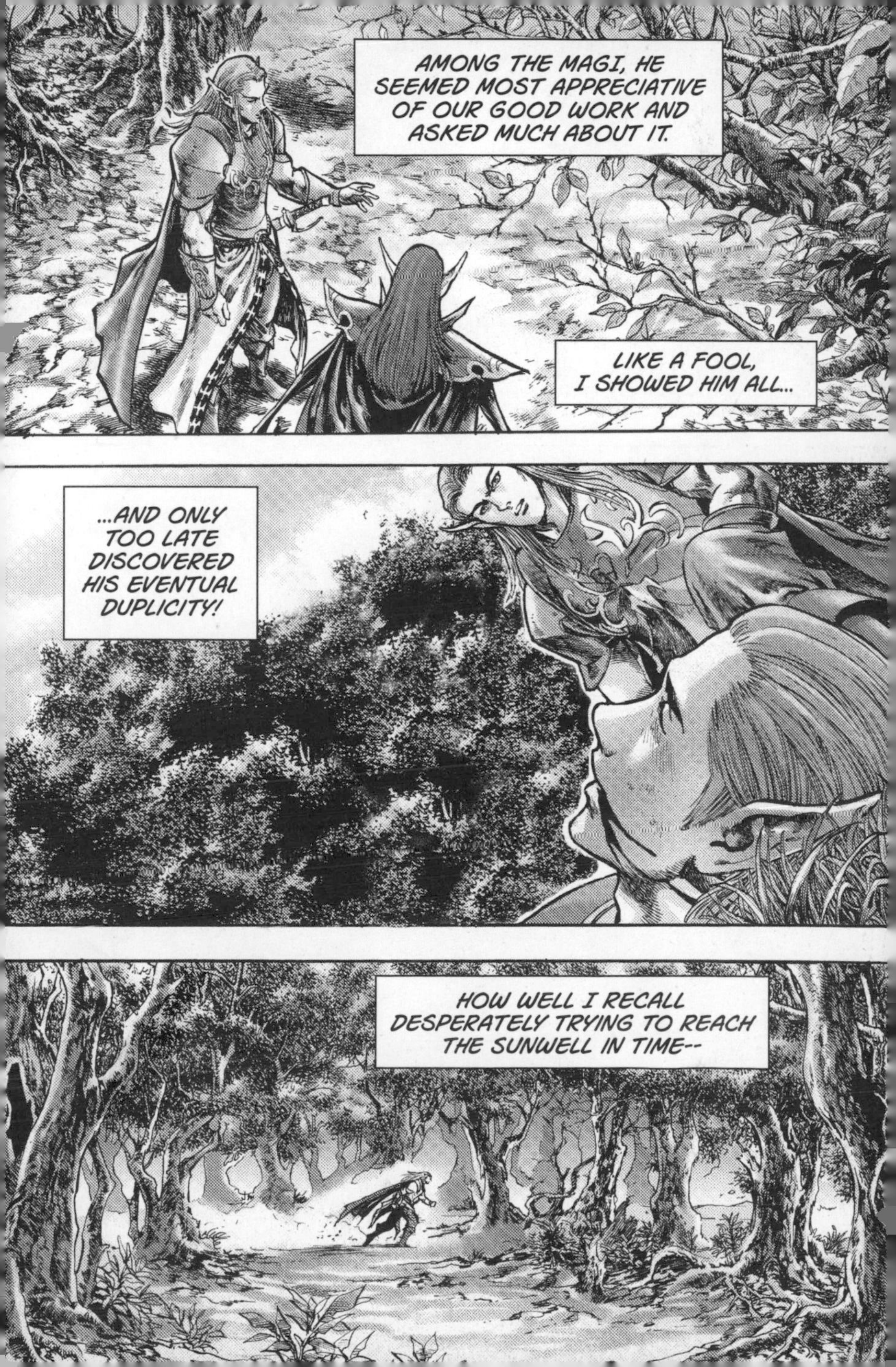
AMONG THE MAGI, HE SEEMED MOST APPRECIATIVE OF OUR GOOD WORK AND ASKED MUCH ABOUT IT.
LIKE A FOOL, I SHOWED HIM ALL...
...AND ONLY TOO LATE DISCOVERED HIS EVENTUAL DUPLICITY!
HOW WELL I RECALL DESPERATELY TRYING TO REACH THE SUNWELL IN TIME--

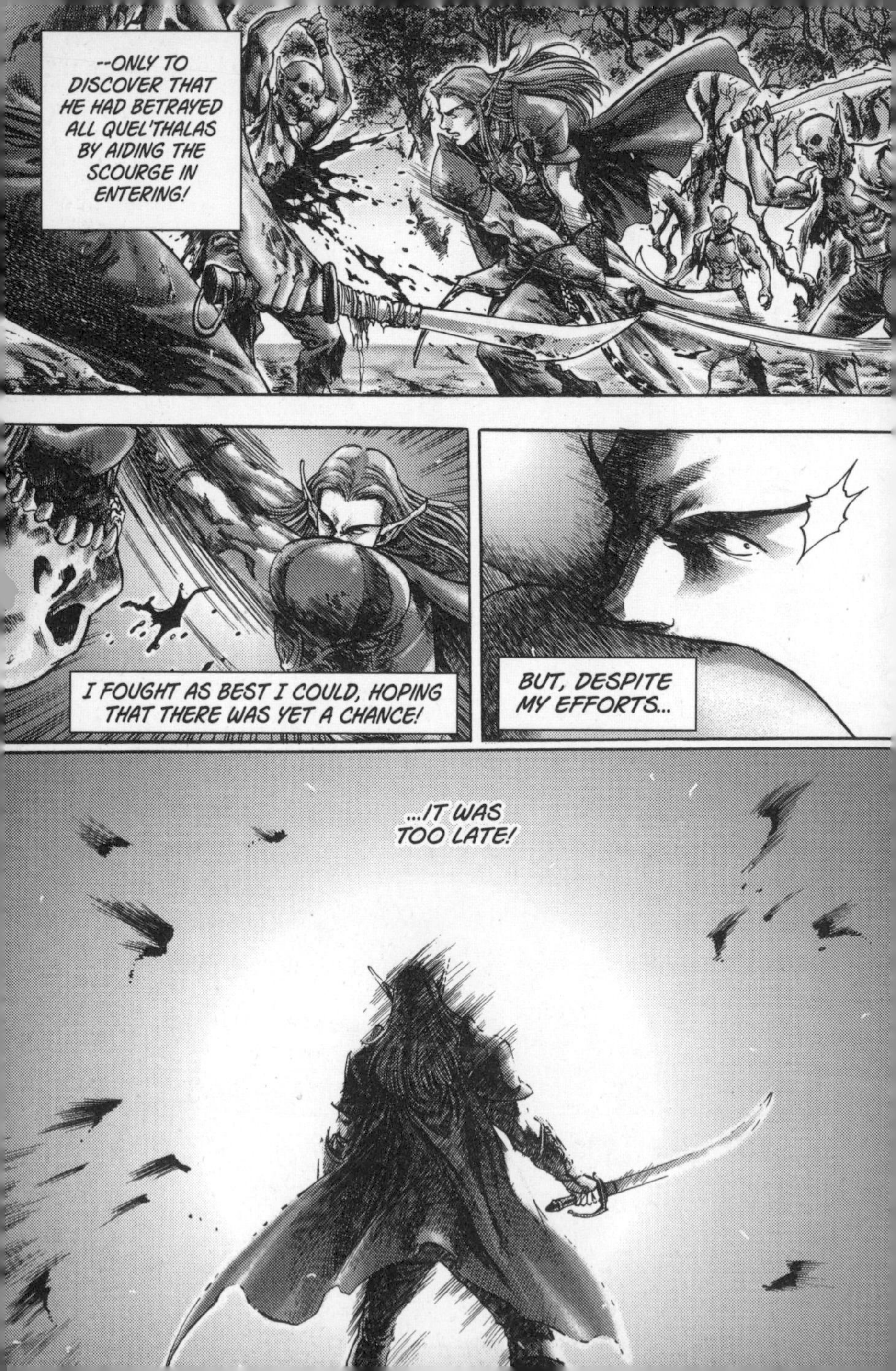
--ONLY TO DISCOVER THAT HE HAD BETRAYED ALL QUEL'THALAS BY AIDING THE SCOURGE IN ENTERING!
I FOUGHT AS BEST I COULD, HOPING THAT THERE WAS YET A CHANCE!
BUT, DESPITE MY EFFORTS...
...IT WAS TOO LATE!

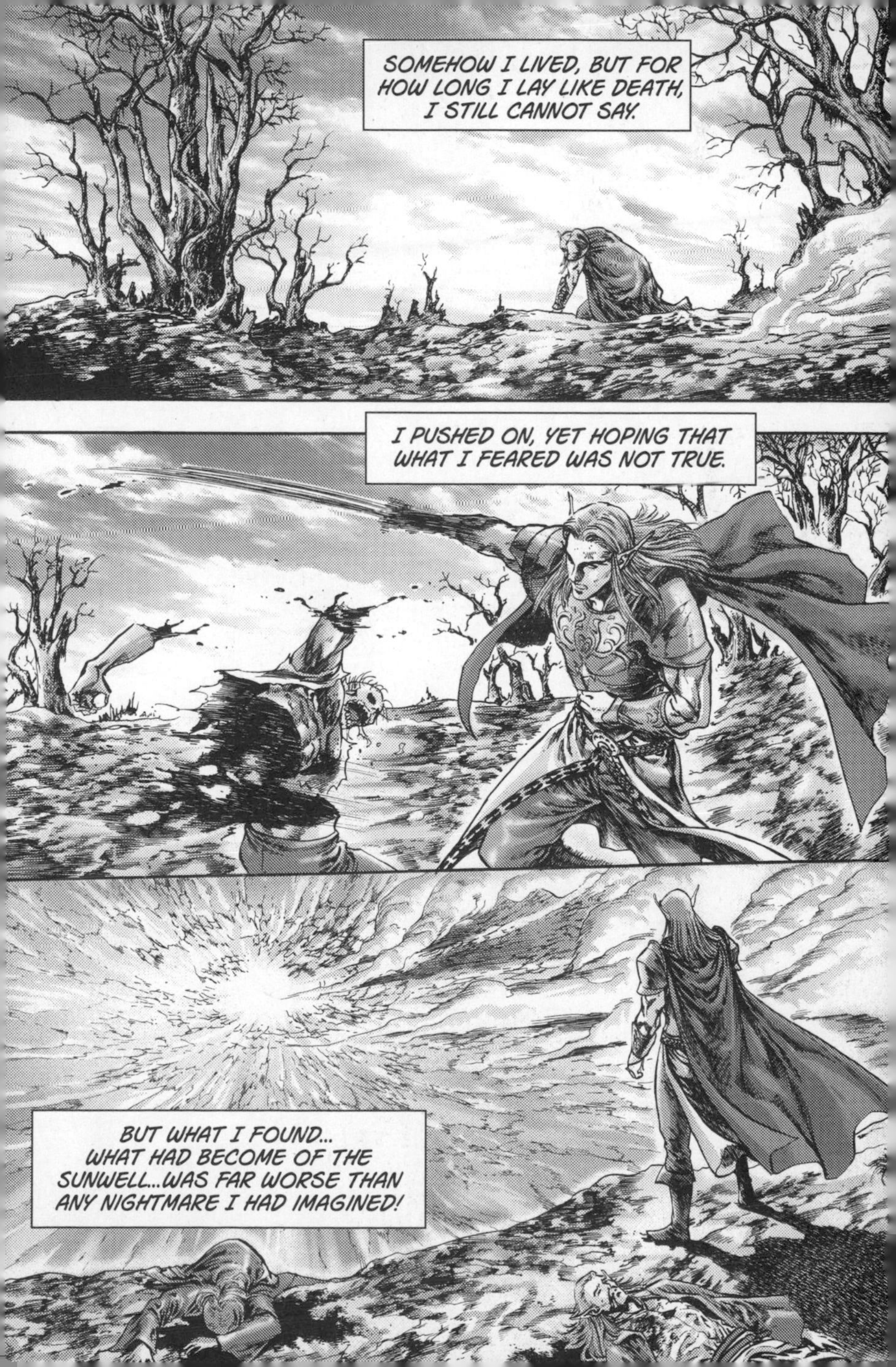
SOMEHOW I LIVED, BUT FOR HOW LONG I LAY LIKE DEATH, I STILL CANNOT SAY.
I PUSHED ON, YET HOPING THAT WHAT I FEARED WAS NOT TRUE.
BUT WHAT I FOUND... WHAT HAD BECOME OF THE SUNWELL...WAS FAR WORSE THAN ANY NIGHTMARE I HAD IMAGINED!

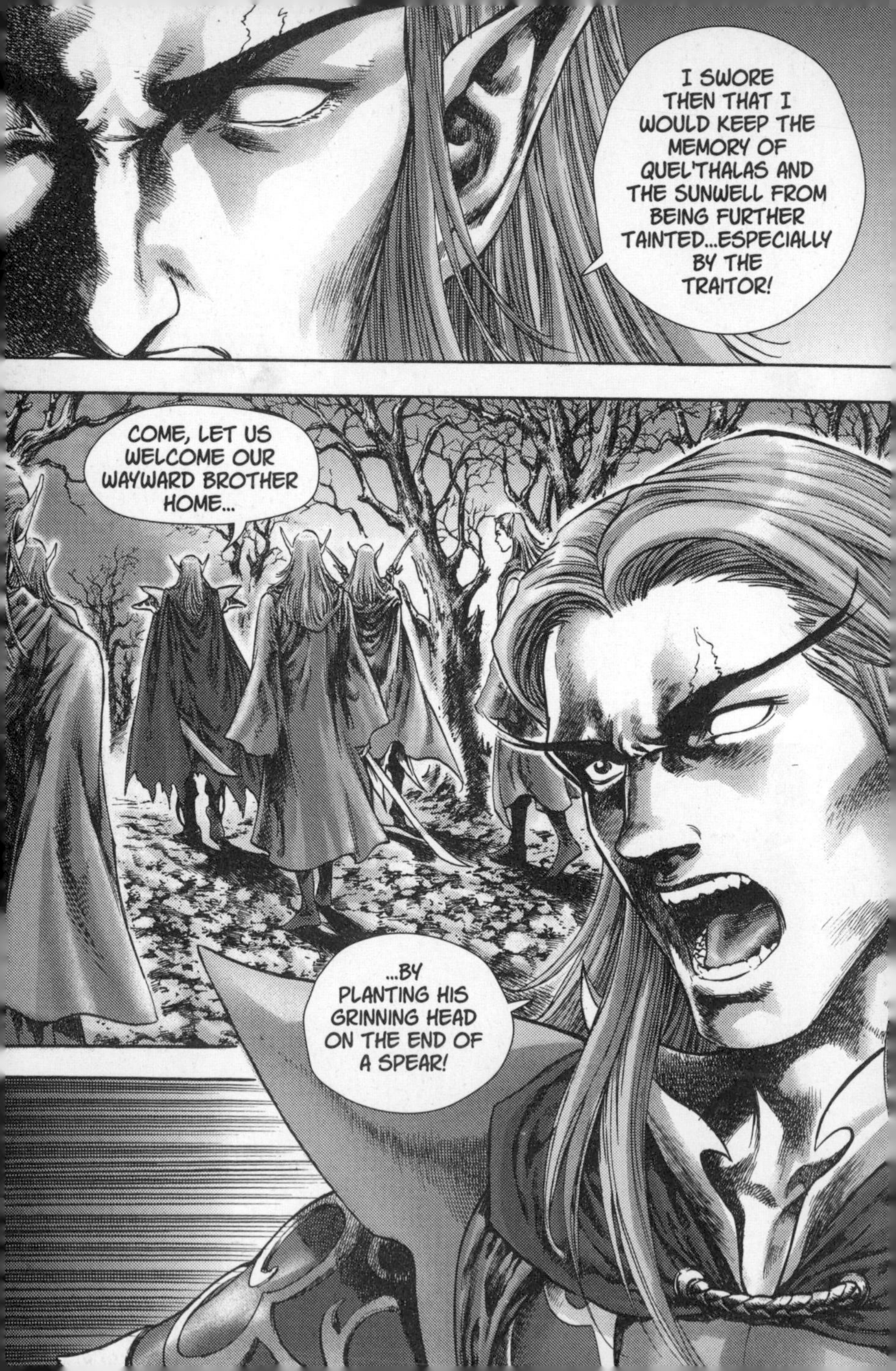
I SWORE THEN THAT I WOULD KEEP THE MEMORY OF QUEL'THALAS AND THE SUNWELL FROM BEING FURTHER TAINTED...ESPECIALLY BY THE TRAITOR!
COME, LET US WELCOME OUR WAYWARD BROTHER HOME...
...BY PLANTING HIS GRINNING HEAD ON THE END OF A SPEAR!

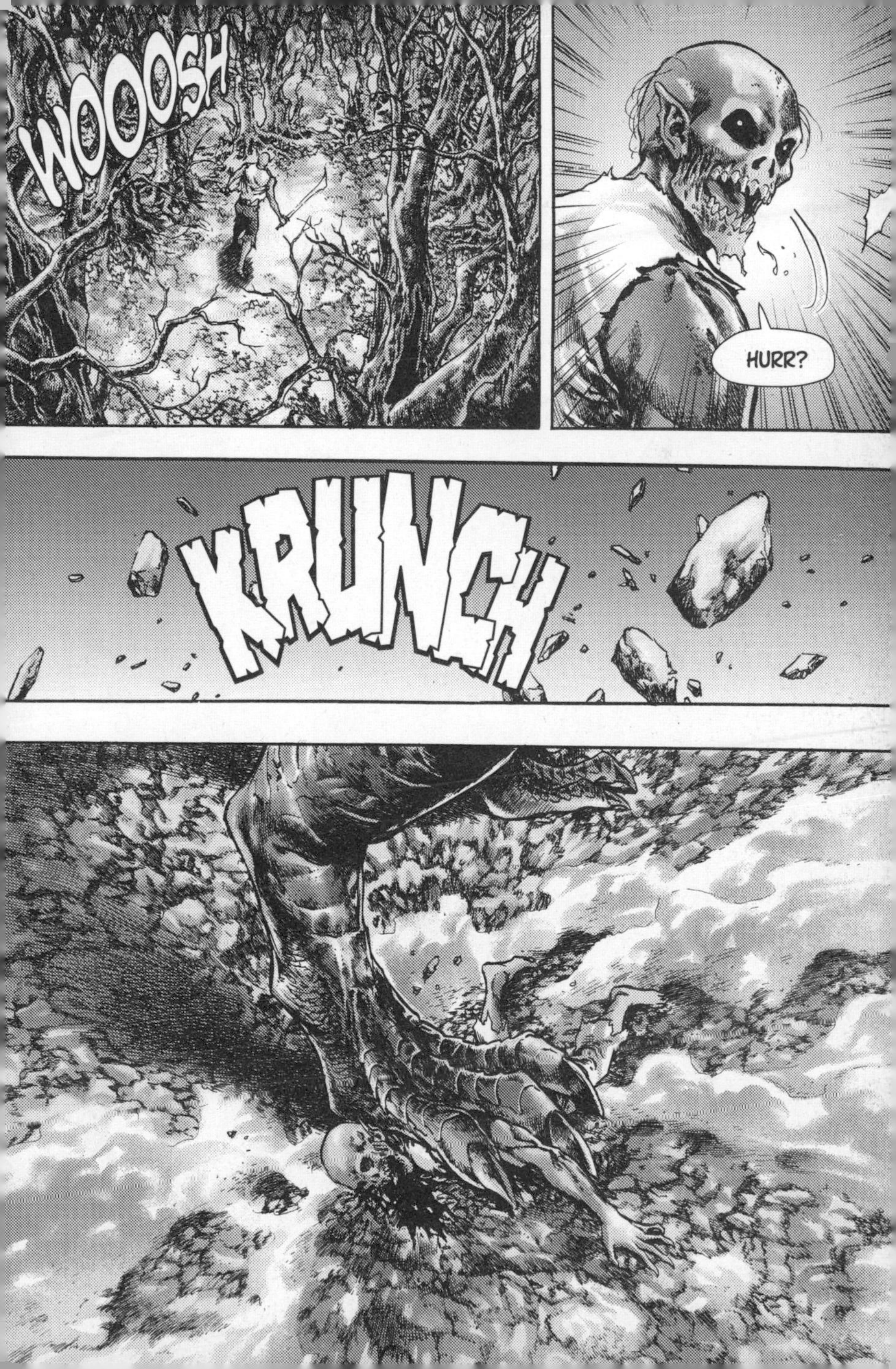
WOOOSH
HURR?
KRUNCH

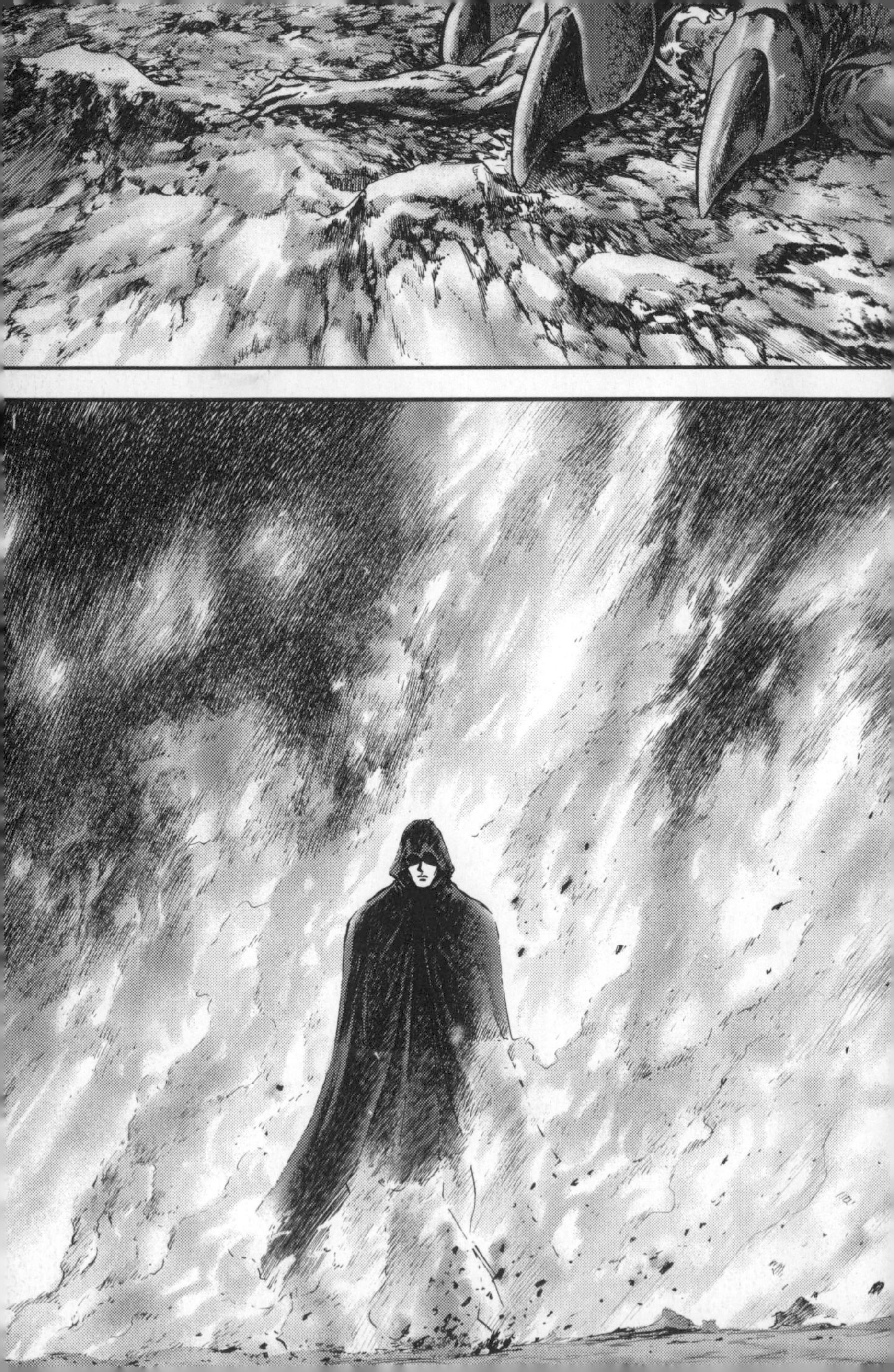

CHAPTER TWO

MASTER OF THE DEAD

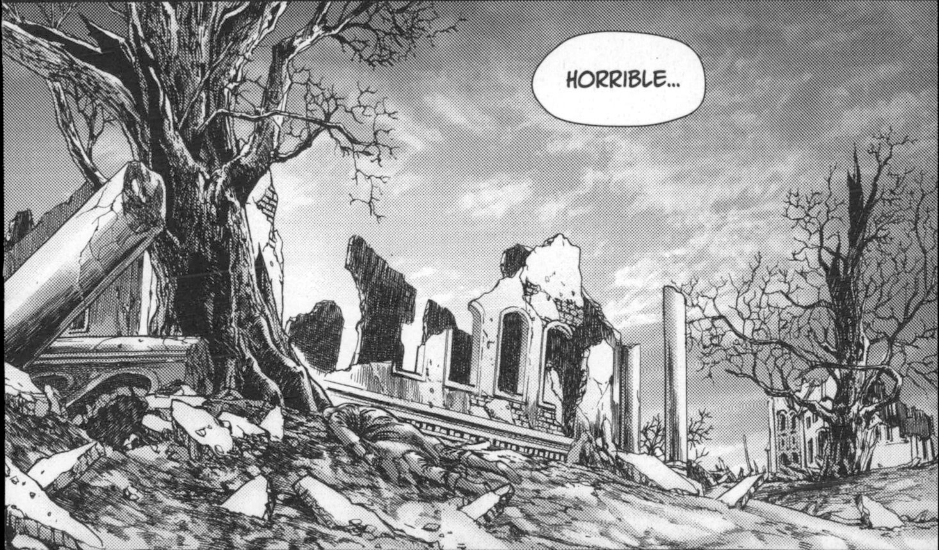
HORRIBLE...

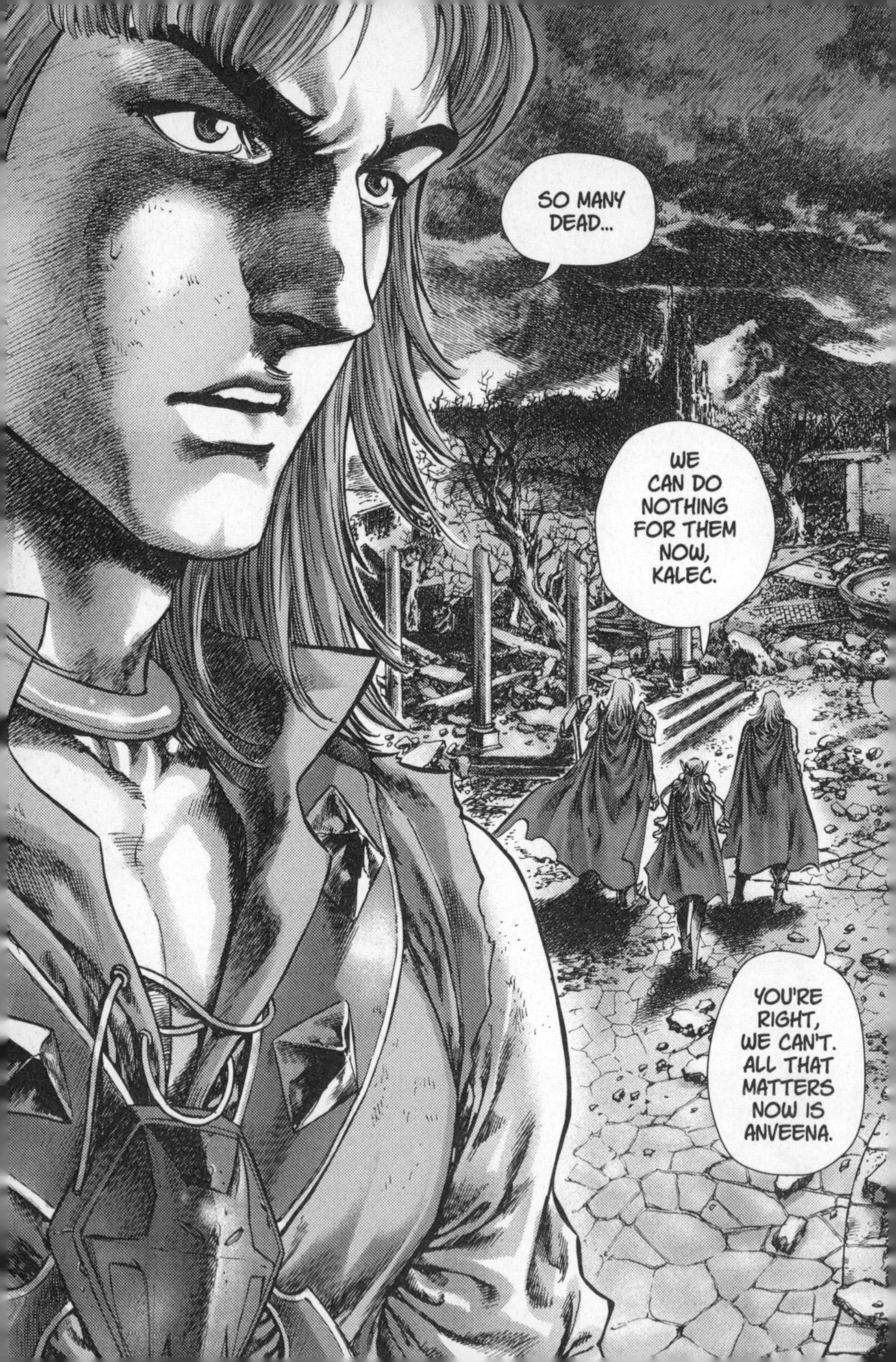
SO MANY DEAD...
WE CAN DO NOTHING FOR THEM NOW, KALEC.
YOU'RE RIGHT, WE CAN'T. ALL THAT MATTERS NOW IS ANVEENA.

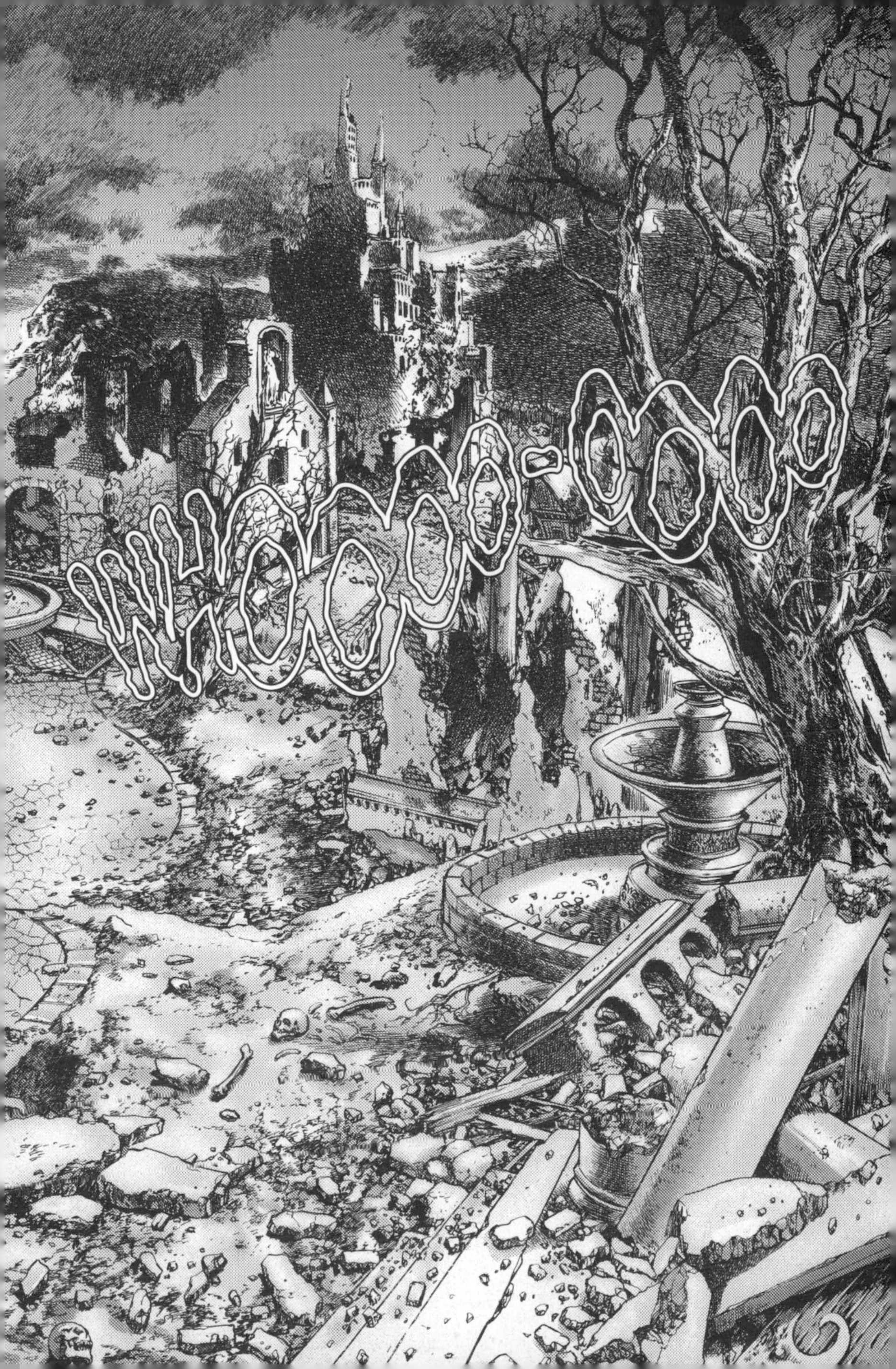
WHOOOO-OOOO

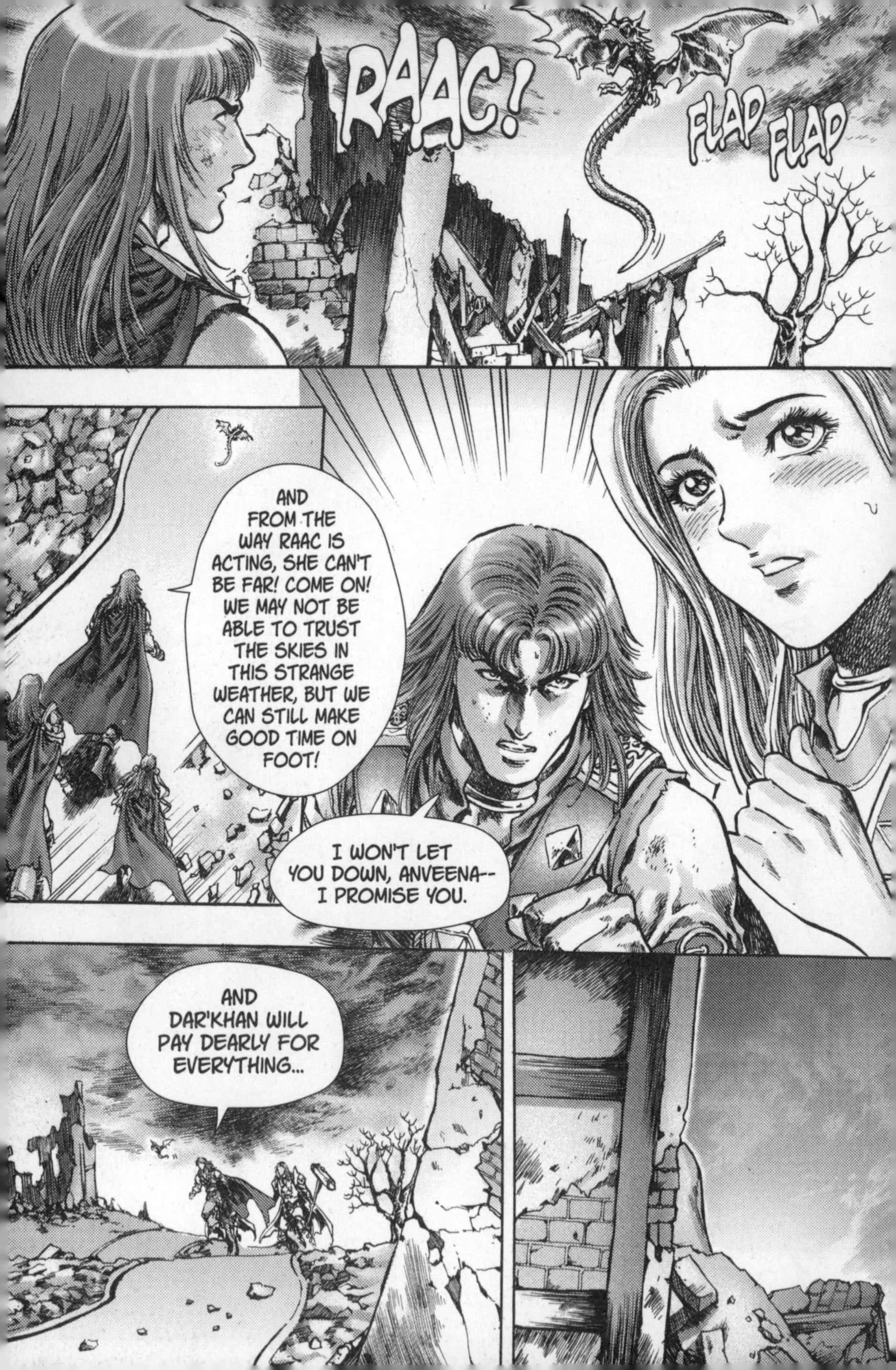
RAAC!
FLAP FLAP
AND FROM THE WAY RAAC IS ACTING, SHE CAN'T BE FAR! COME ON! WE MAY NOT BE ABLE TO TRUST THE SKIES IN THIS STRANGE WEATHER, BUT WE CAN STILL MAKE GOOD TIME ON FOOT!
I WON'T LET YOU DOWN, ANVEENA-- I PROMISE YOU.
AND DAR'KHAN WILL PAY DEARLY FOR EVERYTHING...

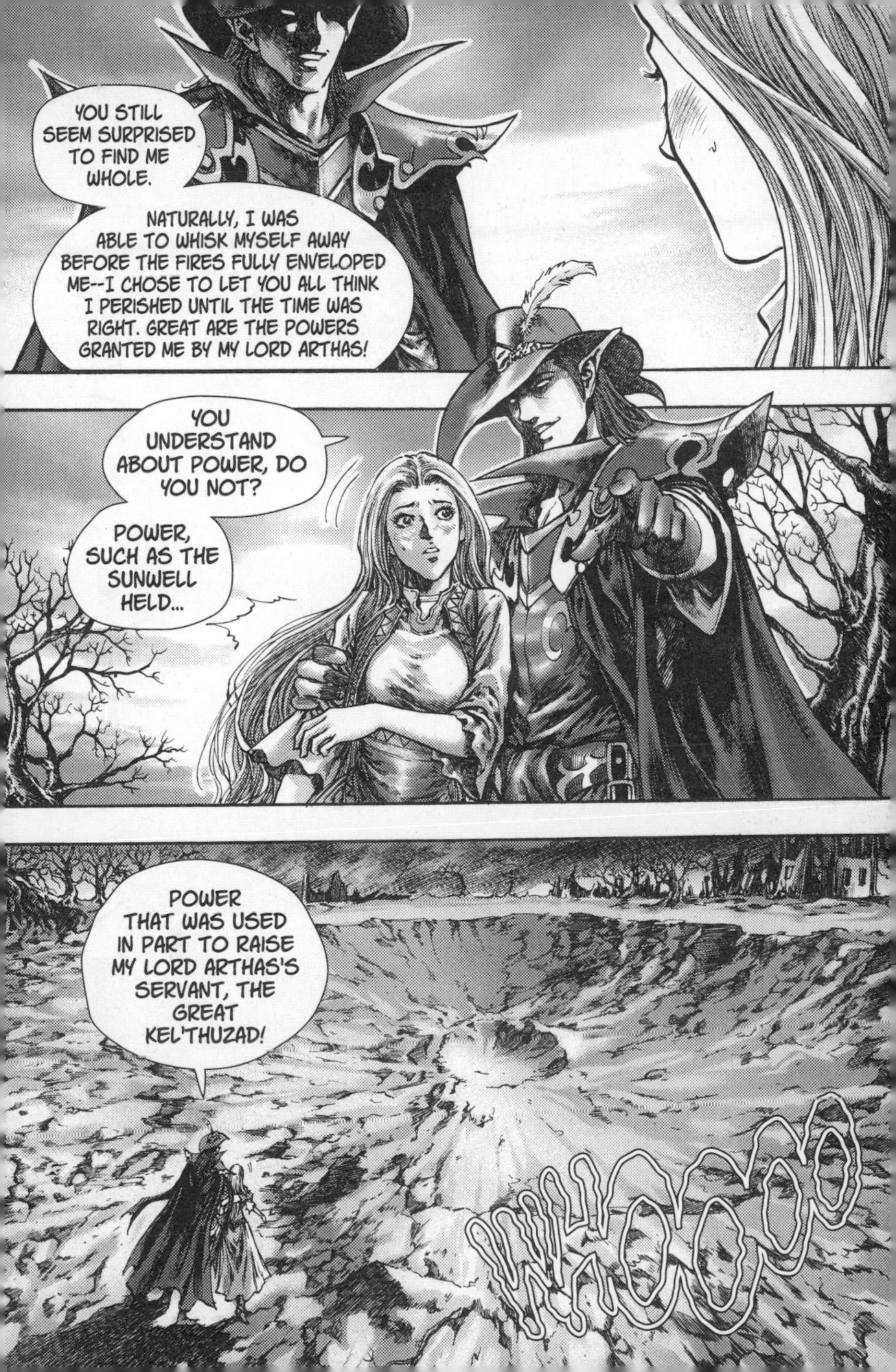

YOU STILL SEEM SURPRISED TO FIND ME WHOLE.
NATURALLY, I WAS ABLE TO WHISK MYSELF AWAY BEFORE THE FIRES FULLY ENVELOPED ME--I CHOSE TO LET YOU ALL THINK I PERISHED UNTIL THE TIME WAS RIGHT. GREAT ARE THE POWERS GRANTED ME BY MY LORD ARTHAS!
YOU UNDERSTAND ABOUT POWER, DO YOU NOT?
POWER, SUCH AS THE SUNWELL HELD...
POWER THAT WAS USED IN PART TO RAISE MY LORD ARTHAS'S SERVANT, THE GREAT KEL'THUZAD!
WHOOOOO

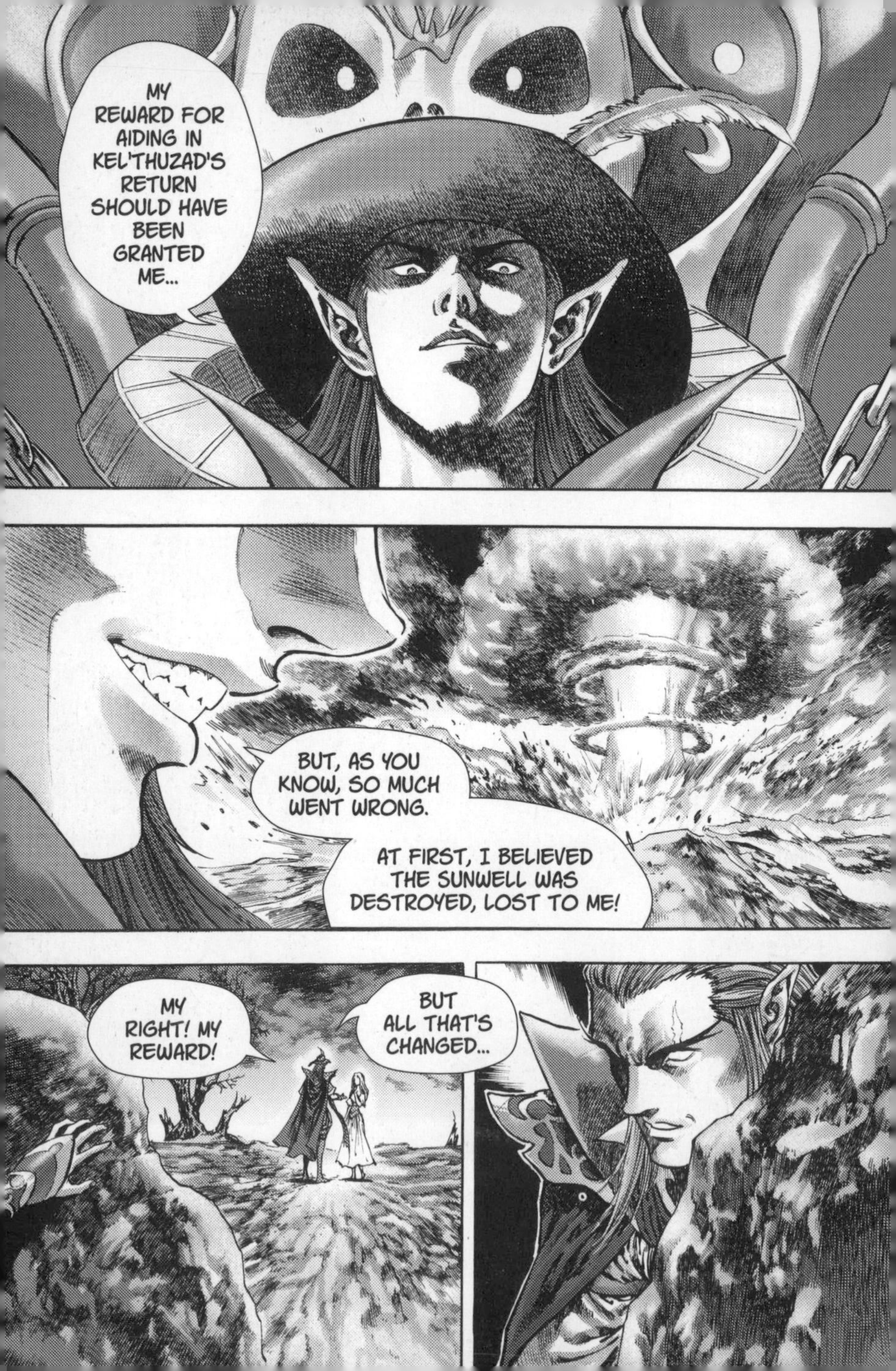
MY REWARD FOR AIDING IN KEL'THUZAD'S RETURN SHOULD HAVE BEEN GRANTED ME...
BUT, AS YOU KNOW, SO MUCH WENT WRONG.
AT FIRST, I BELIEVED THE SUNWELL WAS DESTROYED, LOST TO ME!
MY RIGHT! MY REWARD!
BUT ALL THAT'S CHANGED...

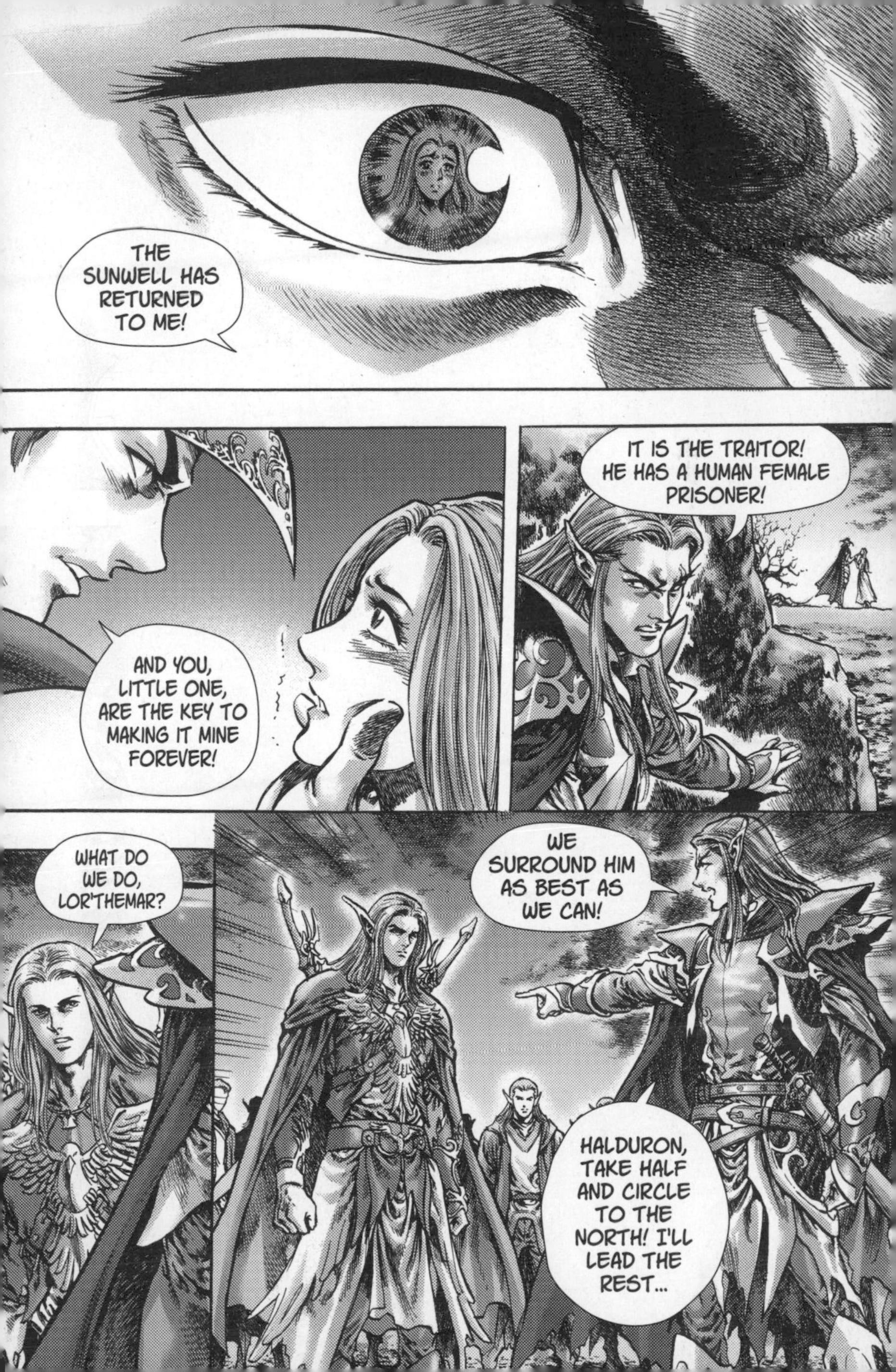
THE SUNWELL HAS RETURNED TO ME!
AND YOU, LITTLE ONE, ARE THE KEY TO MAKING IT MINE FOREVER!
IT IS THE TRAITOR! HE HAS A HUMAN FEMALE PRISONER!
WHAT DO WE DO, LOR'THEMAR?
WE SURROUND HIM AS BEST AS WE CAN!
HALDURON, TAKE HALF AND CIRCLE TO THE NORTH! I'LL LEAD THE REST...

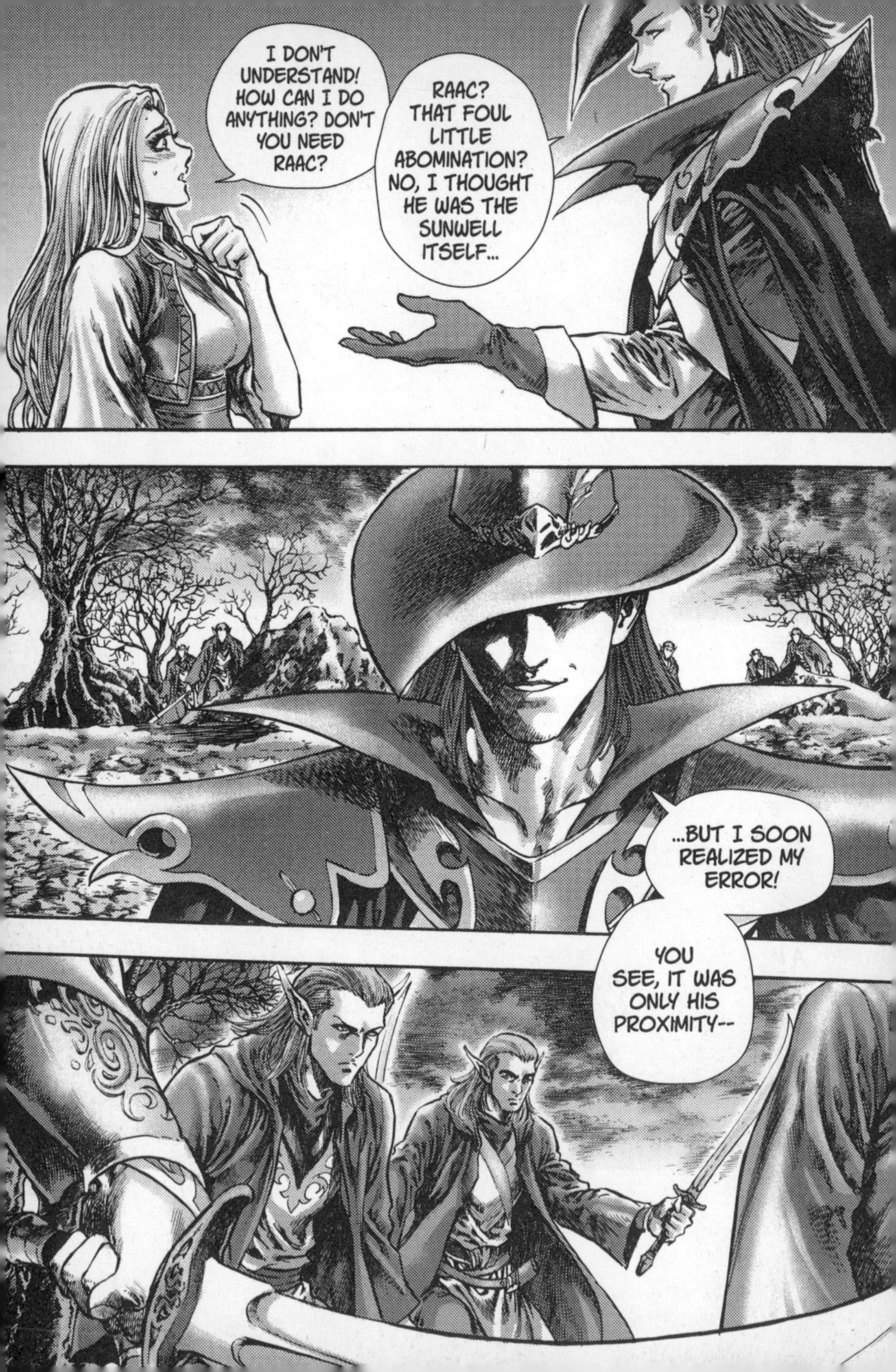
I DON'T UNDERSTAND! HOW CAN I DO ANYTHING? DON'T YOU NEED RAAC?
RAAC? THAT FOUL LITTLE ABOMINATION? NO, I THOUGHT HE WAS THE SUNWELL ITSELF...
...BUT I SOON REALIZED MY ERROR!
YOU SEE, IT WAS ONLY HIS PROXIMITY--

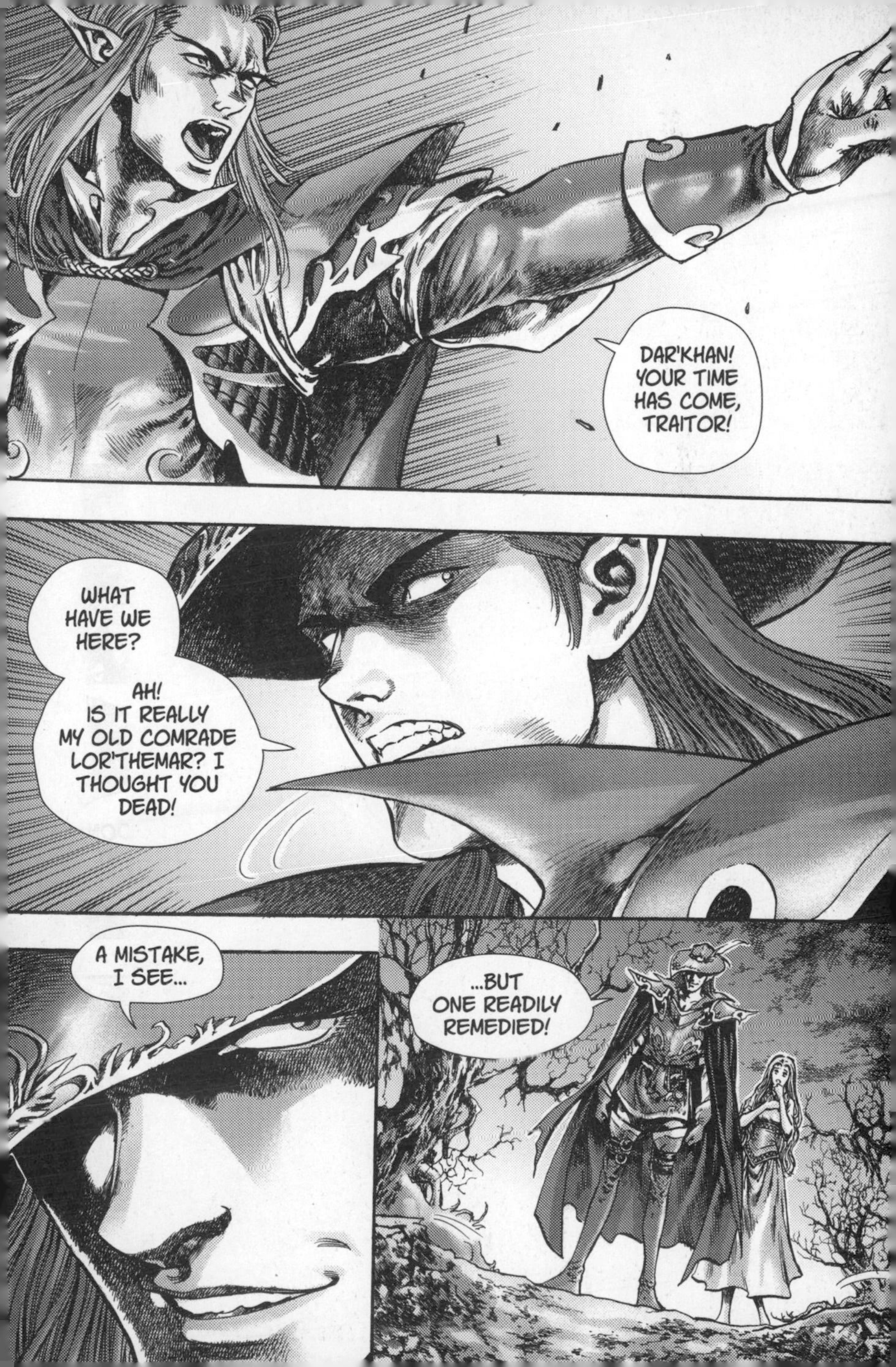
DAR'KHAN! YOUR TIME HAS COME, TRAITOR!
WHAT HAVE WE HERE?
AH! IS IT REALLY MY OLD COMRADE LOR'THEMAR? I THOUGHT YOU DEAD!
A MISTAKE, I SEE...
...BUT ONE READILY REMEDIED!

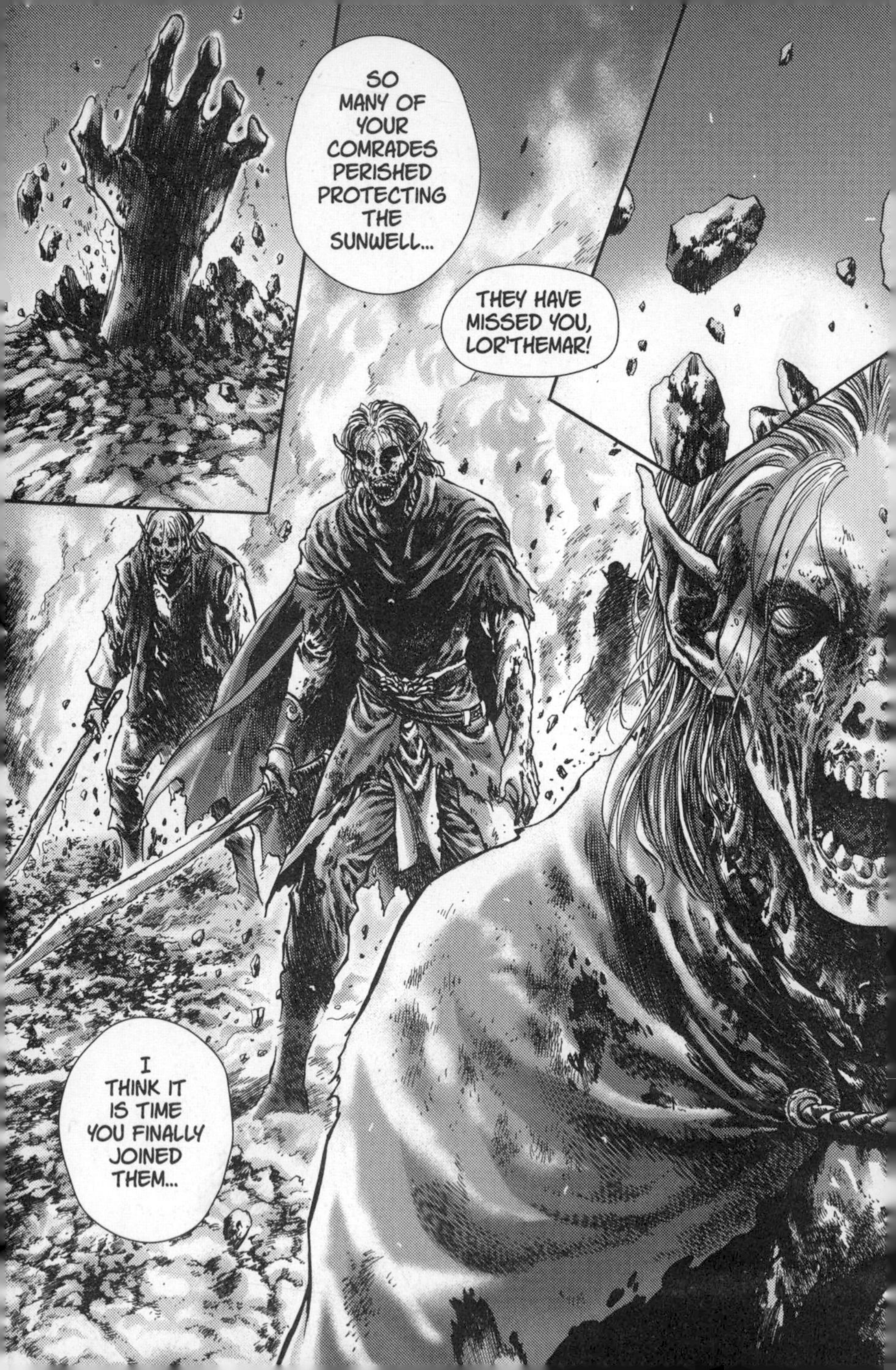
SO MANY OF YOUR COMRADES PERISHED PROTECTING THE SUNWELL...
THEY HAVE MISSED YOU, LOR'THEMAR!
I THINK IT IS TIME YOU FINALLY JOINED THEM...

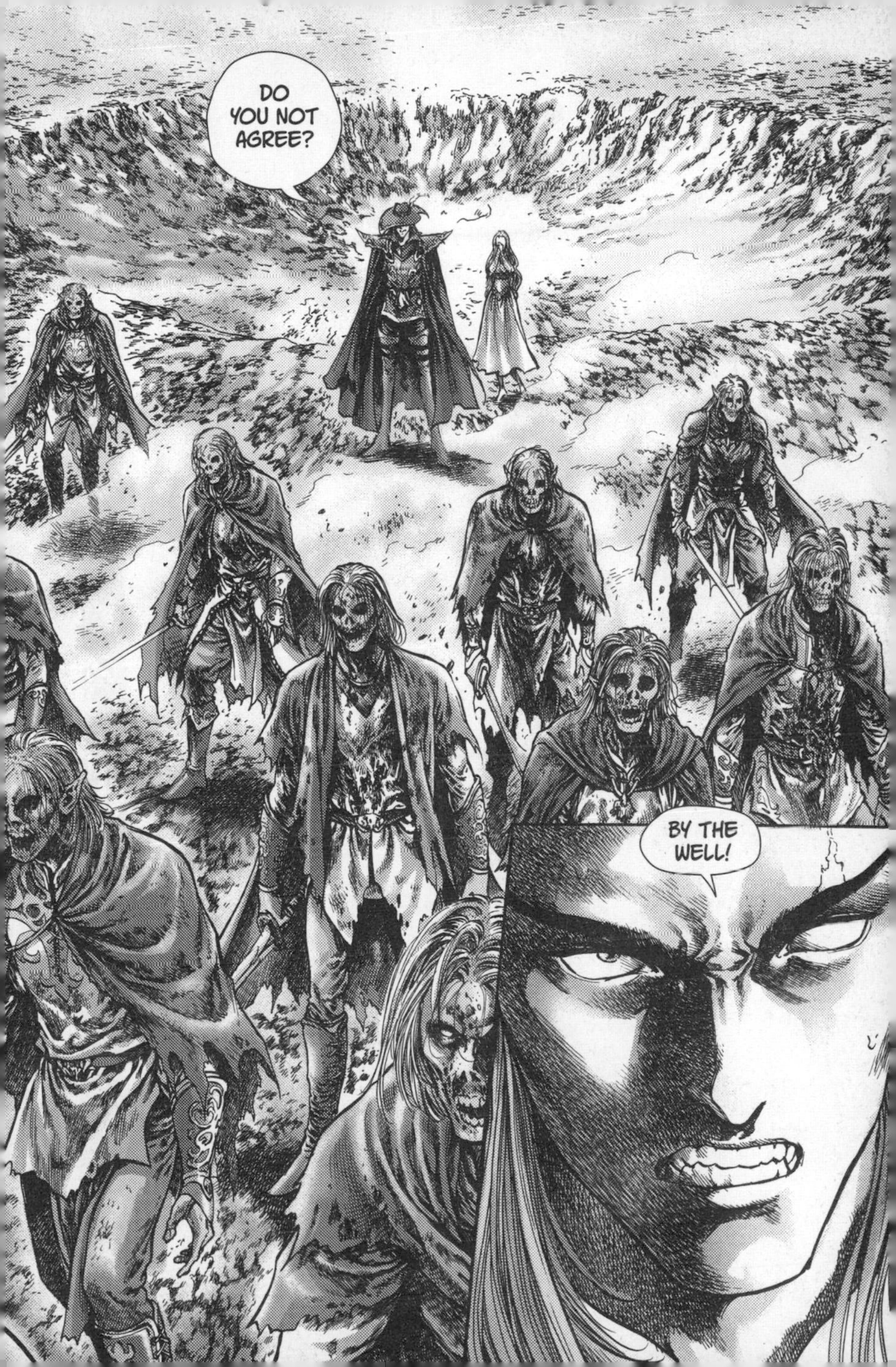
DO YOU NOT AGREE?
BY THE WELL!

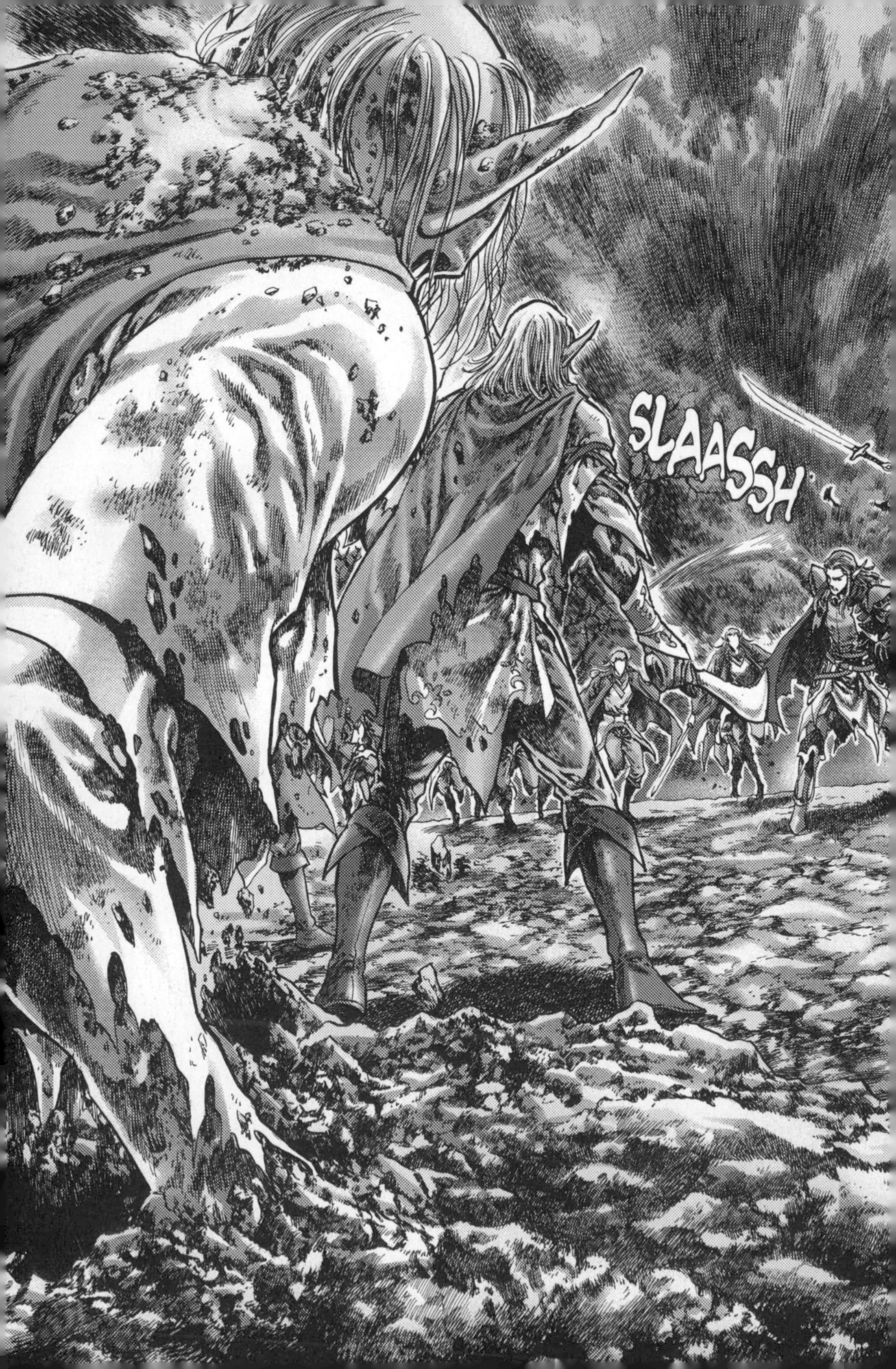
SLAASSH

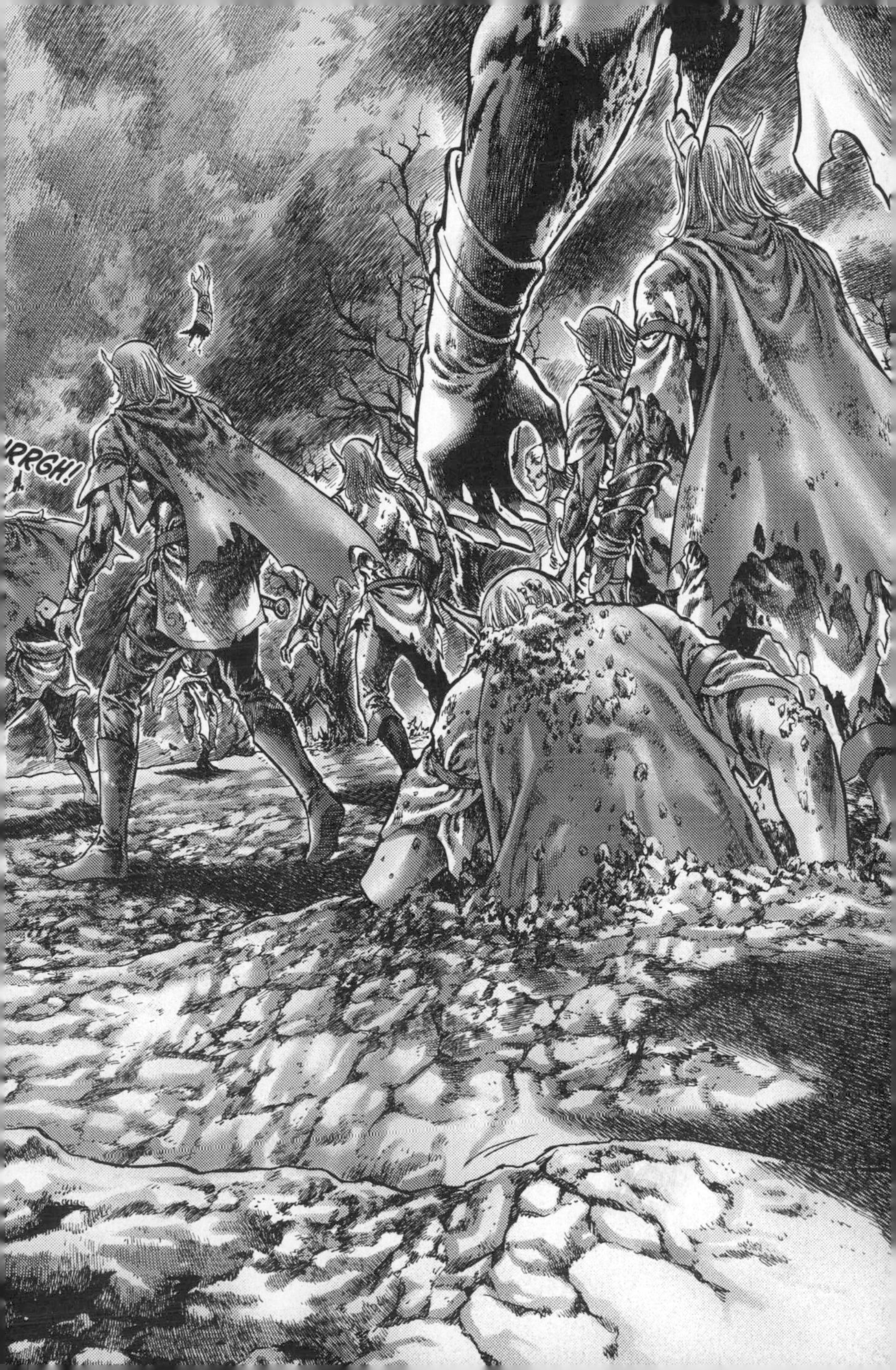
RRGH!

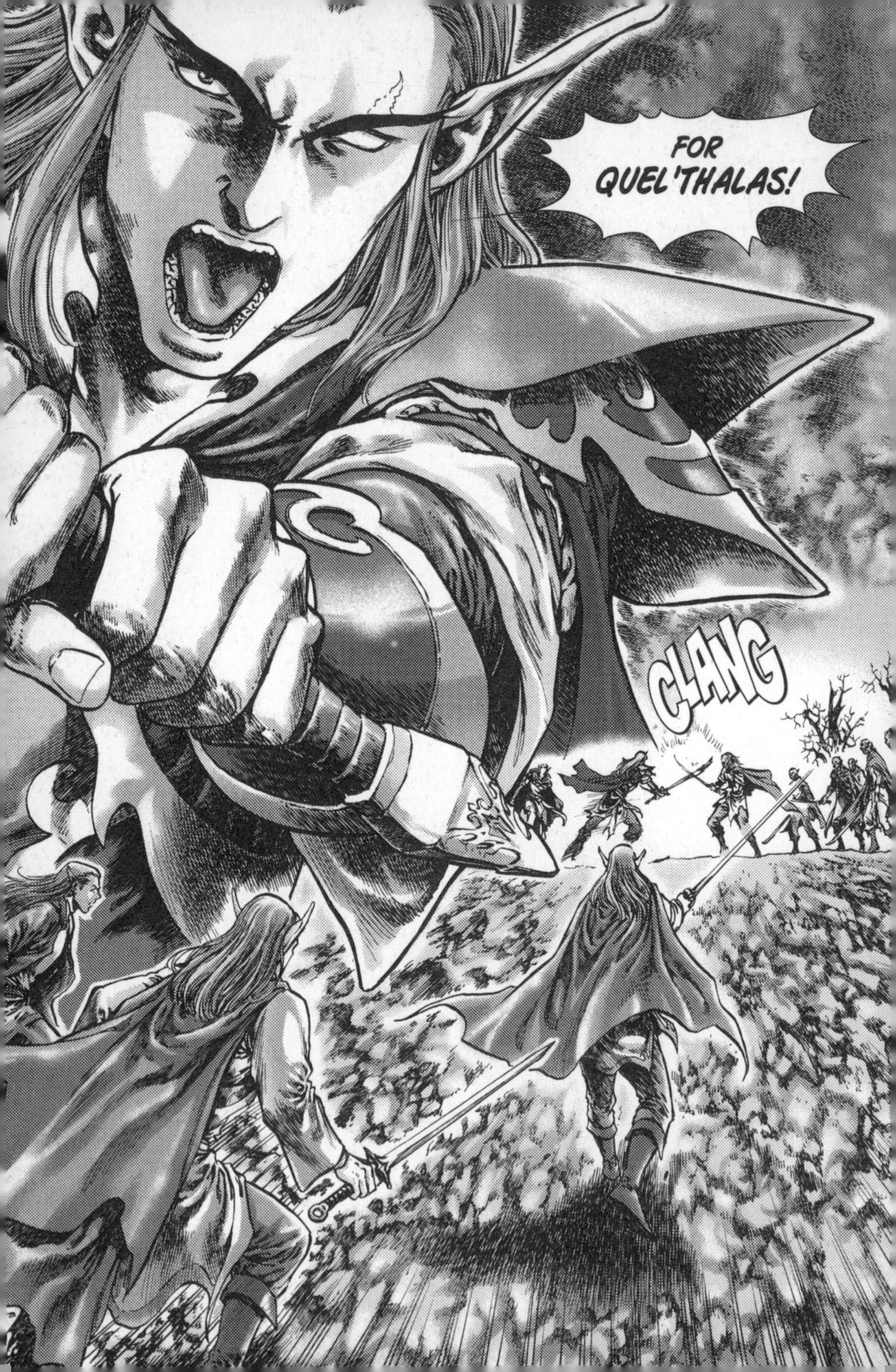
FOR QUEL'THALAS!
CLANG

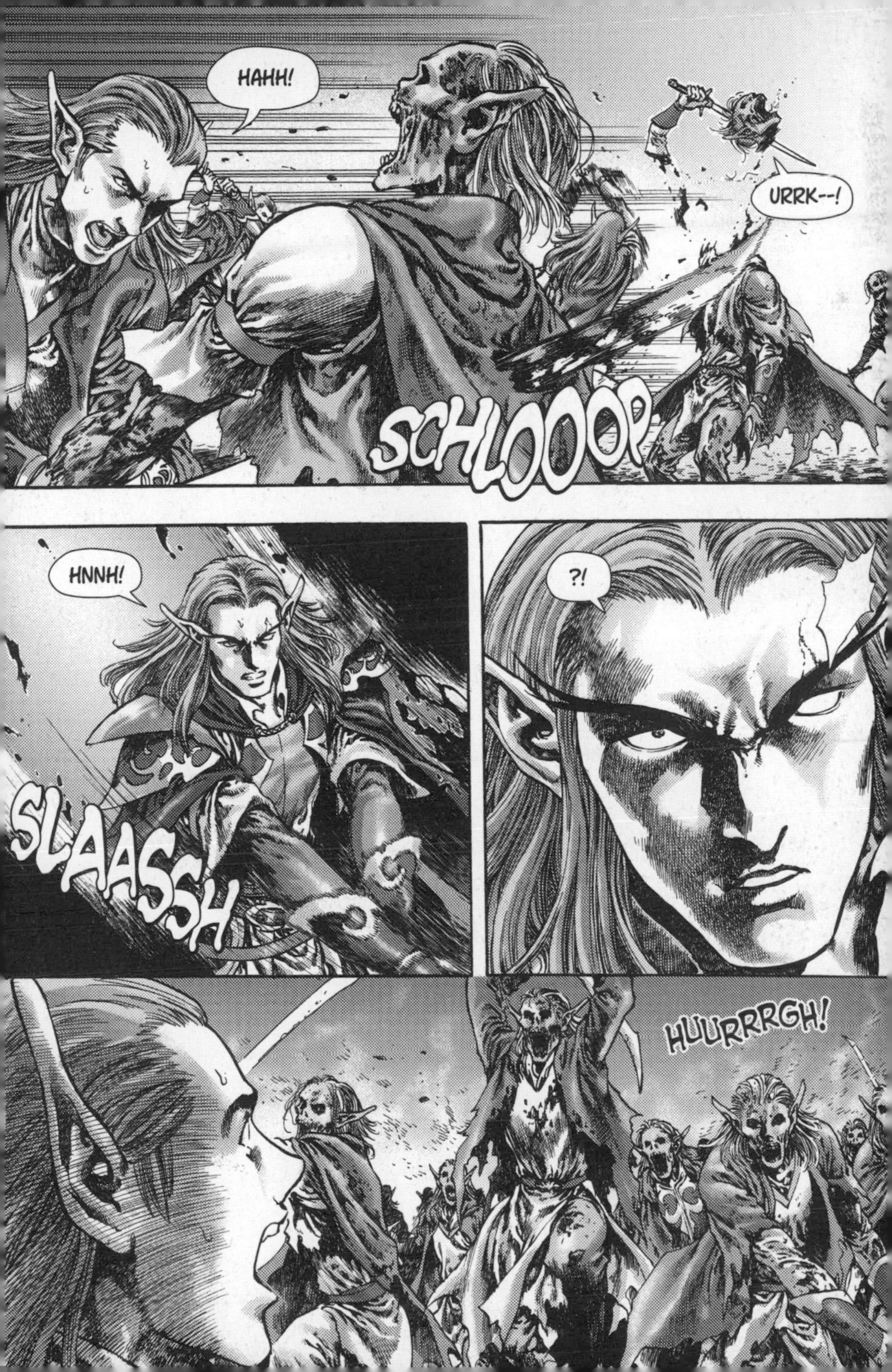
HAHH!
URRK--!
SCHLOOOP
HNNH!
SLAASSH
?!
HUURRRGH!

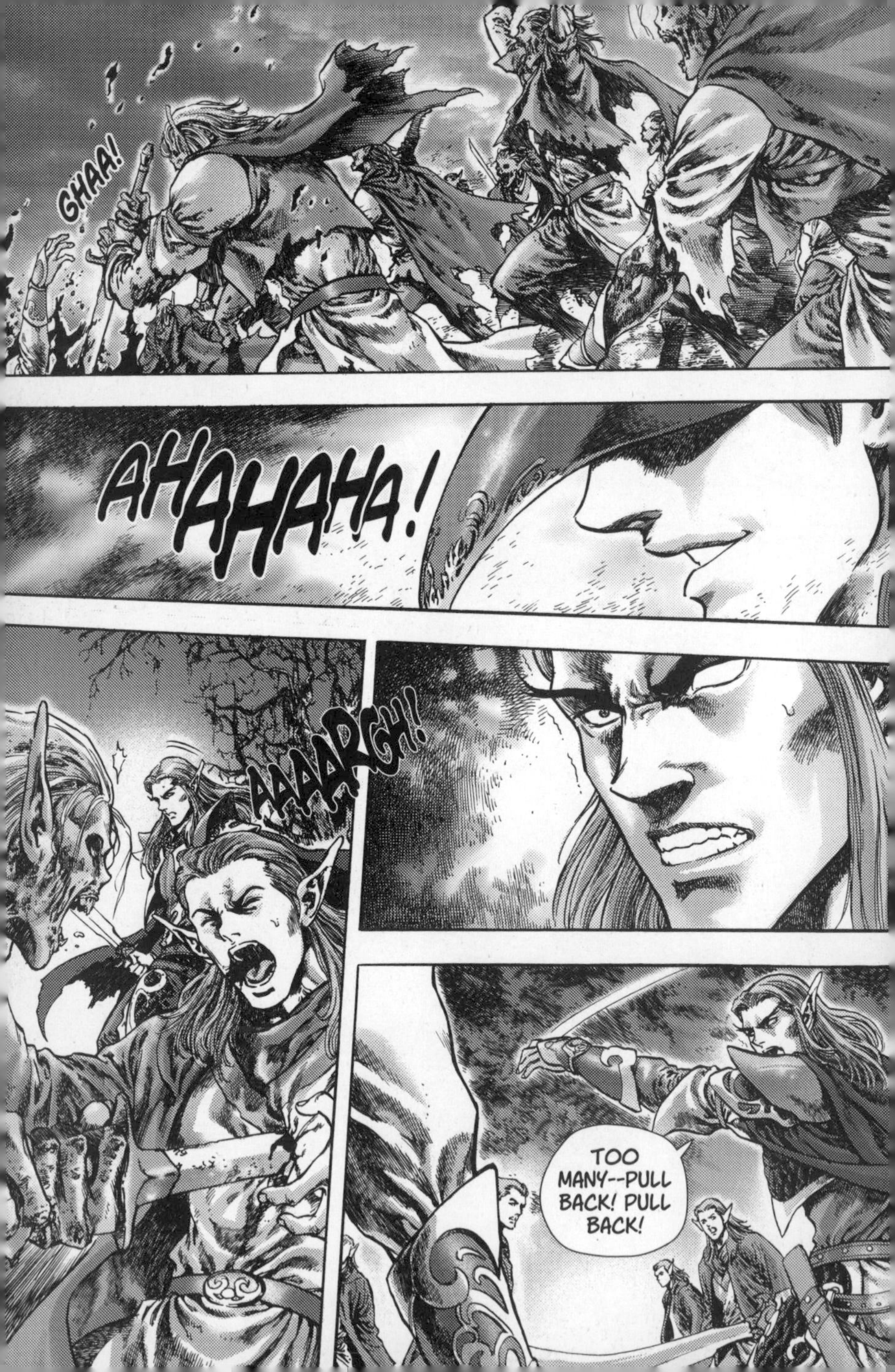
GHAA!
AHAHAHA!
AAAARGH!
TOO MANY--PULL BACK! PULL BACK!

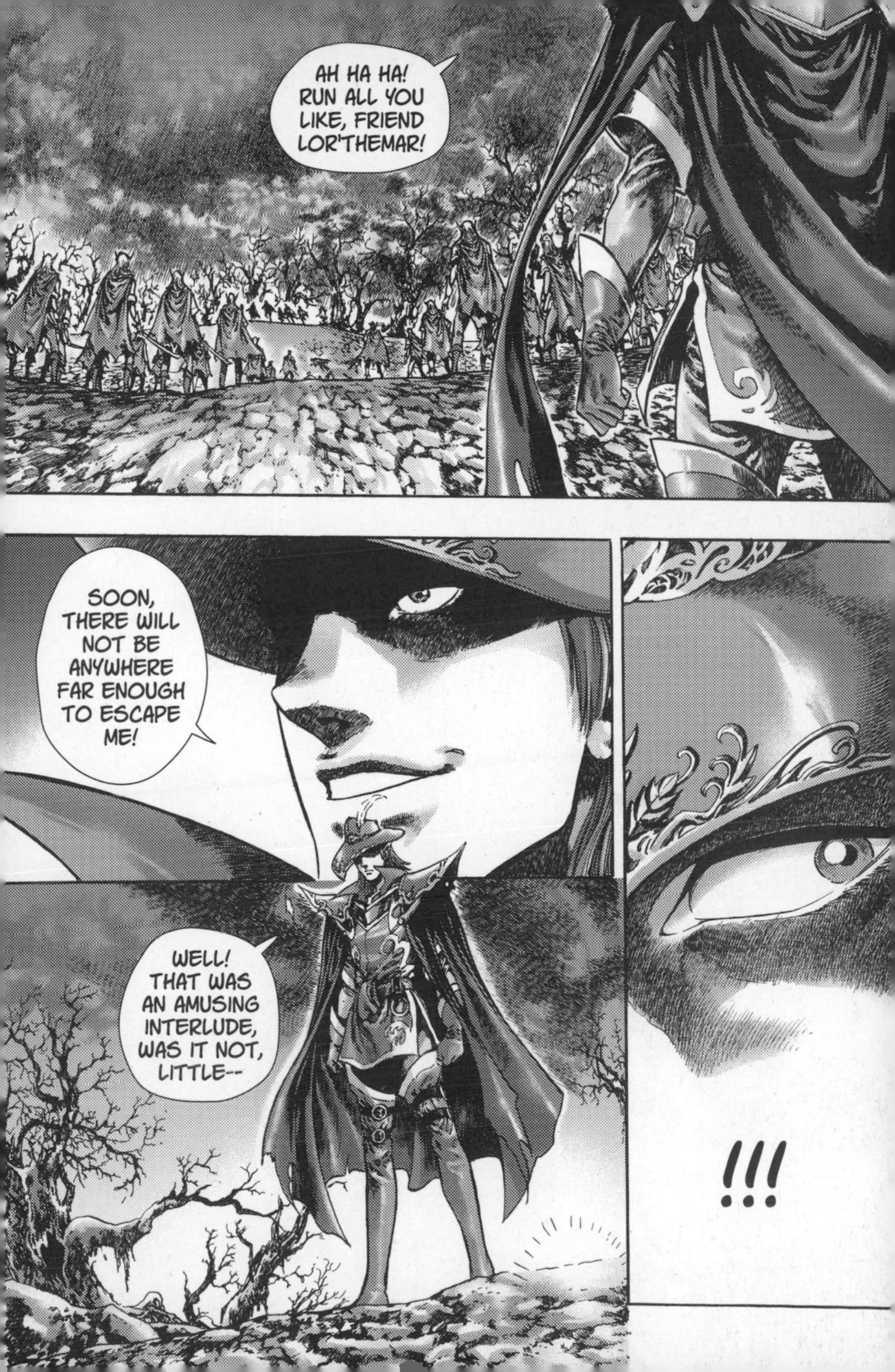
AH HA HA! RUN ALL YOU LIKE, FRIEND LOR'THEMAR!
SOON, THERE WILL NOT BE ANYWHERE FAR ENOUGH TO ESCAPE ME!
WELL! THAT WAS AN AMUSING INTERLUDE, WAS IT NOT, LITTLE--
!!!

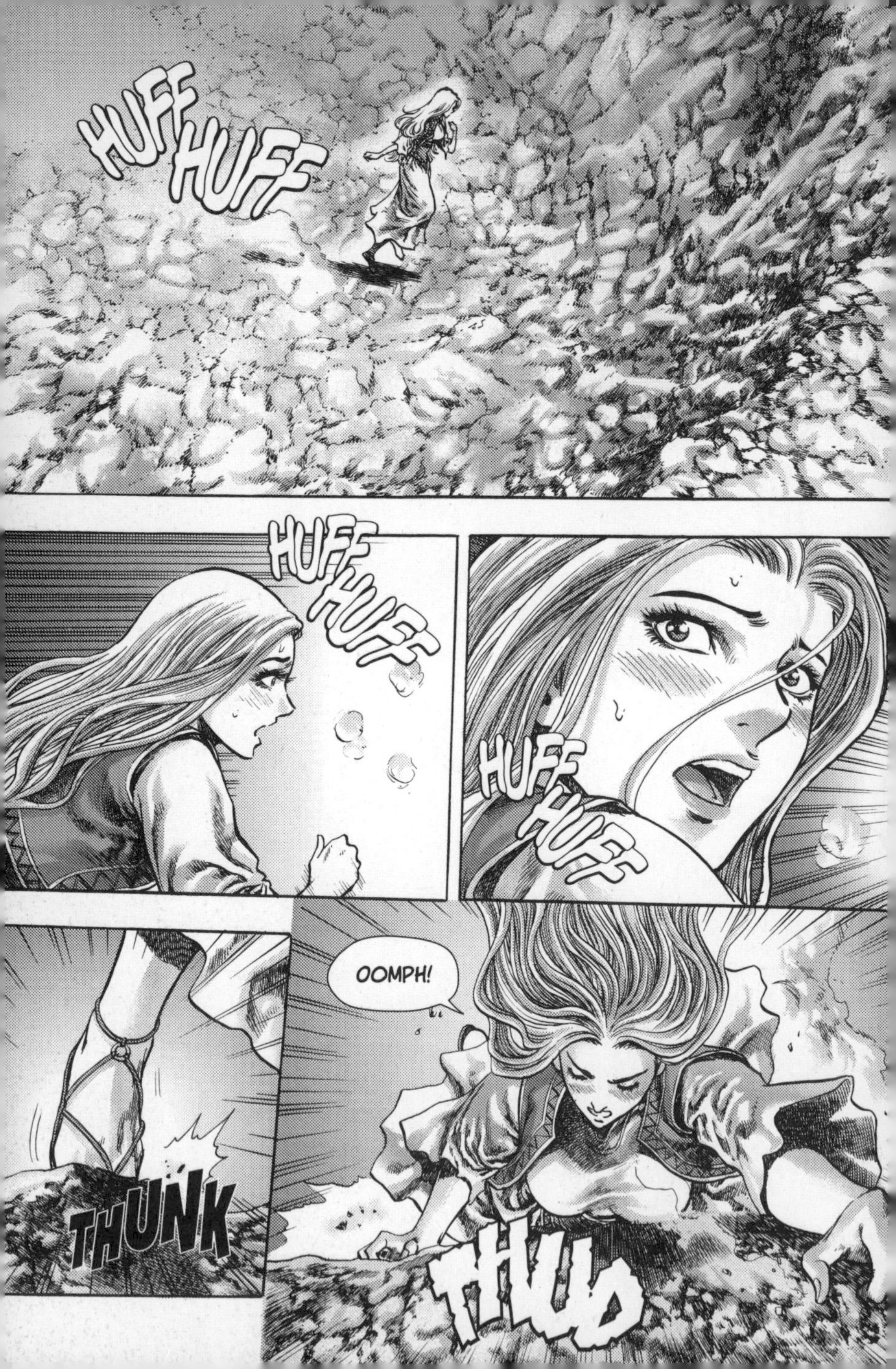
HUFF HUFF
HUFF HUFF
HUFF HUFF
OOMPH!
THUNK
THUD

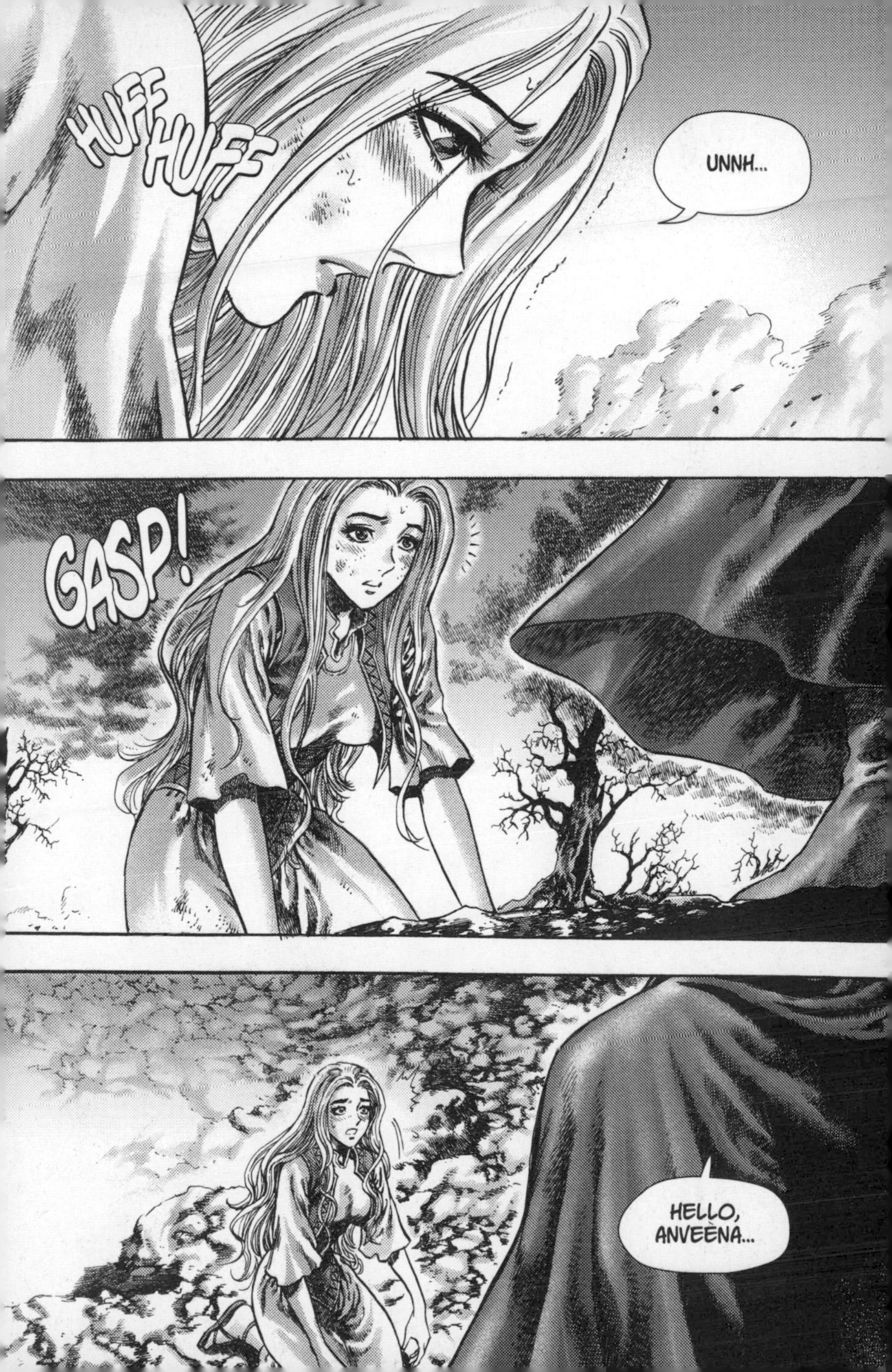
HUFF HUFF
UNNH...
GASP!
HELLO, ANVEÈNA...

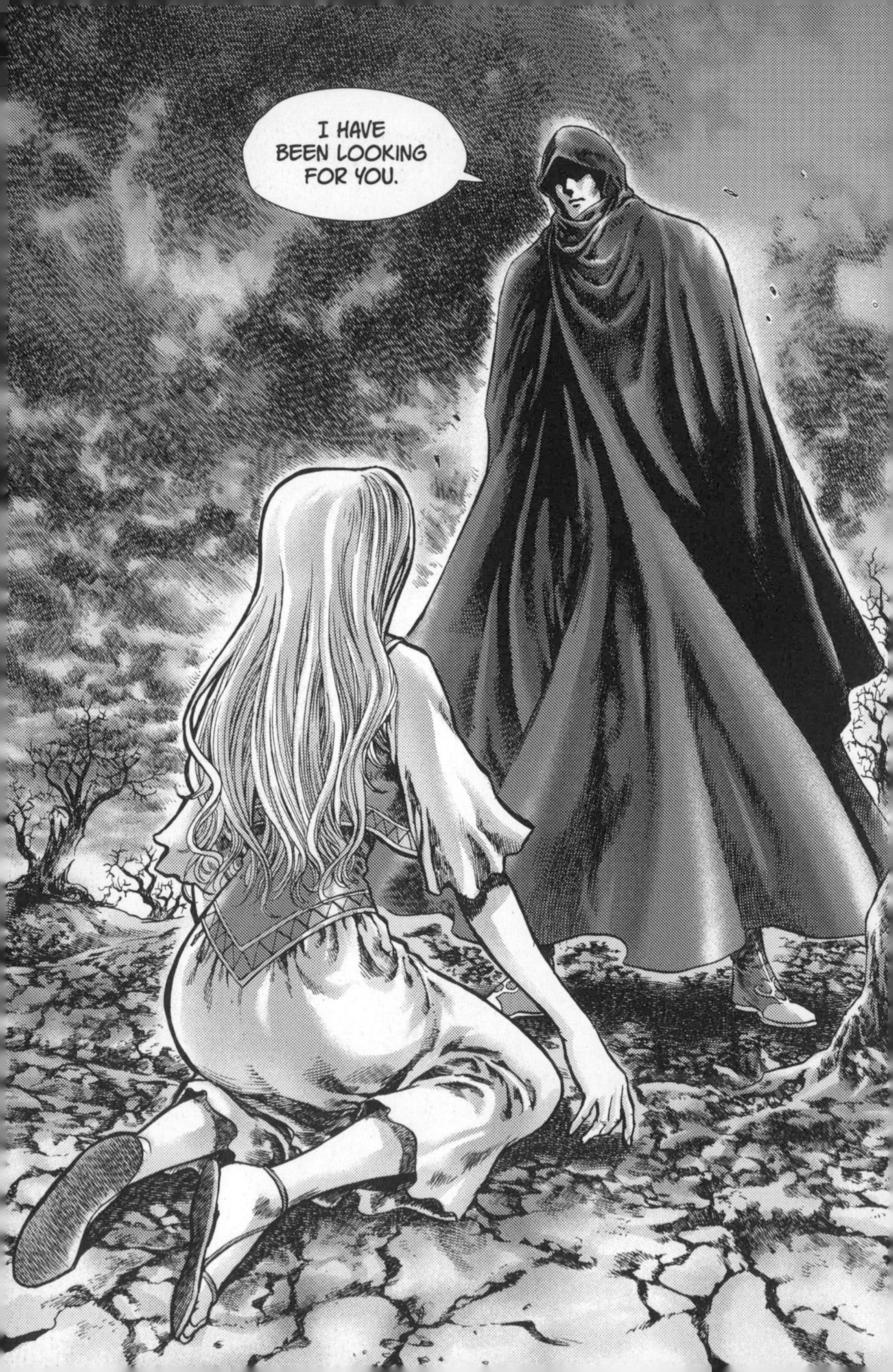
I HAVE BEEN LOOKING FOR YOU.

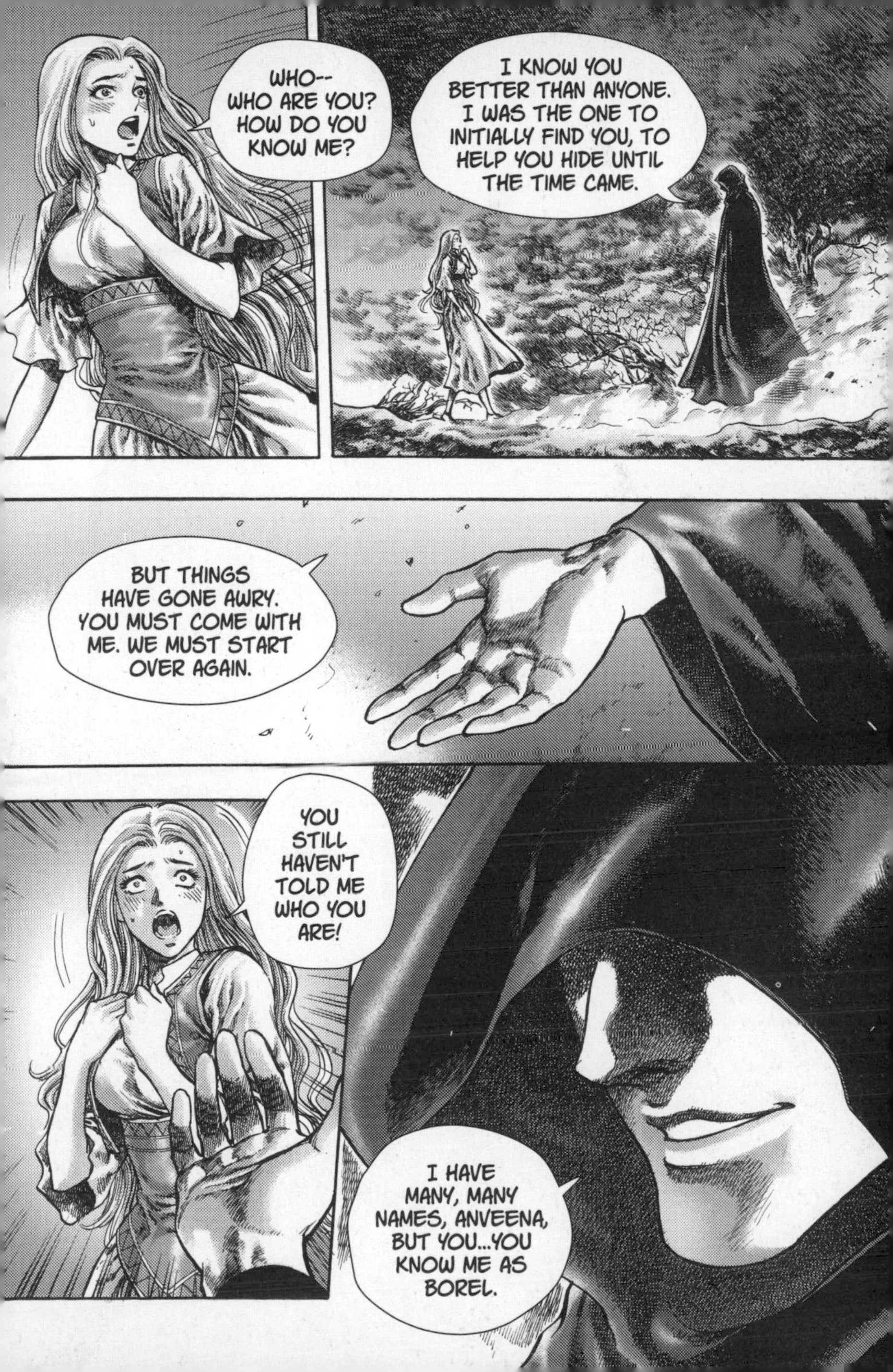
WHO-- WHO ARE YOU? HOW DO YOU KNOW ME?
I KNOW YOU BETTER THAN ANYONE. I WAS THE ONE TO INITIALLY FIND YOU, TO HELP YOU HIDE UNTIL THE TIME CAME.
BUT THINGS HAVE GONE AWRY. YOU MUST COME WITH ME. WE MUST START OVER AGAIN.
YOU STILL HAVEN'T TOLD ME WHO YOU ARE!
I HAVE MANY, MANY NAMES, ANVEENA, BUT YOU...YOU KNOW ME AS BOREL.

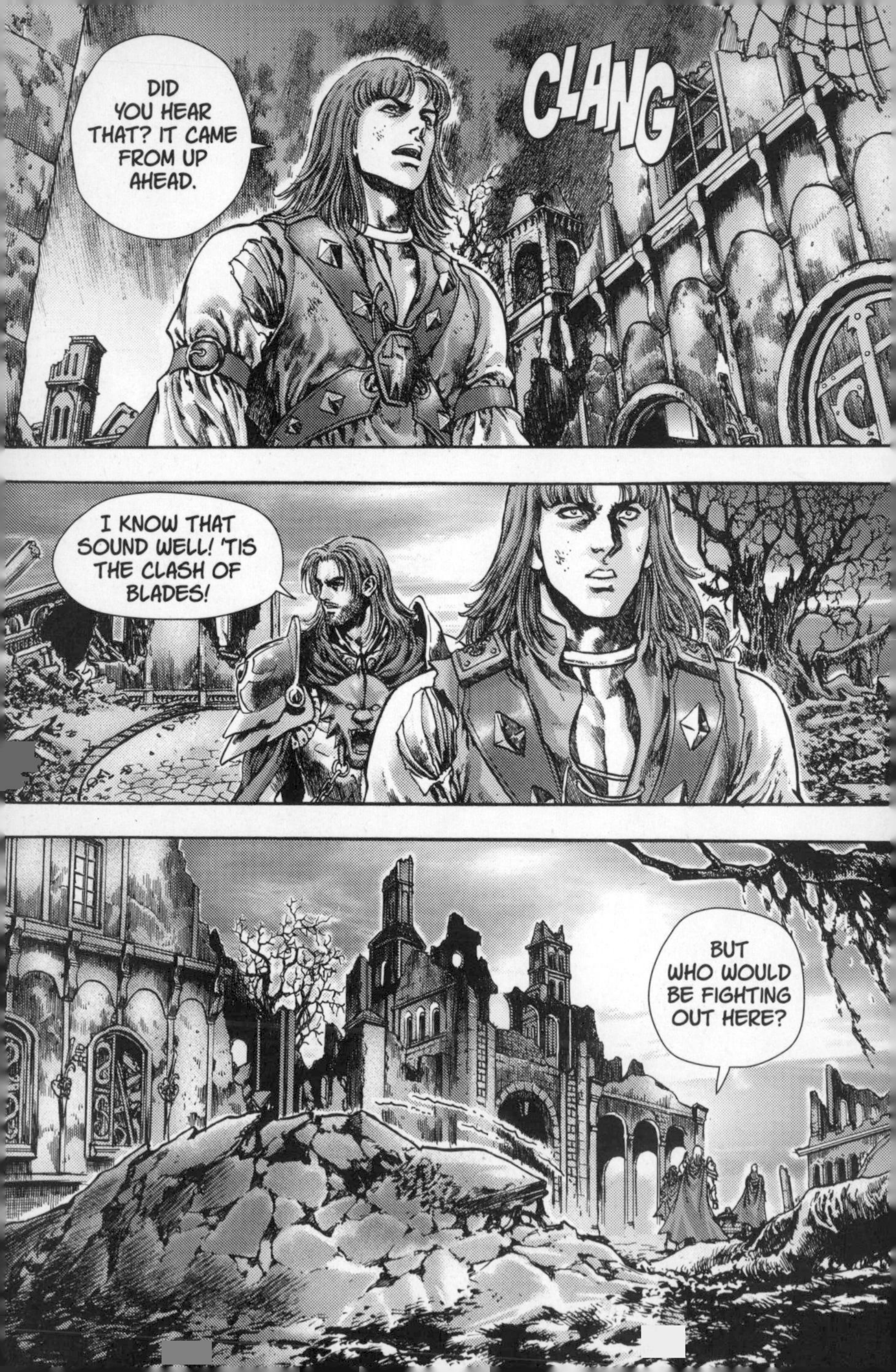
DID YOU HEAR THAT? IT CAME FROM UP AHEAD.
CLANG
I KNOW THAT SOUND WELL! 'TIS THE CLASH OF BLADES!
BUT WHO WOULD BE FIGHTING OUT HERE?

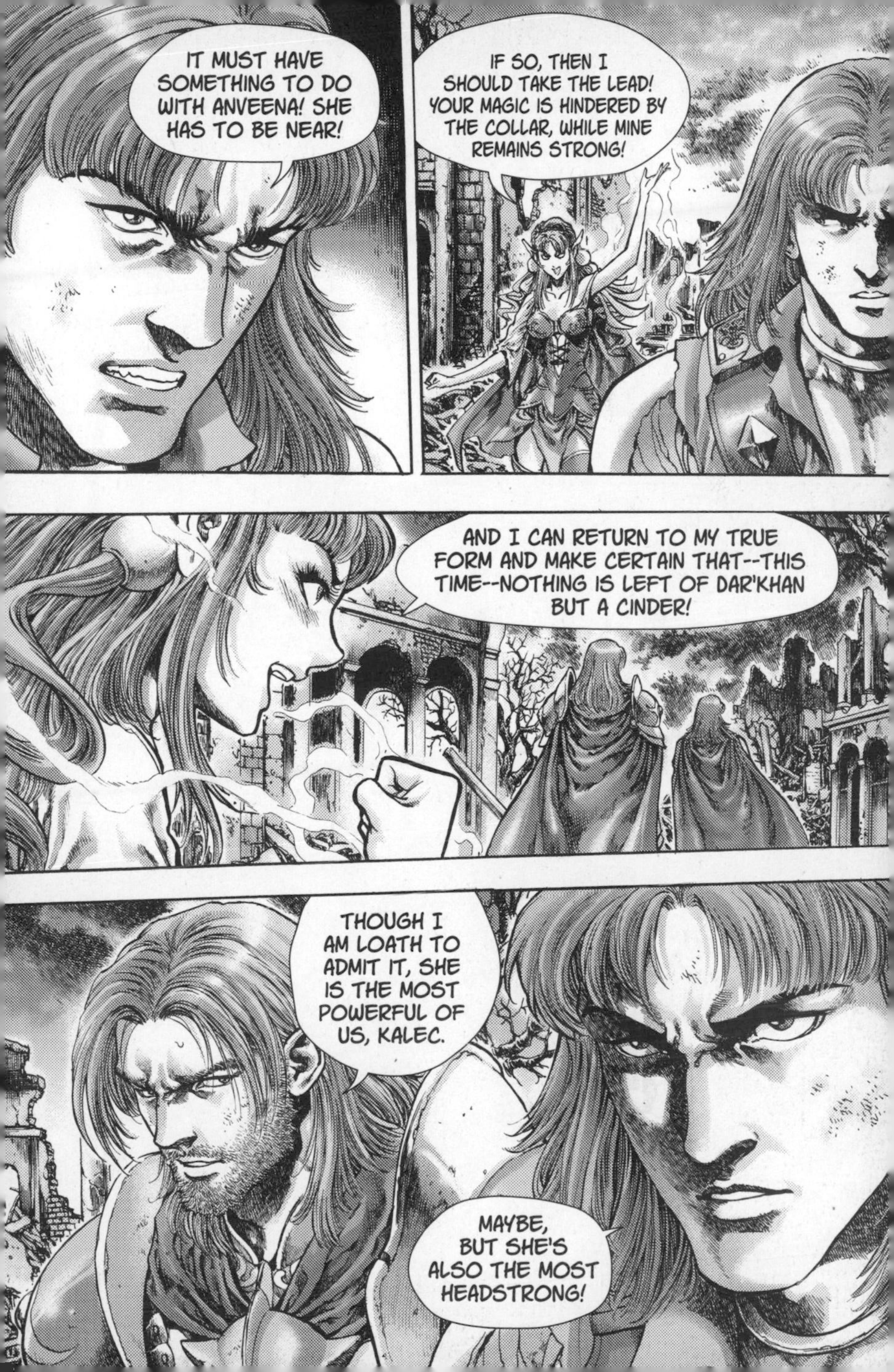
IT MUST HAVE SOMETHING TO DO WITH ANVEENA! SHE HAS TO BE NEAR!
IF SO, THEN I SHOULD TAKE THE LEAD! YOUR MAGIC IS HINDERED BY THE COLLAR, WHILE MINE REMAINS STRONG!
AND I CAN RETURN TO MY TRUE FORM AND MAKE CERTAIN THAT--THIS TIME--NOTHING IS LEFT OF DAR'KHAN BUT A CINDER!
THOUGH I AM LOATH TO ADMIT IT, SHE IS THE MOST POWERFUL OF US, KALEC.
MAYBE, BUT SHE'S ALSO THE MOST HEADSTRONG!

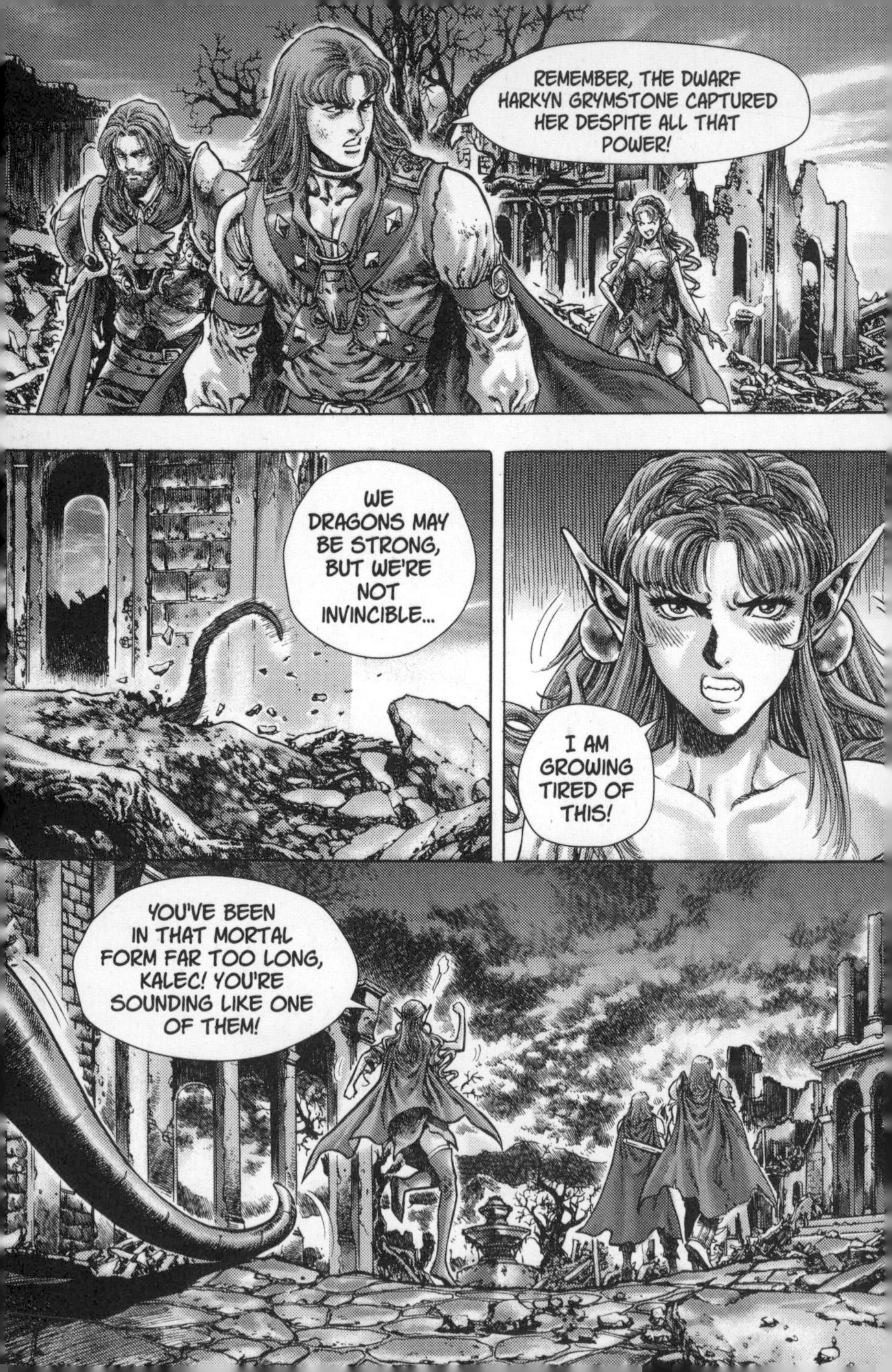
REMEMBER, THE DWARF HARKYN GRYMSTONE CAPTURED HER DESPITE ALL THAT POWER!
WE DRAGONS MAY BE STRONG, BUT WE'RE NOT INVINCIBLE...
I AM GROWING TIRED OF THIS!
YOU'VE BEEN IN THAT MORTAL FORM FAR TOO LONG, KALEC! YOU'RE SOUNDING LIKE ONE OF THEM!

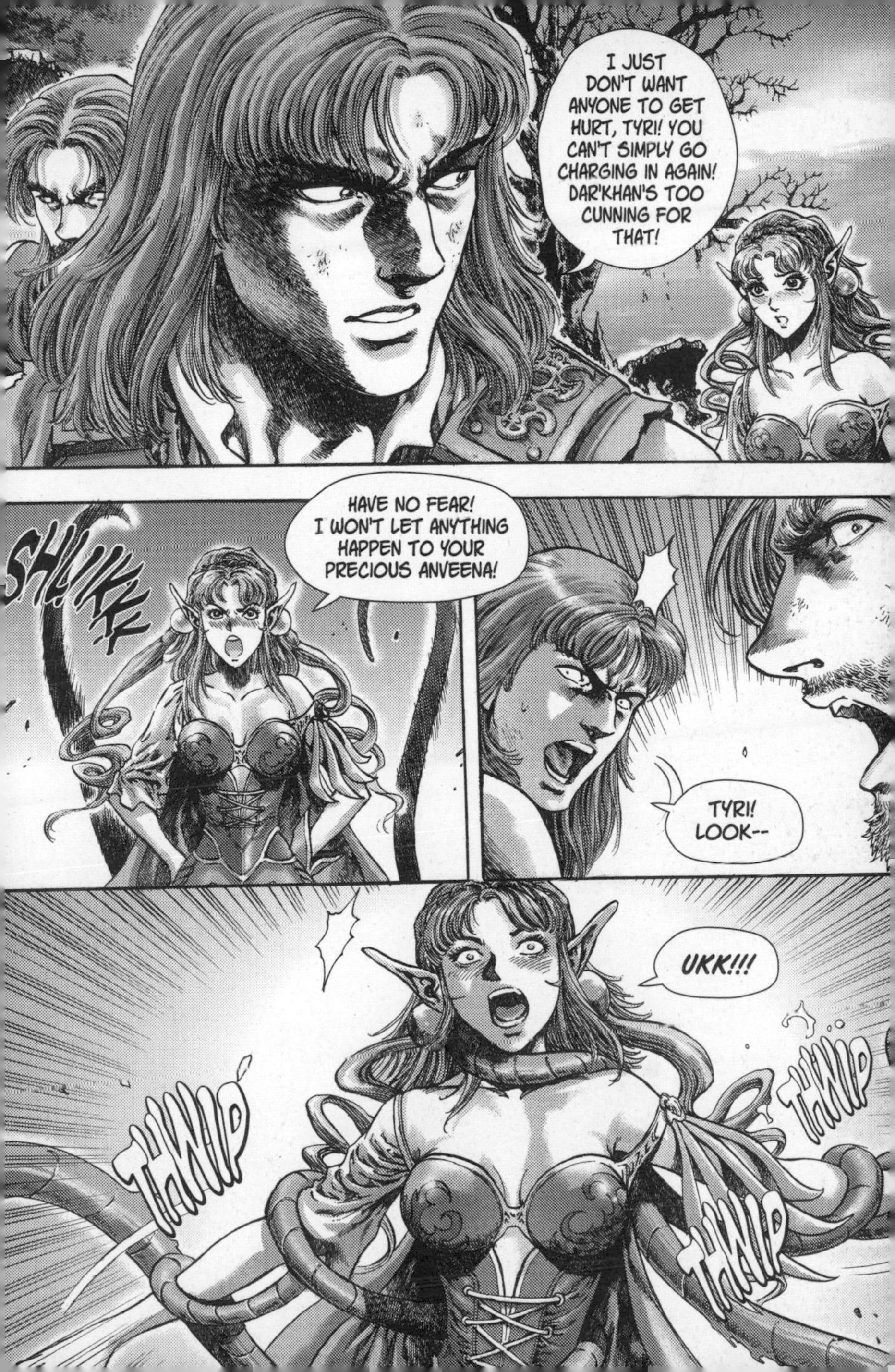

I JUST DON'T WANT ANYONE TO GET HURT, TYRI! YOU CAN'T SIMPLY GO CHARGING IN AGAIN! DAR'KHAN'S TOO CUNNING FOR THAT!
SHUKKK
HAVE NO FEAR! I WON'T LET ANYTHING HAPPEN TO YOUR PRECIOUS ANVEENA!
TYRI! LOOK--
UKK!!!
THWIP
THWIP
THWIP

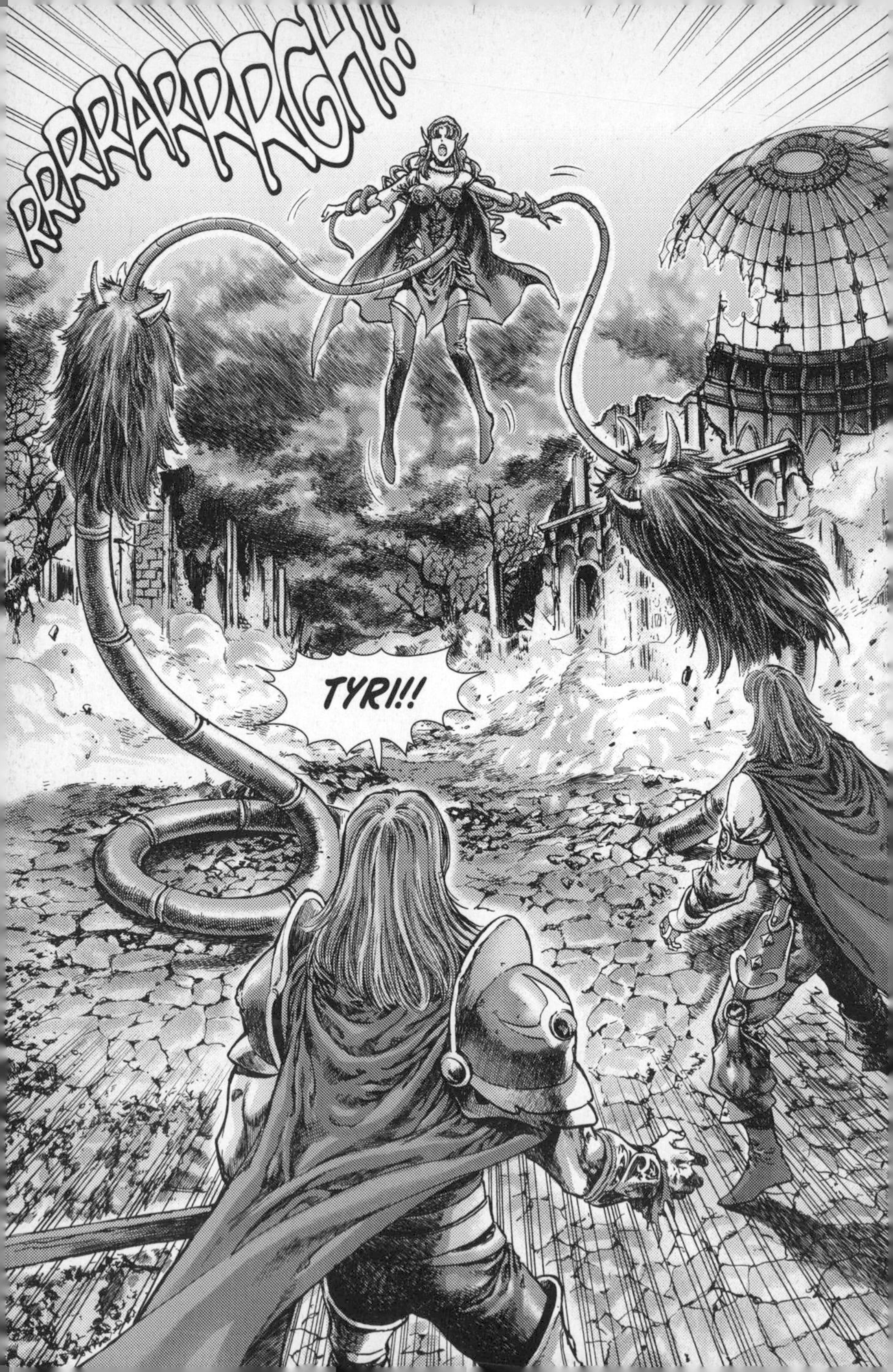
RRRRARRRGH!!
TYRI!!

CHAPTER THREE

CRY OF THE BANSHEE

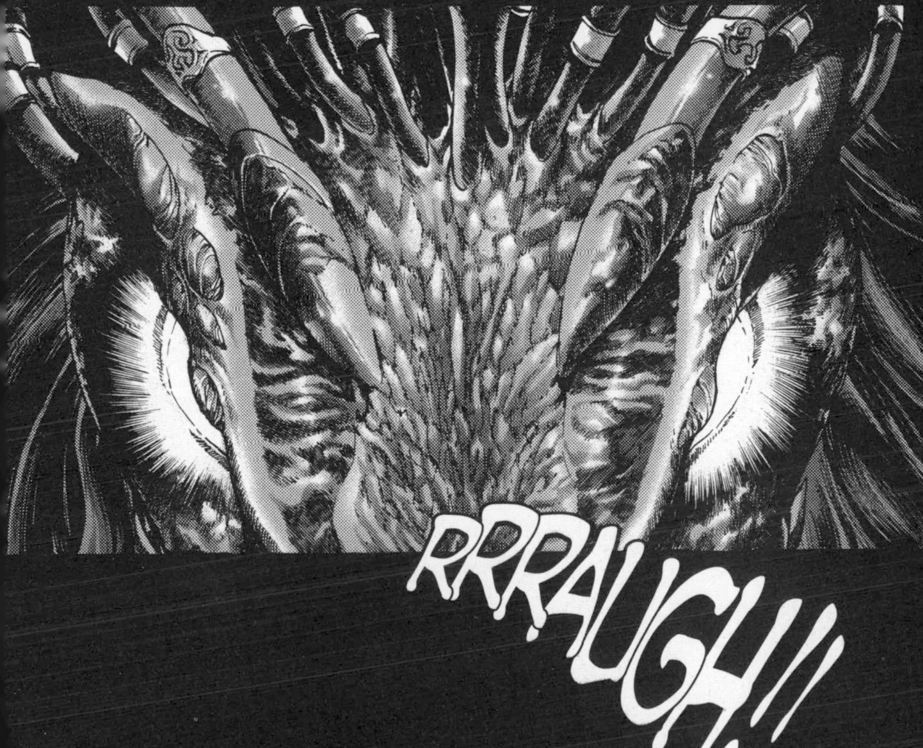
RRRAUGH!!

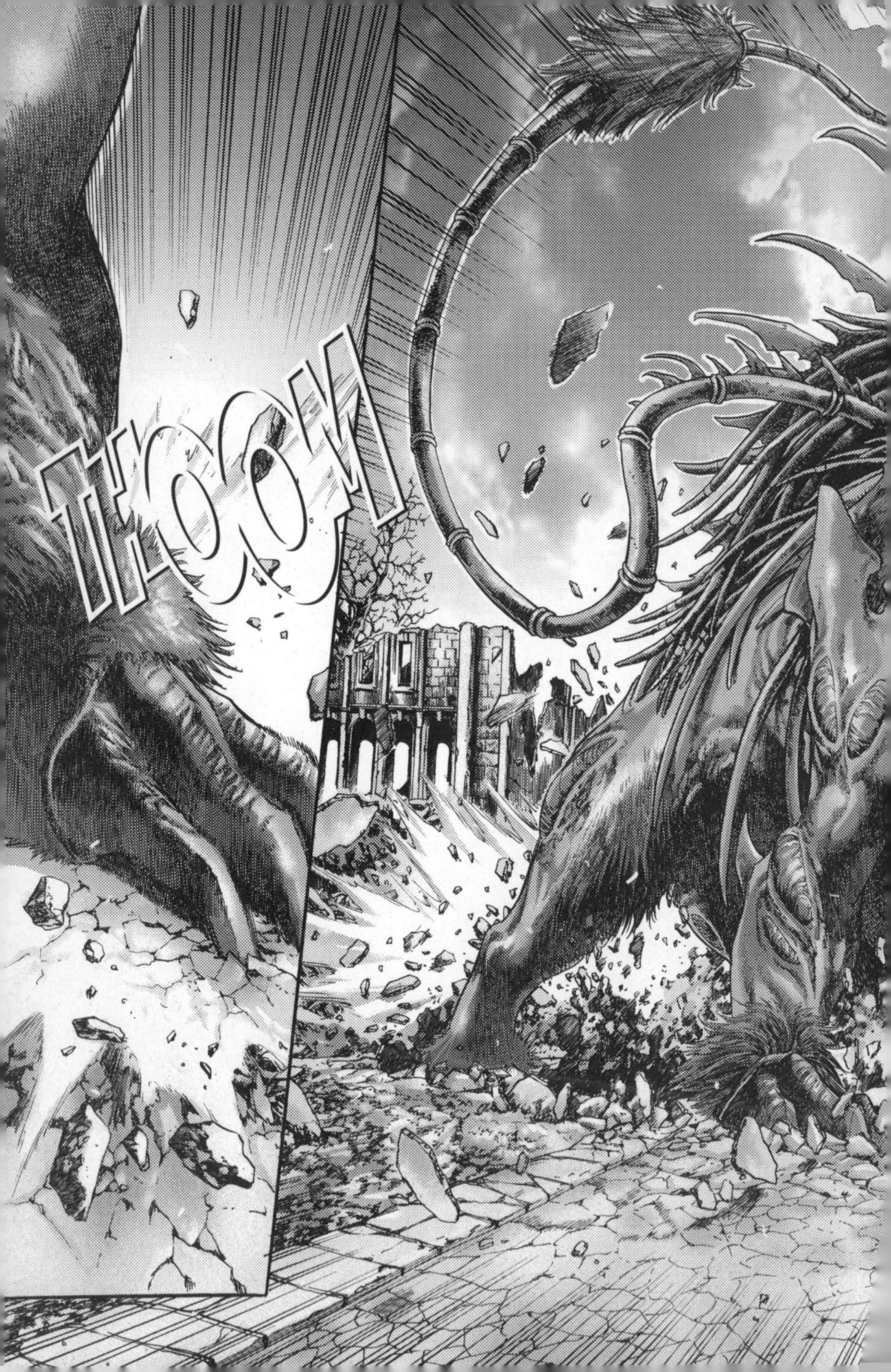
THOOM

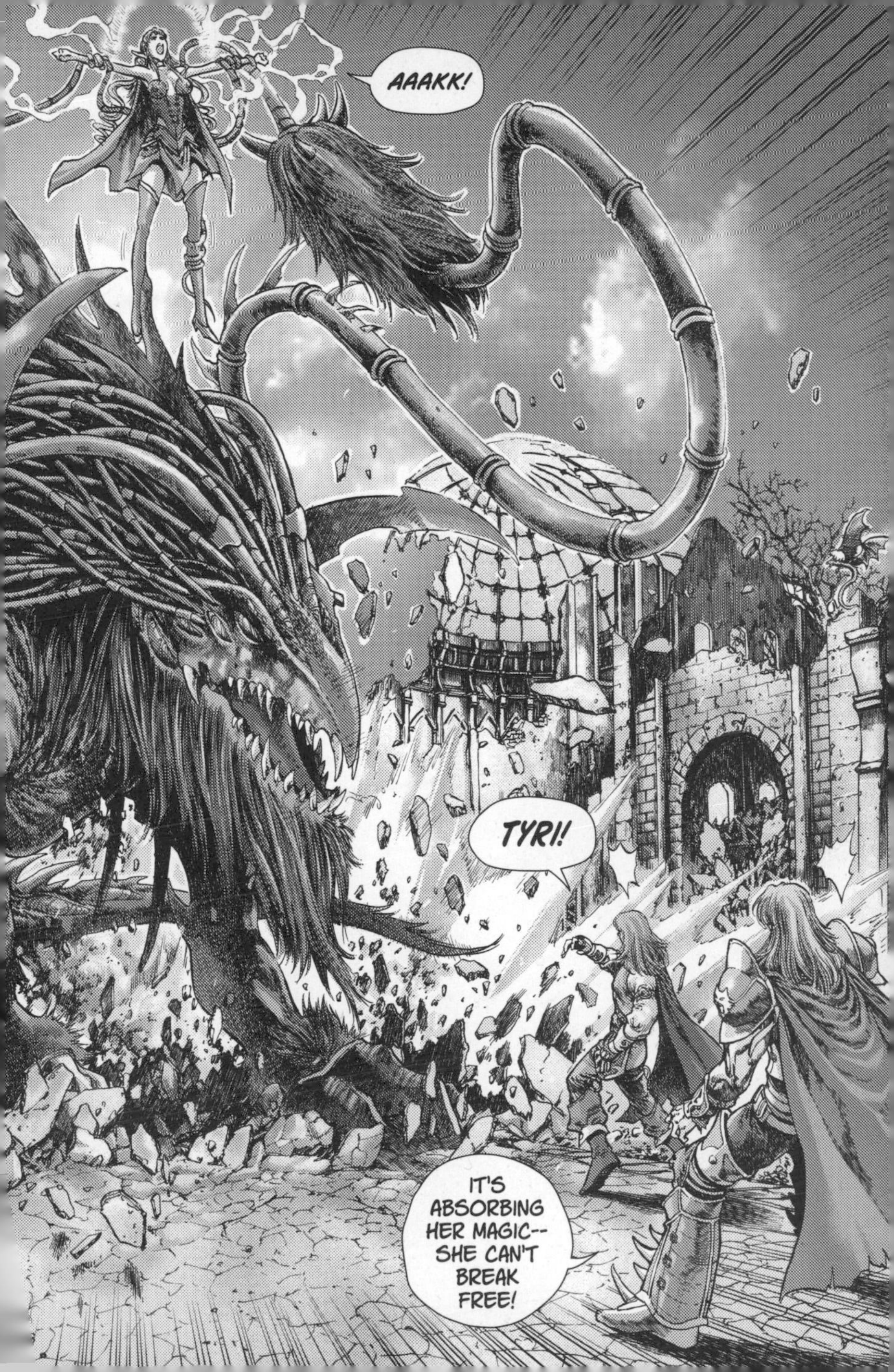
AAAKK!
TYRI!
IT'S ABSORBING HER MAGIC--SHE CAN'T BREAK FREE!

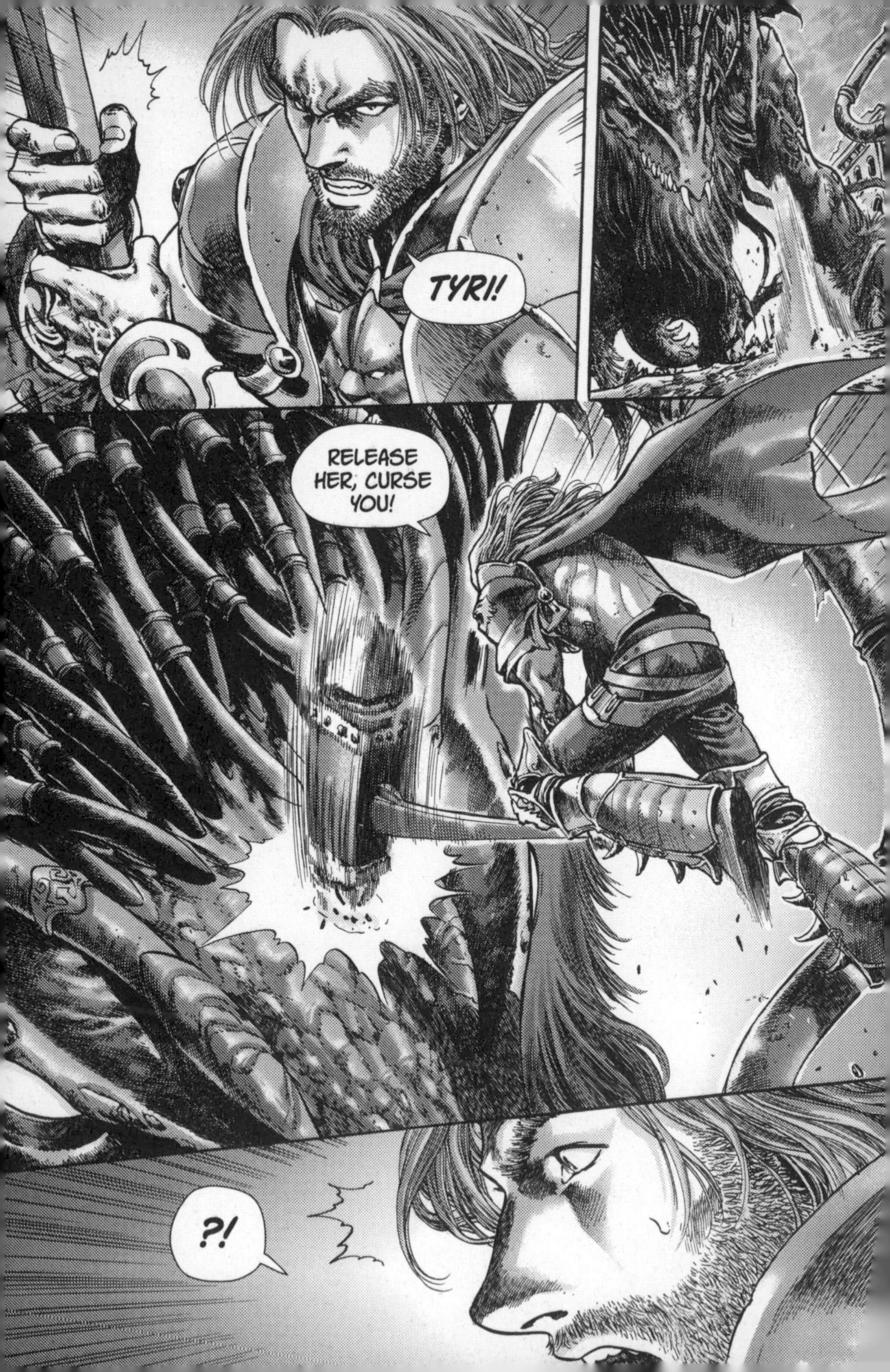
TYRI!
RELEASE HER, CURSE YOU!
?!

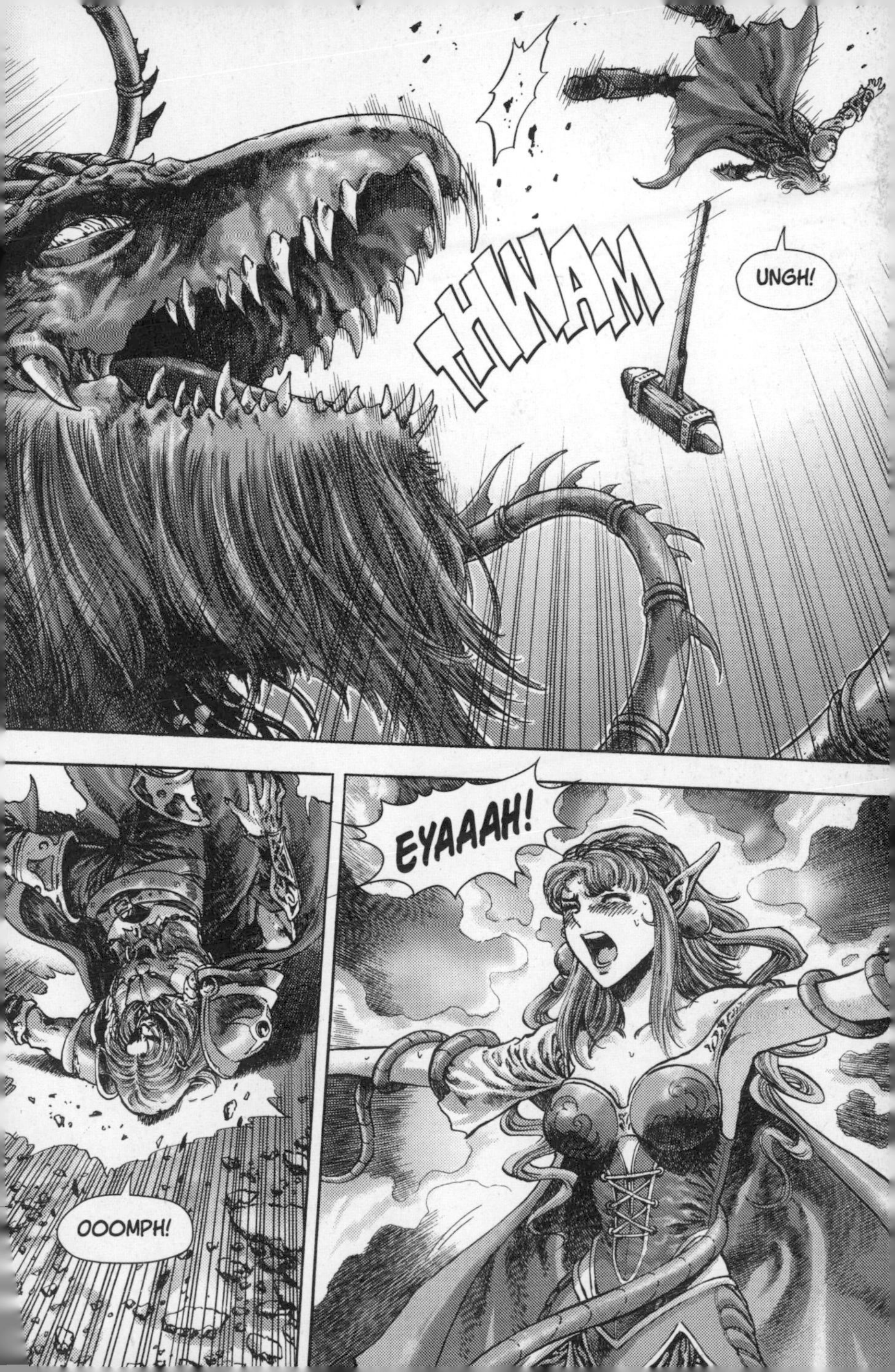
THWAM
UNGH!
OOOMPH!
EYAAAH!

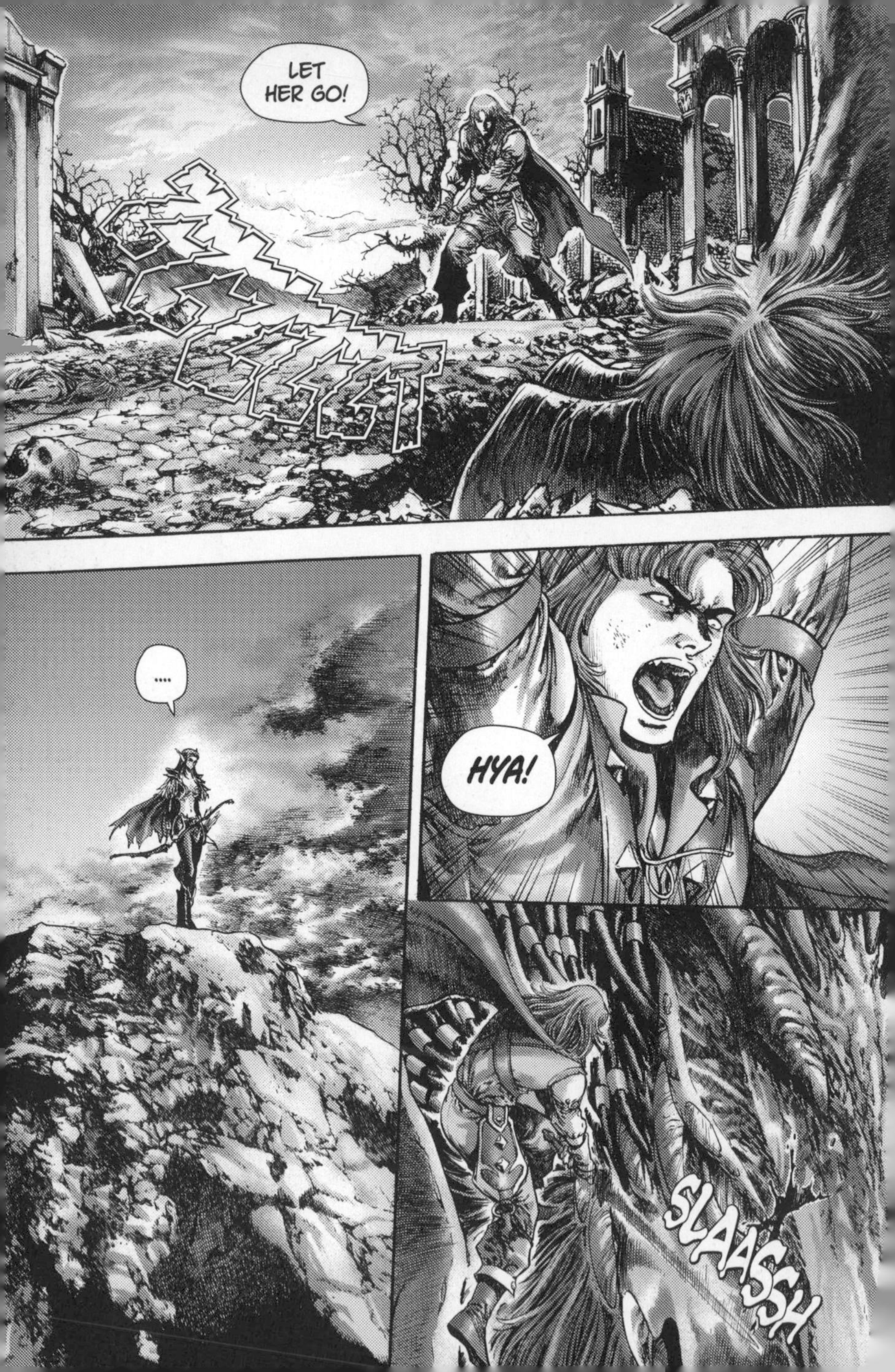
LET HER GO!
....
HYA!
SLAASSH

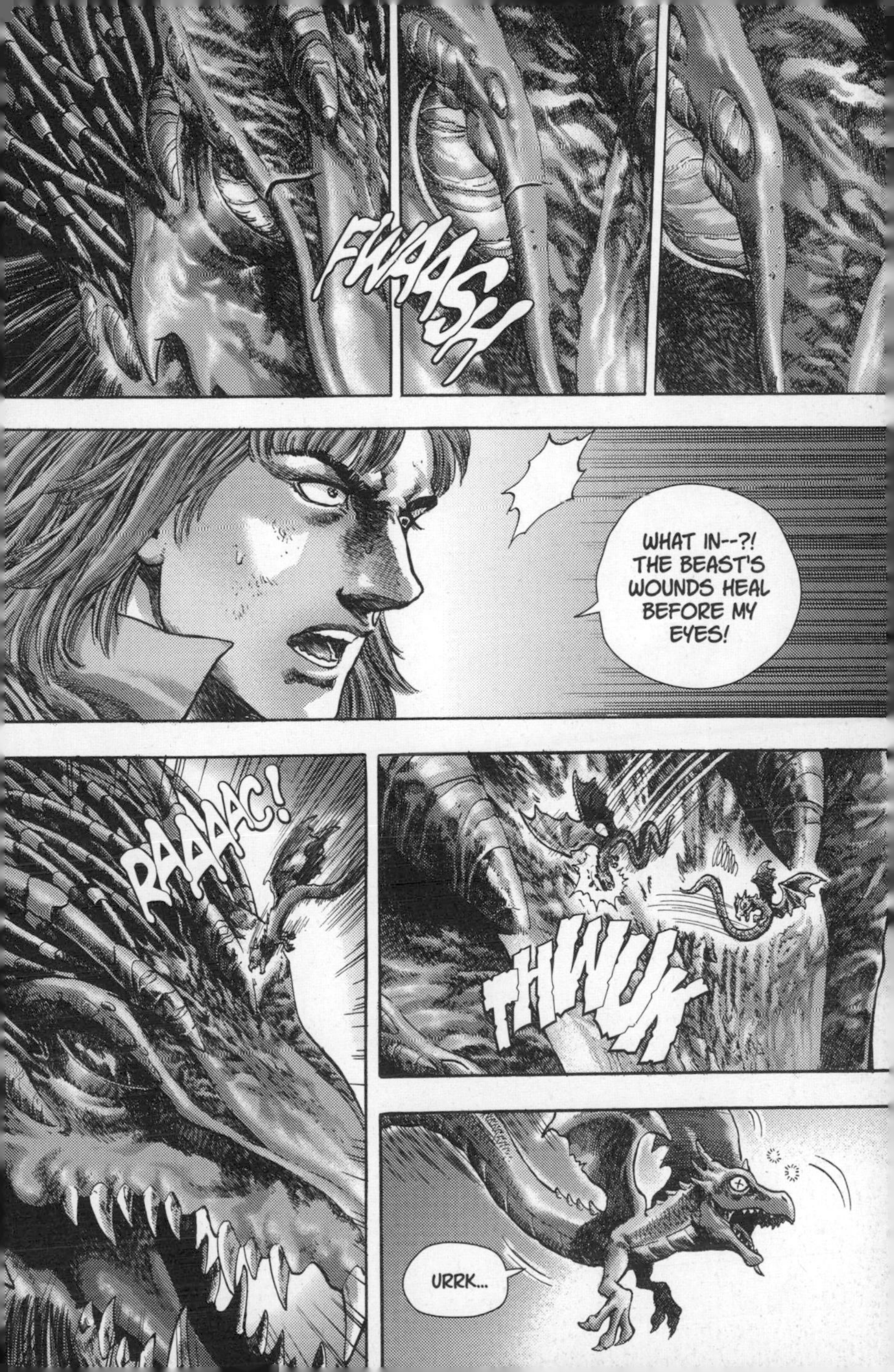
FWAASH
WHAT IN--?! THE BEAST'S WOUNDS HEAL BEFORE MY EYES!
RAAAAC!
THWUK
URRK...

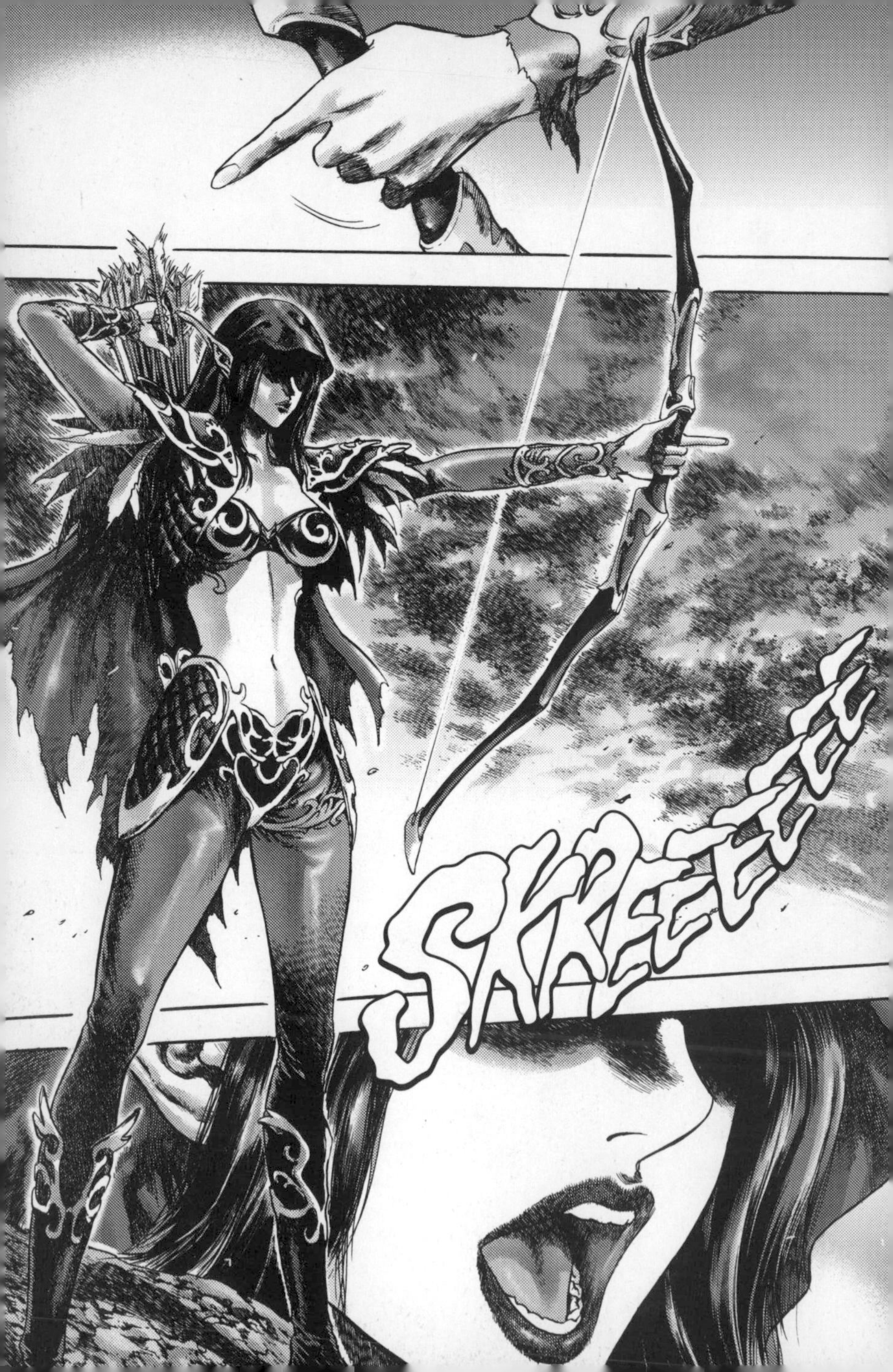
SKREEEEEEEE

EEEEEEEEEEEEEEEEEEEEEEEEEEEE

!!!

HER!

RRRAUGH!!

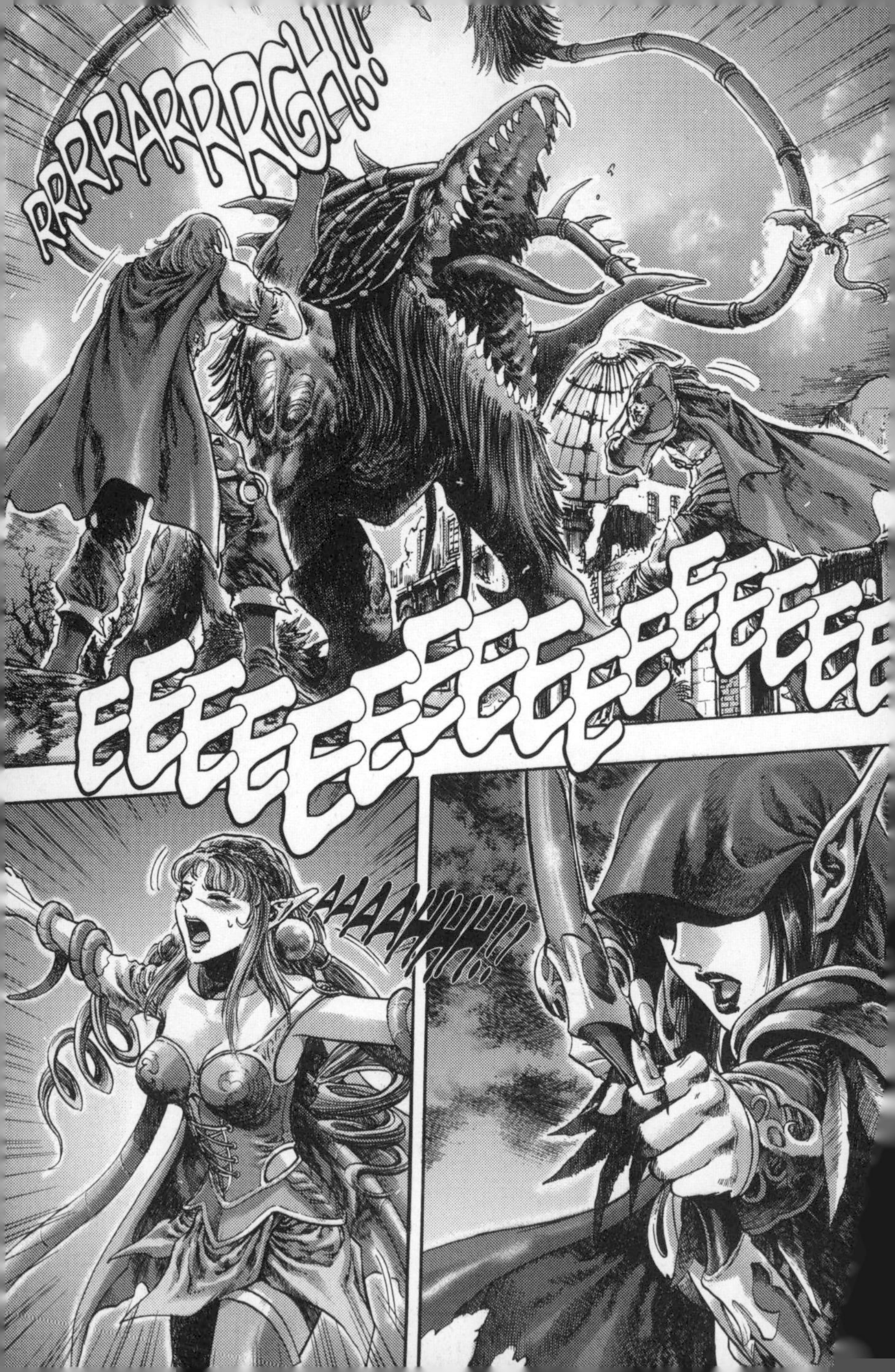
RRRRARRRRGH!!!
EEEEEEEEEEEEEEEEEE
AAAAHHHH!!!

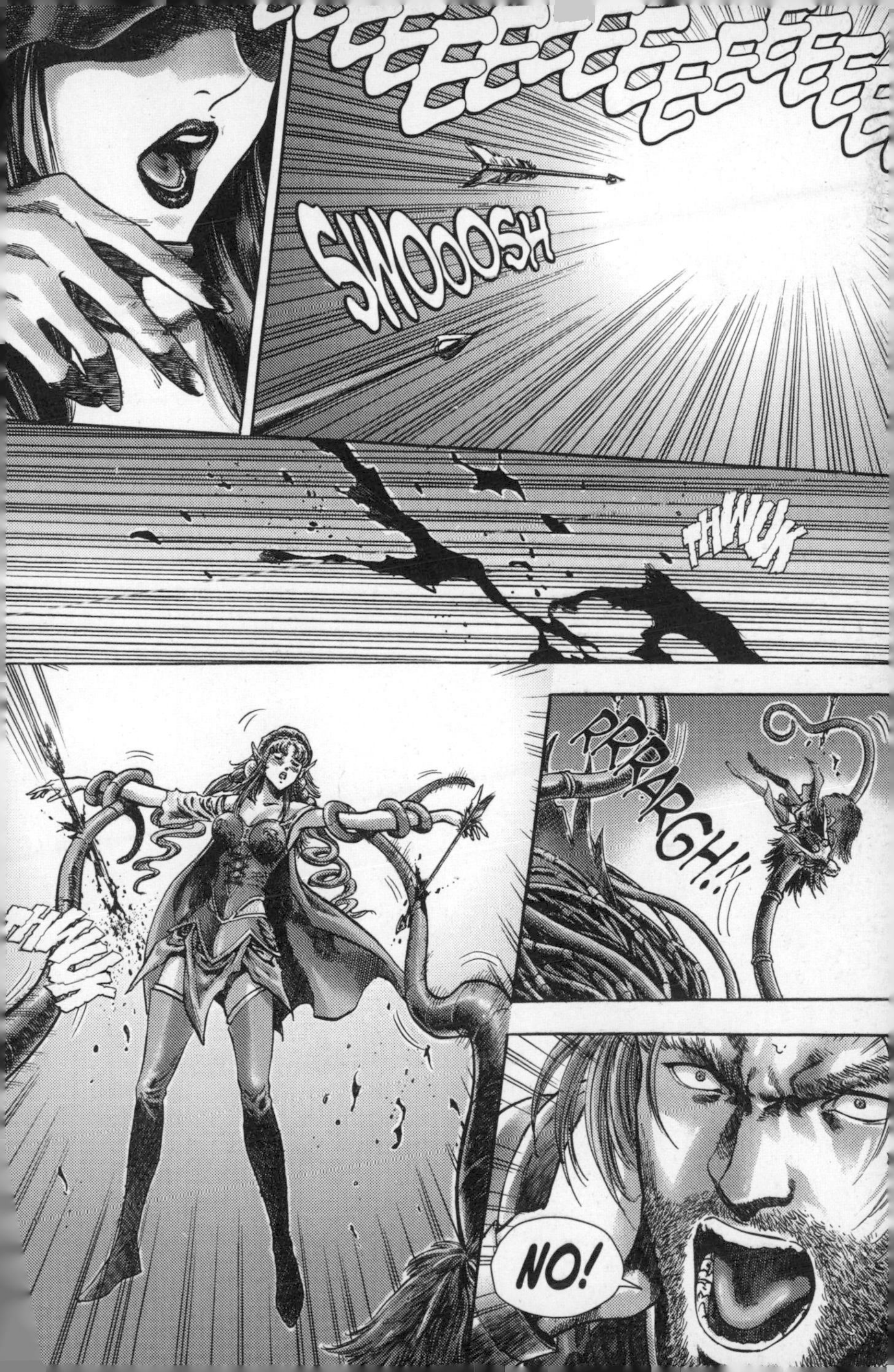
EEEEEEEEEEEEEEEEE
SWOOOSH
THWUK
THWUK
RRRARGH!!
NO!

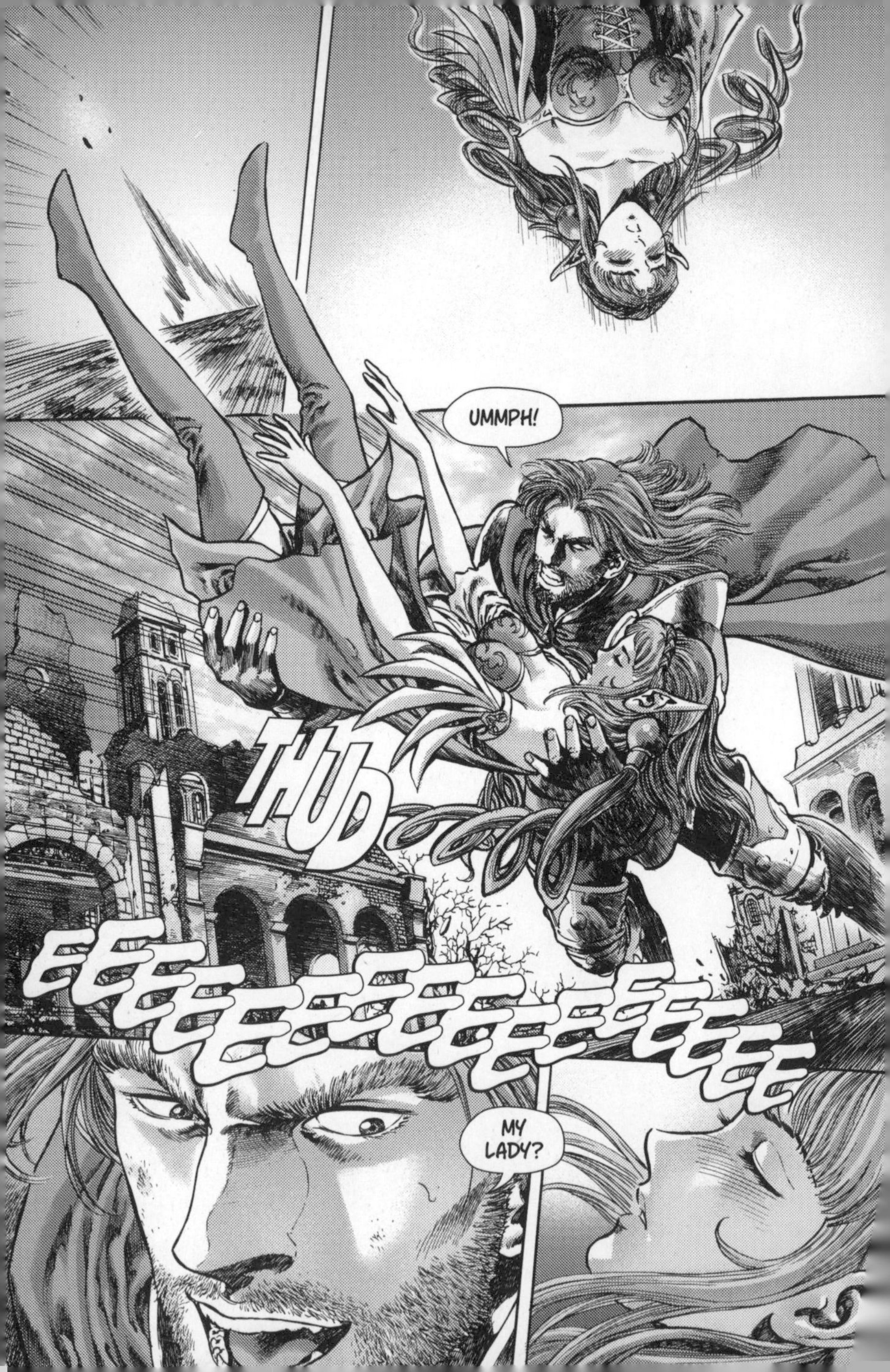
UMMPH!
THUD
EEEEEEEEEEEEEEEEEEEEEEEE
MY LADY?

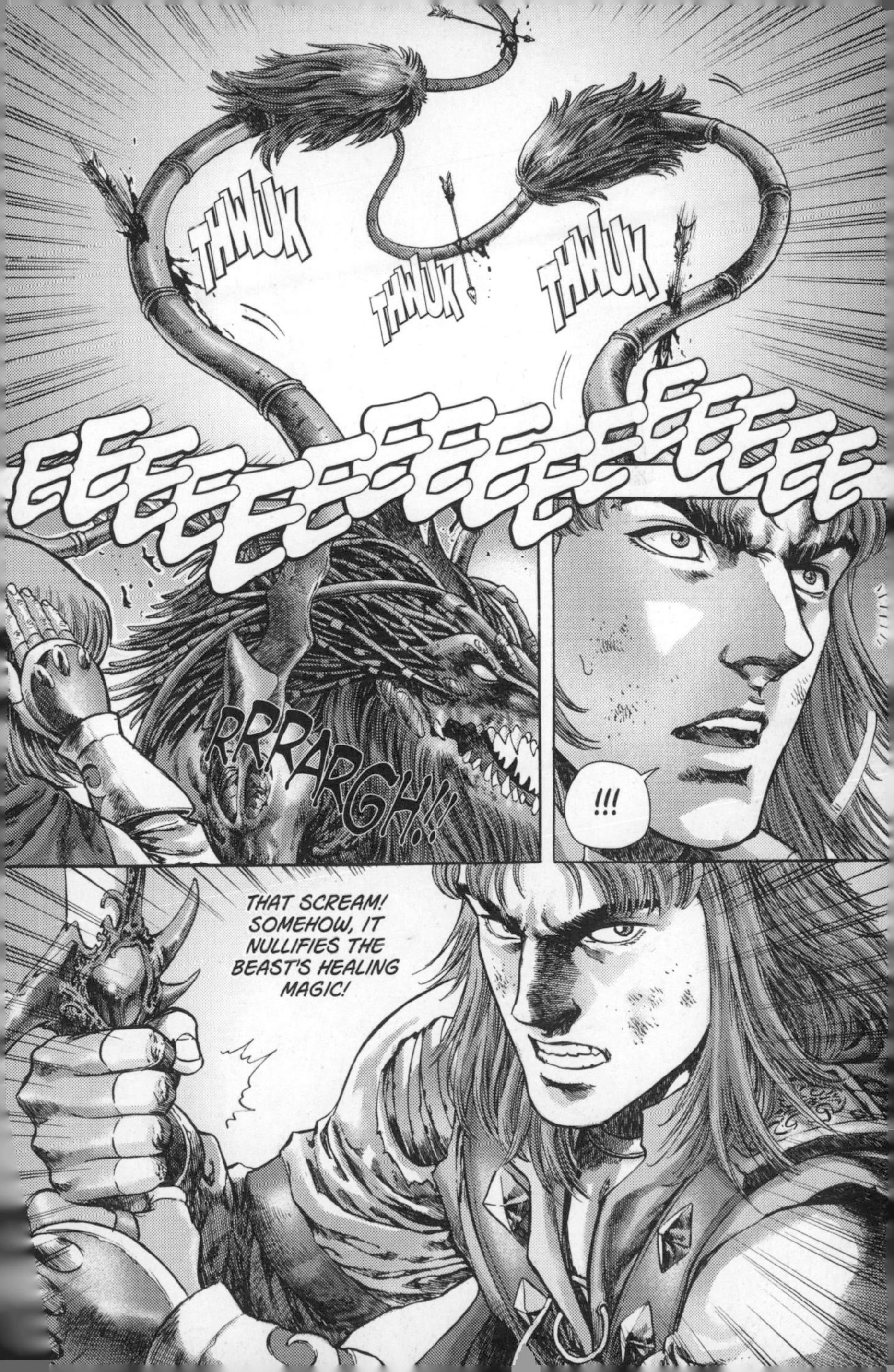
THWUK
THWUK
THWUK
EEEEEEEEEEEEEEEEEEEEEEEE
RRRARGH!!
!!!
THAT SCREAM! SOMEHOW, IT NULLIFIES THE BEAST'S HEALING MAGIC!

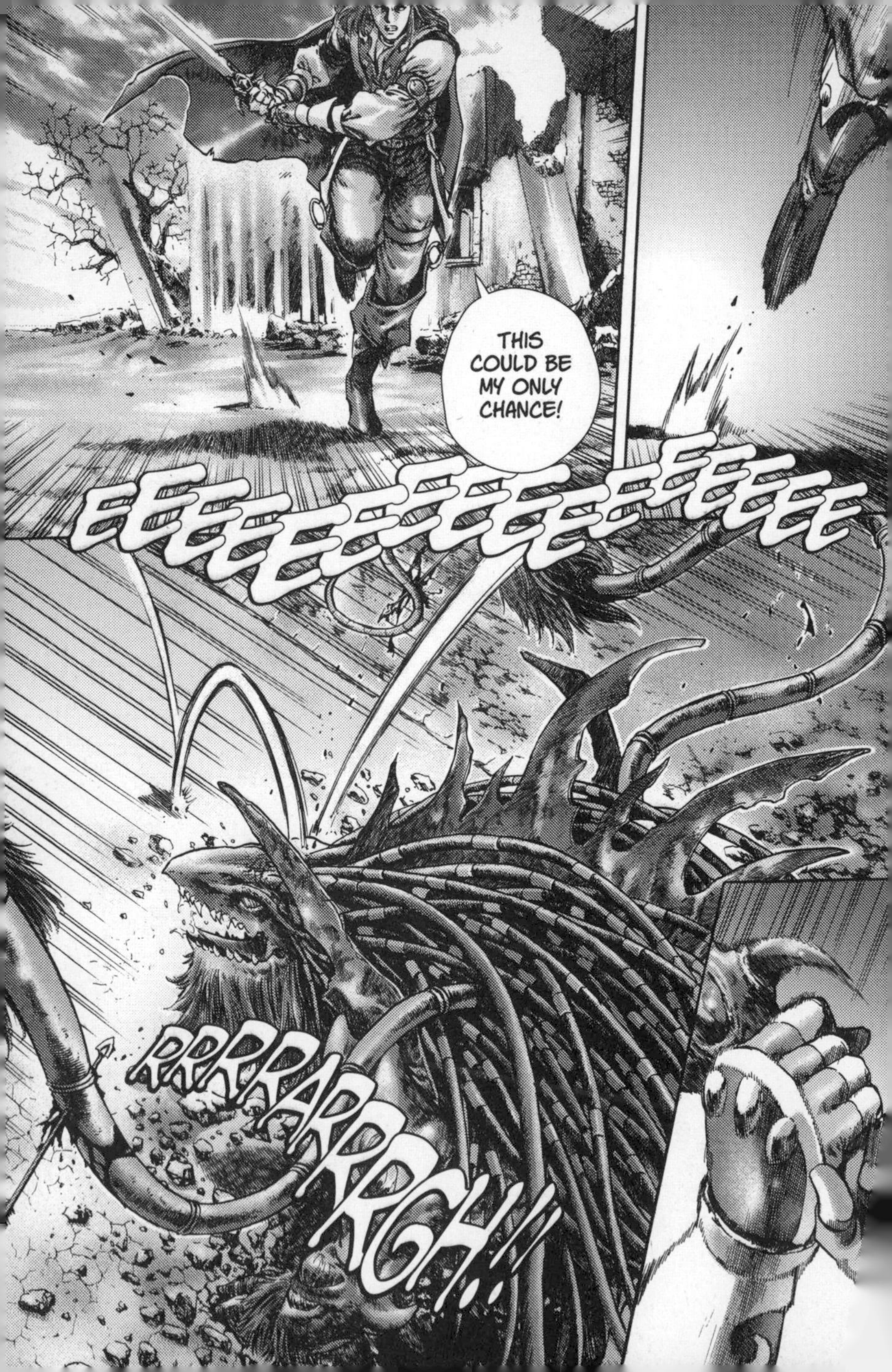
THIS COULD BE MY ONLY CHANCE!
EEEEEEEEEEEEEEEEEEEEEEE
RRRRARRRGH!!

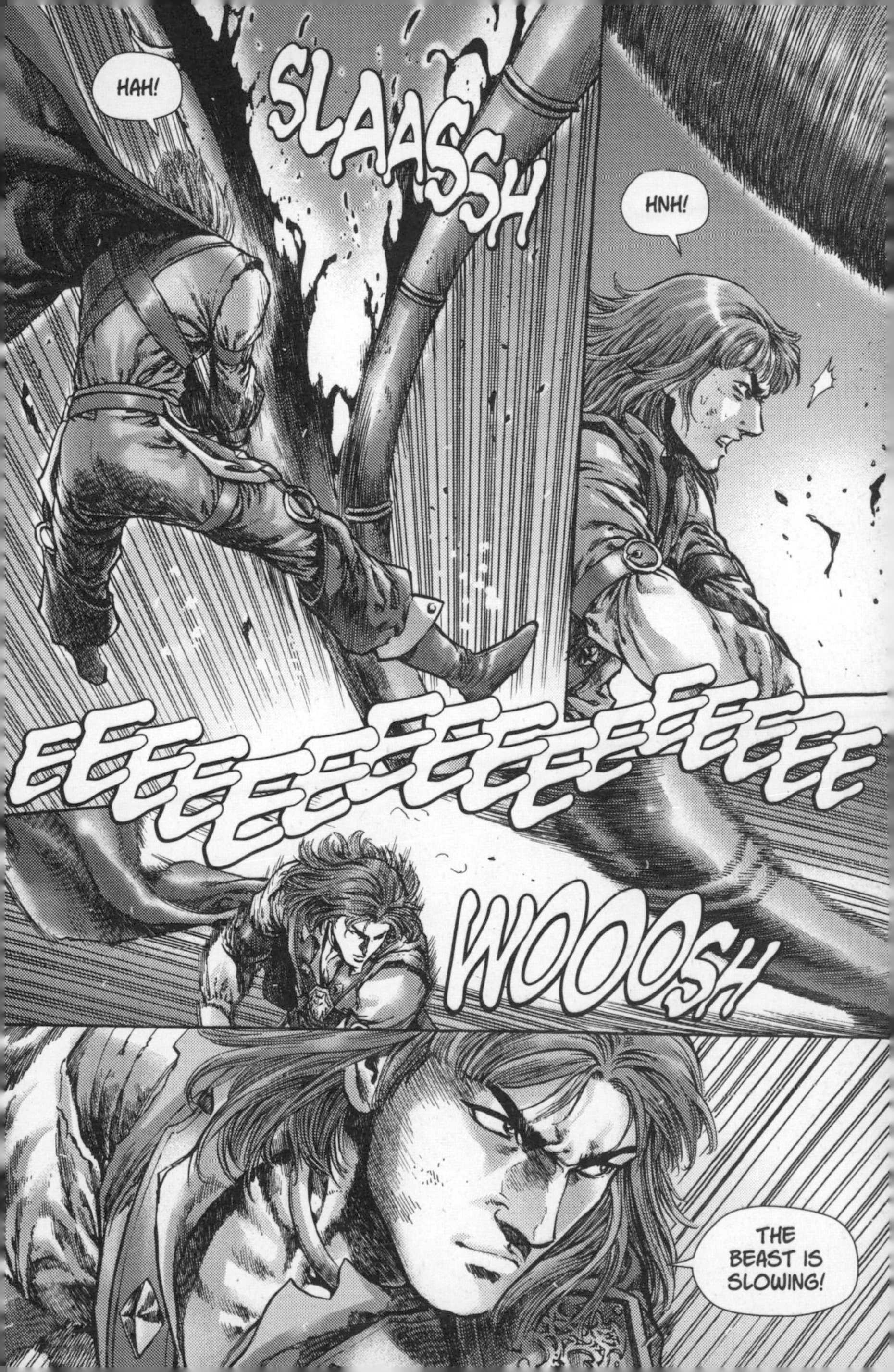
HAH!
SLAASSH
HNH!
EEEEEEEEEEEEEEEEEEEEEEEEE
WOOOSH
THE BEAST IS SLOWING!

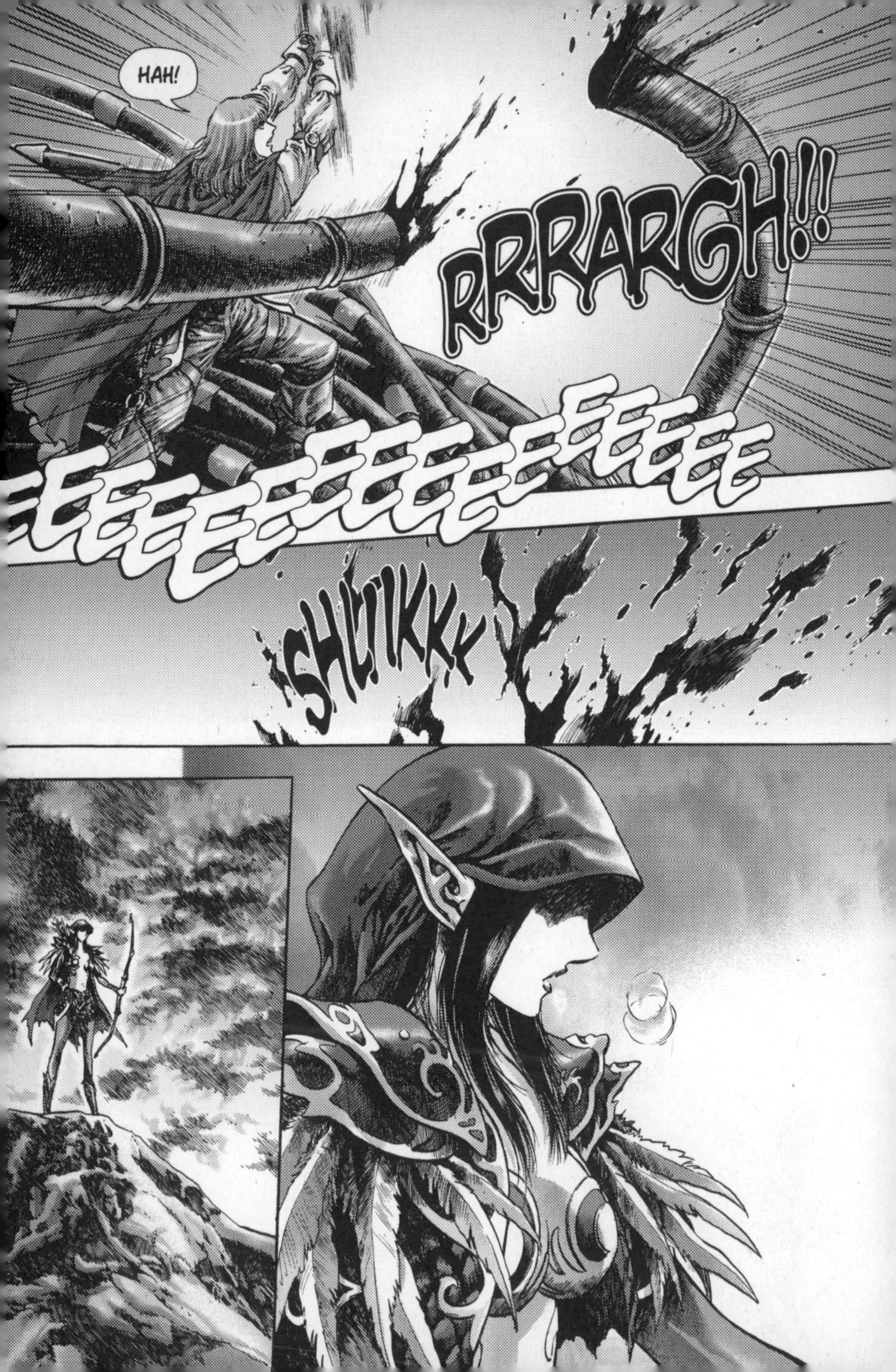
HAH!
RRRARGH!!!
EEEEEEEEEEEEEEEEEE
SHUIKKK

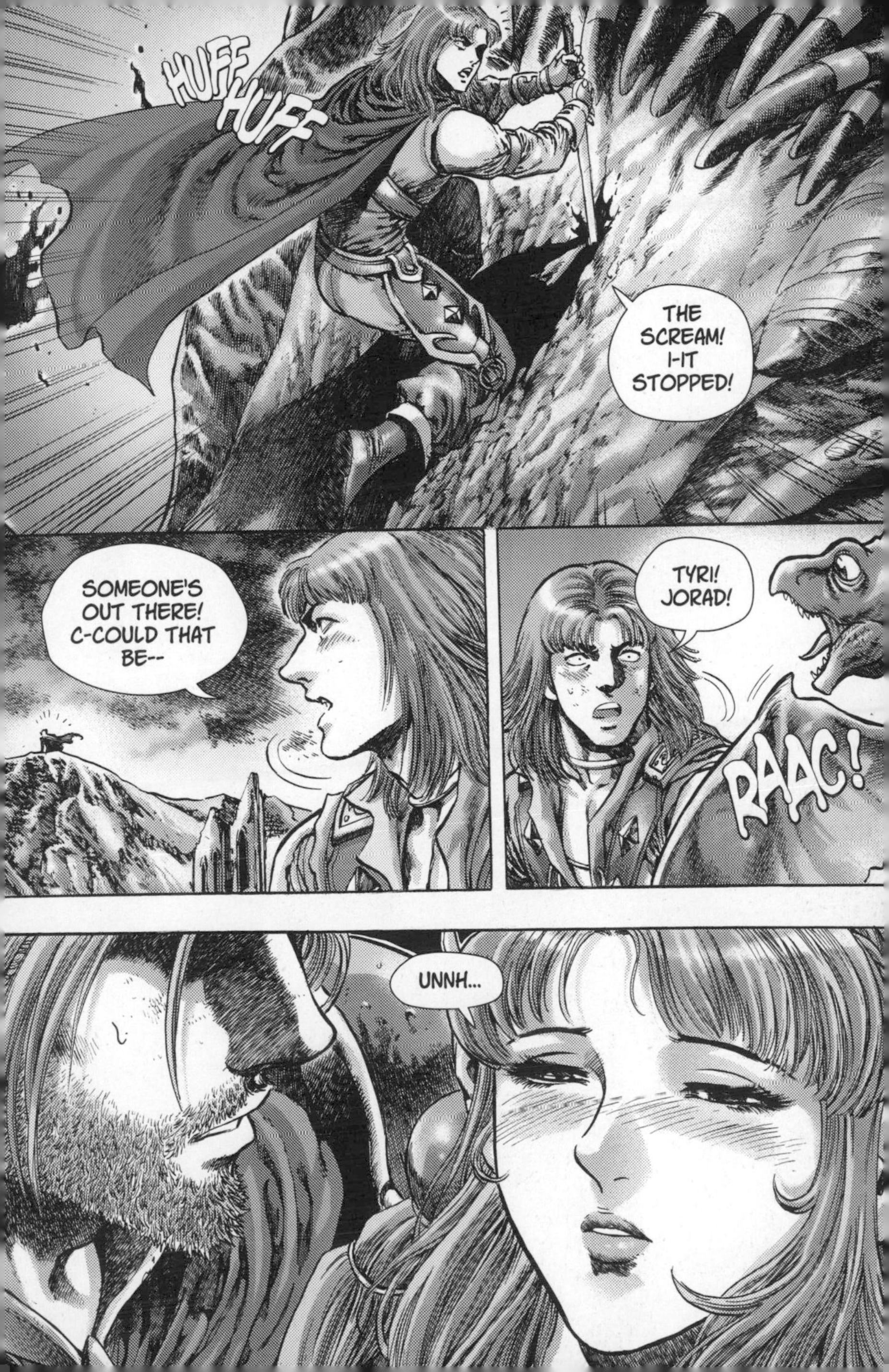
HUFF HUFF
THE SCREAM! I-IT STOPPED!
SOMEONE'S OUT THERE! C-COULD THAT BE--
TYRI! JORAD!
RAAC!
UNNH...

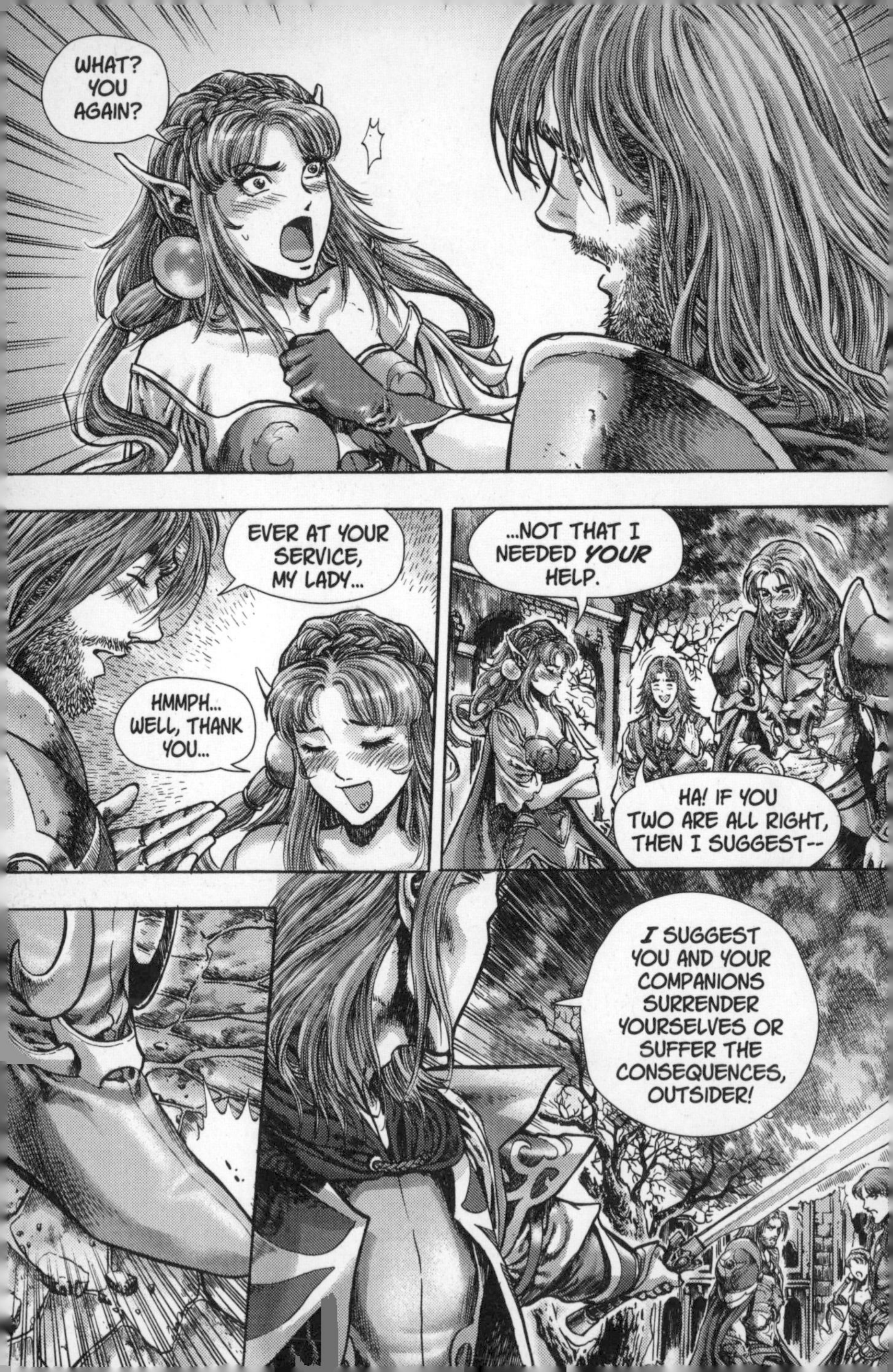
WHAT? YOU AGAIN?
EVER AT YOUR SERVICE, MY LADY...
HMMPH... WELL, THANK YOU...
...NOT THAT I NEEDED *YOUR* HELP.
HA! IF YOU TWO ARE ALL RIGHT, THEN I SUGGEST--
I SUGGEST YOU AND YOUR COMPANIONS SURRENDER YOURSELVES OR SUFFER THE CONSEQUENCES, OUTSIDER!

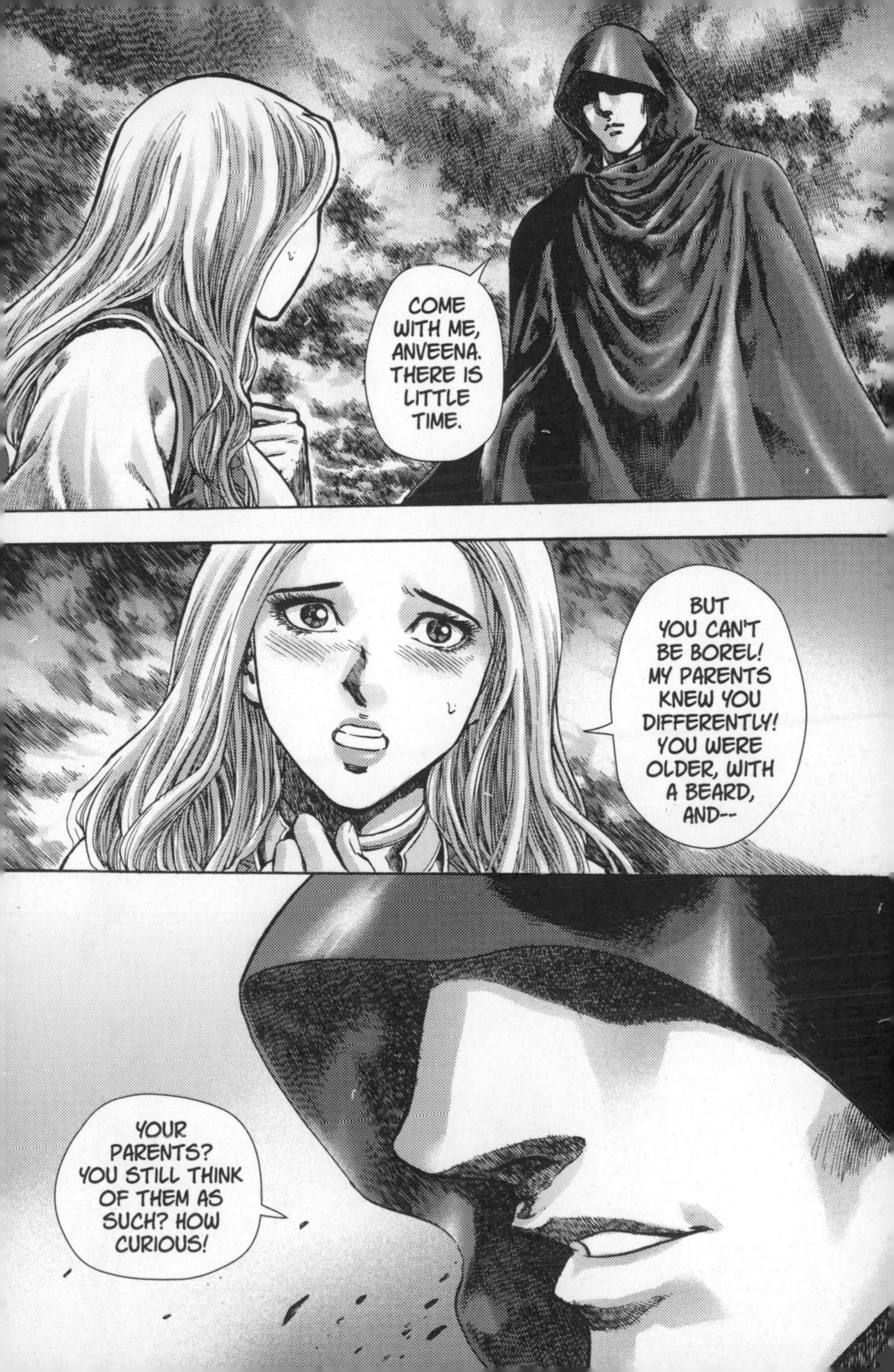
COME WITH ME, ANVEENA. THERE IS LITTLE TIME.
BUT YOU CAN'T BE BOREL! MY PARENTS KNEW YOU DIFFERENTLY! YOU WERE OLDER, WITH A BEARD, AND--
YOUR PARENTS? YOU STILL THINK OF THEM AS SUCH? HOW CURIOUS!

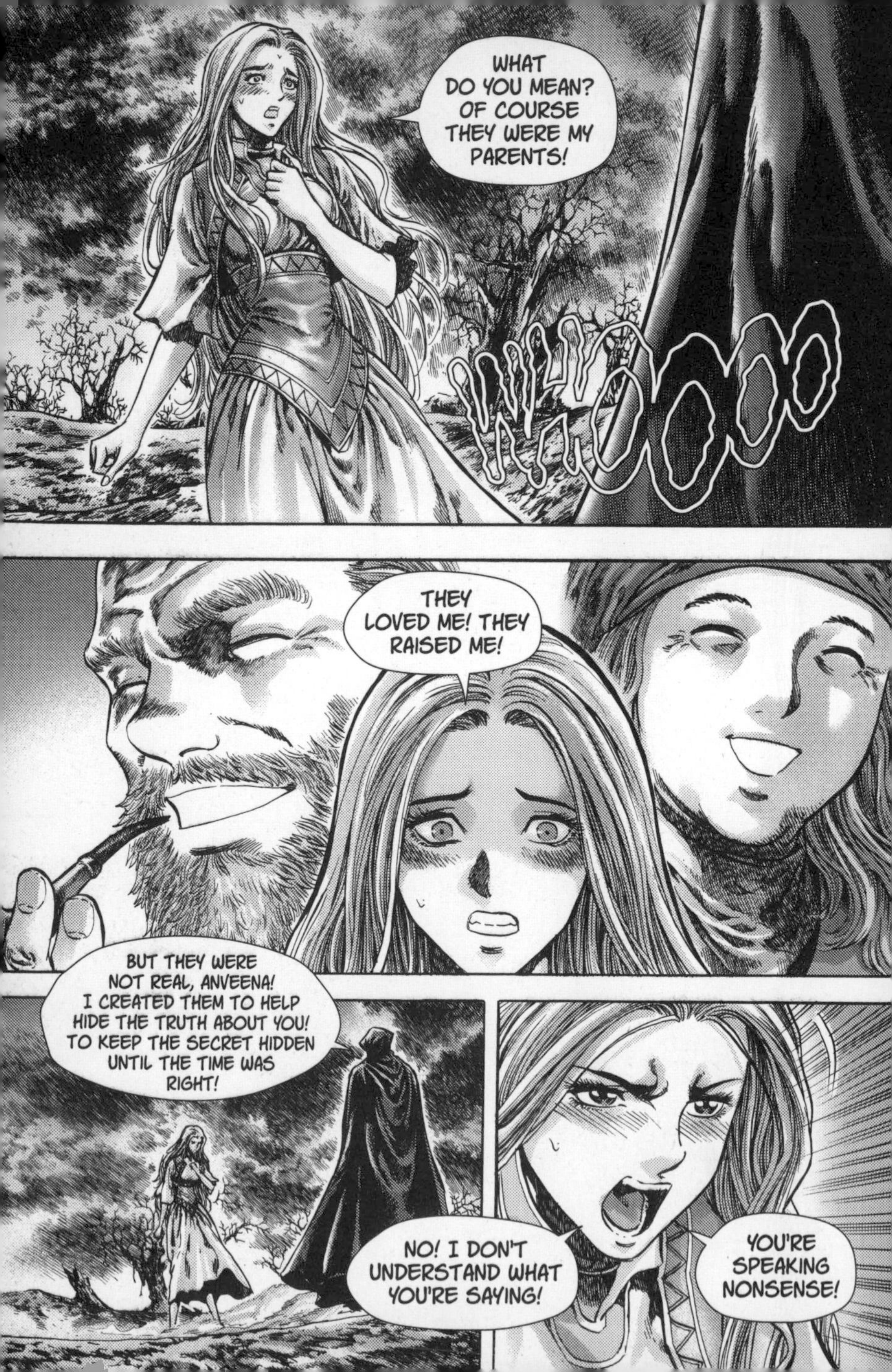
WHAT DO YOU MEAN? OF COURSE THEY WERE MY PARENTS!
WHOOOOOO
THEY LOVED ME! THEY RAISED ME!
BUT THEY WERE NOT REAL, ANVEENA! I CREATED THEM TO HELP HIDE THE TRUTH ABOUT YOU! TO KEEP THE SECRET HIDDEN UNTIL THE TIME WAS RIGHT!
NO! I DON'T UNDERSTAND WHAT YOU'RE SAYING!
YOU'RE SPEAKING NONSENSE!

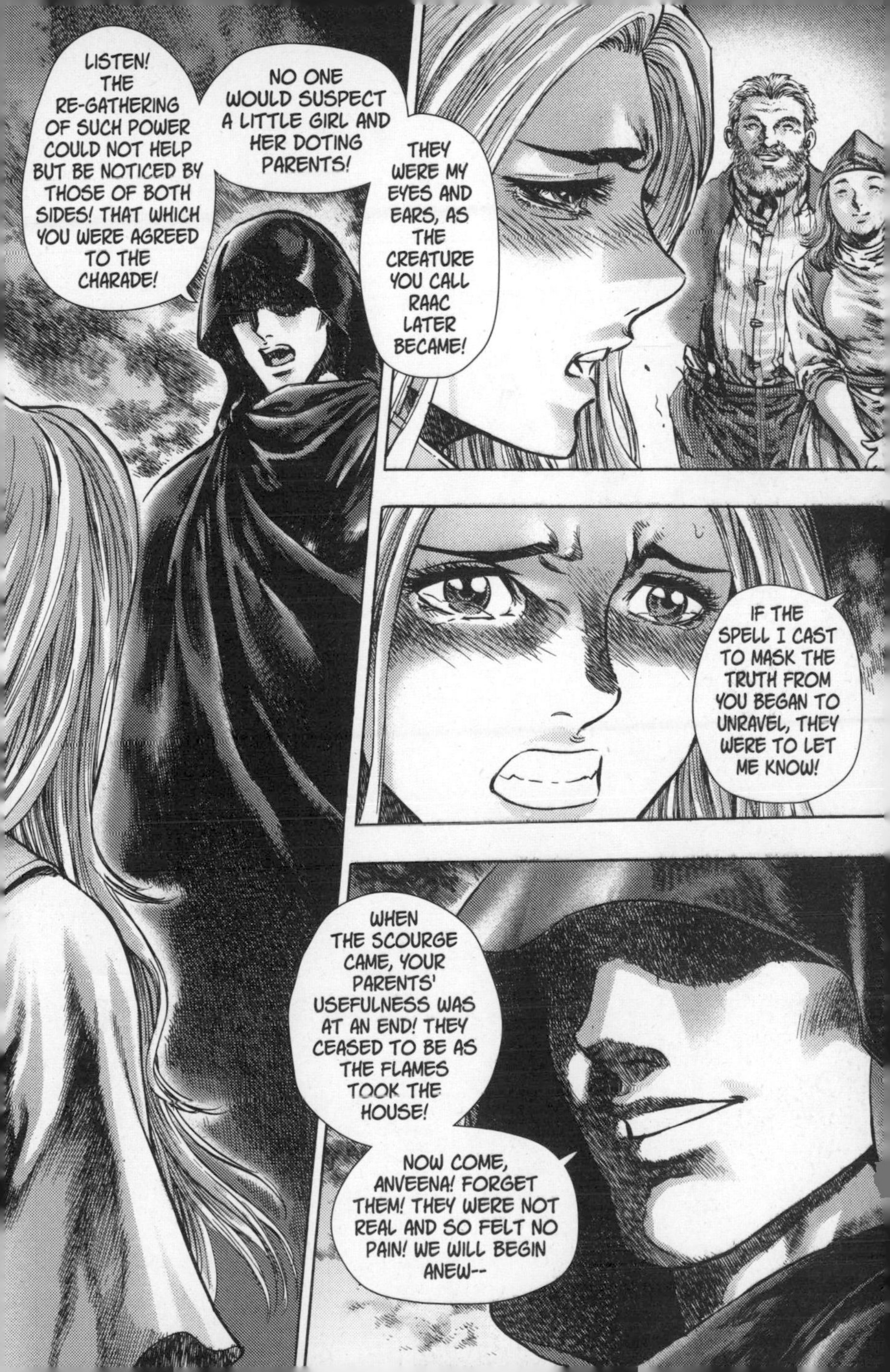
LISTEN! THE RE-GATHERING OF SUCH POWER COULD NOT HELP BUT BE NOTICED BY THOSE OF BOTH SIDES! THAT WHICH YOU WERE AGREED TO THE CHARADE!
NO ONE WOULD SUSPECT A LITTLE GIRL AND HER DOTING PARENTS!
THEY WERE MY EYES AND EARS, AS THE CREATURE YOU CALL RAAC LATER BECAME!
IF THE SPELL I CAST TO MASK THE TRUTH FROM YOU BEGAN TO UNRAVEL, THEY WERE TO LET ME KNOW!
WHEN THE SCOURGE CAME, YOUR PARENTS' USEFULNESS WAS AT AN END! THEY CEASED TO BE AS THE FLAMES TOOK THE HOUSE!
NOW COME, ANVEENA! FORGET THEM! THEY WERE NOT REAL AND SO FELT NO PAIN! WE WILL BEGIN ANEW--

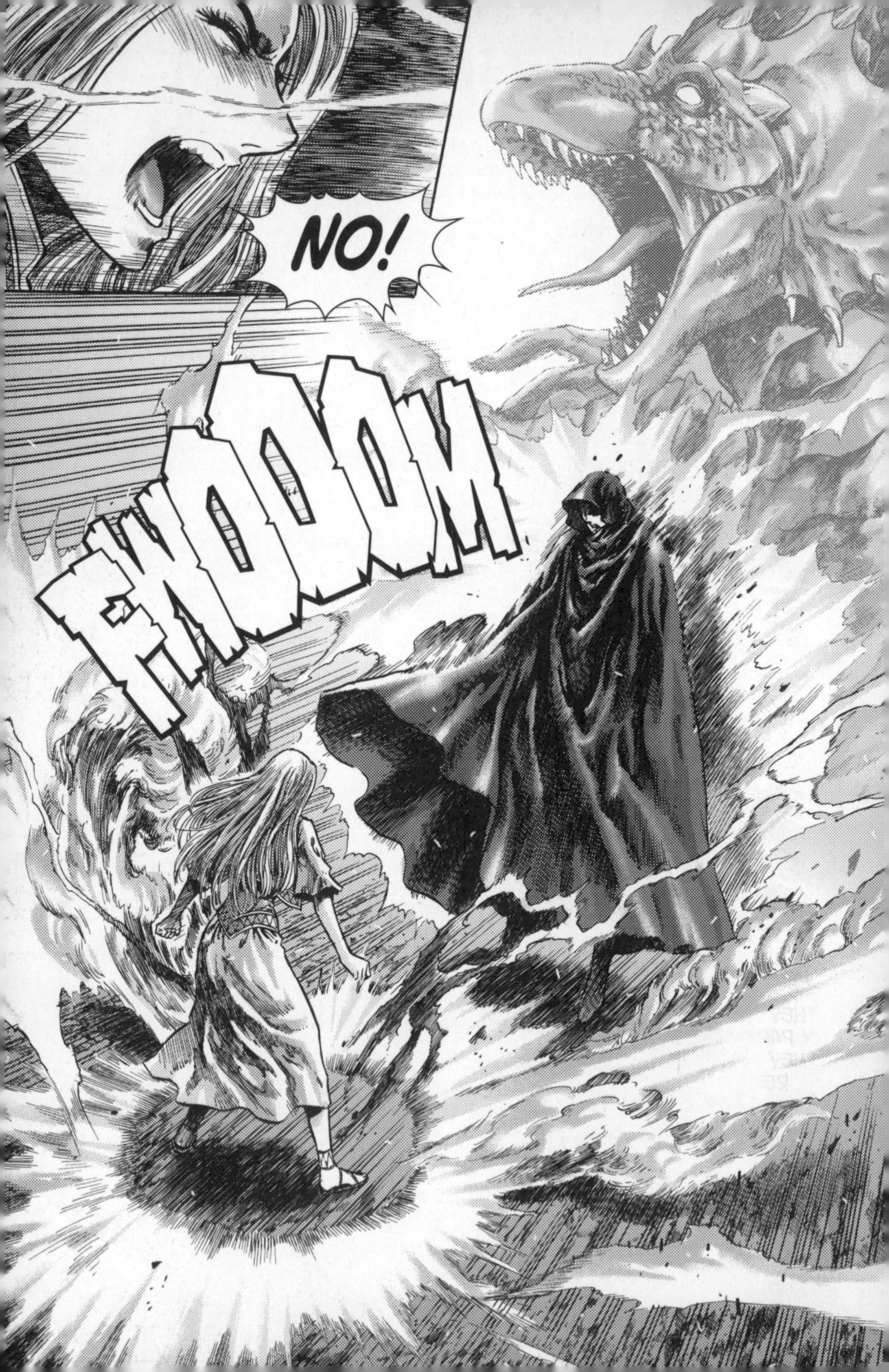
NO!
FWOOOM

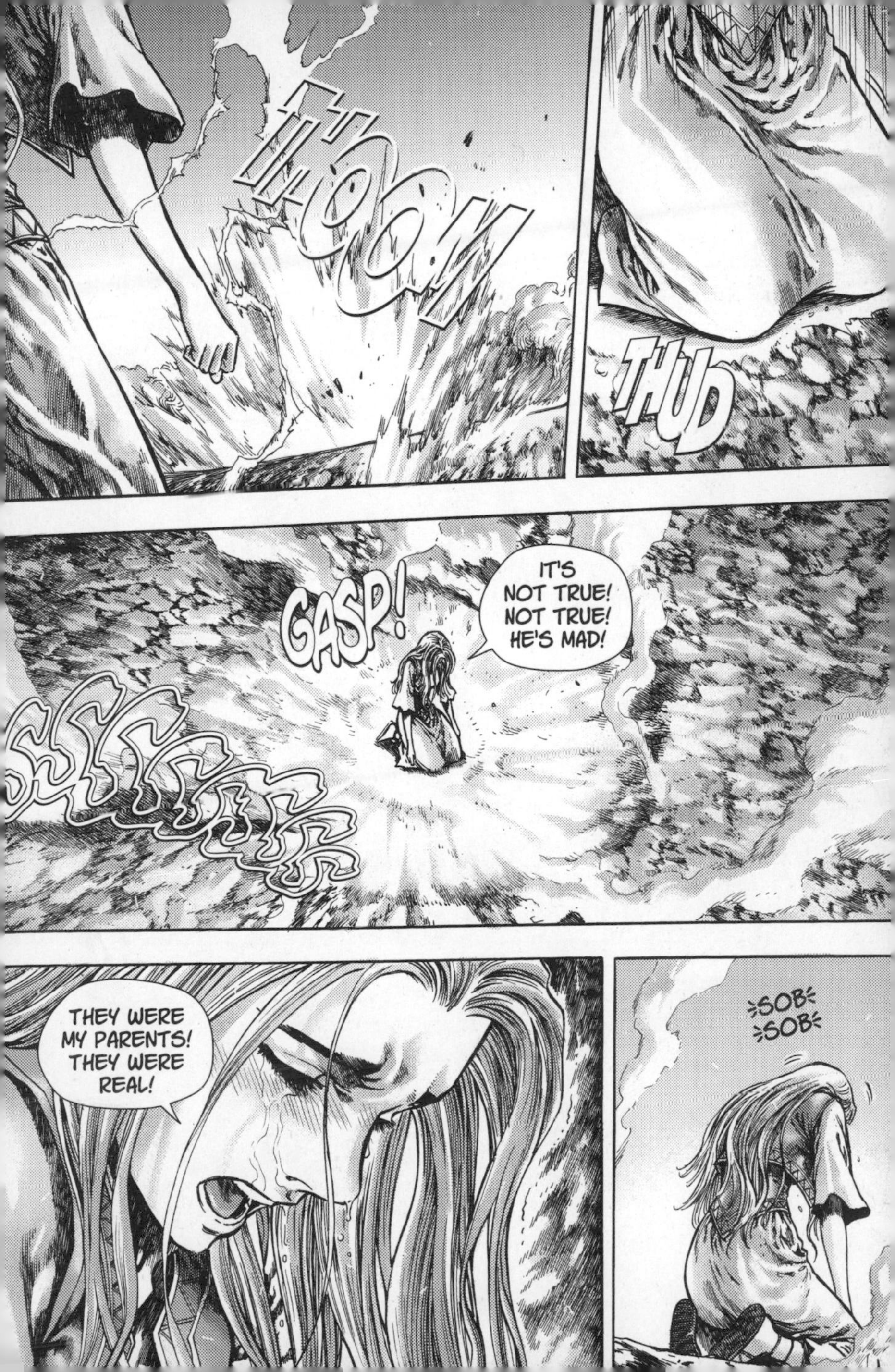
FOOM
THUD
GASP!
IT'S NOT TRUE! NOT TRUE! HE'S MAD!
THEY WERE MY PARENTS! THEY WERE REAL!
SOB
SOB

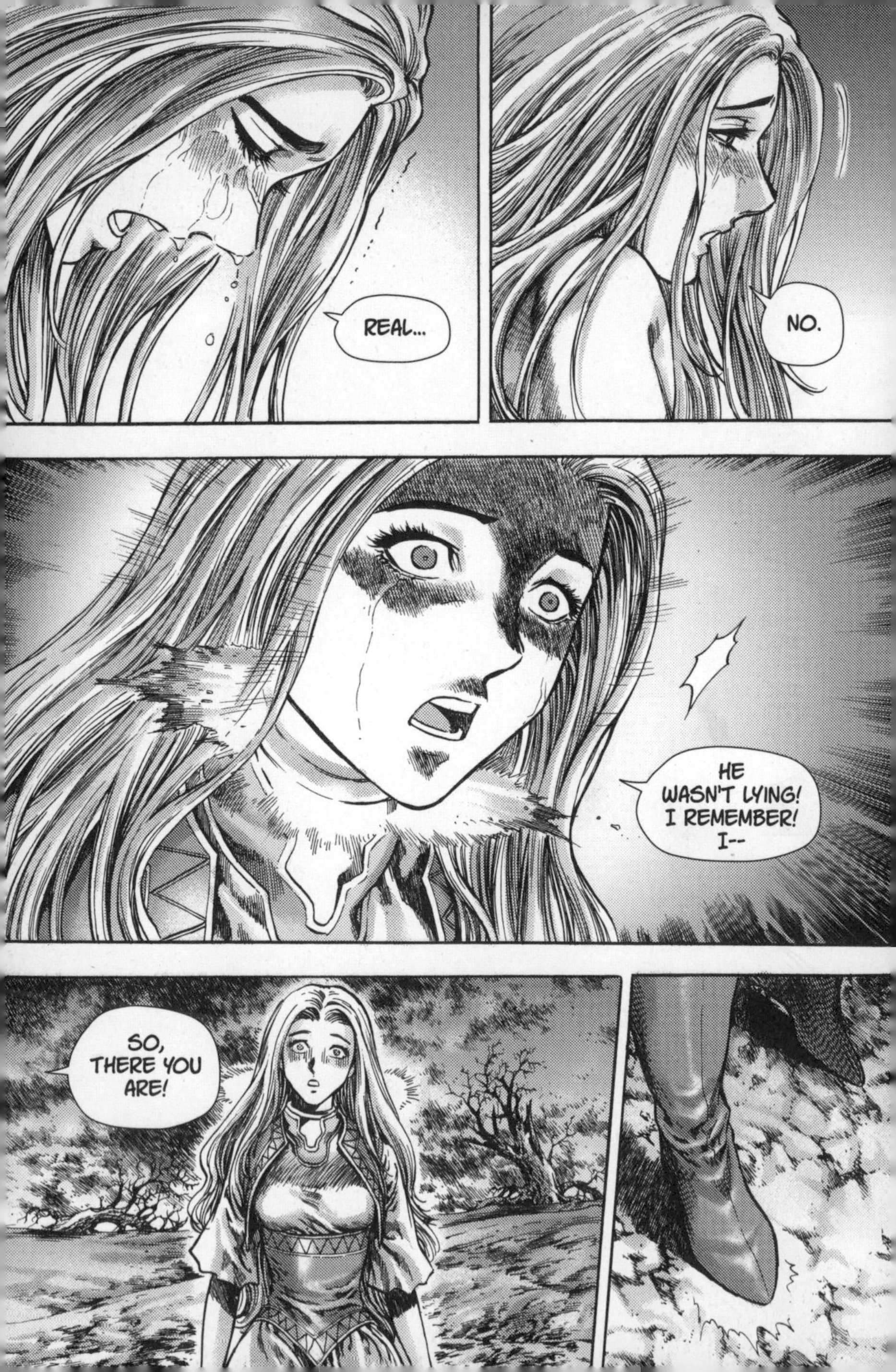
REAL...
NO.
HE WASN'T LYING! I REMEMBER! I--
SO, THERE YOU ARE!

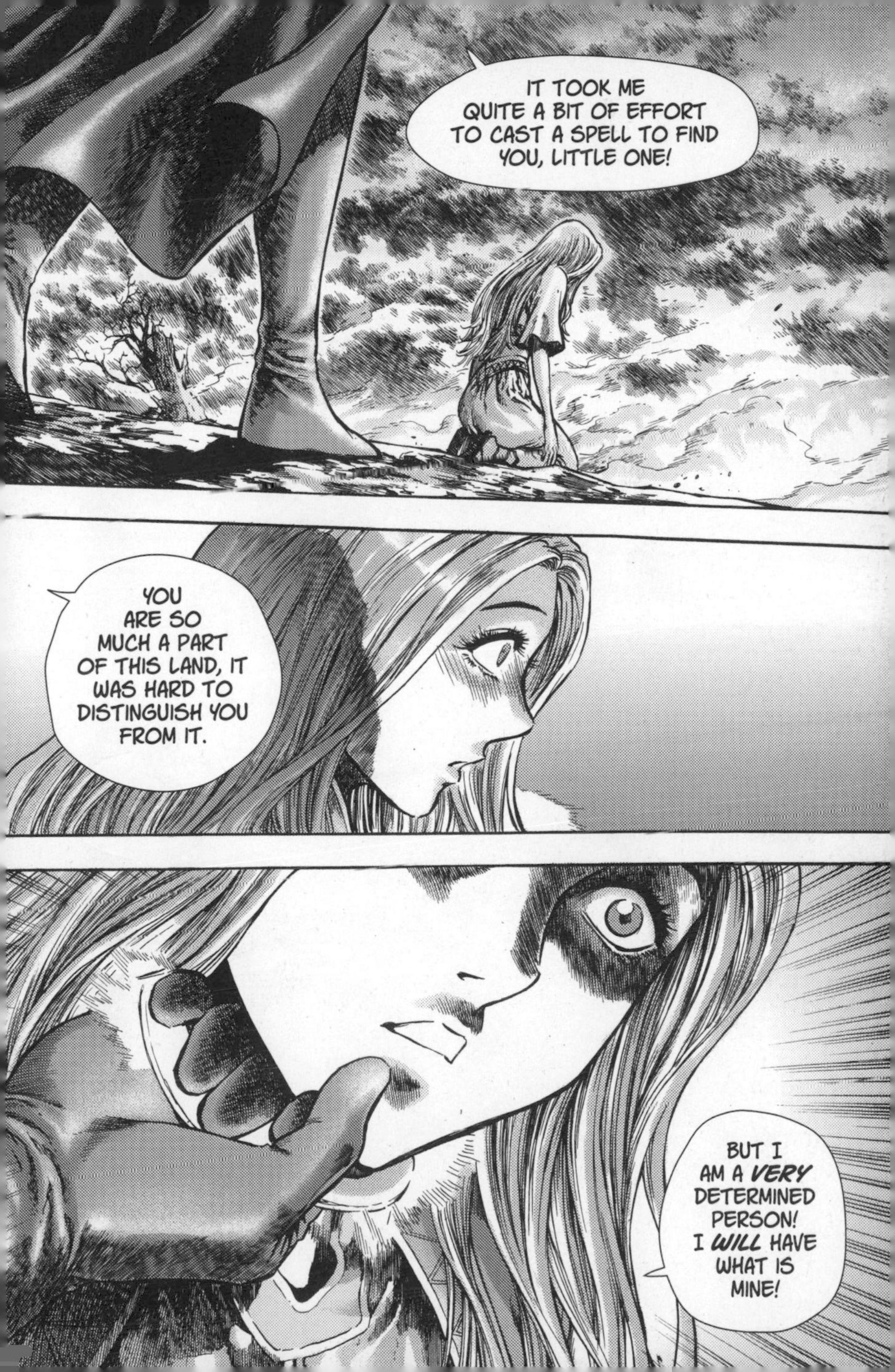
IT TOOK ME QUITE A BIT OF EFFORT TO CAST A SPELL TO FIND YOU, LITTLE ONE!
YOU ARE SO MUCH A PART OF THIS LAND, IT WAS HARD TO DISTINGUISH YOU FROM IT.
BUT I AM A ***VERY*** DETERMINED PERSON! I ***WILL*** HAVE WHAT IS MINE!

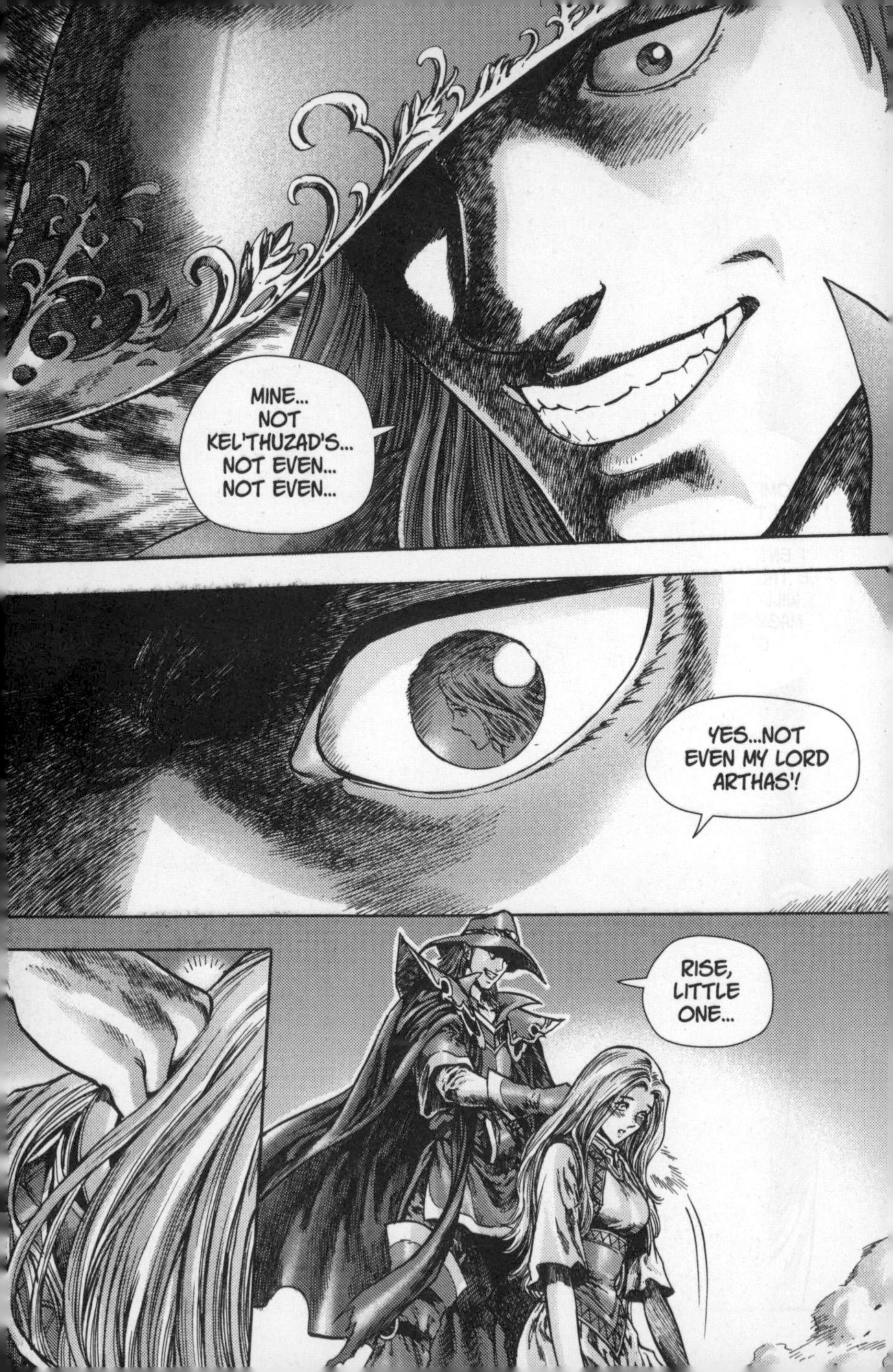
MINE... NOT KEL'THUZAD'S... NOT EVEN... NOT EVEN...
YES...NOT EVEN MY LORD ARTHAS'!
RISE, LITTLE ONE...

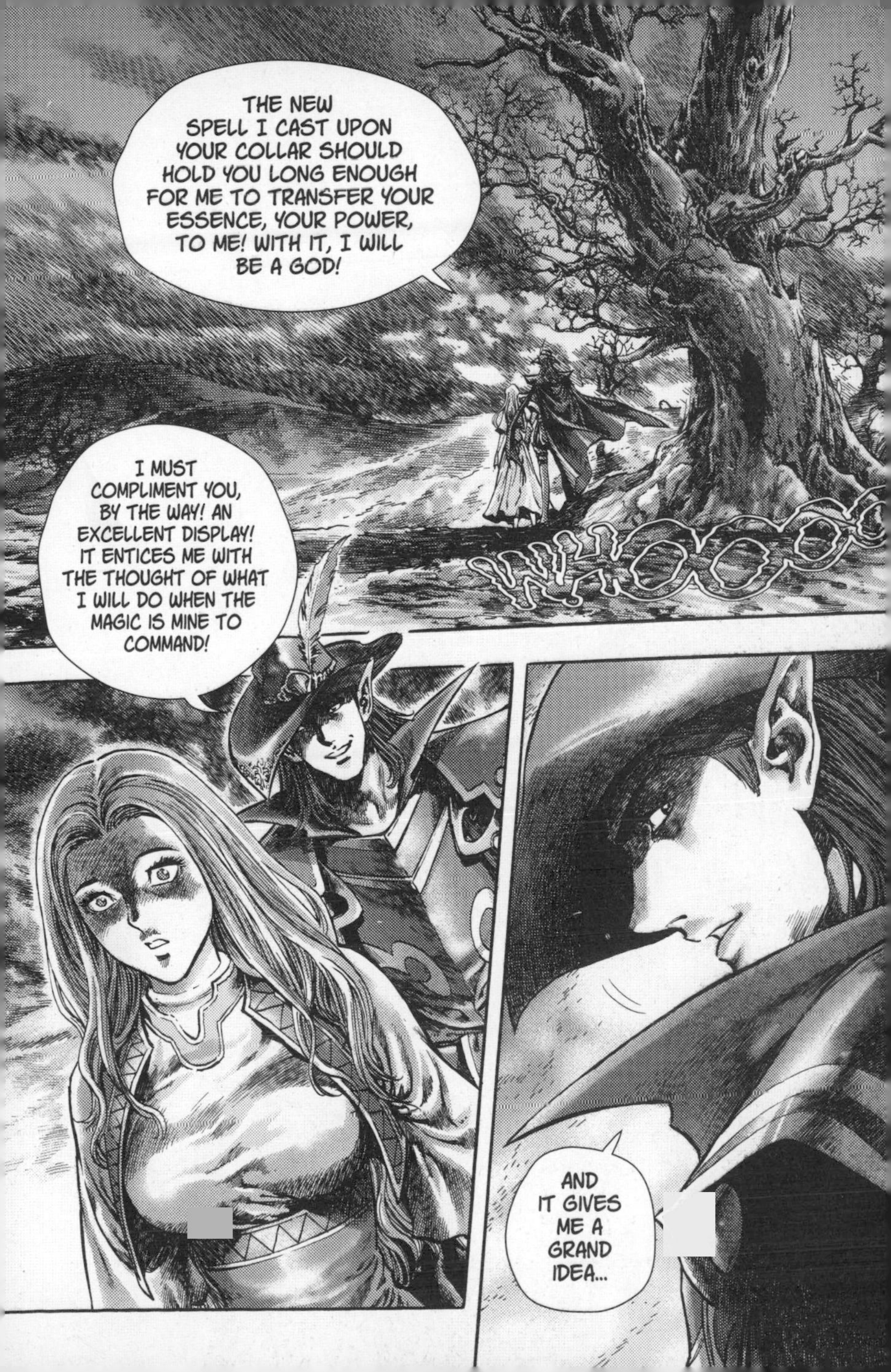
THE NEW SPELL I CAST UPON YOUR COLLAR SHOULD HOLD YOU LONG ENOUGH FOR ME TO TRANSFER YOUR ESSENCE, YOUR POWER, TO ME! WITH IT, I WILL BE A GOD!
I MUST COMPLIMENT YOU, BY THE WAY! AN EXCELLENT DISPLAY! IT ENTICES ME WITH THE THOUGHT OF WHAT I WILL DO WHEN THE MAGIC IS MINE TO COMMAND!
AND IT GIVES ME A GRAND IDEA...

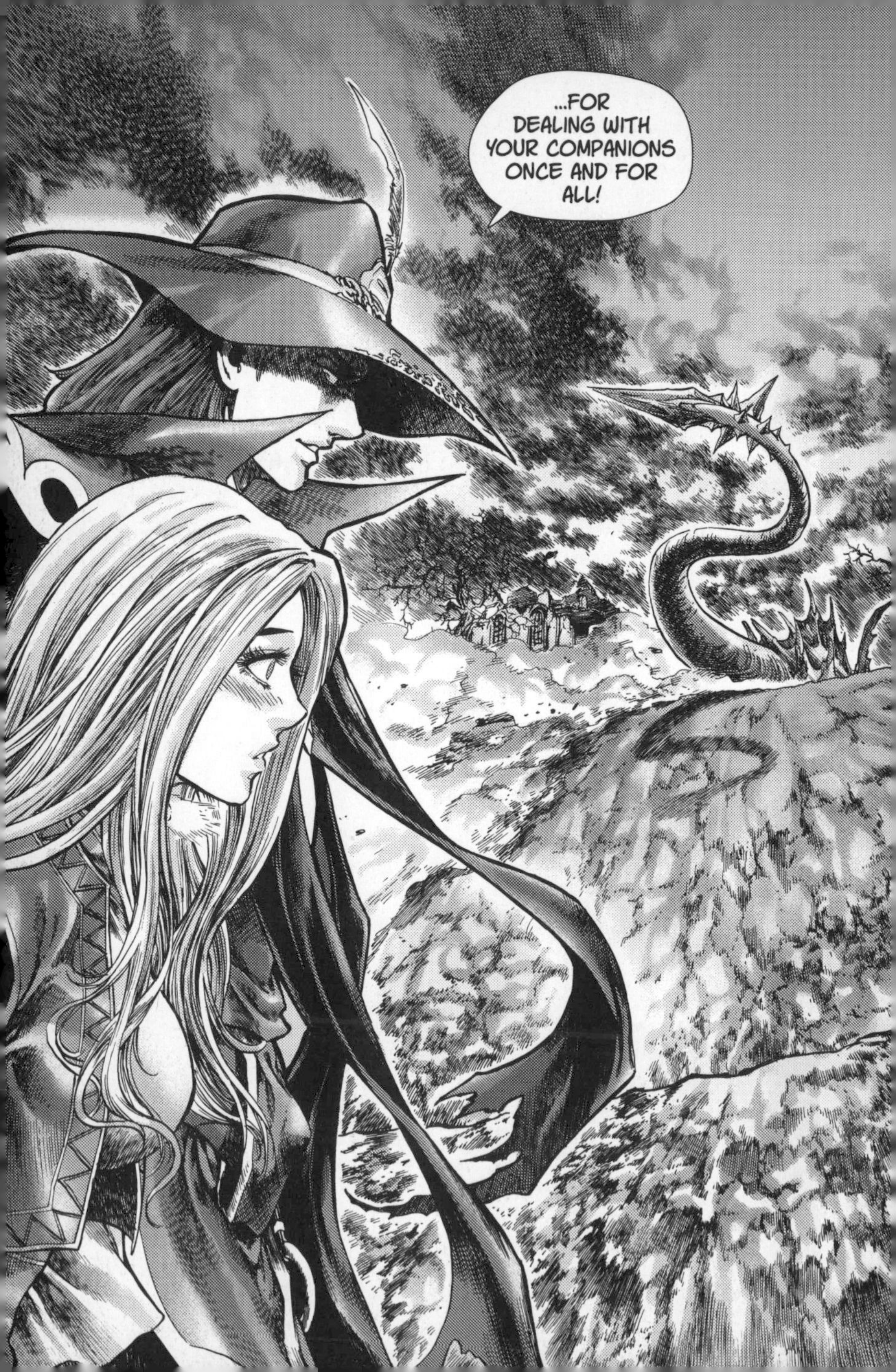
...FOR DEALING WITH YOUR COMPANIONS ONCE AND FOR ALL!

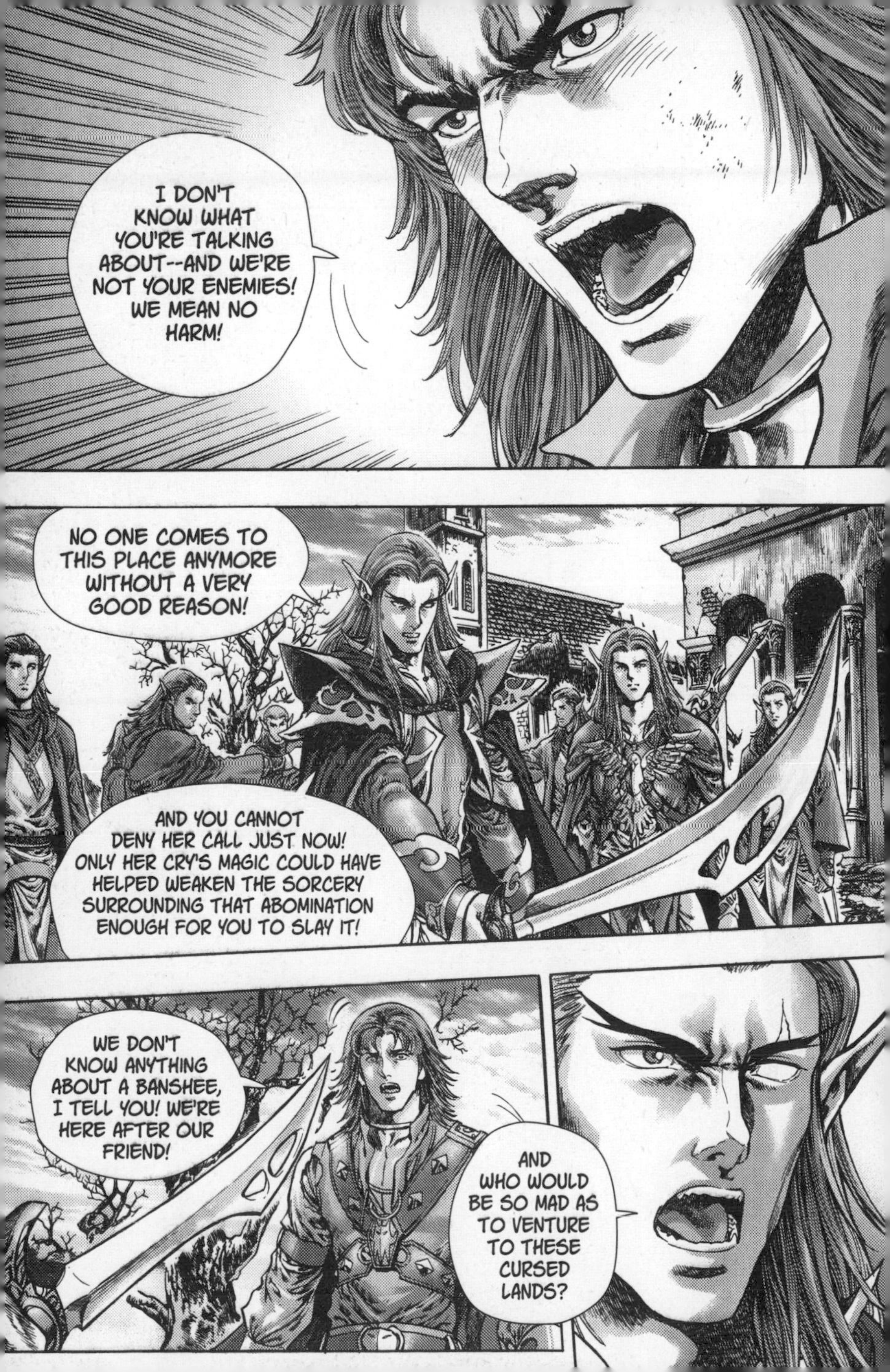

I DON'T KNOW WHAT YOU'RE TALKING ABOUT--AND WE'RE NOT YOUR ENEMIES! WE MEAN NO HARM!
NO ONE COMES TO THIS PLACE ANYMORE WITHOUT A VERY GOOD REASON!
AND YOU CANNOT DENY HER CALL JUST NOW! ONLY HER CRY'S MAGIC COULD HAVE HELPED WEAKEN THE SORCERY SURROUNDING THAT ABOMINATION ENOUGH FOR YOU TO SLAY IT!
WE DON'T KNOW ANYTHING ABOUT A BANSHEE, I TELL YOU! WE'RE HERE AFTER OUR FRIEND!
AND WHO WOULD BE SO MAD AS TO VENTURE TO THESE CURSED LANDS?

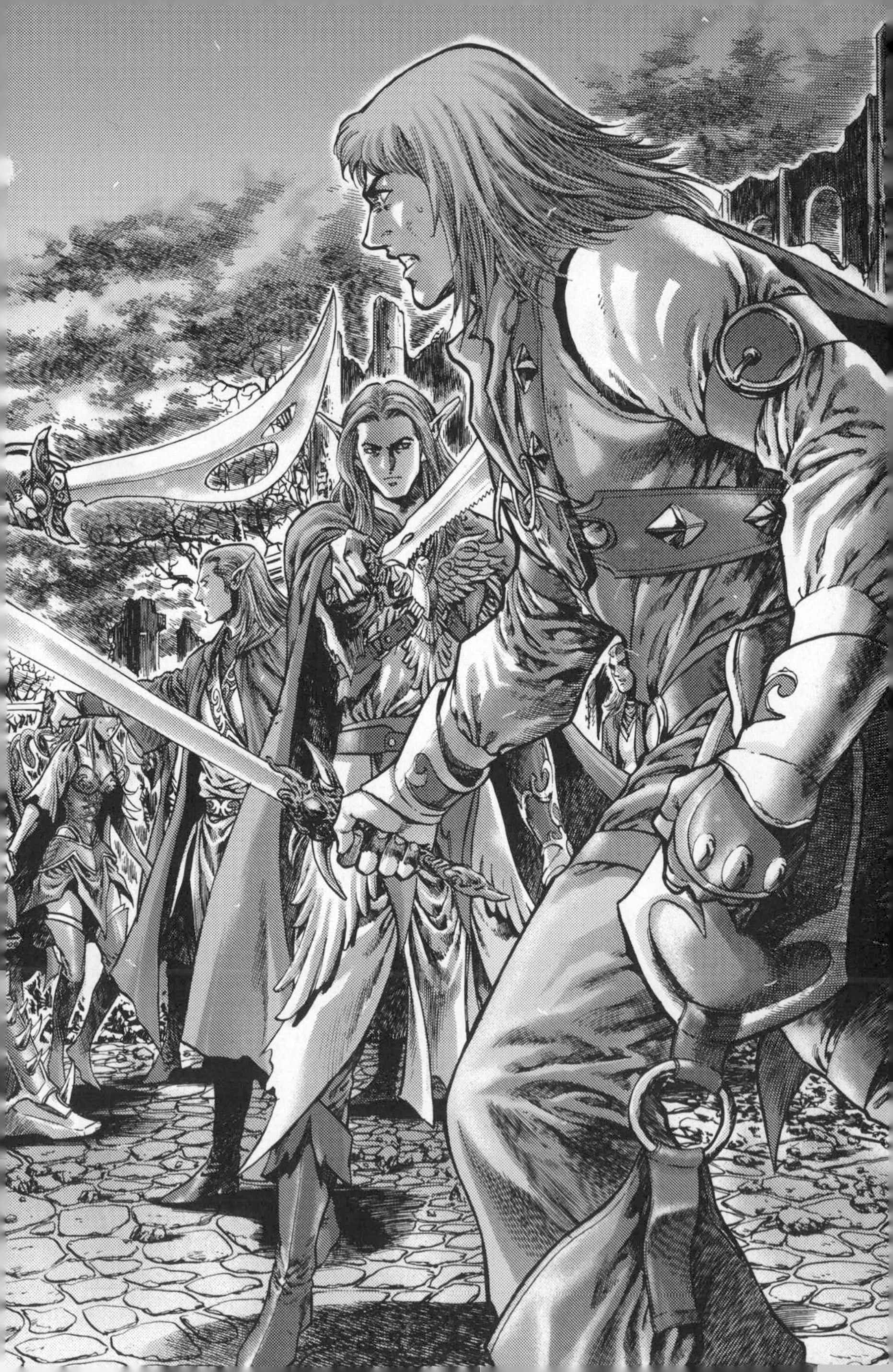

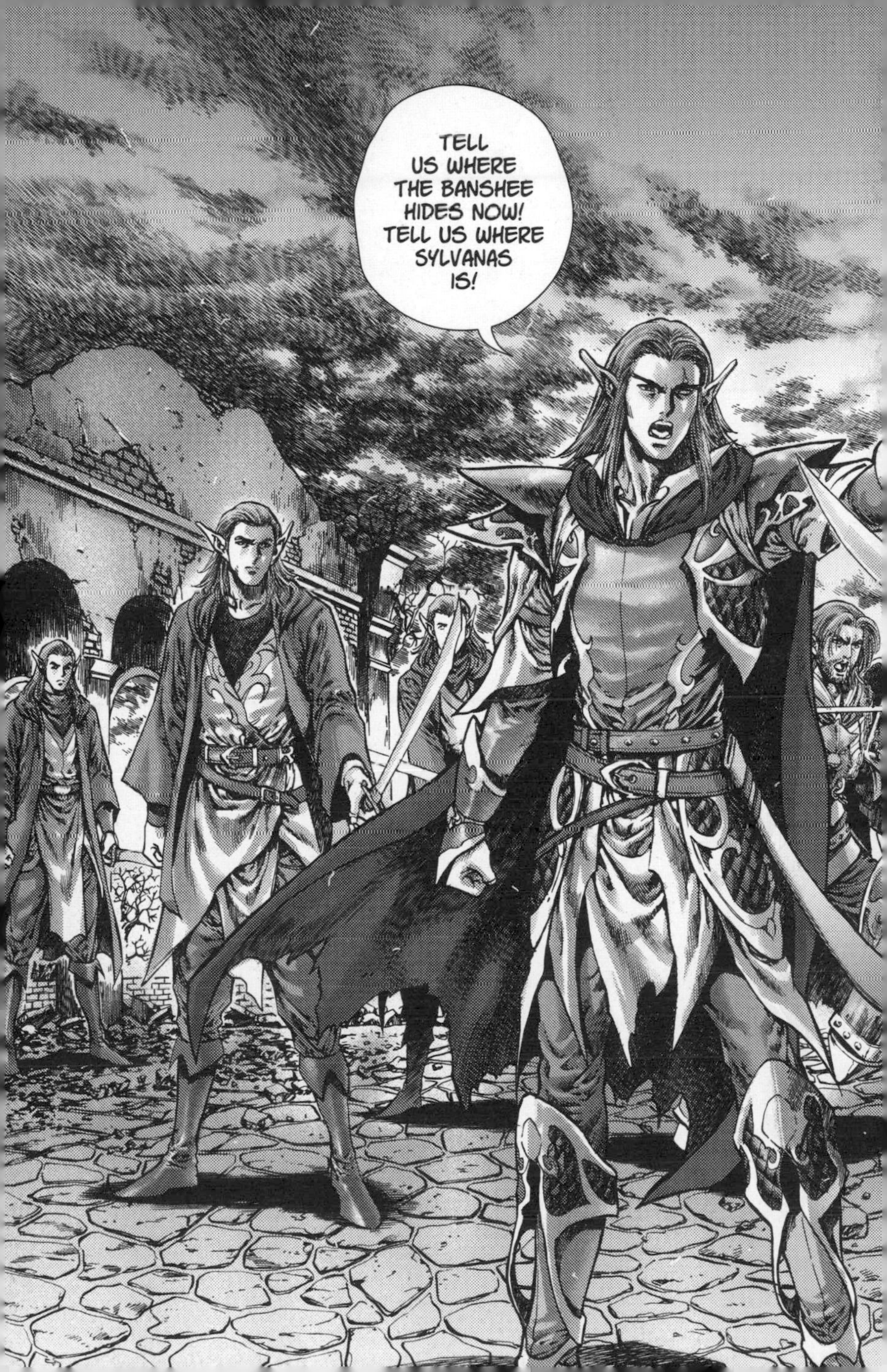
TELL US WHERE THE BANSHEE HIDES NOW! TELL US WHERE SYLVANAS IS!

CHAPTER FOUR
DARK REUNION

YOU HAVE BUT ONE CHANCE TO LIVE...

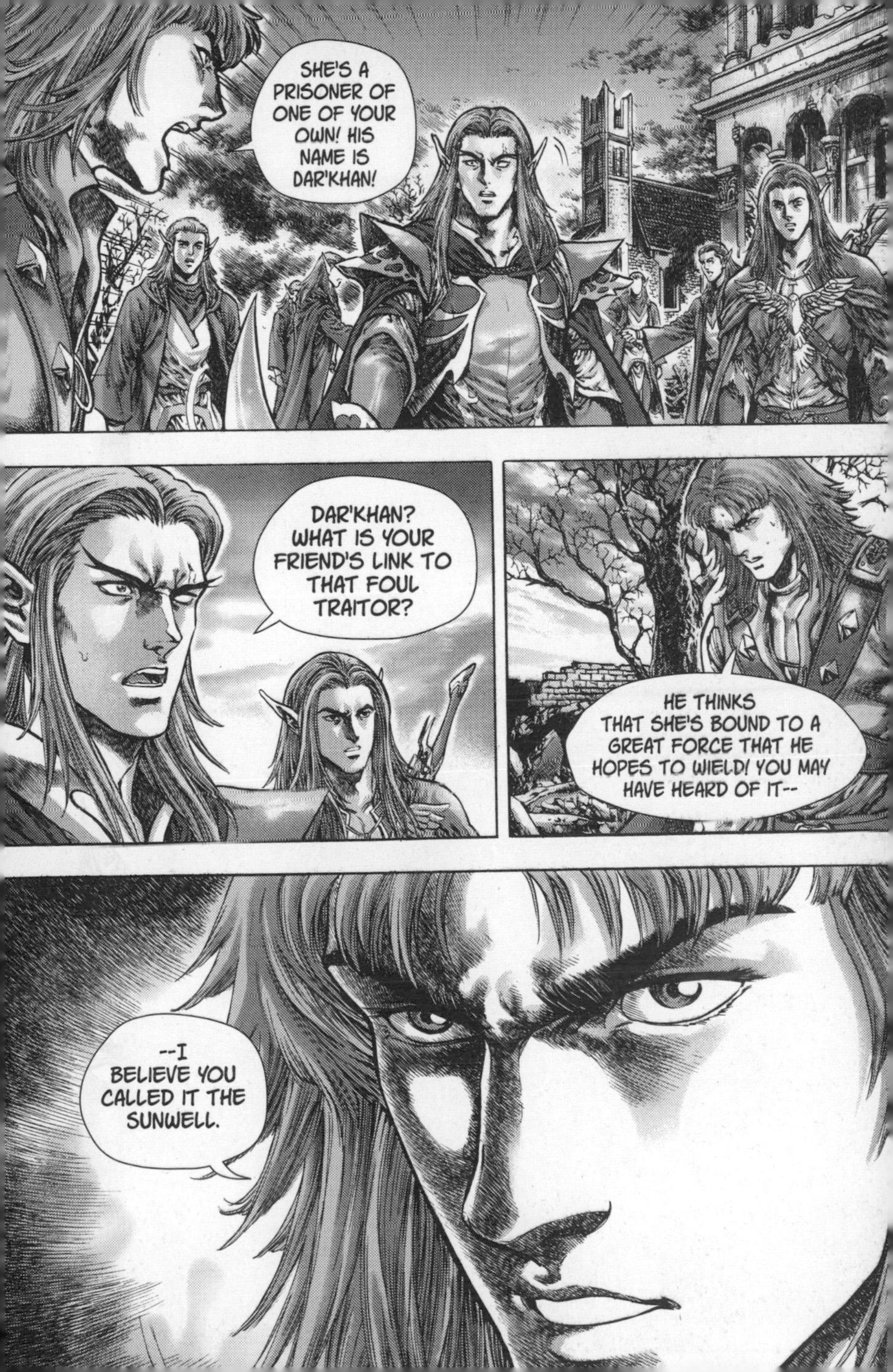
SHE'S A PRISONER OF ONE OF YOUR OWN! HIS NAME IS DAR'KHAN!
DAR'KHAN? WHAT IS YOUR FRIEND'S LINK TO THAT FOUL TRAITOR?
HE THINKS THAT SHE'S BOUND TO A GREAT FORCE THAT HE HOPES TO WIELD! YOU MAY HAVE HEARD OF IT--
--I BELIEVE YOU CALLED IT THE SUNWELL.

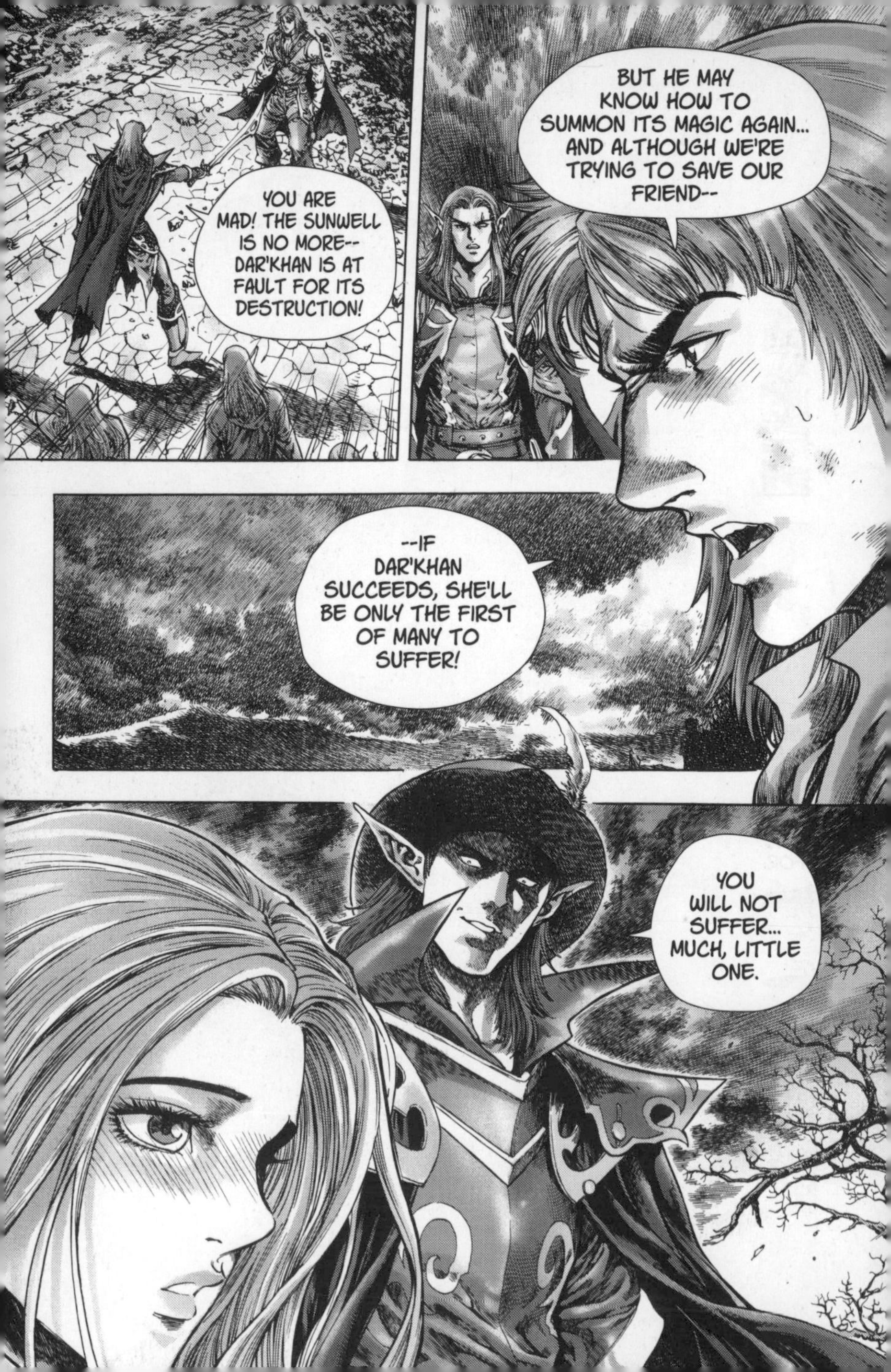
YOU ARE MAD! THE SUNWELL IS NO MORE-- DAR'KHAN IS AT FAULT FOR ITS DESTRUCTION!
BUT HE MAY KNOW HOW TO SUMMON ITS MAGIC AGAIN... AND ALTHOUGH WE'RE TRYING TO SAVE OUR FRIEND--
--IF DAR'KHAN SUCCEEDS, SHE'LL BE ONLY THE FIRST OF MANY TO SUFFER!
YOU WILL NOT SUFFER... MUCH, LITTLE ONE.

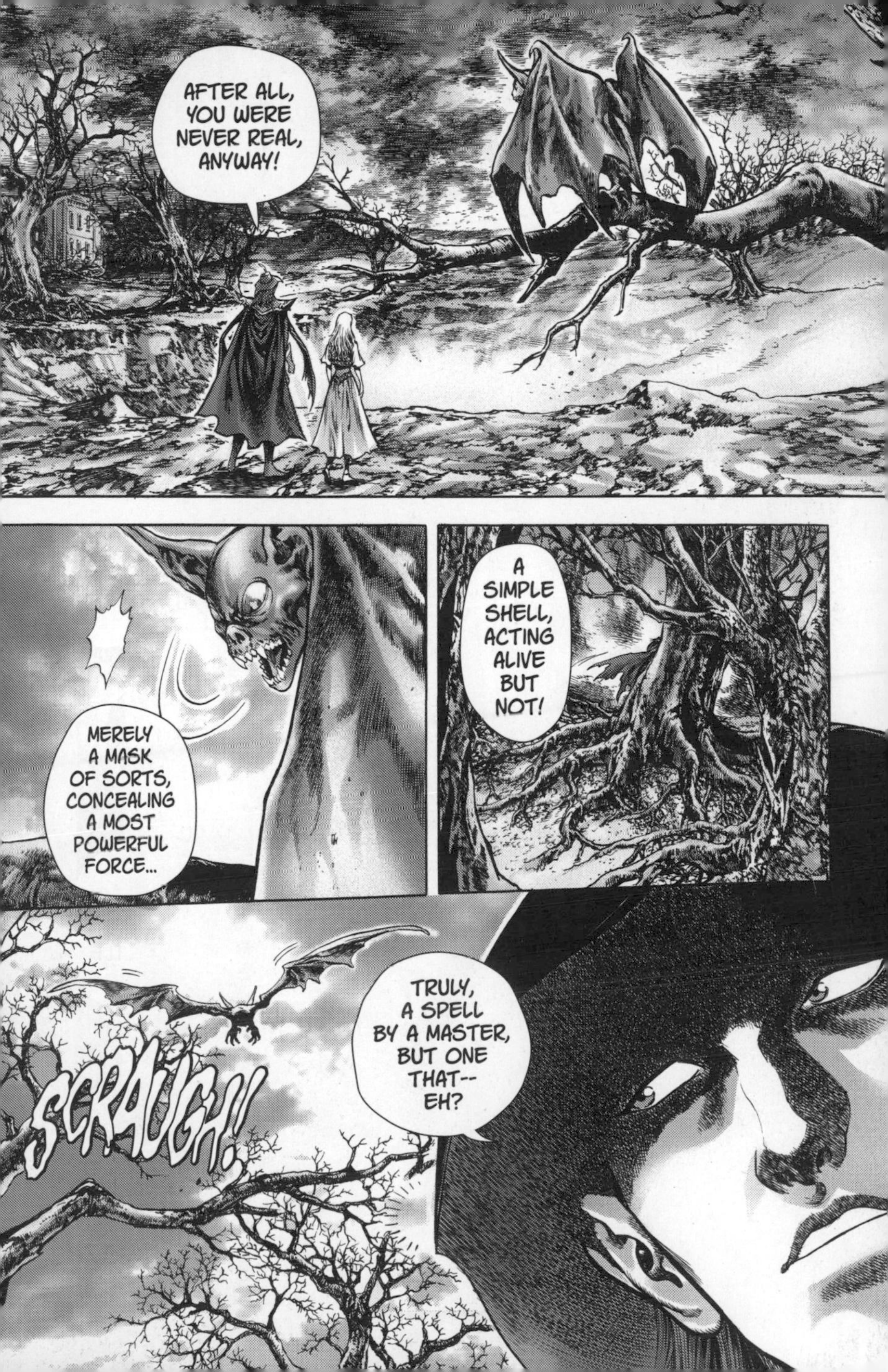
AFTER ALL, YOU WERE NEVER REAL, ANYWAY!
MERELY A MASK OF SORTS, CONCEALING A MOST POWERFUL FORCE...
A SIMPLE SHELL, ACTING ALIVE BUT NOT!
SCRAUGH!!
TRULY, A SPELL BY A MASTER, BUT ONE THAT-- EH?

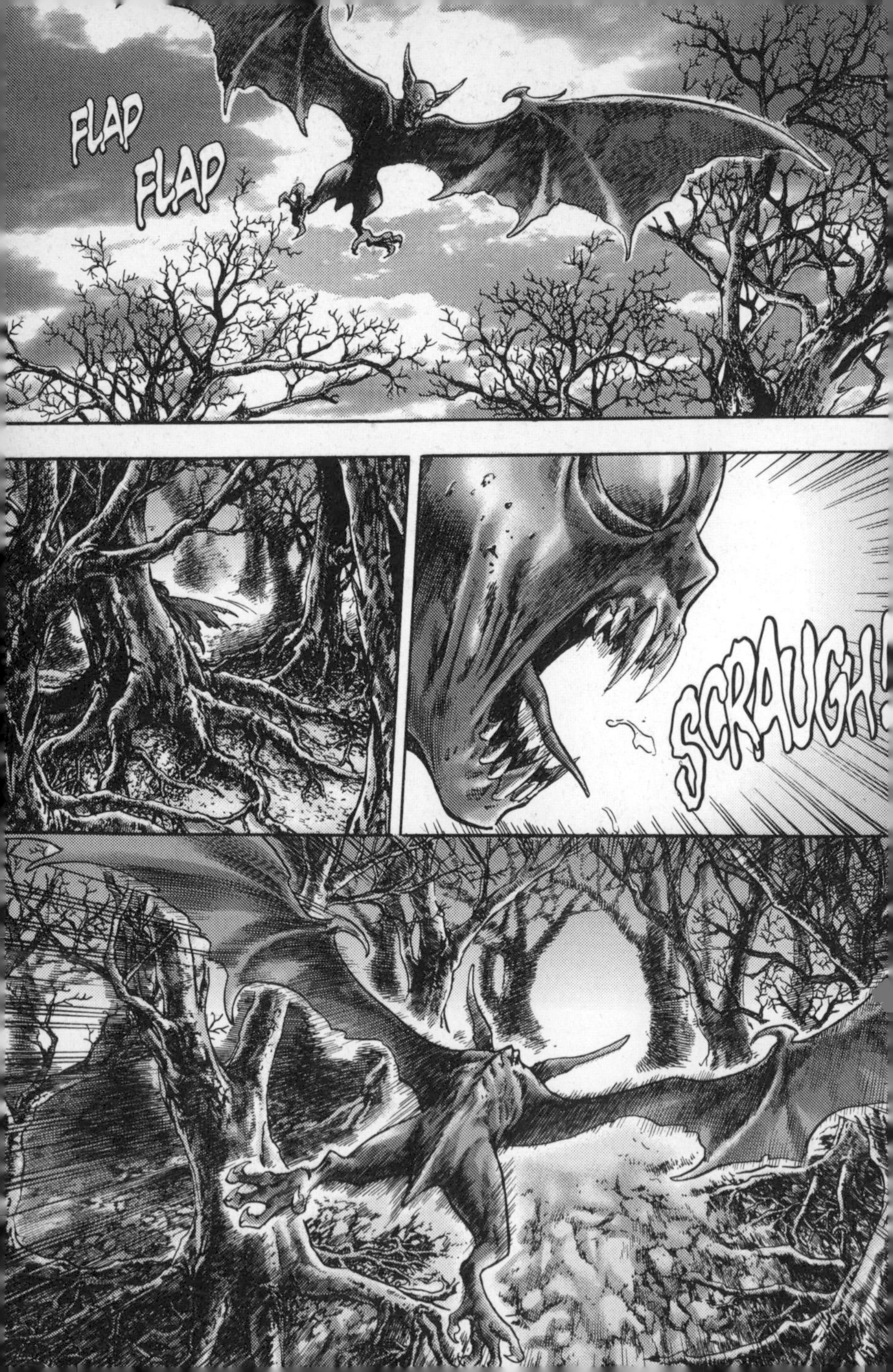
FLAP
FLAP
SCRAUGH!

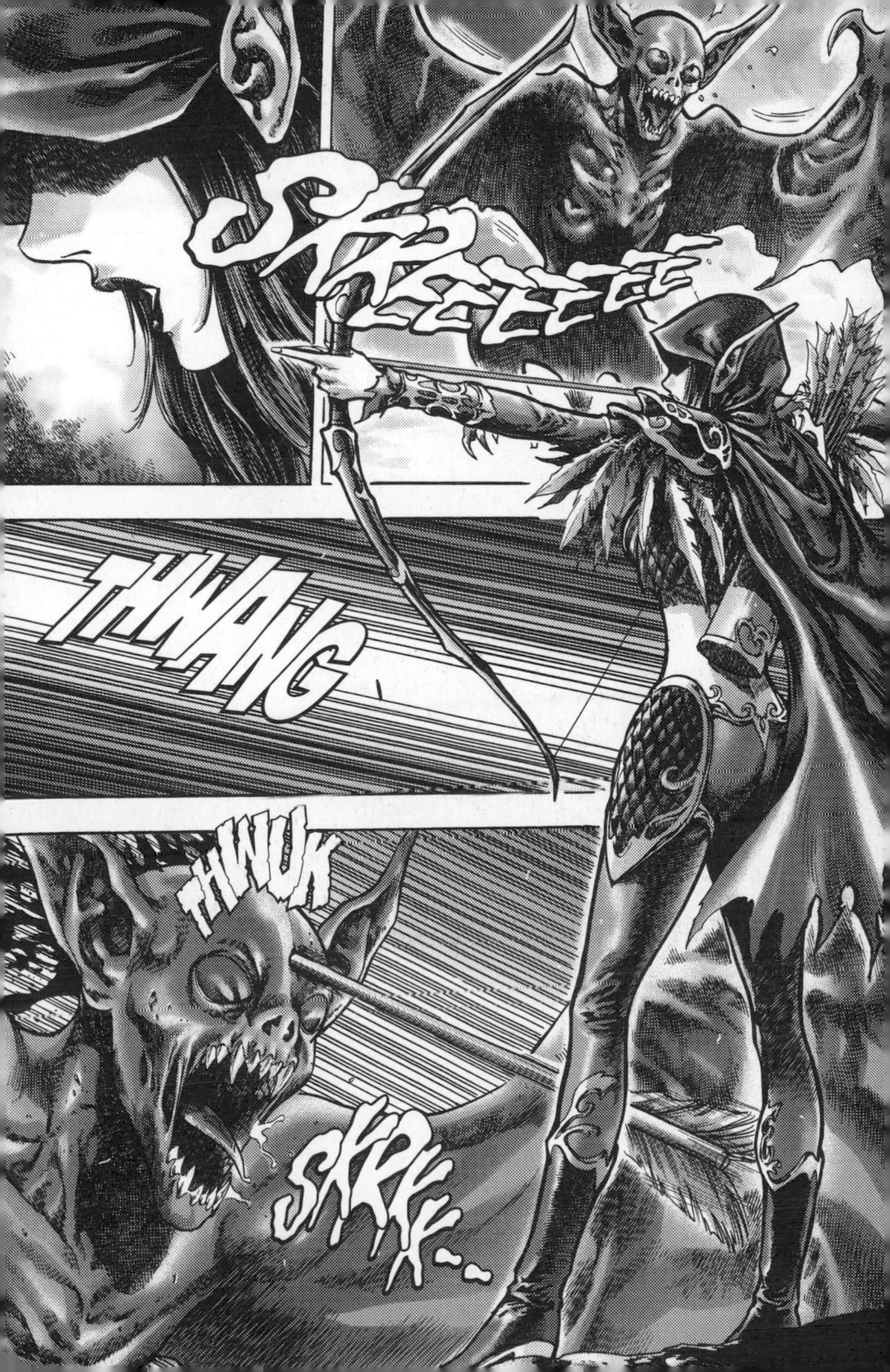
SKREEEEEE
THWANG
THWUK
SKRKK--

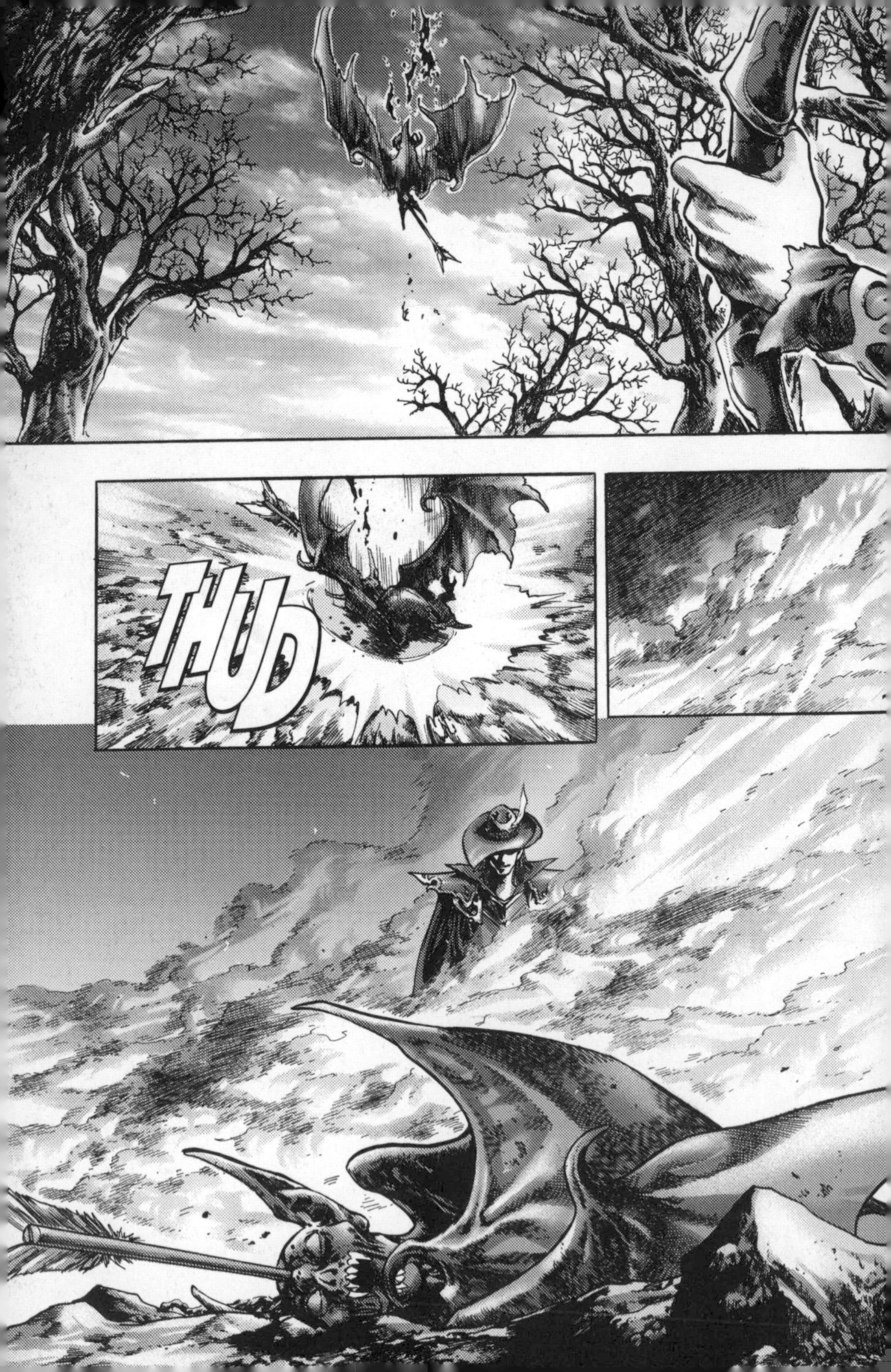
THUD

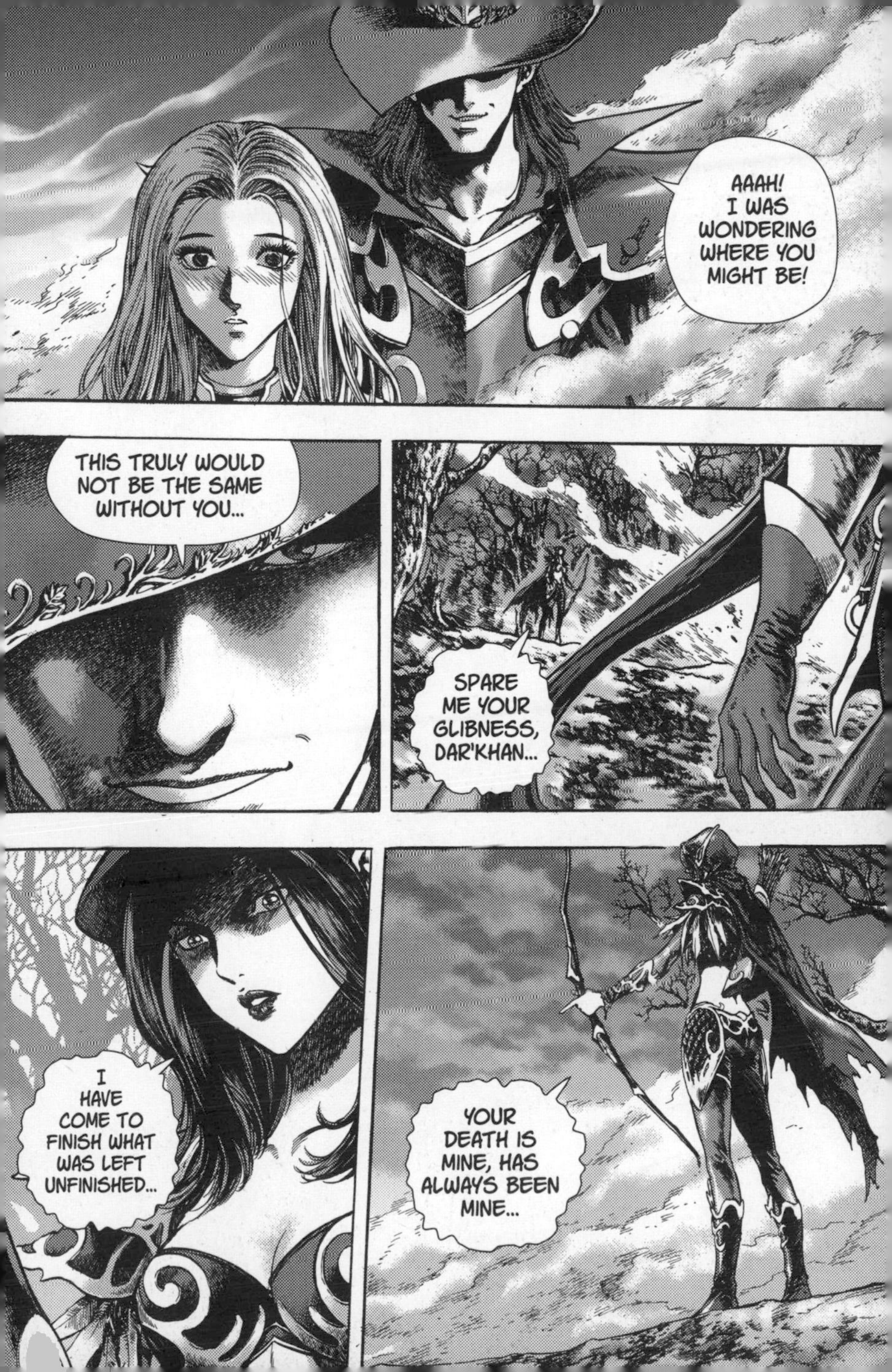
AAAH! I WAS WONDERING WHERE YOU MIGHT BE!
THIS TRULY WOULD NOT BE THE SAME WITHOUT YOU...
SPARE ME YOUR GLIBNESS, DAR'KHAN...
I HAVE COME TO FINISH WHAT WAS LEFT UNFINISHED...
YOUR DEATH IS MINE, HAS ALWAYS BEEN MINE...

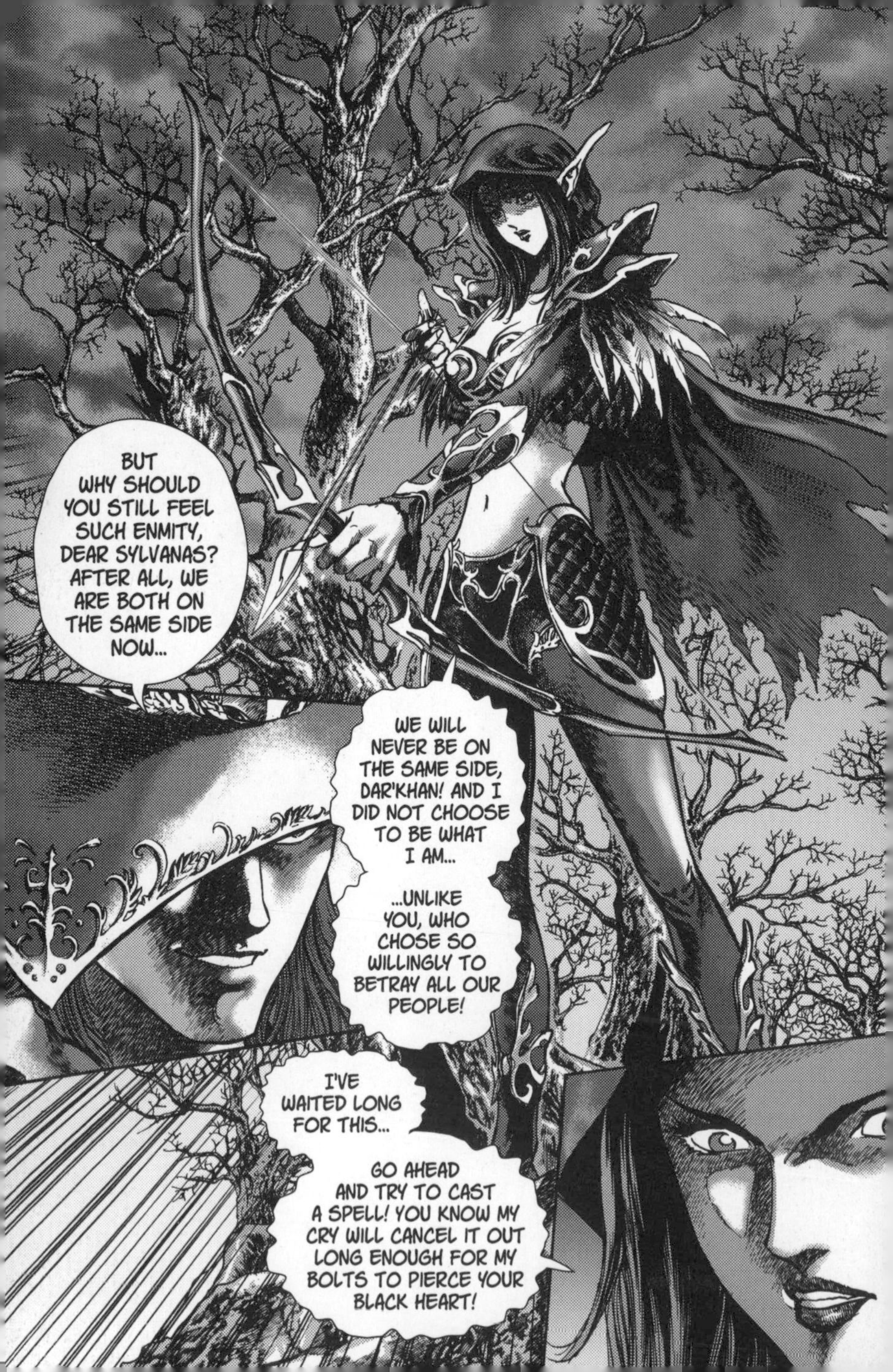
BUT WHY SHOULD YOU STILL FEEL SUCH ENMITY, DEAR SYLVANAS? AFTER ALL, WE ARE BOTH ON THE SAME SIDE NOW...
WE WILL NEVER BE ON THE SAME SIDE, DAR'KHAN! AND I DID NOT CHOOSE TO BE WHAT I AM...
...UNLIKE YOU, WHO CHOSE SO WILLINGLY TO BETRAY ALL OUR PEOPLE!
I'VE WAITED LONG FOR THIS...
GO AHEAD AND TRY TO CAST A SPELL! YOU KNOW MY CRY WILL CANCEL IT OUT LONG ENOUGH FOR MY BOLTS TO PIERCE YOUR BLACK HEART!

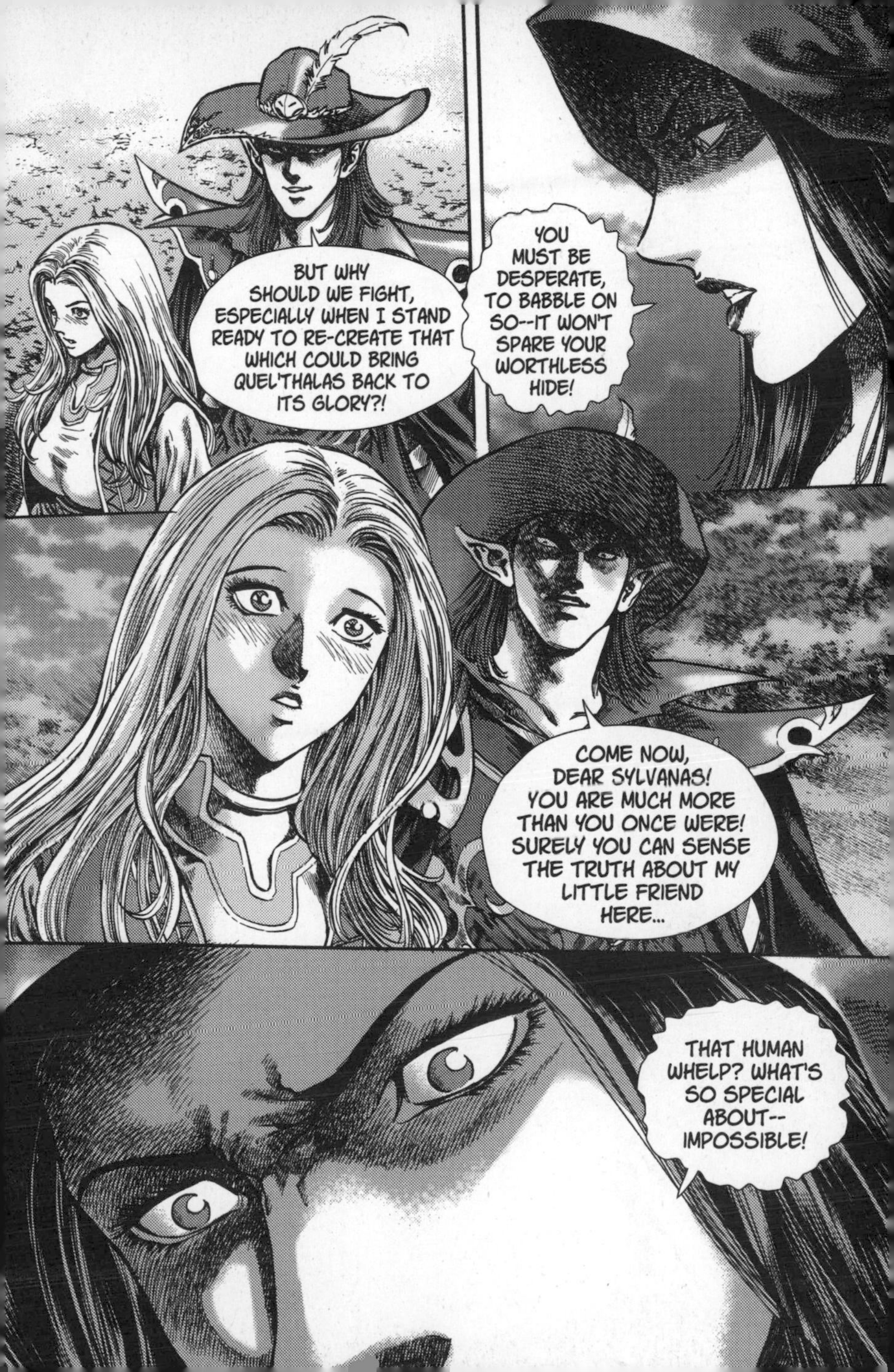
BUT WHY SHOULD WE FIGHT, ESPECIALLY WHEN I STAND READY TO RE-CREATE THAT WHICH COULD BRING QUEL'THALAS BACK TO ITS GLORY?!
YOU MUST BE DESPERATE, TO BABBLE ON SO--IT WON'T SPARE YOUR WORTHLESS HIDE!
COME NOW, DEAR SYLVANAS! YOU ARE MUCH MORE THAN YOU ONCE WERE! SURELY YOU CAN SENSE THE TRUTH ABOUT MY LITTLE FRIEND HERE...
THAT HUMAN WHELP? WHAT'S SO SPECIAL ABOUT-- IMPOSSIBLE!

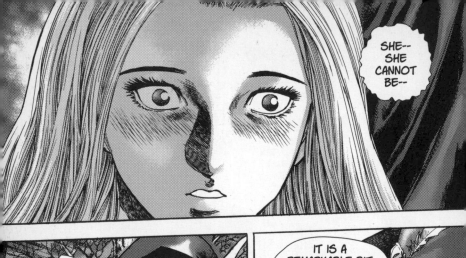

SHE--SHE CANNOT BE--

THAT LITTLE WHELP CANNOT HOLD IN HER THE ESSENCE OF THE BLESSED SUNWELL!

IT IS A REMARKABLE BIT OF DECEPTION, ISN'T IT? WHO WOULD SUSPECT?

BUT THE POINT IS, NOW I HAVE HER AND I WILL RESTORE HER TO WHAT SHE TRULY IS.

AND AFTERWARD, NOBLY RETURN OUR HOMELAND TO ITS PRISTINE PERFECTION? I DOUBT THAT OF YOU, TRAITOR!

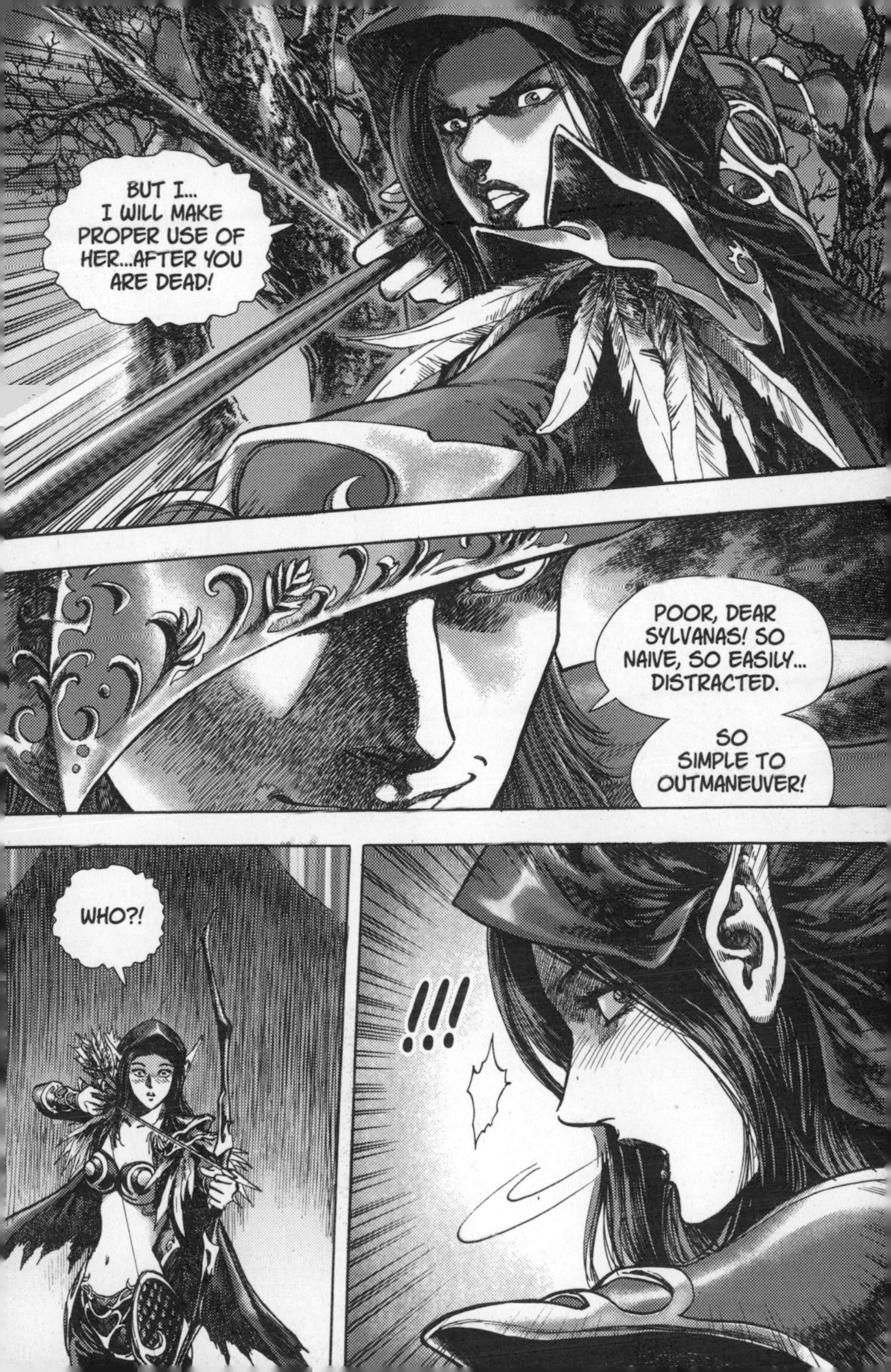
BUT I... I WILL MAKE PROPER USE OF HER...AFTER YOU ARE DEAD!
POOR, DEAR SYLVANAS! SO NAIVE, SO EASILY... DISTRACTED.
SO SIMPLE TO OUTMANEUVER!
WHO?!
!!!

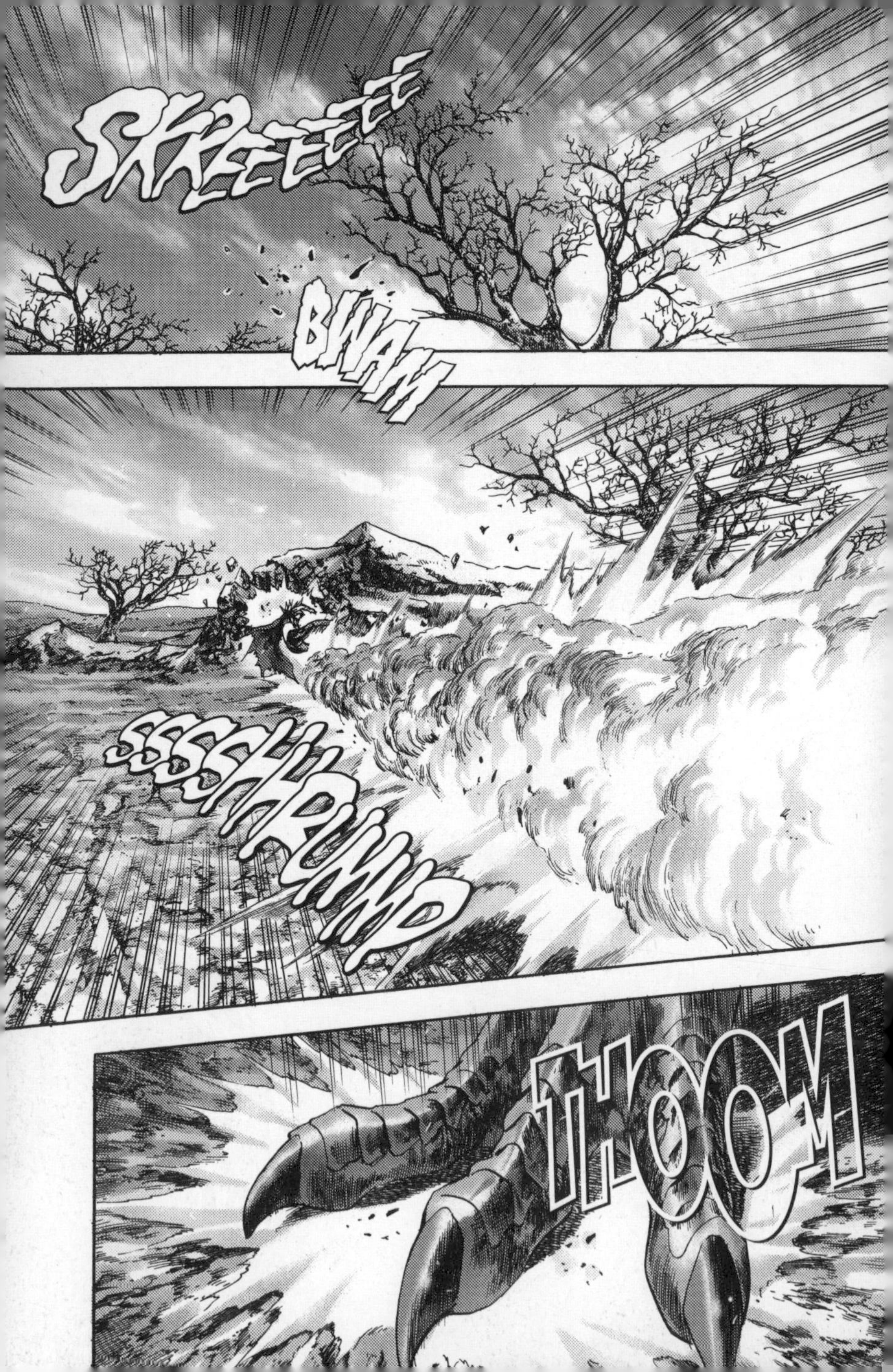
SKREEEEEE
BWAM
SSSSCHRUMMP
THOOM

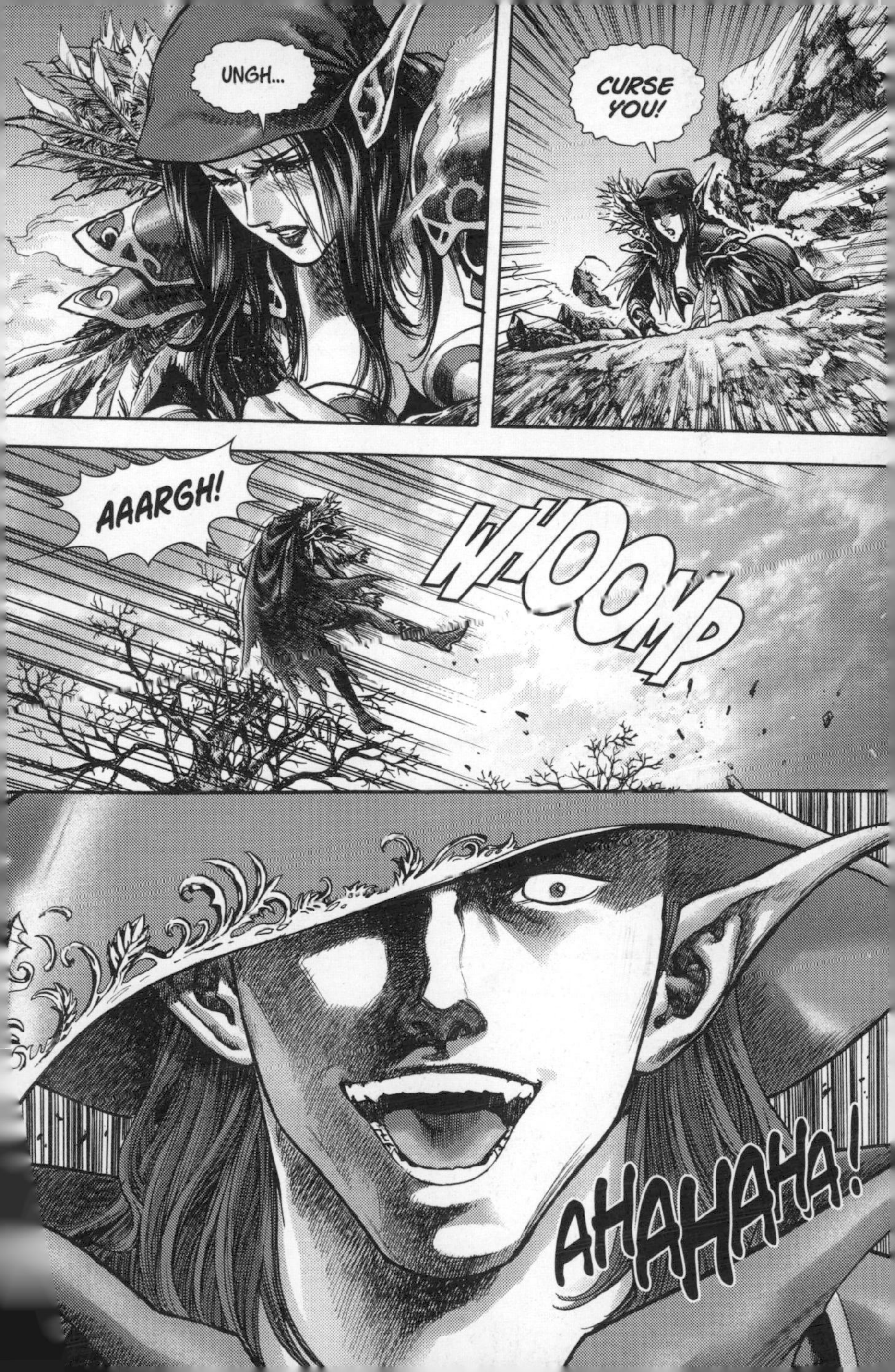
UNGH...
CURSE YOU!
AAARGH!
WHOOMP
AHAHAHA!

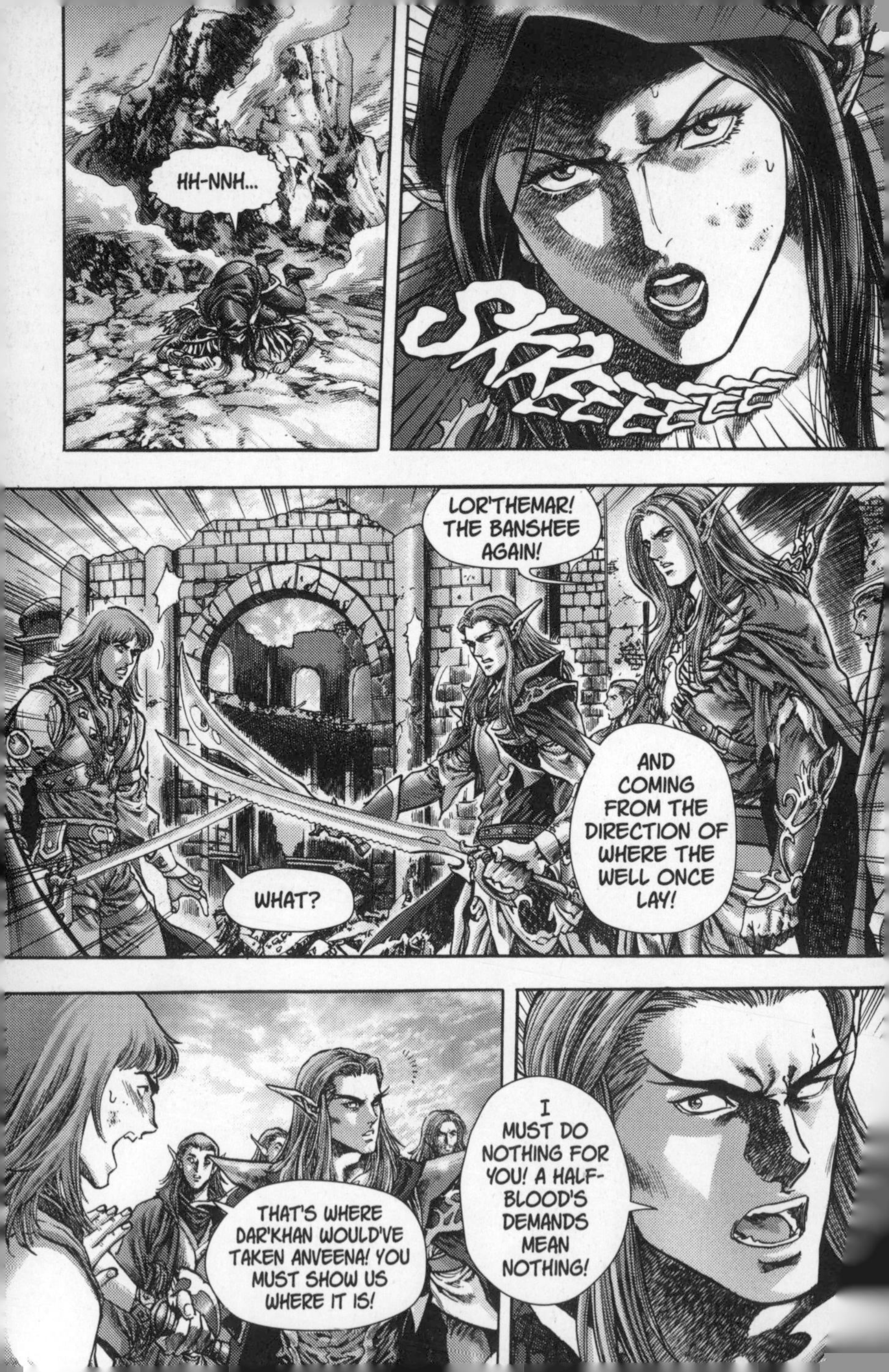
HH-NNH...
SKREEEEEE
LOR'THEMAR! THE BANSHEE AGAIN!
WHAT?
AND COMING FROM THE DIRECTION OF WHERE THE WELL ONCE LAY!
THAT'S WHERE DAR'KHAN WOULD'VE TAKEN ANVEENA! YOU MUST SHOW US WHERE IT IS!
I MUST DO NOTHING FOR YOU! A HALF-BLOOD'S DEMANDS MEAN NOTHING!

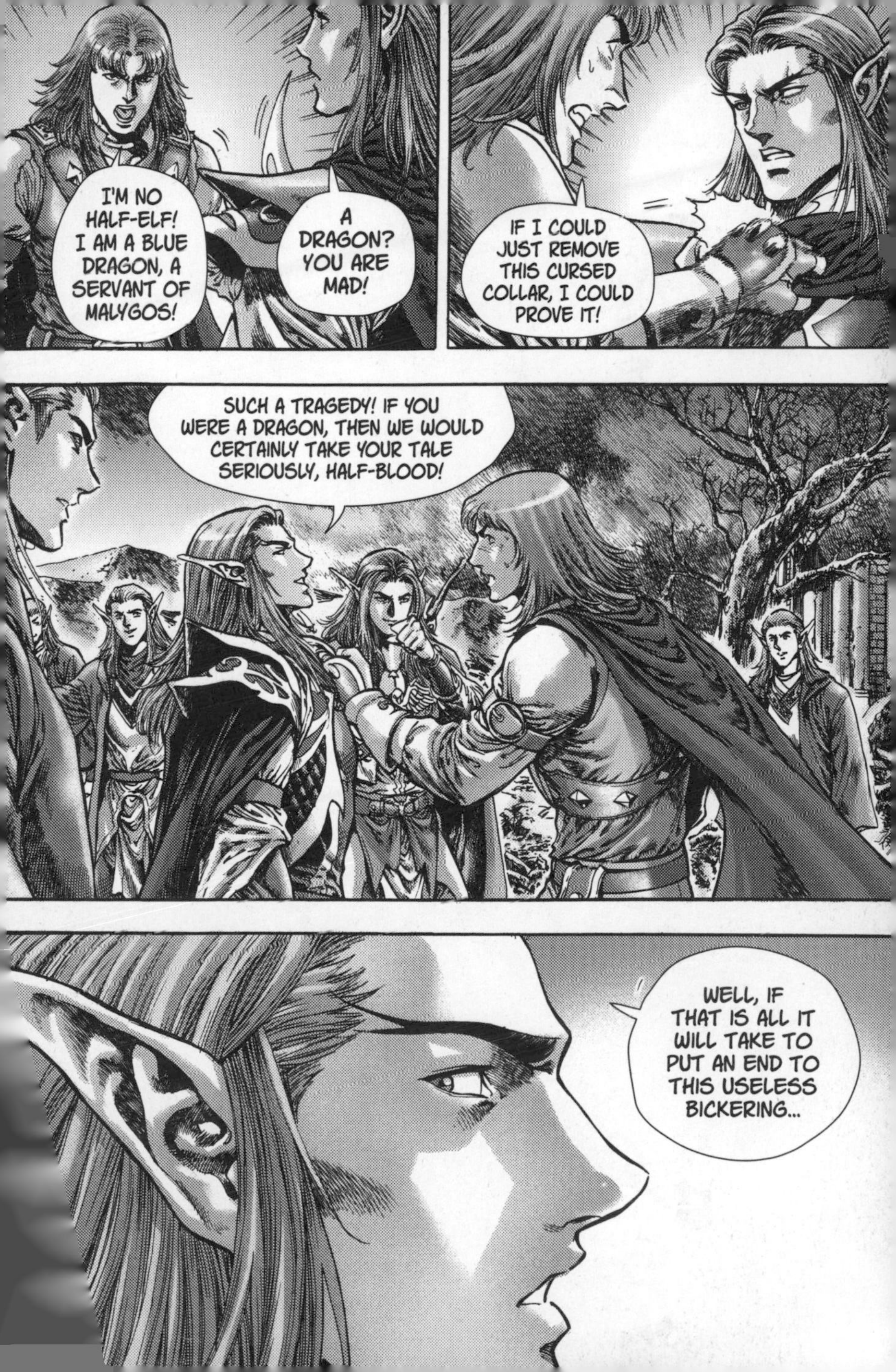
I'M NO HALF-ELF! I AM A BLUE DRAGON, A SERVANT OF MALYGOS!
A DRAGON? YOU ARE MAD!
IF I COULD JUST REMOVE THIS CURSED COLLAR, I COULD PROVE IT!
SUCH A TRAGEDY! IF YOU WERE A DRAGON, THEN WE WOULD CERTAINLY TAKE YOUR TALE SERIOUSLY, HALF-BLOOD!
WELL, IF THAT IS ALL IT WILL TAKE TO PUT AN END TO THIS USELESS BICKERING...

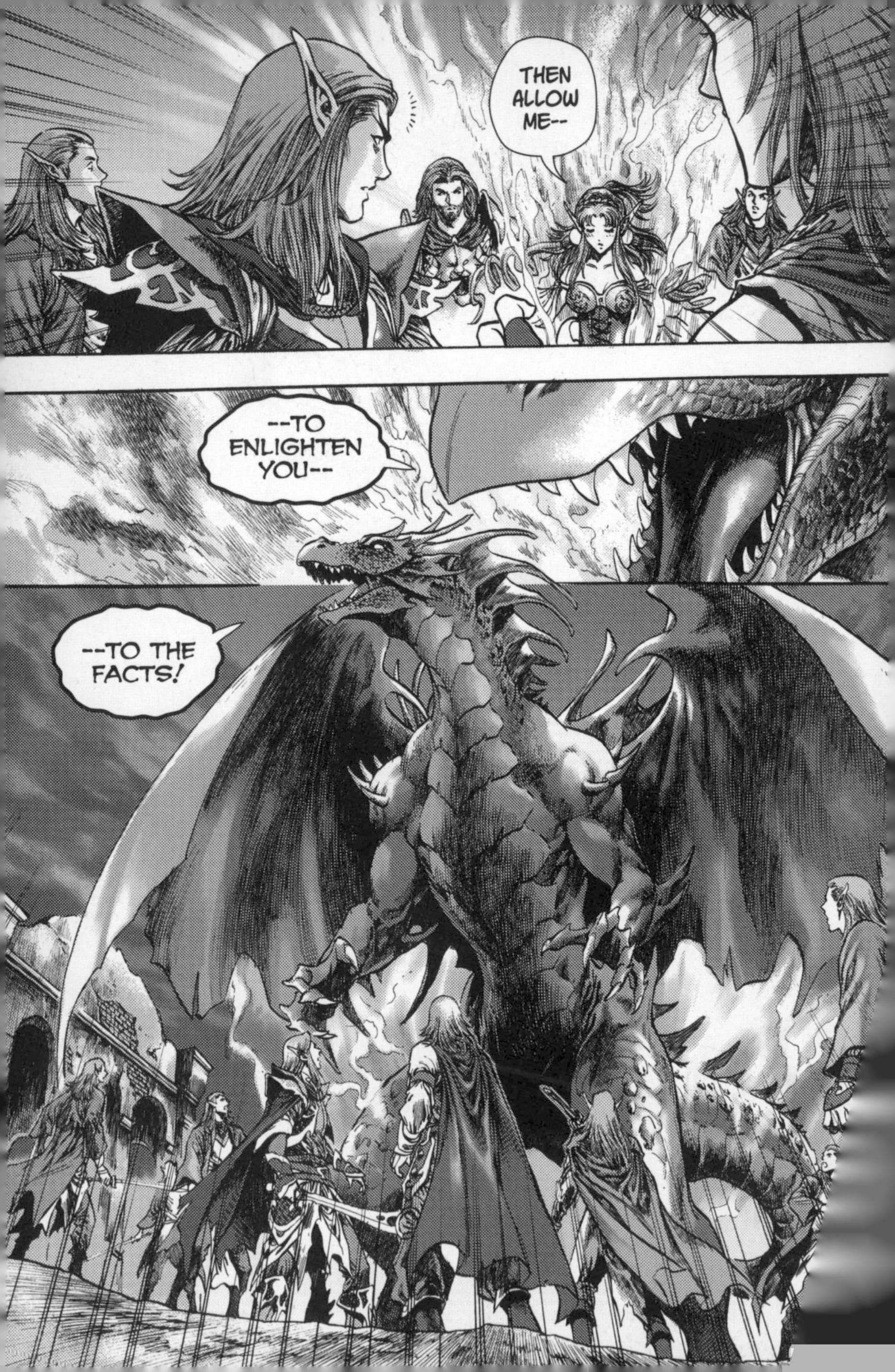
THEN ALLOW ME--
--TO ENLIGHTEN YOU--
--TO THE FACTS!

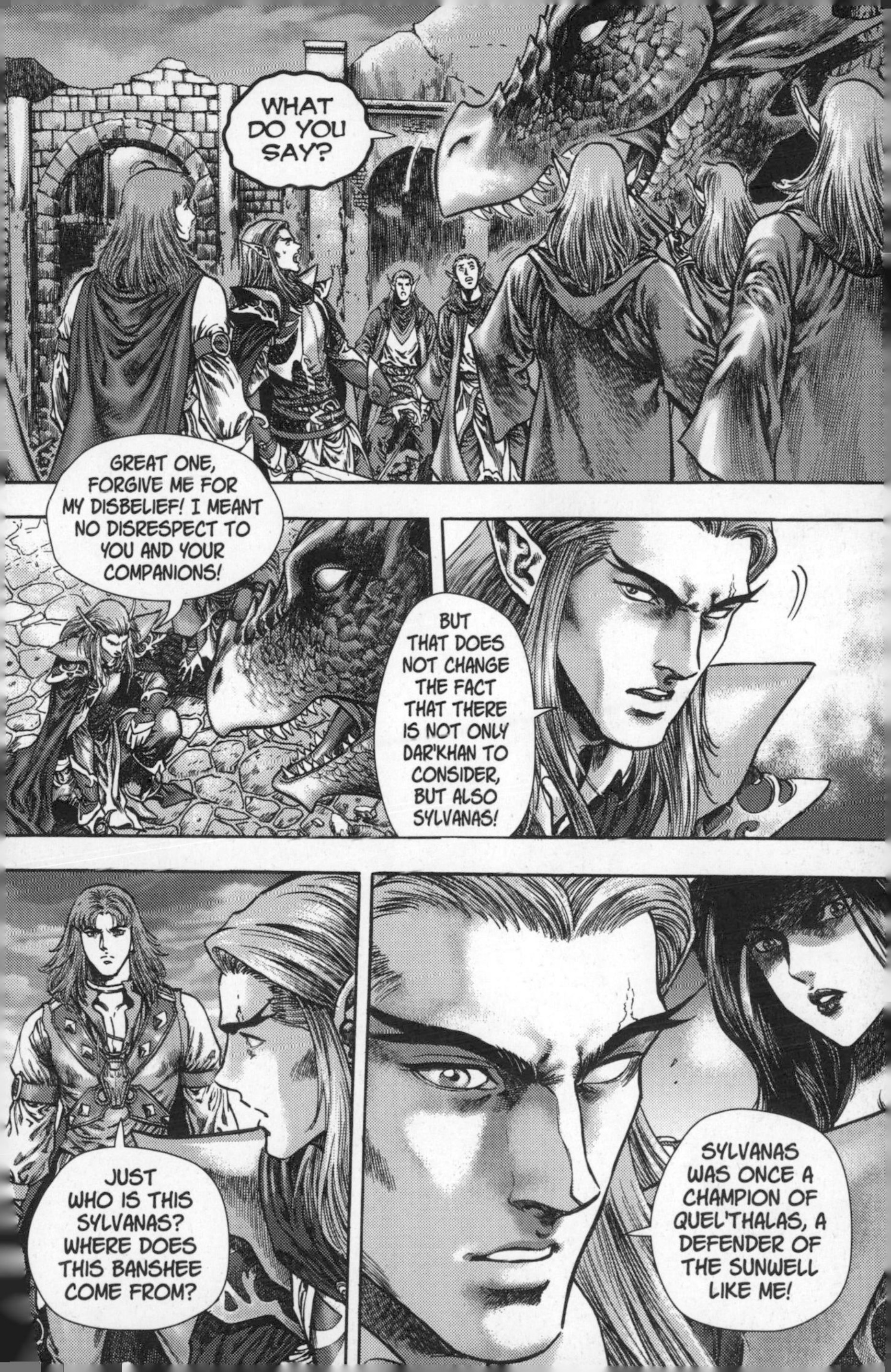
WHAT DO YOU SAY?
GREAT ONE, FORGIVE ME FOR MY DISBELIEF! I MEANT NO DISRESPECT TO YOU AND YOUR COMPANIONS!
BUT THAT DOES NOT CHANGE THE FACT THAT THERE IS NOT ONLY DAR'KHAN TO CONSIDER, BUT ALSO SYLVANAS!
JUST WHO IS THIS SYLVANAS? WHERE DOES THIS BANSHEE COME FROM?
SYLVANAS WAS ONCE A CHAMPION OF QUEL'THALAS, A DEFENDER OF THE SUNWELL LIKE ME!

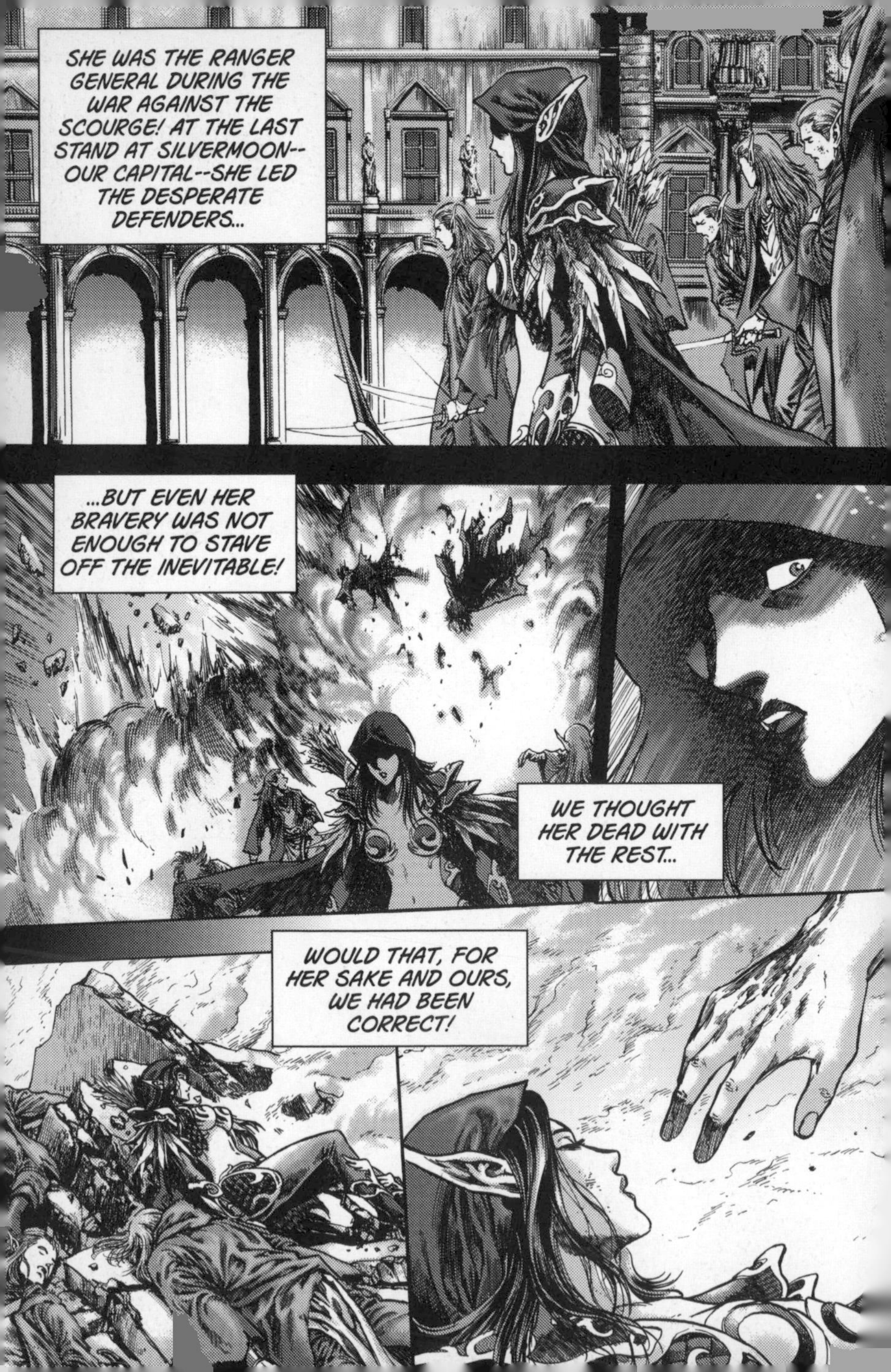
SHE WAS THE RANGER GENERAL DURING THE WAR AGAINST THE SCOURGE! AT THE LAST STAND AT SILVERMOON--OUR CAPITAL--SHE LED THE DESPERATE DEFENDERS...
...BUT EVEN HER BRAVERY WAS NOT ENOUGH TO STAVE OFF THE INEVITABLE!
WE THOUGHT HER DEAD WITH THE REST...
WOULD THAT, FOR HER SAKE AND OURS, WE HAD BEEN CORRECT!

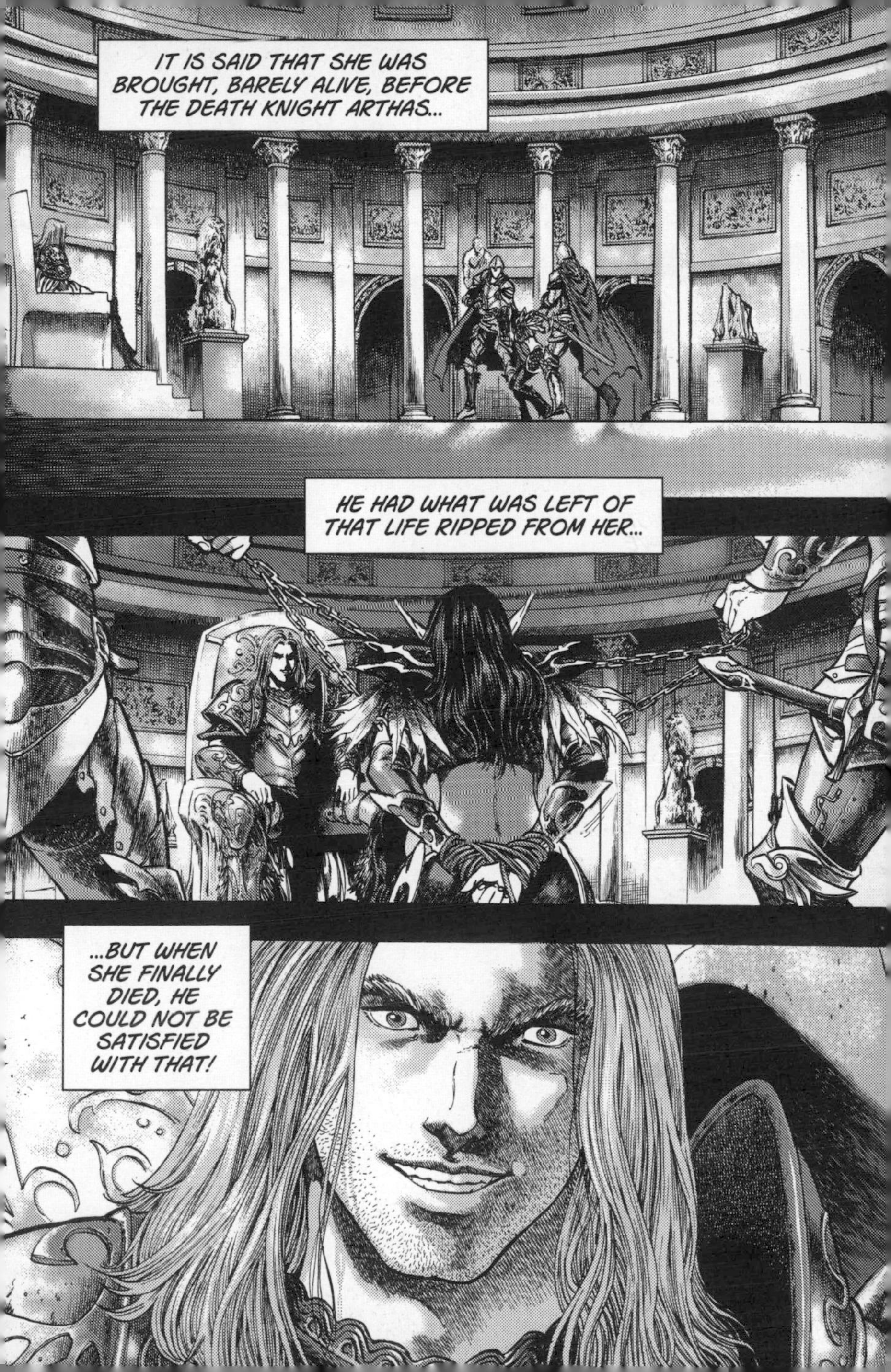
IT IS SAID THAT SHE WAS BROUGHT, BARELY ALIVE, BEFORE THE DEATH KNIGHT ARTHAS...
HE HAD WHAT WAS LEFT OF THAT LIFE RIPPED FROM HER...
...BUT WHEN SHE FINALLY DIED, HE COULD NOT BE SATISFIED WITH THAT!

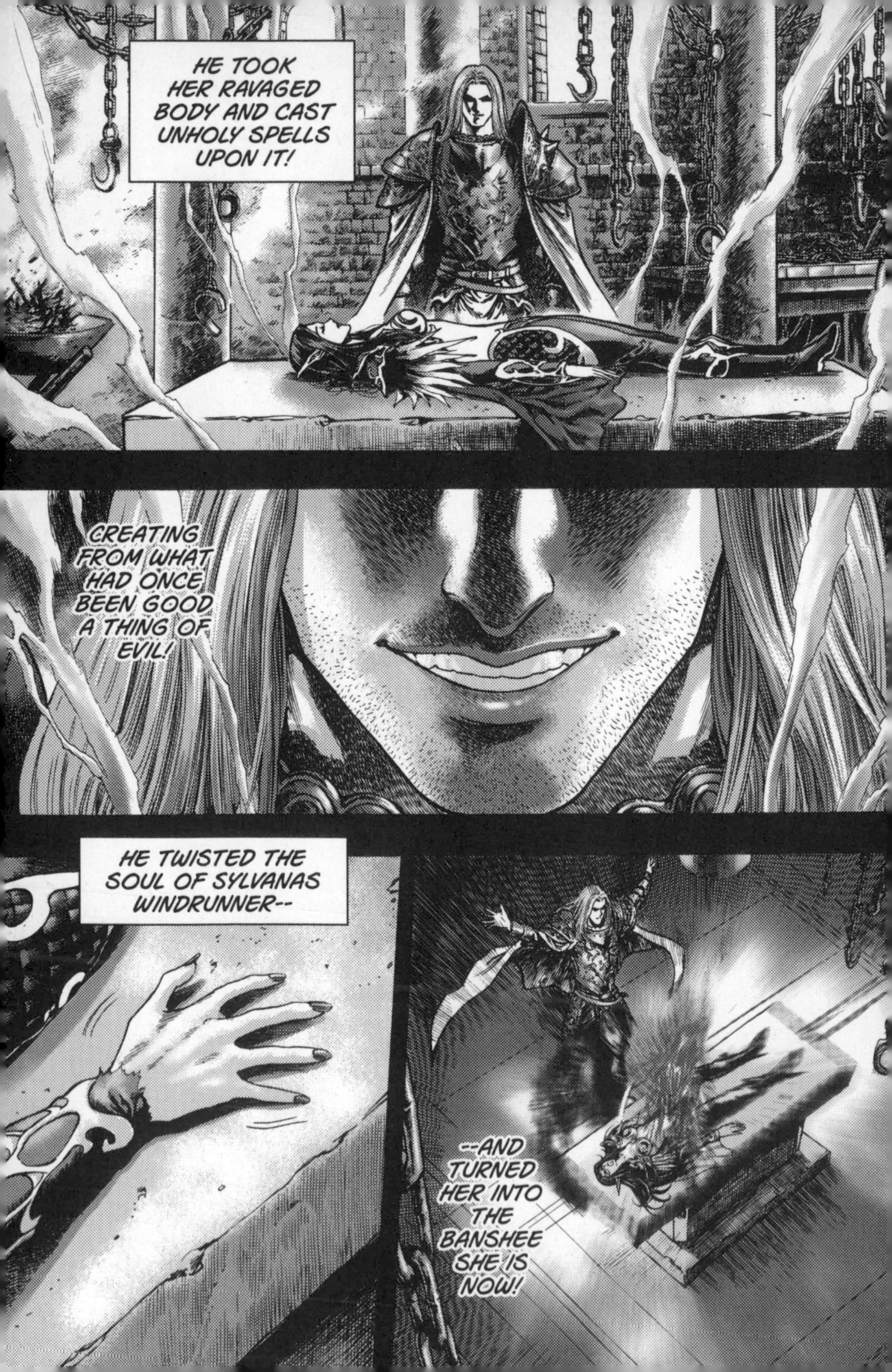
HE TOOK HER RAVAGED BODY AND CAST UNHOLY SPELLS UPON IT!
CREATING FROM WHAT HAD ONCE BEEN GOOD A THING OF EVIL!
HE TWISTED THE SOUL OF SYLVANAS WINDRUNNER--
--AND TURNED HER INTO THE BANSHEE SHE IS NOW!

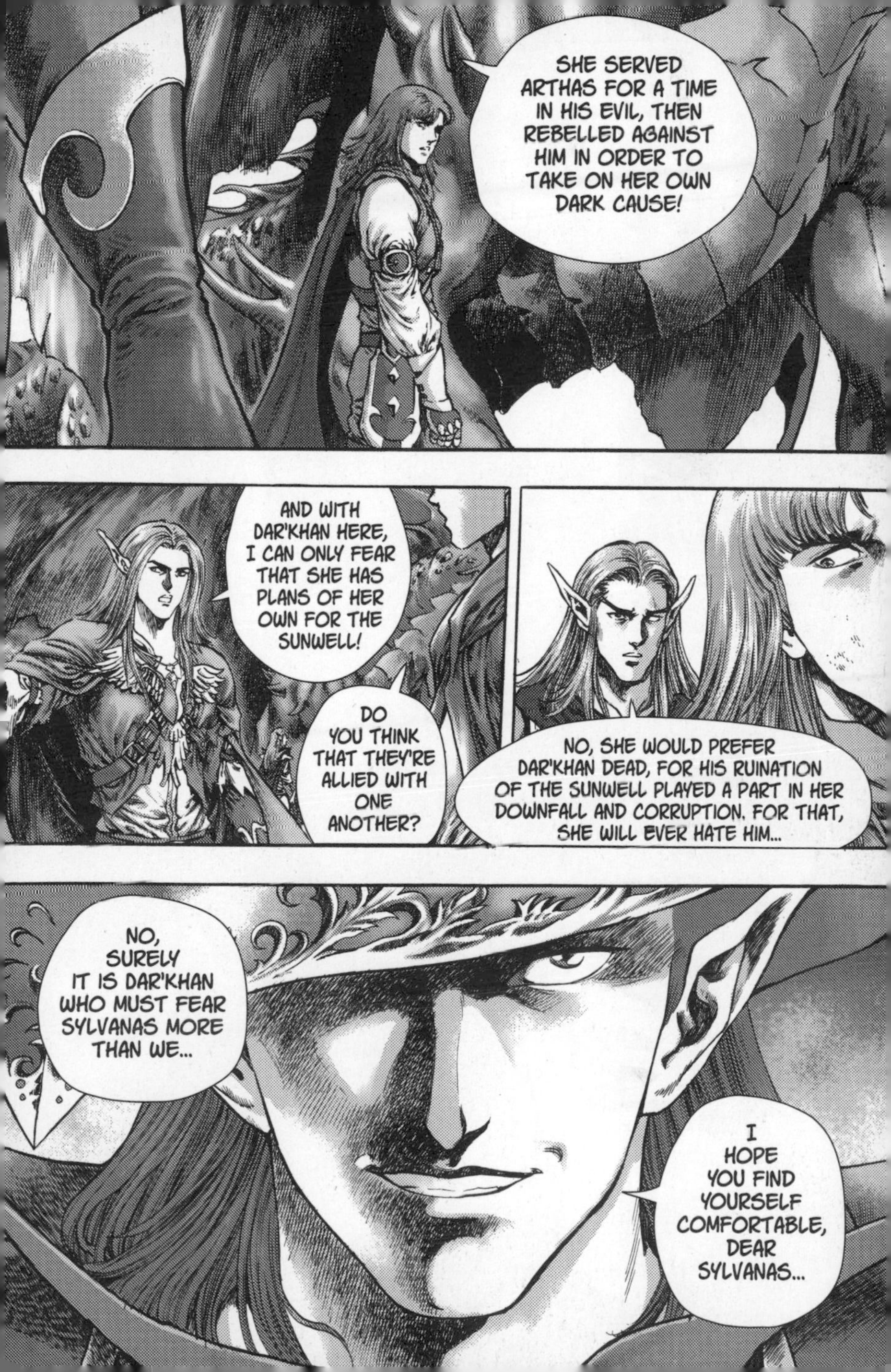
SHE SERVED ARTHAS FOR A TIME IN HIS EVIL, THEN REBELLED AGAINST HIM IN ORDER TO TAKE ON HER OWN DARK CAUSE!
AND WITH DAR'KHAN HERE, I CAN ONLY FEAR THAT SHE HAS PLANS OF HER OWN FOR THE SUNWELL!
DO YOU THINK THAT THEY'RE ALLIED WITH ONE ANOTHER?
NO, SHE WOULD PREFER DAR'KHAN DEAD, FOR HIS RUINATION OF THE SUNWELL PLAYED A PART IN HER DOWNFALL AND CORRUPTION. FOR THAT, SHE WILL EVER HATE HIM...
NO, SURELY IT IS DAR'KHAN WHO MUST FEAR SYLVANAS MORE THAN WE...
I HOPE YOU FIND YOURSELF COMFORTABLE, DEAR SYLVANAS...

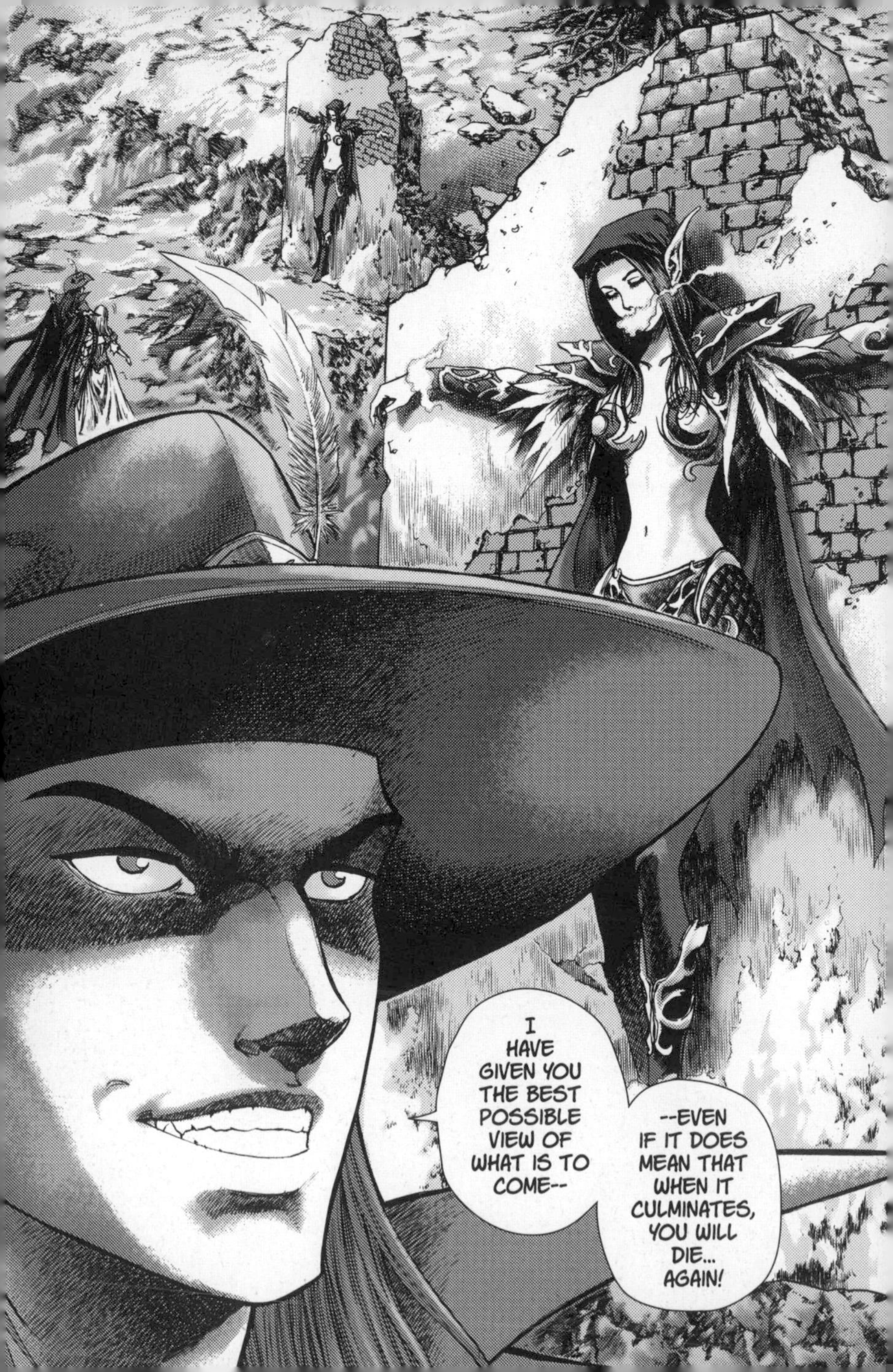
I HAVE GIVEN YOU THE BEST POSSIBLE VIEW OF WHAT IS TO COME--
--EVEN IF IT DOES MEAN THAT WHEN IT CULMINATES, YOU WILL DIE... AGAIN!

CHAPTER FIVE

EDGE OF THE ABYSS

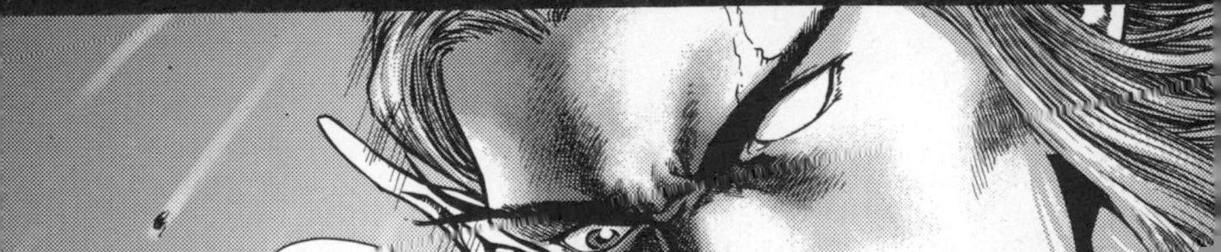
THERE! WE MUST LAND THERE!

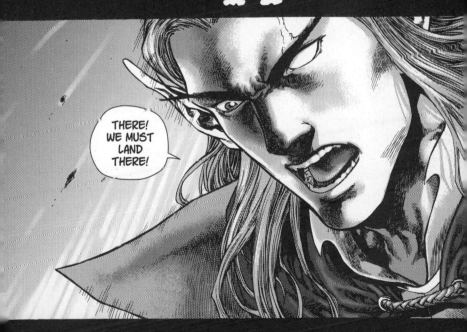

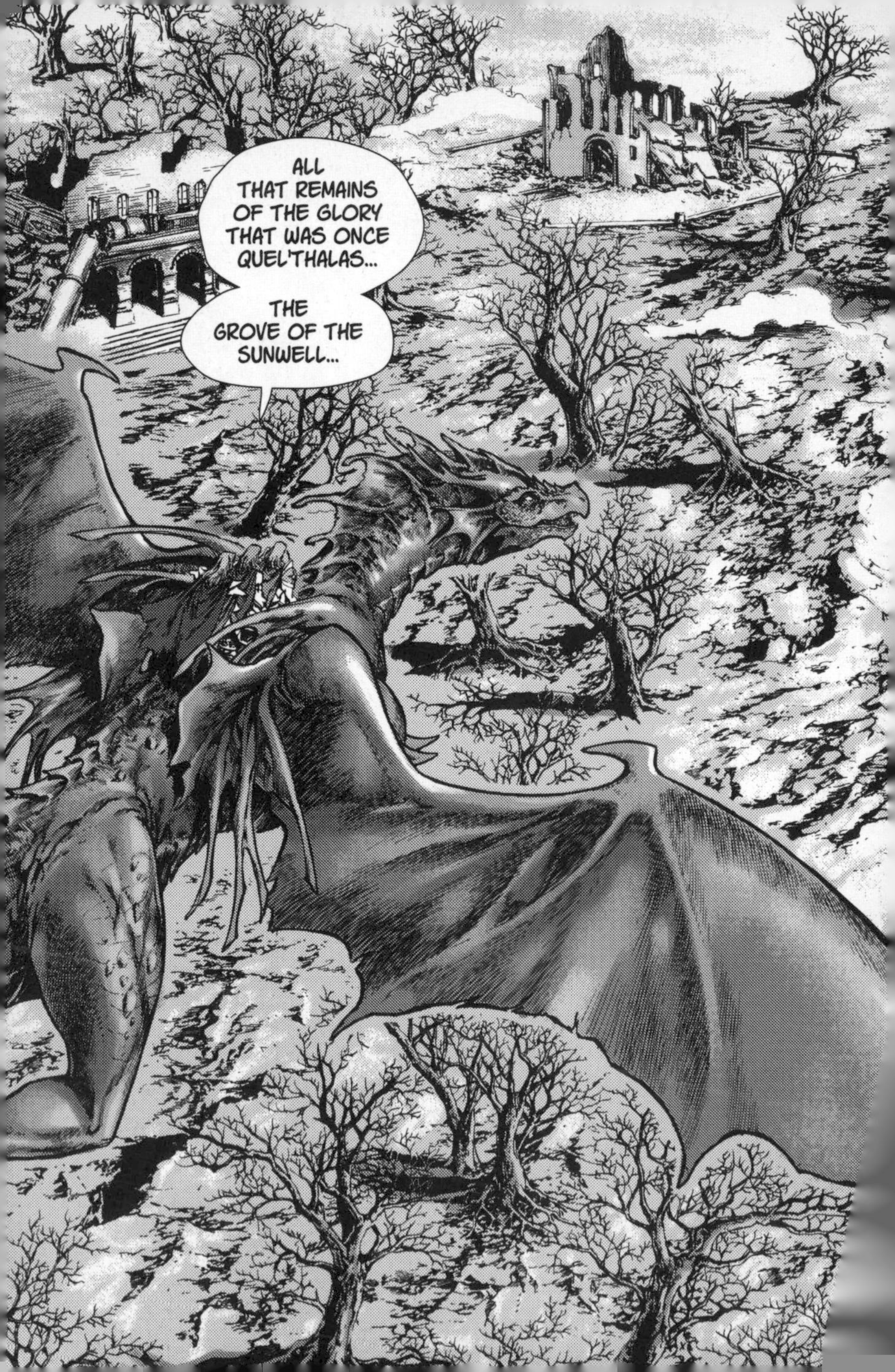
ALL THAT REMAINS OF THE GLORY THAT WAS ONCE QUEL'THALAS...
THE GROVE OF THE SUNWELL...

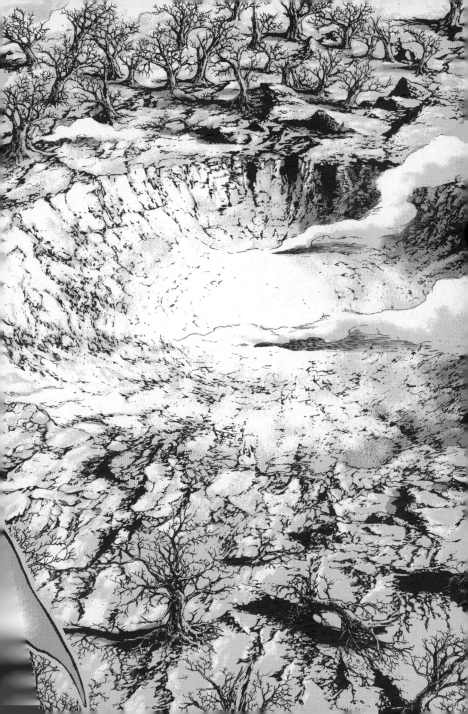

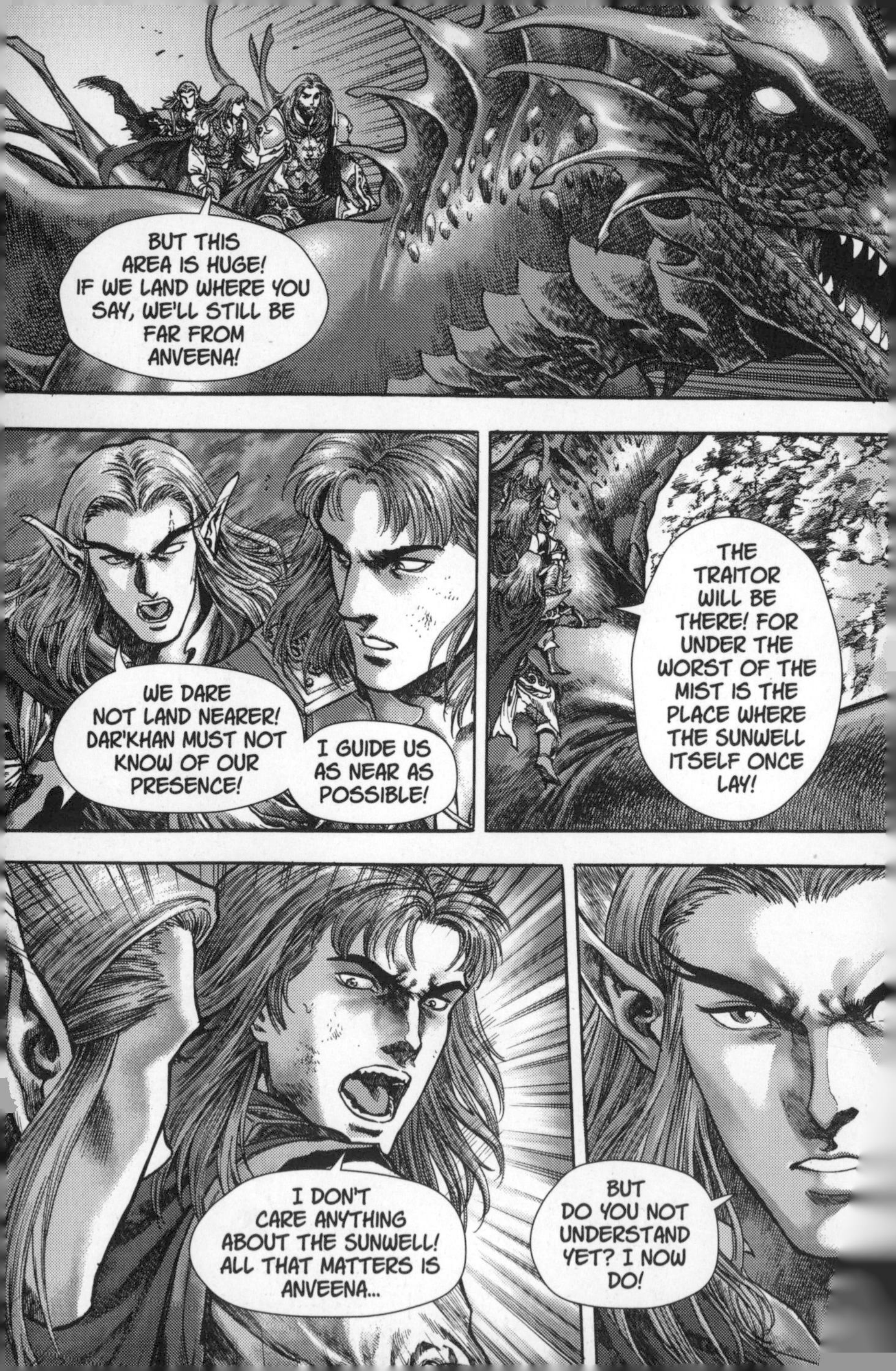
BUT THIS AREA IS HUGE! IF WE LAND WHERE YOU SAY, WE'LL STILL BE FAR FROM ANVEENA!
WE DARE NOT LAND NEARER! DAR'KHAN MUST NOT KNOW OF OUR PRESENCE!
I GUIDE US AS NEAR AS POSSIBLE!
THE TRAITOR WILL BE THERE! FOR UNDER THE WORST OF THE MIST IS THE PLACE WHERE THE SUNWELL ITSELF ONCE LAY!
I DON'T CARE ANYTHING ABOUT THE SUNWELL! ALL THAT MATTERS IS ANVEENA...
BUT DO YOU NOT UNDERSTAND YET? I NOW DO!

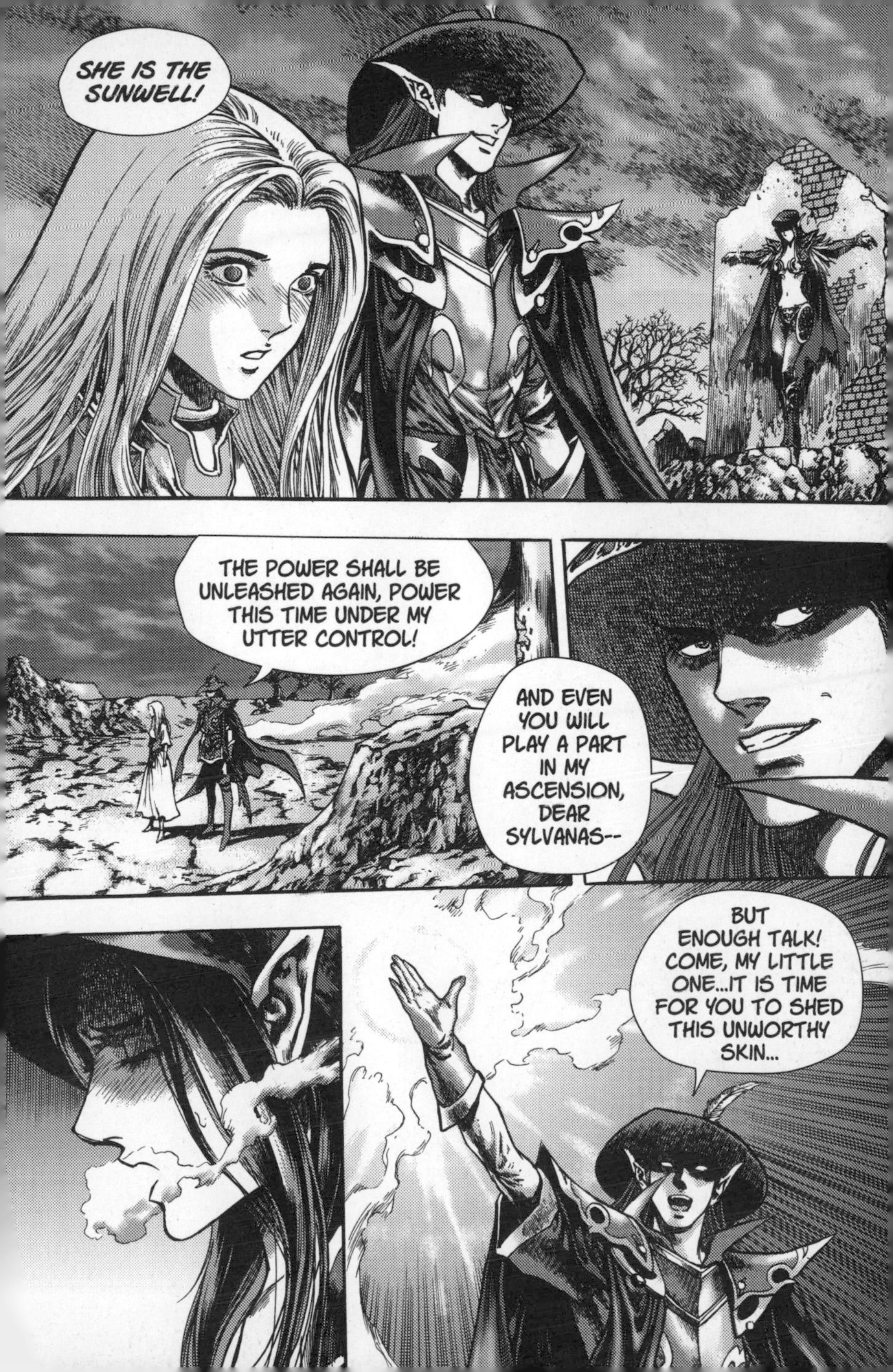
SHE IS THE SUNWELL!
THE POWER SHALL BE UNLEASHED AGAIN, POWER THIS TIME UNDER MY UTTER CONTROL!
AND EVEN YOU WILL PLAY A PART IN MY ASCENSION, DEAR SYLVANAS--
BUT ENOUGH TALK! COME, MY LITTLE ONE...IT IS TIME FOR YOU TO SHED THIS UNWORTHY SKIN...

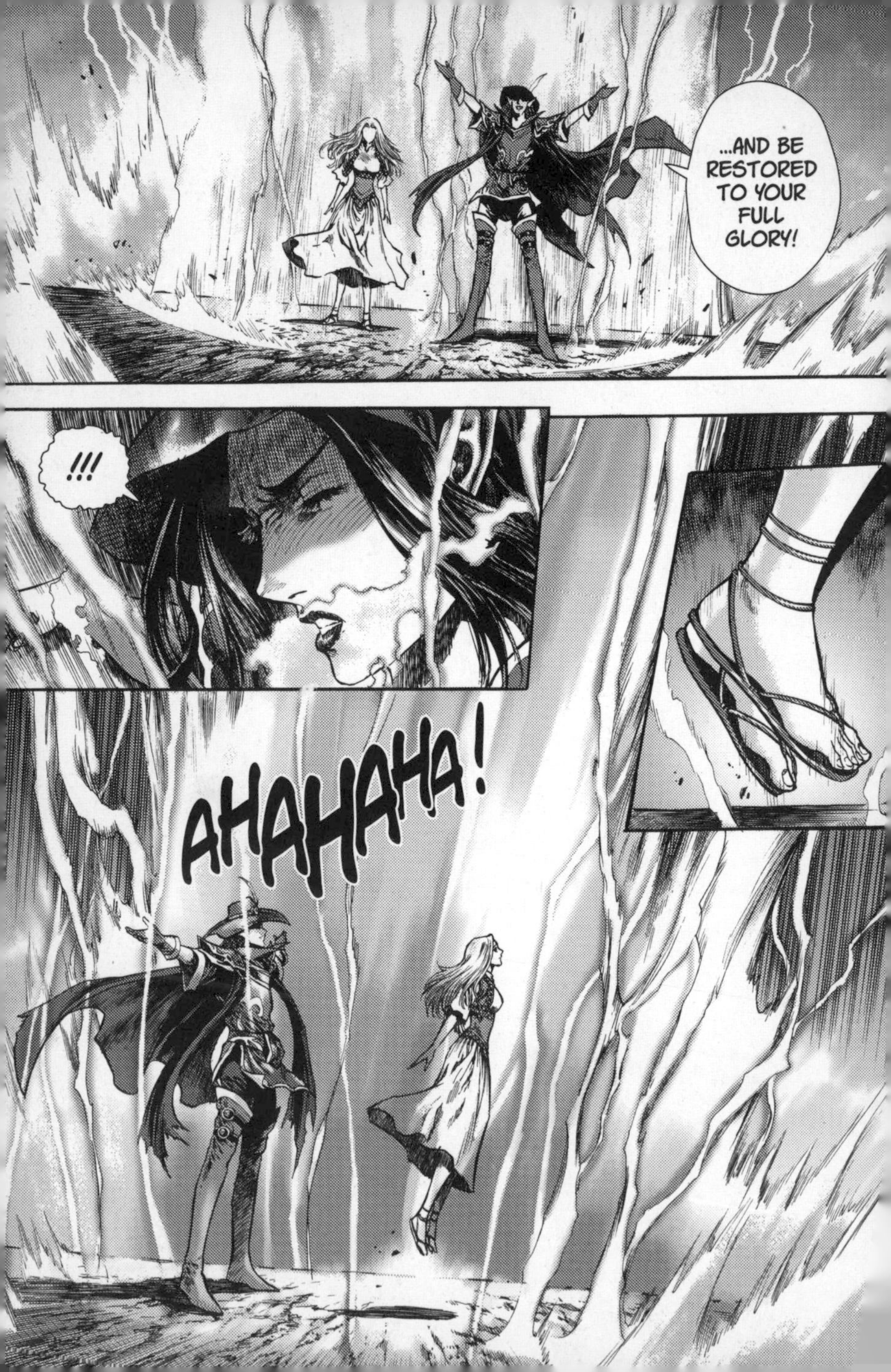
...AND BE RESTORED TO YOUR FULL GLORY!
!!!
AHAHAHA!

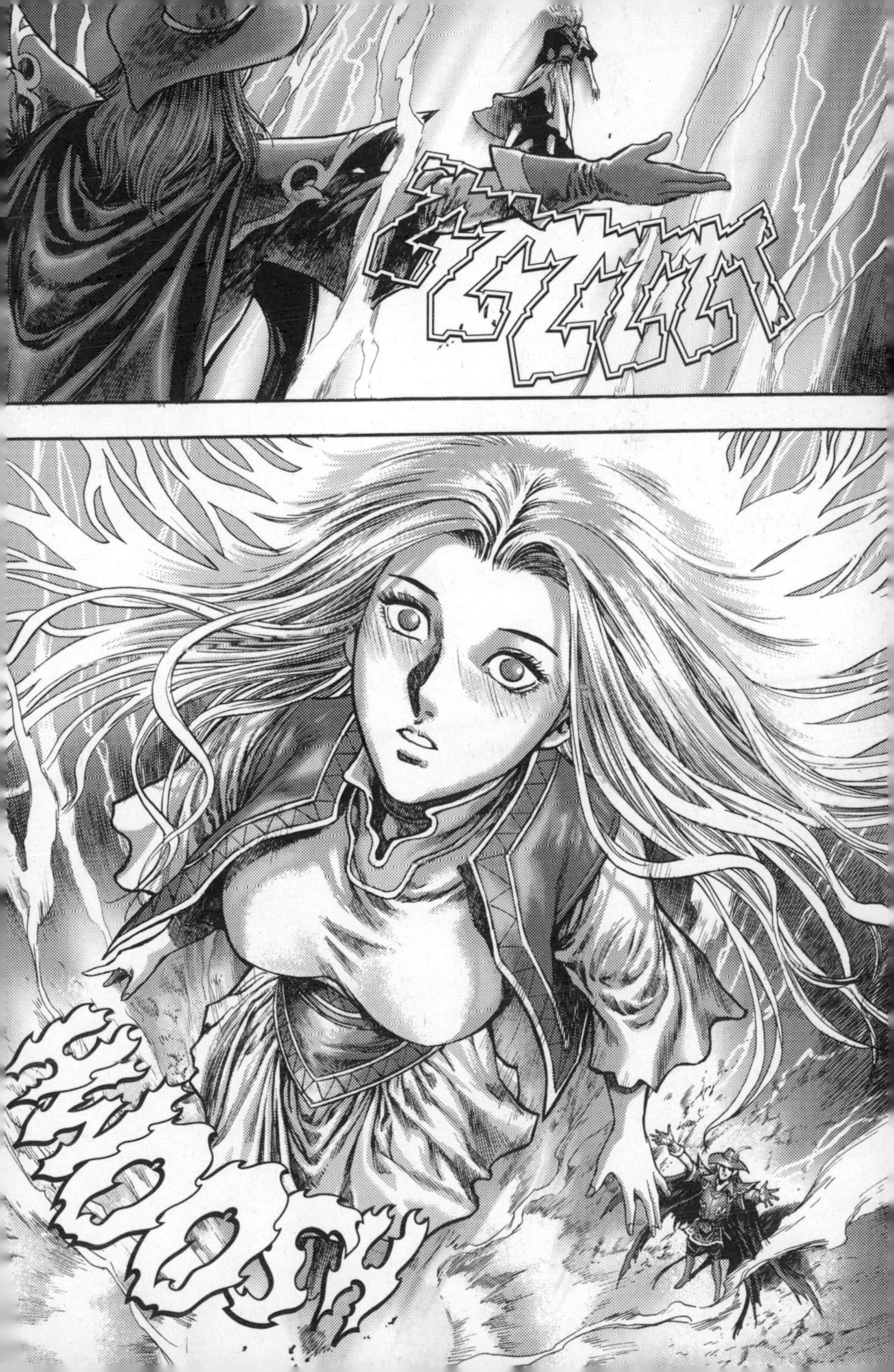

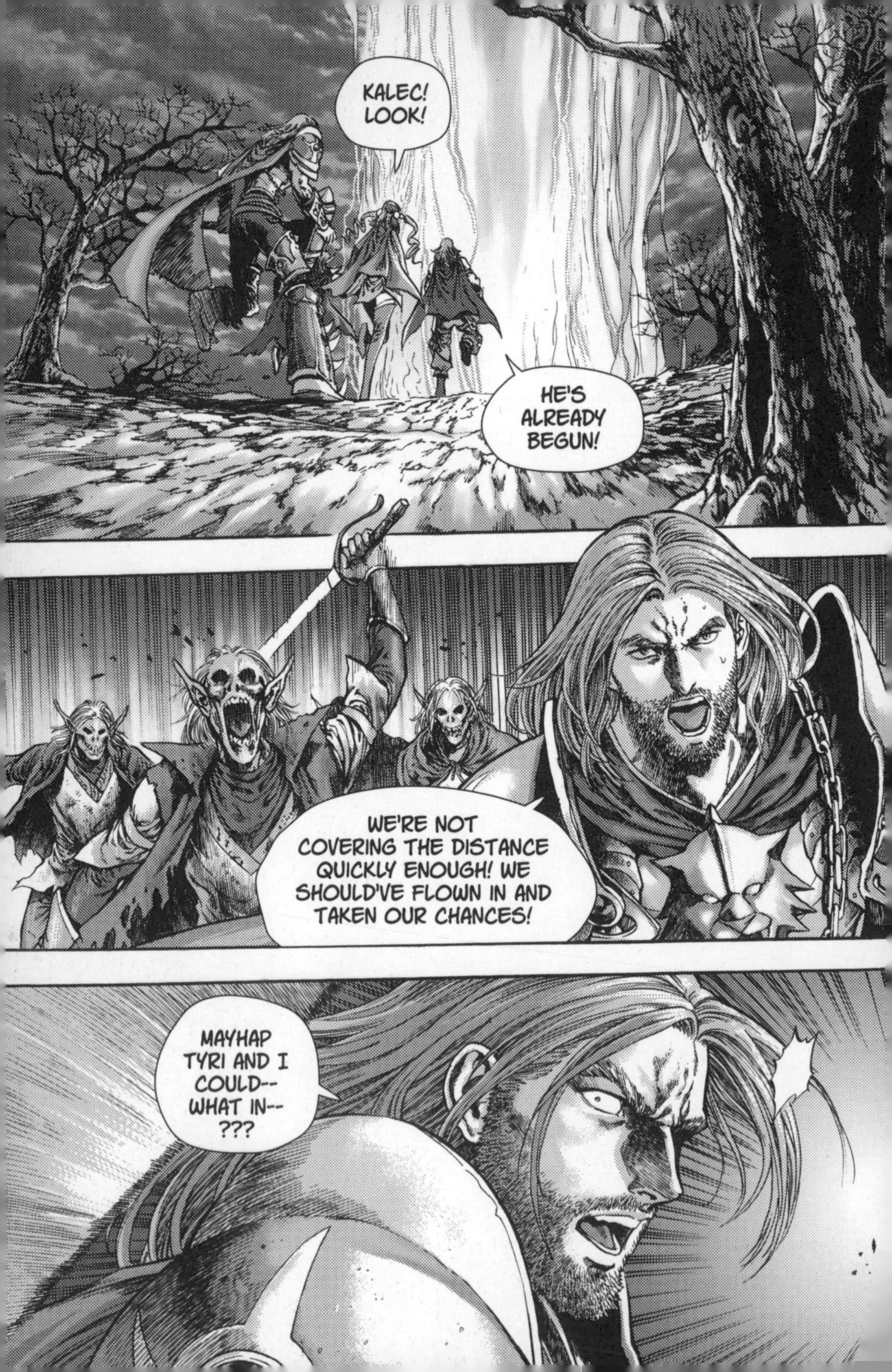
KALEC! LOOK!
HE'S ALREADY BEGUN!
WE'RE NOT COVERING THE DISTANCE QUICKLY ENOUGH! WE SHOULD'VE FLOWN IN AND TAKEN OUR CHANCES!
MAYHAP TYRI AND I COULD-- WHAT IN-- ???

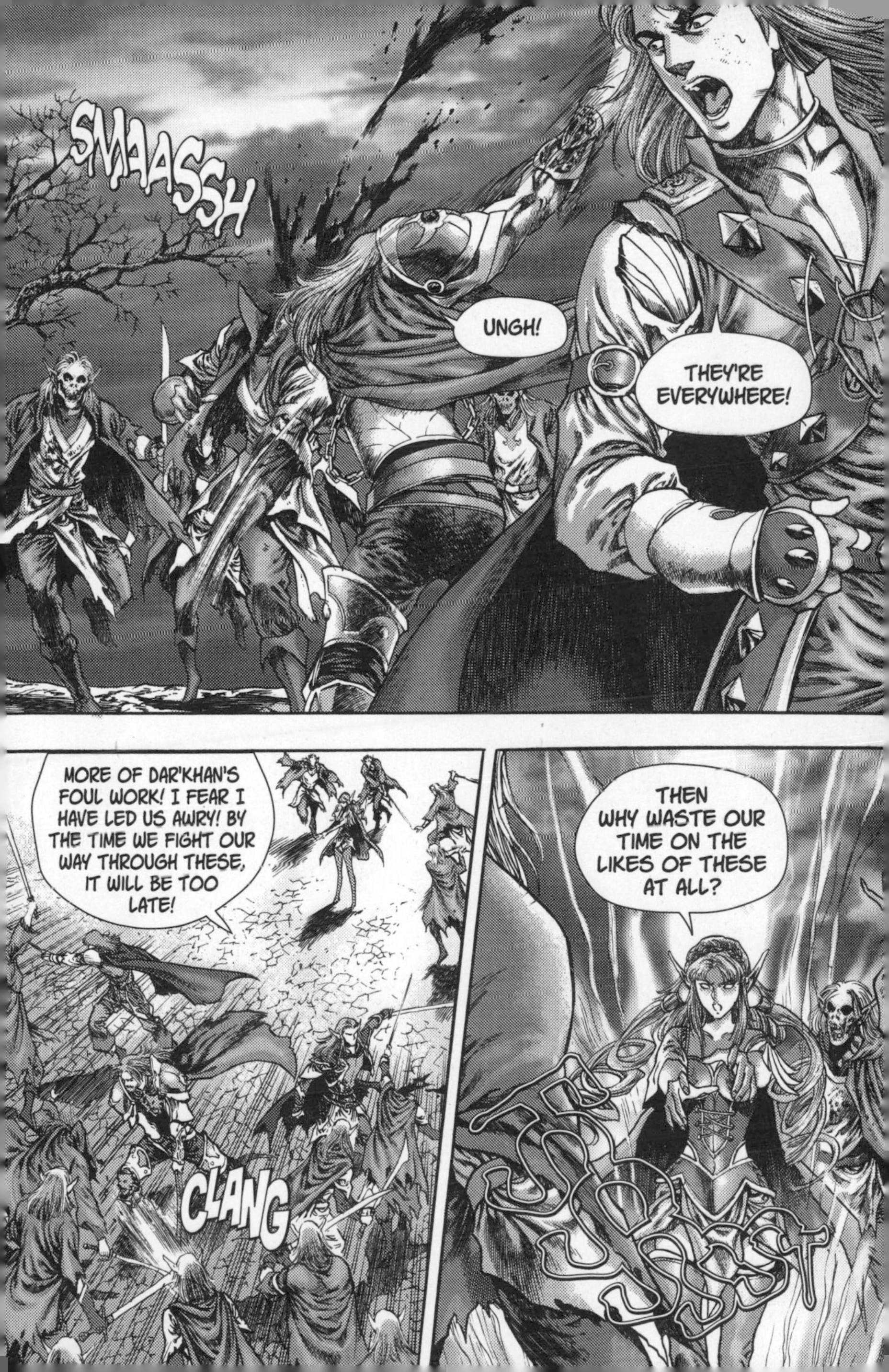
SMAASSH
UNGH!
THEY'RE EVERYWHERE!
MORE OF DAR'KHAN'S FOUL WORK! I FEAR I HAVE LED US AWRY! BY THE TIME WE FIGHT OUR WAY THROUGH THESE, IT WILL BE TOO LATE!
CLANG
THEN WHY WASTE OUR TIME ON THE LIKES OF THESE AT ALL?

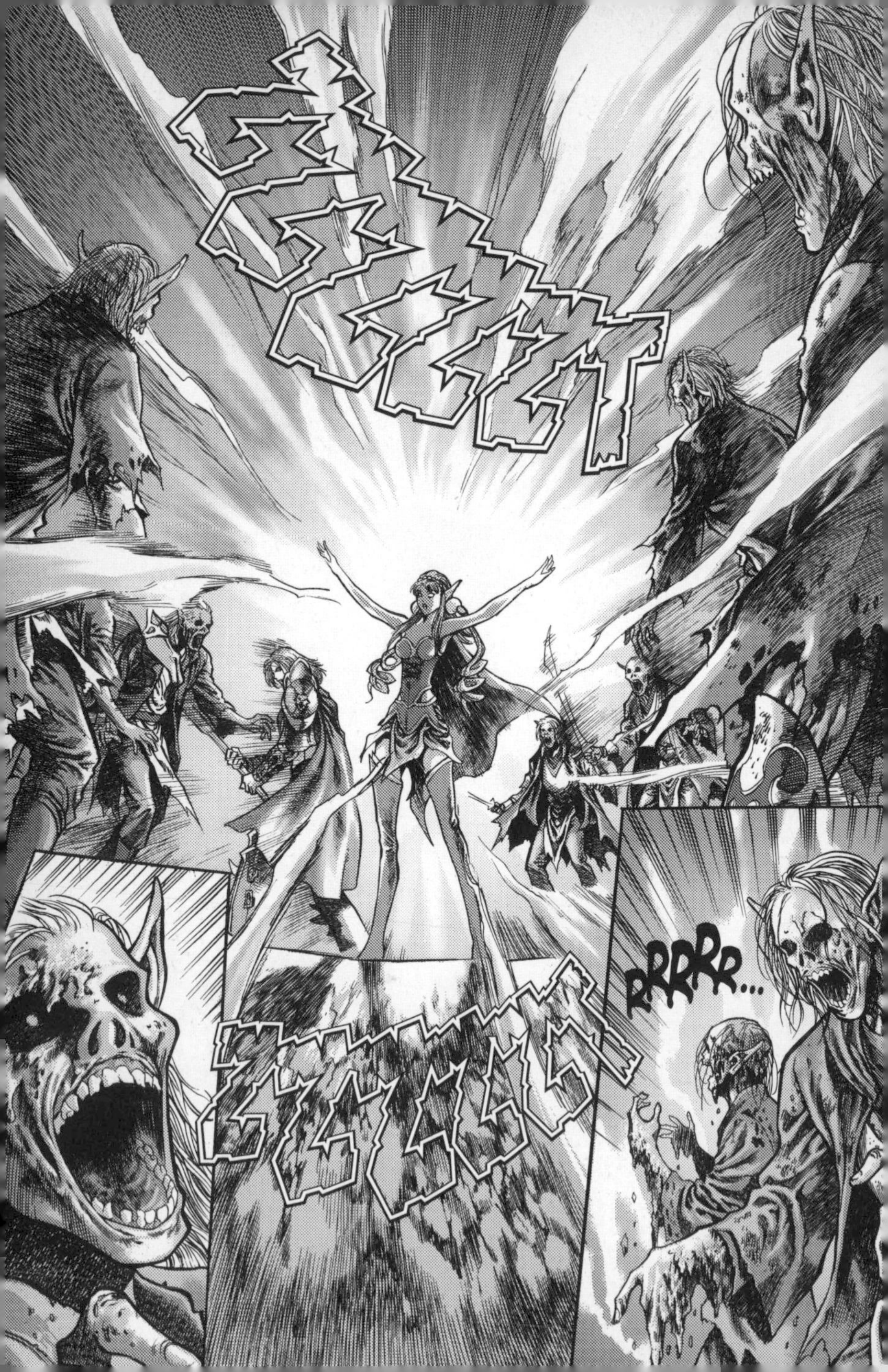
ZZZZT
ZZZZT
RRRRR...

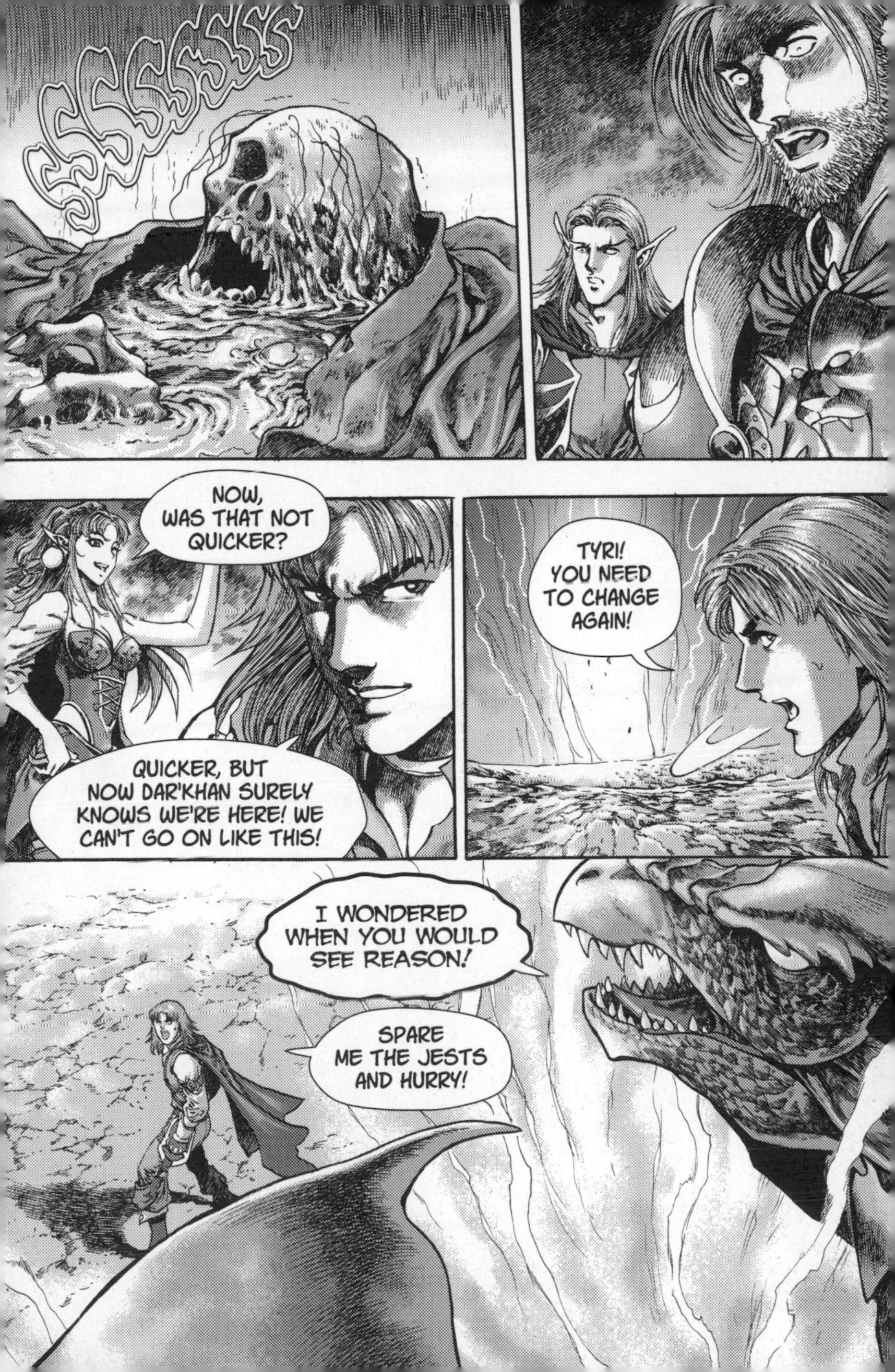
NOW, WAS THAT NOT QUICKER?
QUICKER, BUT NOW DAR'KHAN SURELY KNOWS WE'RE HERE! WE CAN'T GO ON LIKE THIS!
TYRI! YOU NEED TO CHANGE AGAIN!
I WONDERED WHEN YOU WOULD SEE REASON!
SPARE ME THE JESTS AND HURRY!

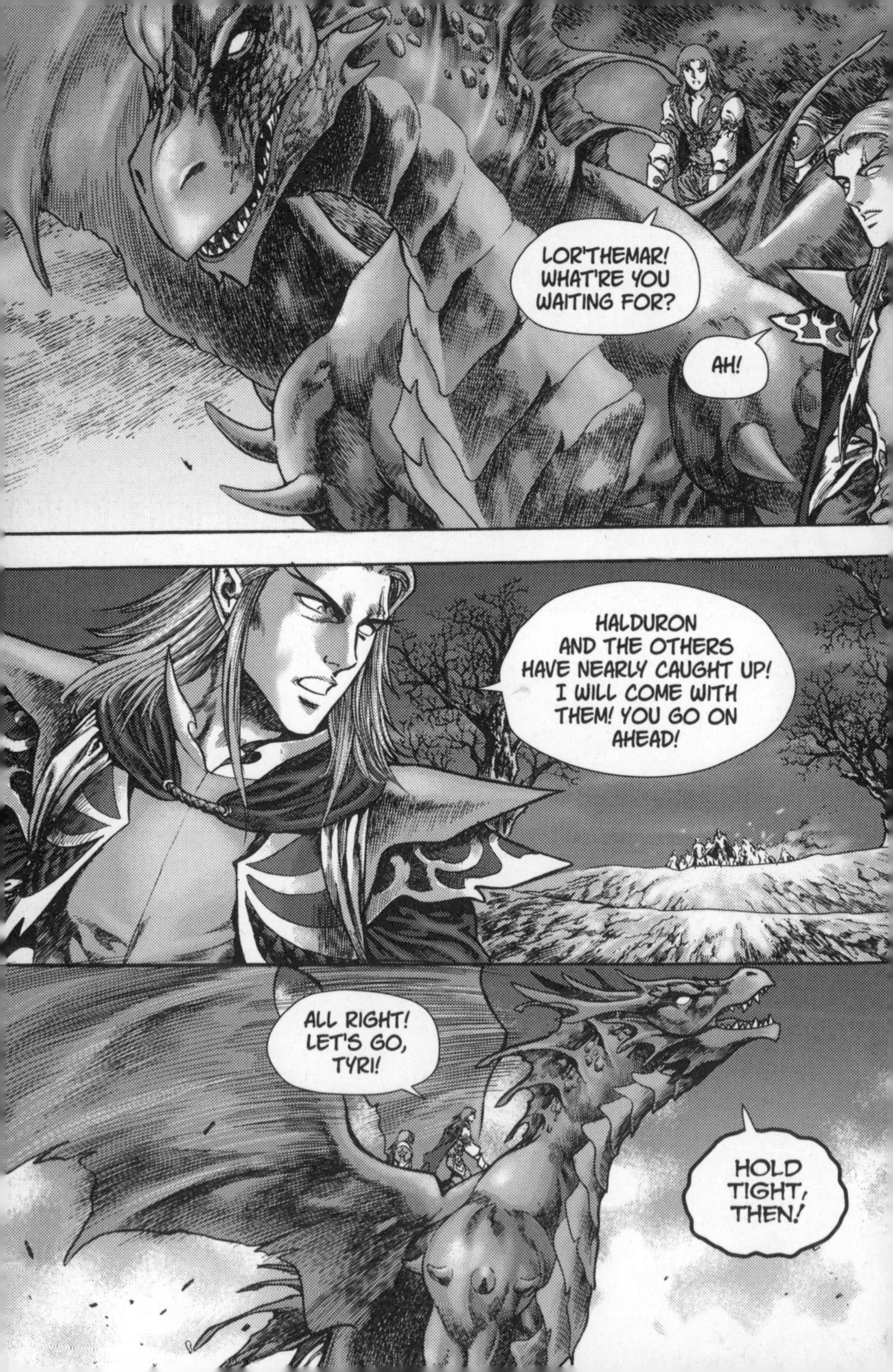
LOR'THEMAR! WHAT'RE YOU WAITING FOR?
AH!
HALDURON AND THE OTHERS HAVE NEARLY CAUGHT UP! I WILL COME WITH THEM! YOU GO ON AHEAD!
ALL RIGHT! LET'S GO, TYRI!
HOLD TIGHT, THEN!

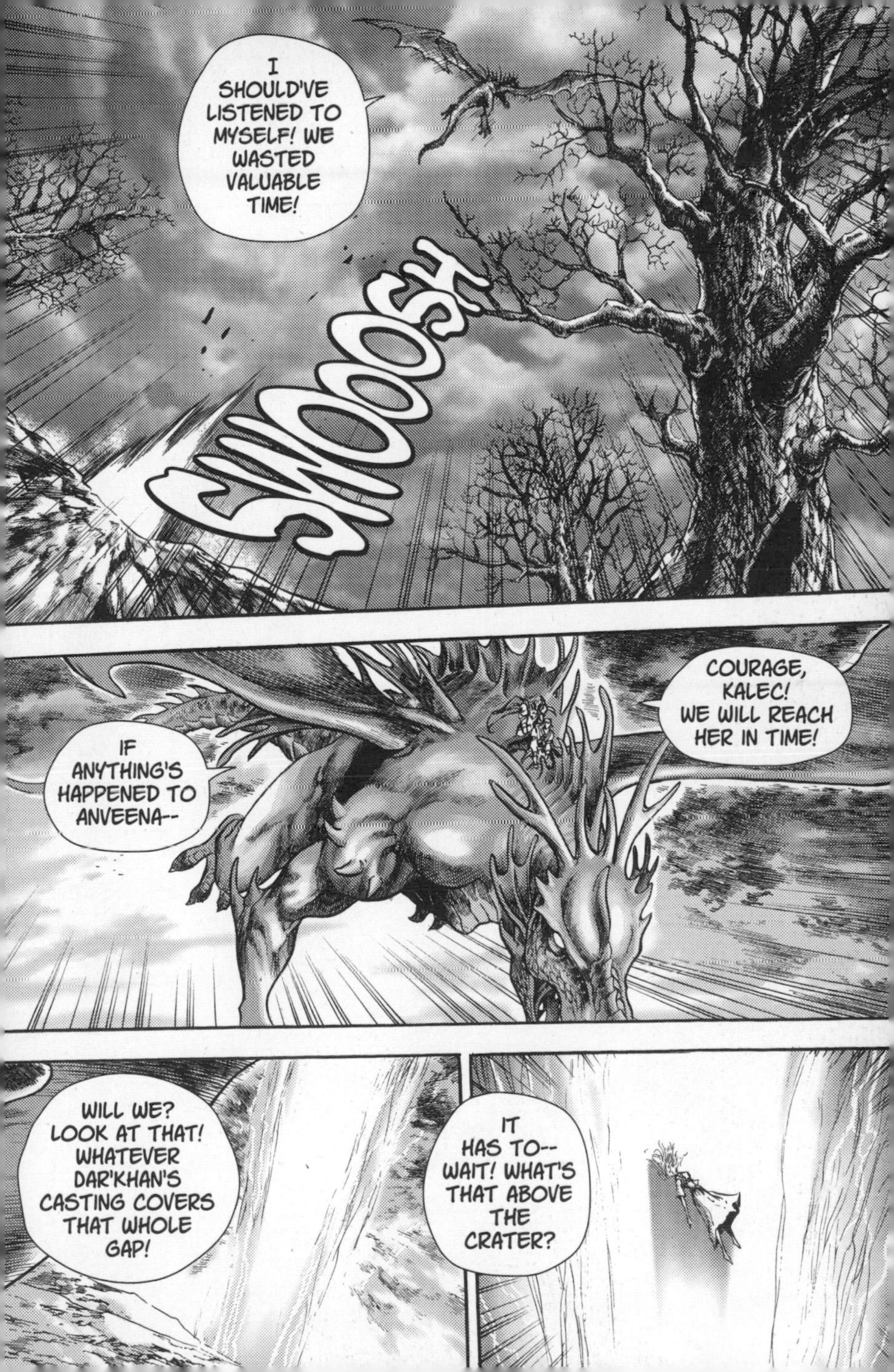
I SHOULD'VE LISTENED TO MYSELF! WE WASTED VALUABLE TIME!
SWOOOSH
IF ANYTHING'S HAPPENED TO ANVEENA--
COURAGE, KALEC! WE WILL REACH HER IN TIME!
WILL WE? LOOK AT THAT! WHATEVER DAR'KHAN'S CASTING COVERS THAT WHOLE GAP!
IT HAS TO-- WAIT! WHAT'S THAT ABOVE THE CRATER?

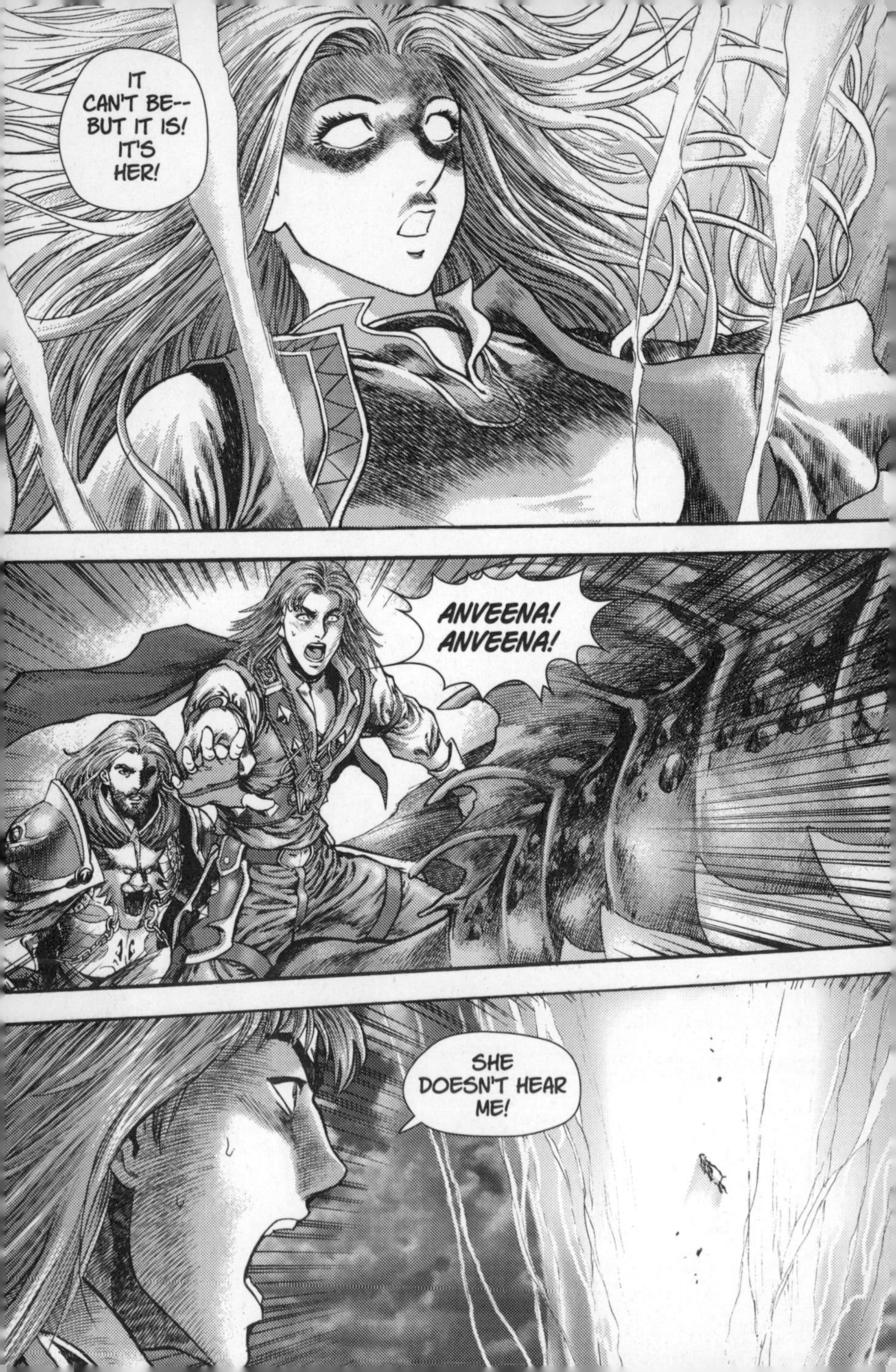
IT CAN'T BE-- BUT IT IS! IT'S HER!
ANVEENA! ANVEENA!
SHE DOESN'T HEAR ME!

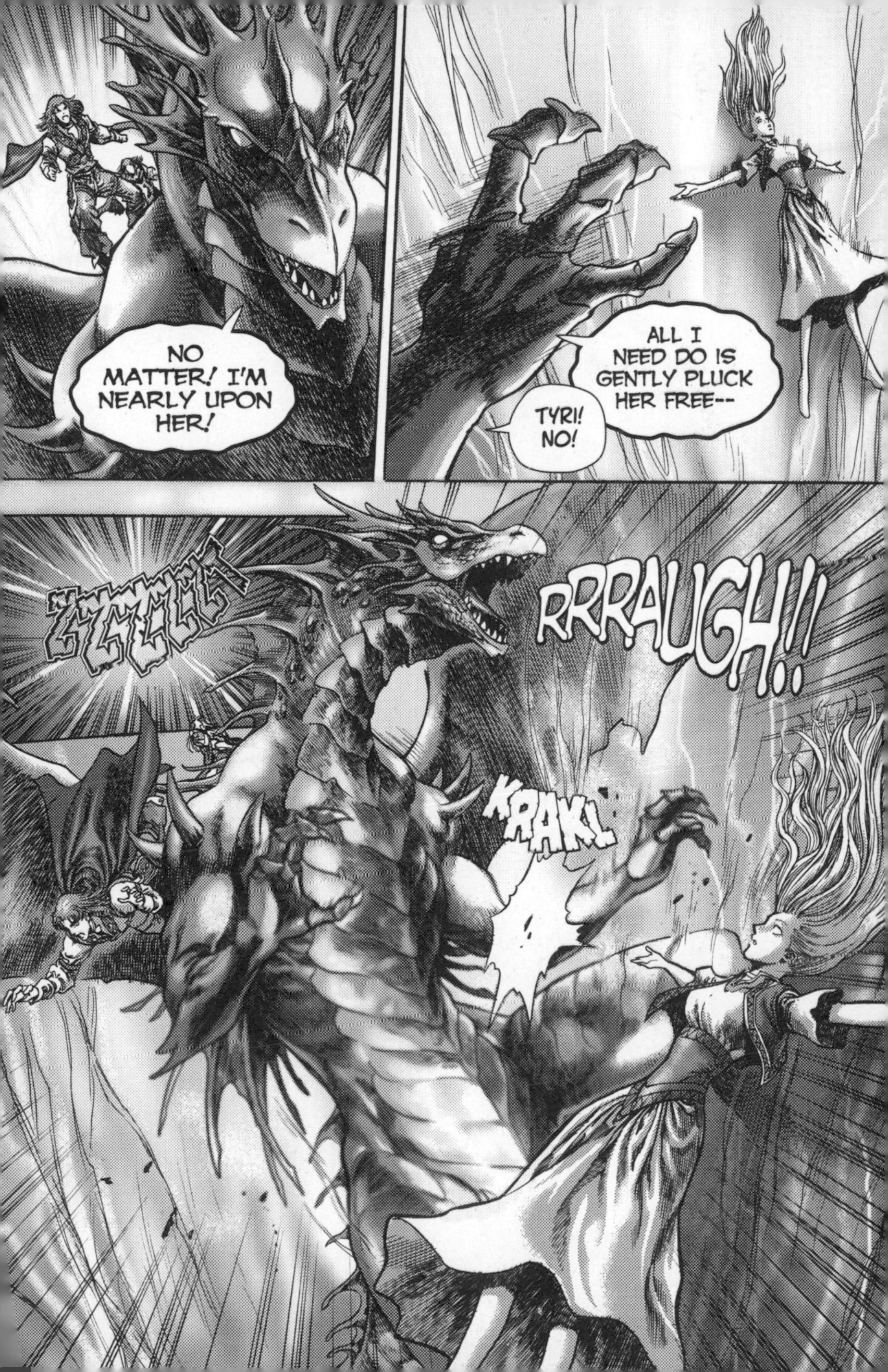
NO MATTER! I'M NEARLY UPON HER!
ALL I NEED DO IS GENTLY PLUCK HER FREE--
TYRI! NO!
RRRAUGH!!
KRAK!

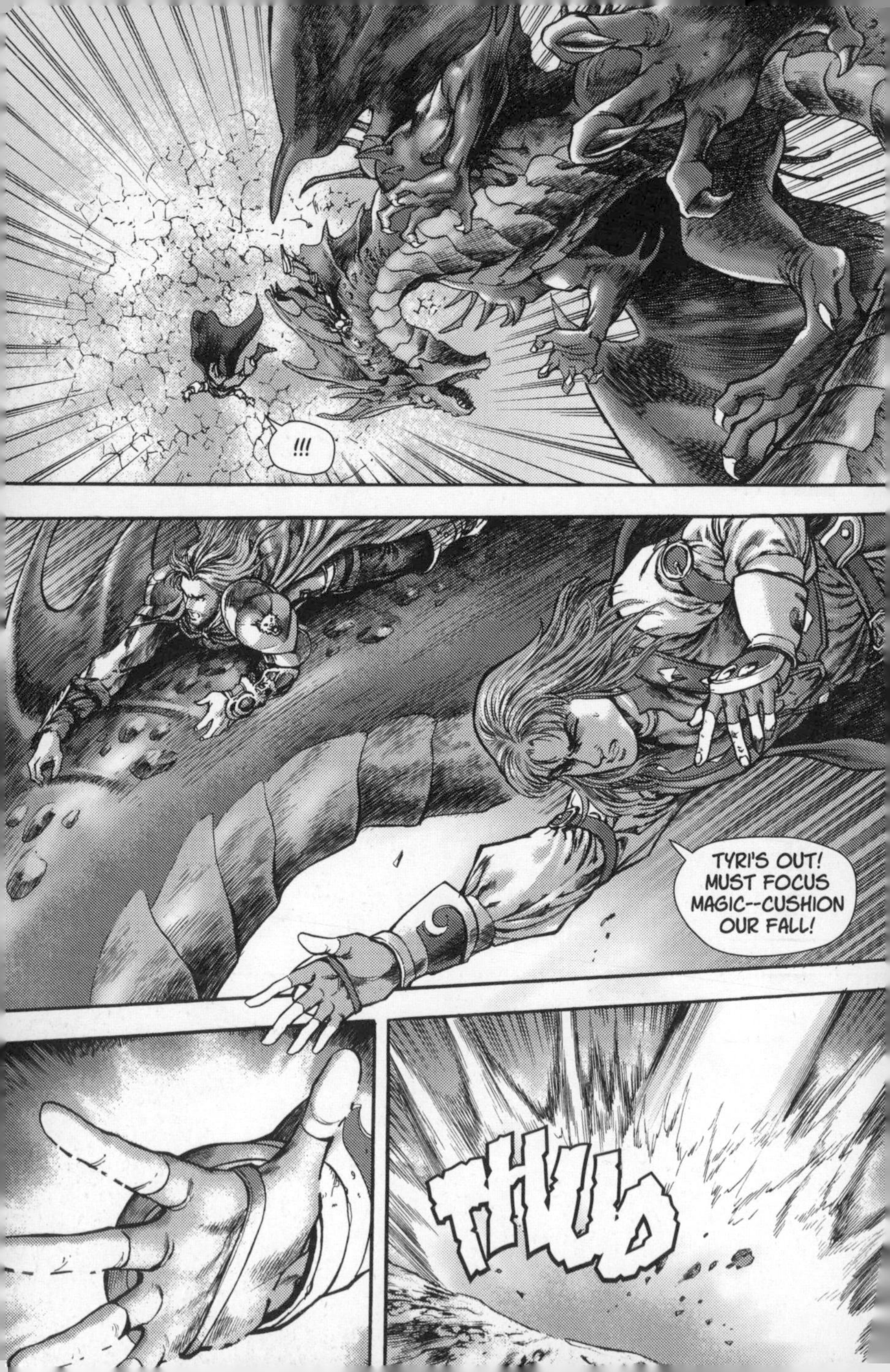
!!!
TYRI'S OUT! MUST FOCUS MAGIC--CUSHION OUR FALL!
THUD

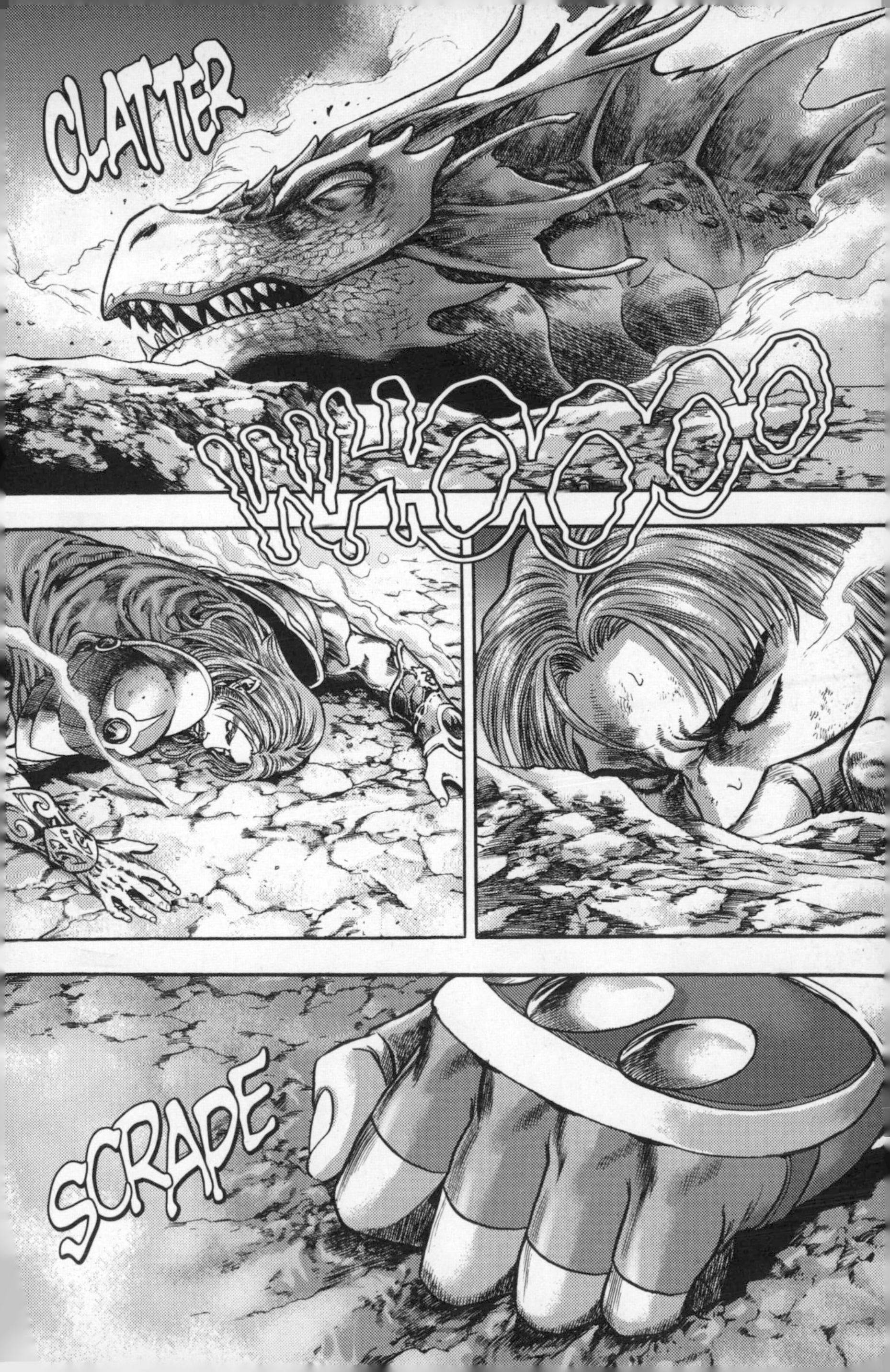
CLATTER
WHOOOOO
SCRAPE

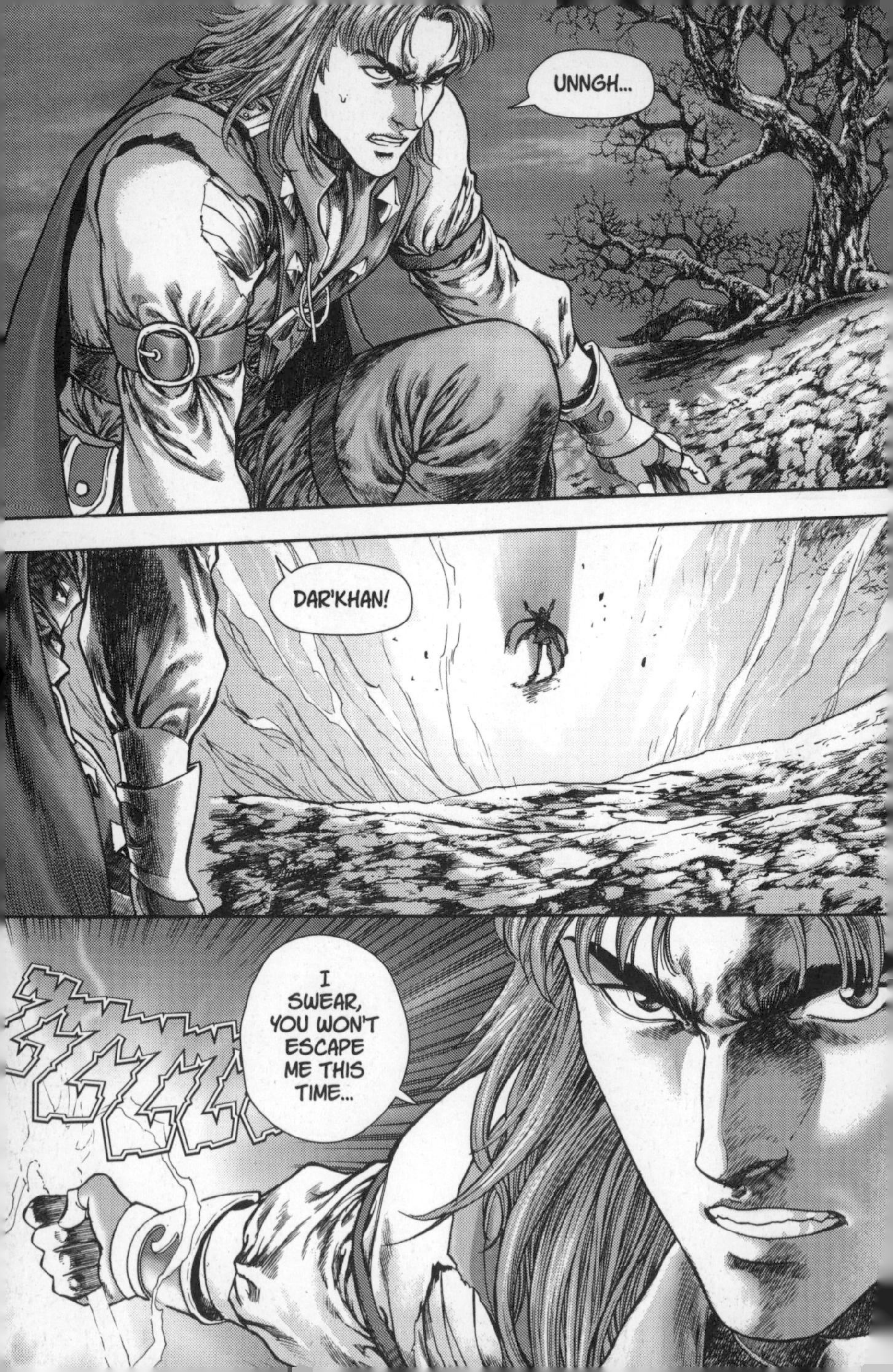
UNNGH...
DAR'KHAN!
I SWEAR, YOU WON'T ESCAPE ME THIS TIME...

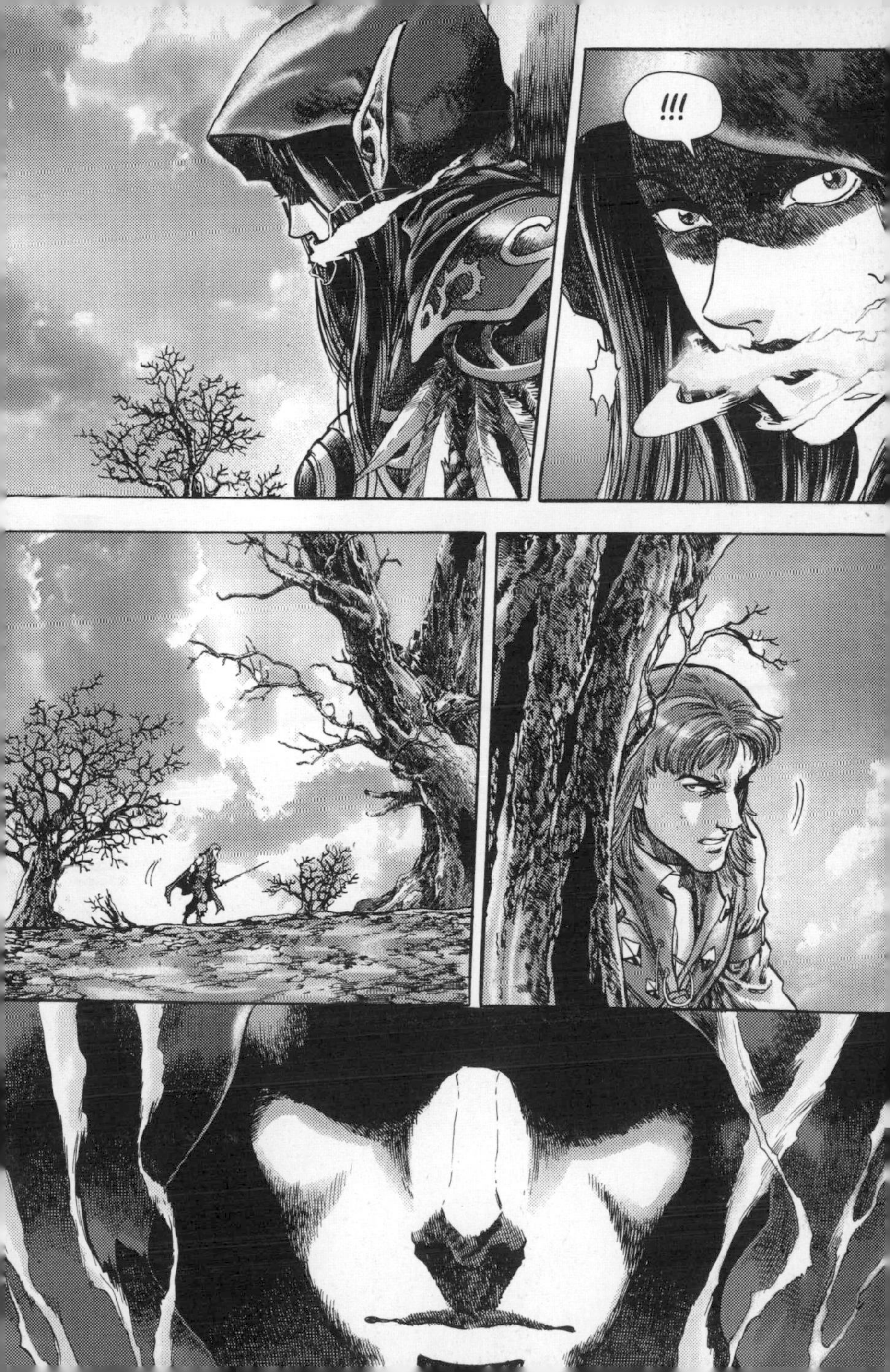
!!!

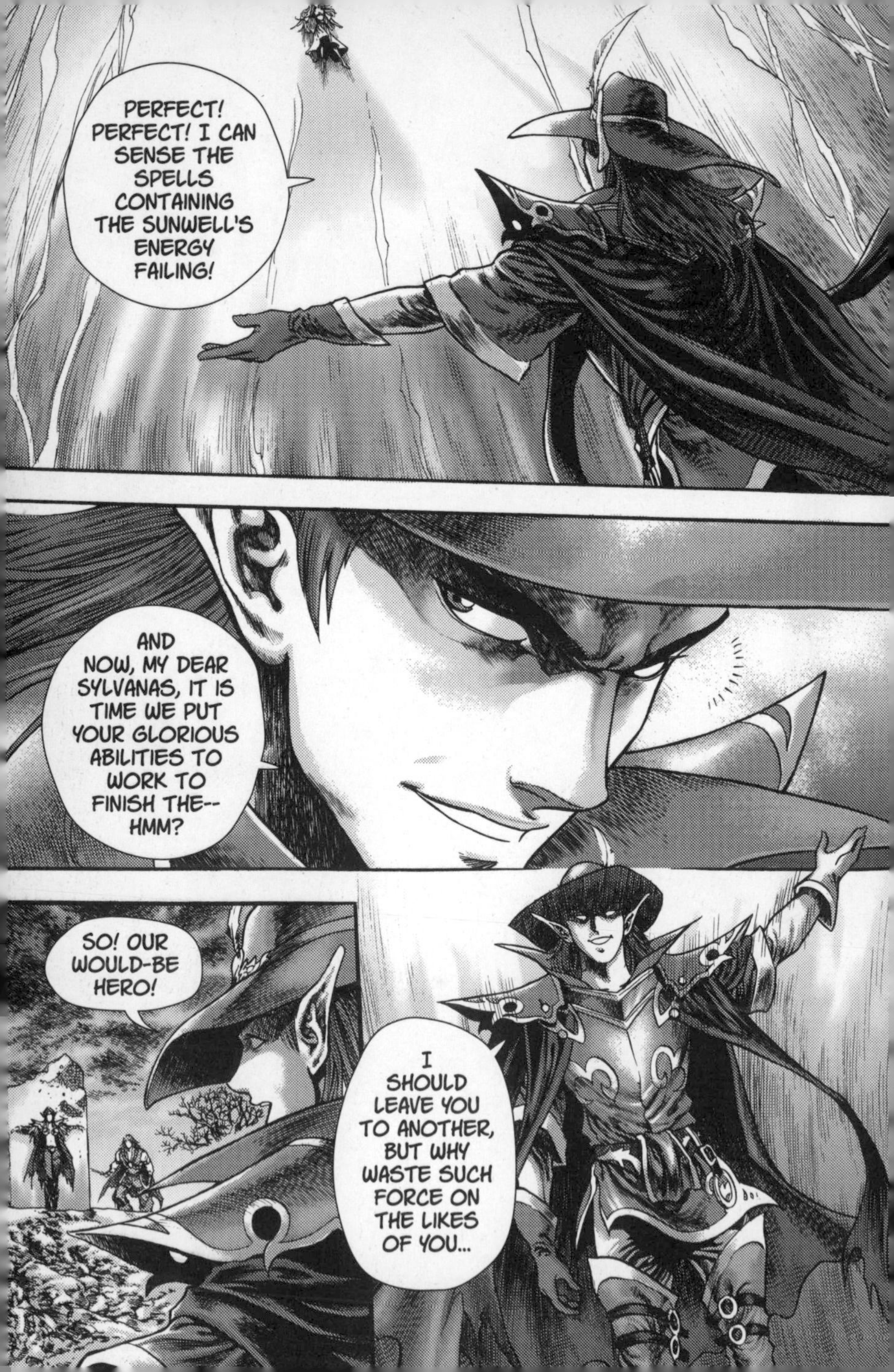
PERFECT! PERFECT! I CAN SENSE THE SPELLS CONTAINING THE SUNWELL'S ENERGY FAILING!
AND NOW, MY DEAR SYLVANAS, IT IS TIME WE PUT YOUR GLORIOUS ABILITIES TO WORK TO FINISH THE-- HMM?
SO! OUR WOULD-BE HERO!
I SHOULD LEAVE YOU TO ANOTHER, BUT WHY WASTE SUCH FORCE ON THE LIKES OF YOU...

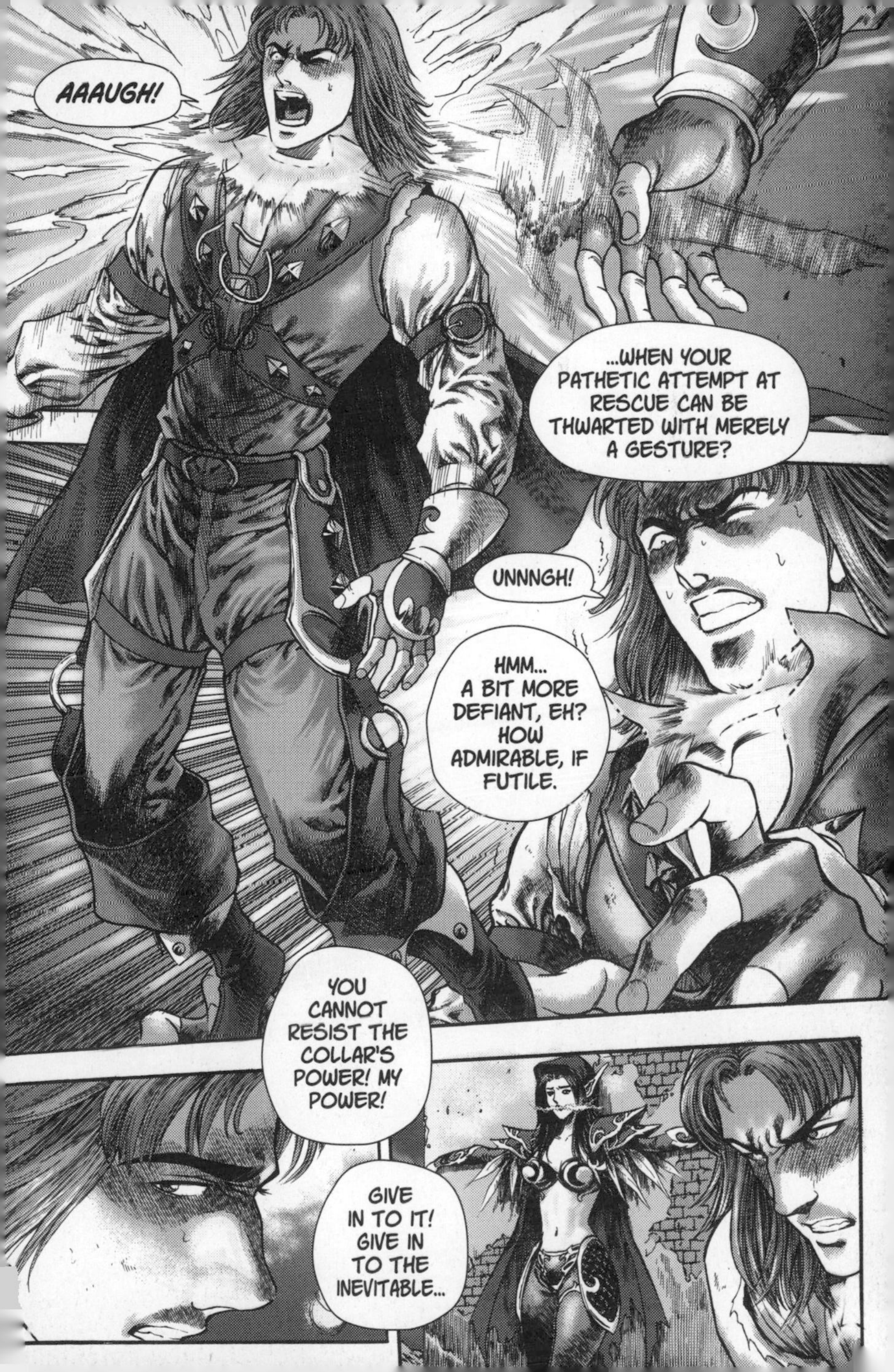
AAAUGH!
...WHEN YOUR PATHETIC ATTEMPT AT RESCUE CAN BE THWARTED WITH MERELY A GESTURE?
UNNNGH!
HMM... A BIT MORE DEFIANT, EH? HOW ADMIRABLE, IF FUTILE.
YOU CANNOT RESIST THE COLLAR'S POWER! MY POWER!
GIVE IN TO IT! GIVE IN TO THE INEVITABLE...

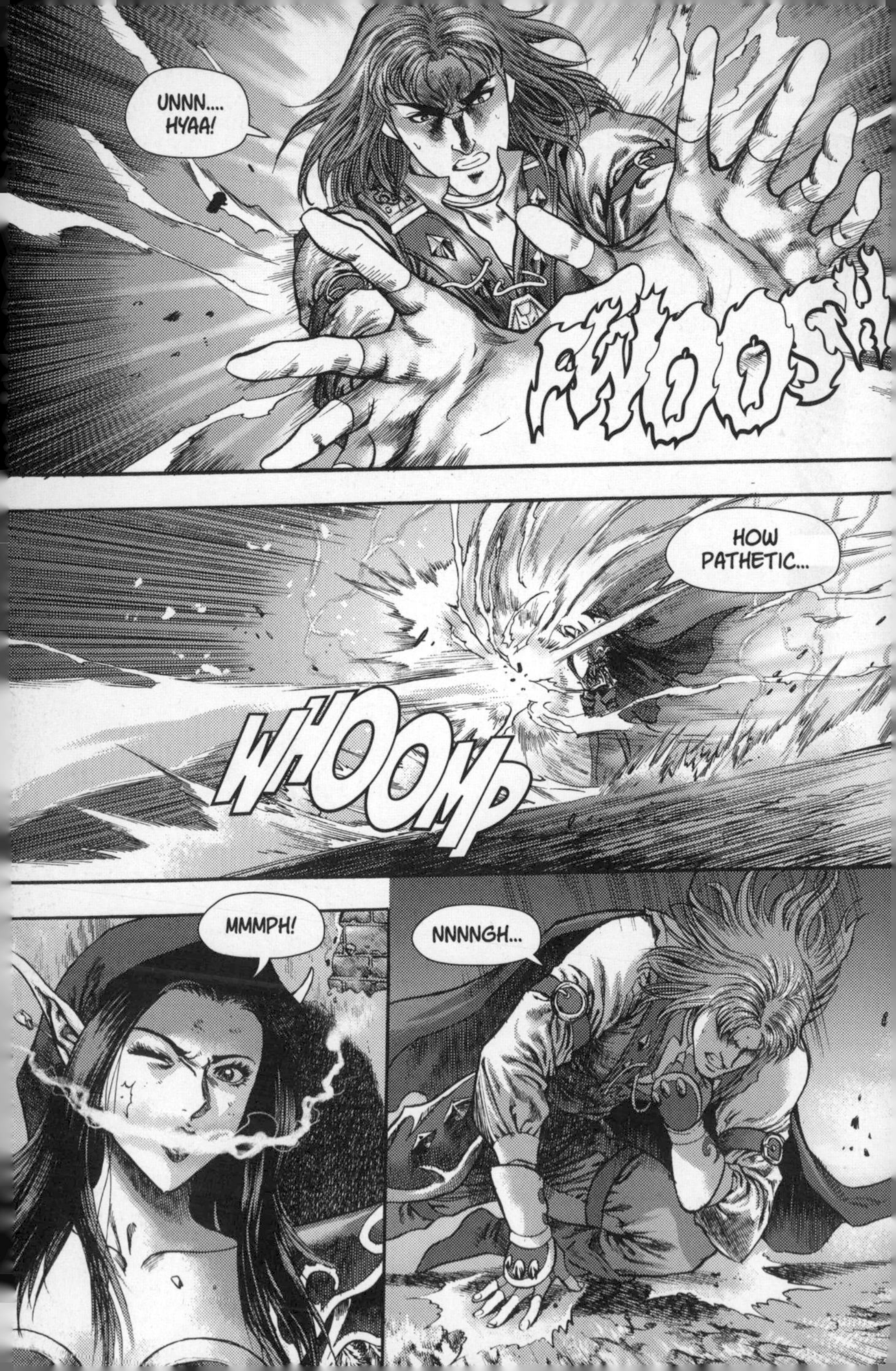
UNNN....
HYAA!
FWOOSH
HOW PATHETIC...
WHOOMP
MMMPH!
NNNNGH...

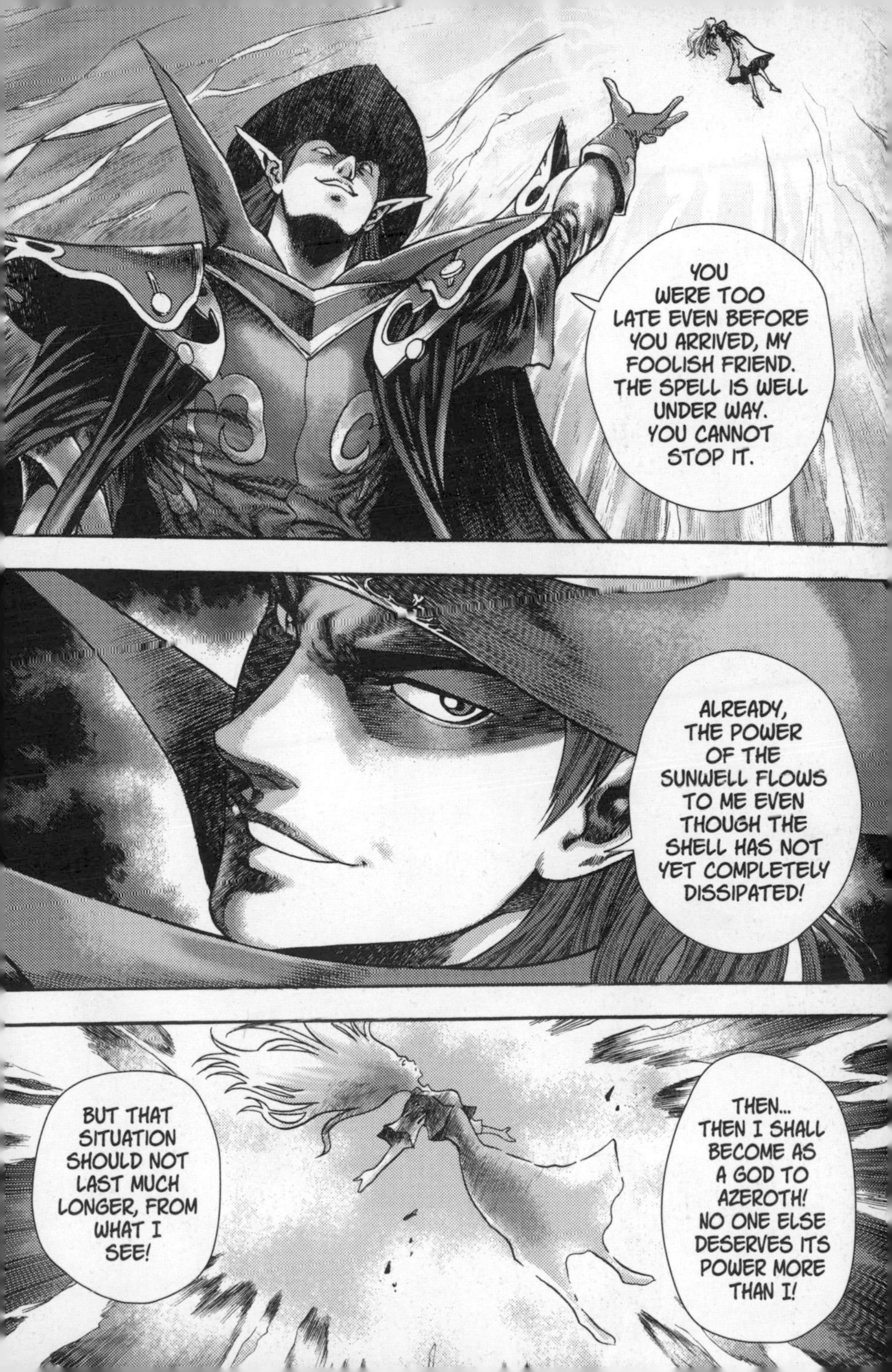
YOU WERE TOO LATE EVEN BEFORE YOU ARRIVED, MY FOOLISH FRIEND. THE SPELL IS WELL UNDER WAY. YOU CANNOT STOP IT.
ALREADY, THE POWER OF THE SUNWELL FLOWS TO ME EVEN THOUGH THE SHELL HAS NOT YET COMPLETELY DISSIPATED!
BUT THAT SITUATION SHOULD NOT LAST MUCH LONGER, FROM WHAT I SEE!
THEN... THEN I SHALL BECOME AS A GOD TO AZEROTH! NO ONE ELSE DESERVES ITS POWER MORE THAN I!

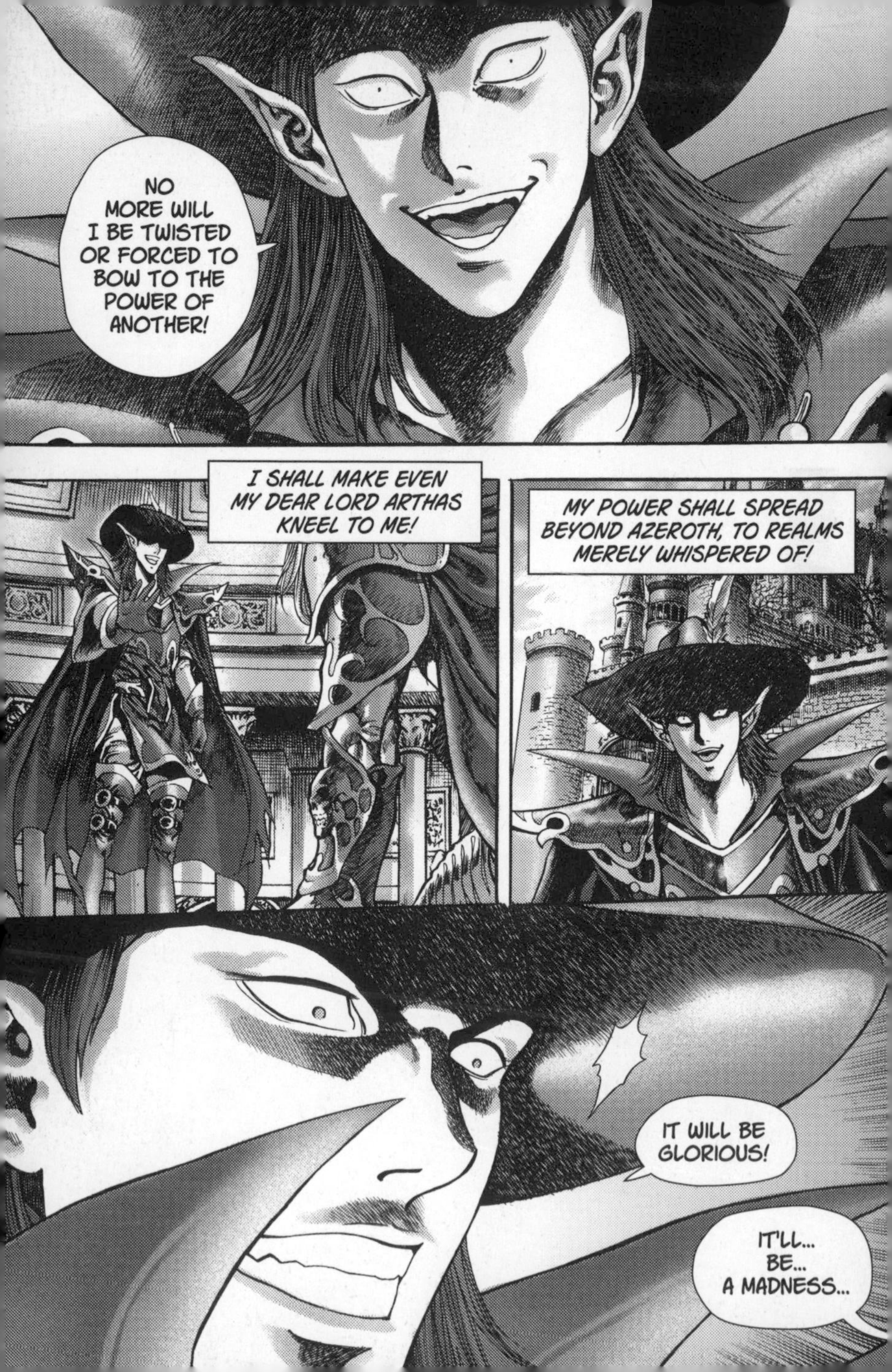
NO MORE WILL I BE TWISTED OR FORCED TO BOW TO THE POWER OF ANOTHER!
I SHALL MAKE EVEN MY DEAR LORD ARTHAS KNEEL TO ME!
MY POWER SHALL SPREAD BEYOND AZEROTH, TO REALMS MERELY WHISPERED OF!
IT WILL BE GLORIOUS!
IT'LL... BE... A MADNESS...

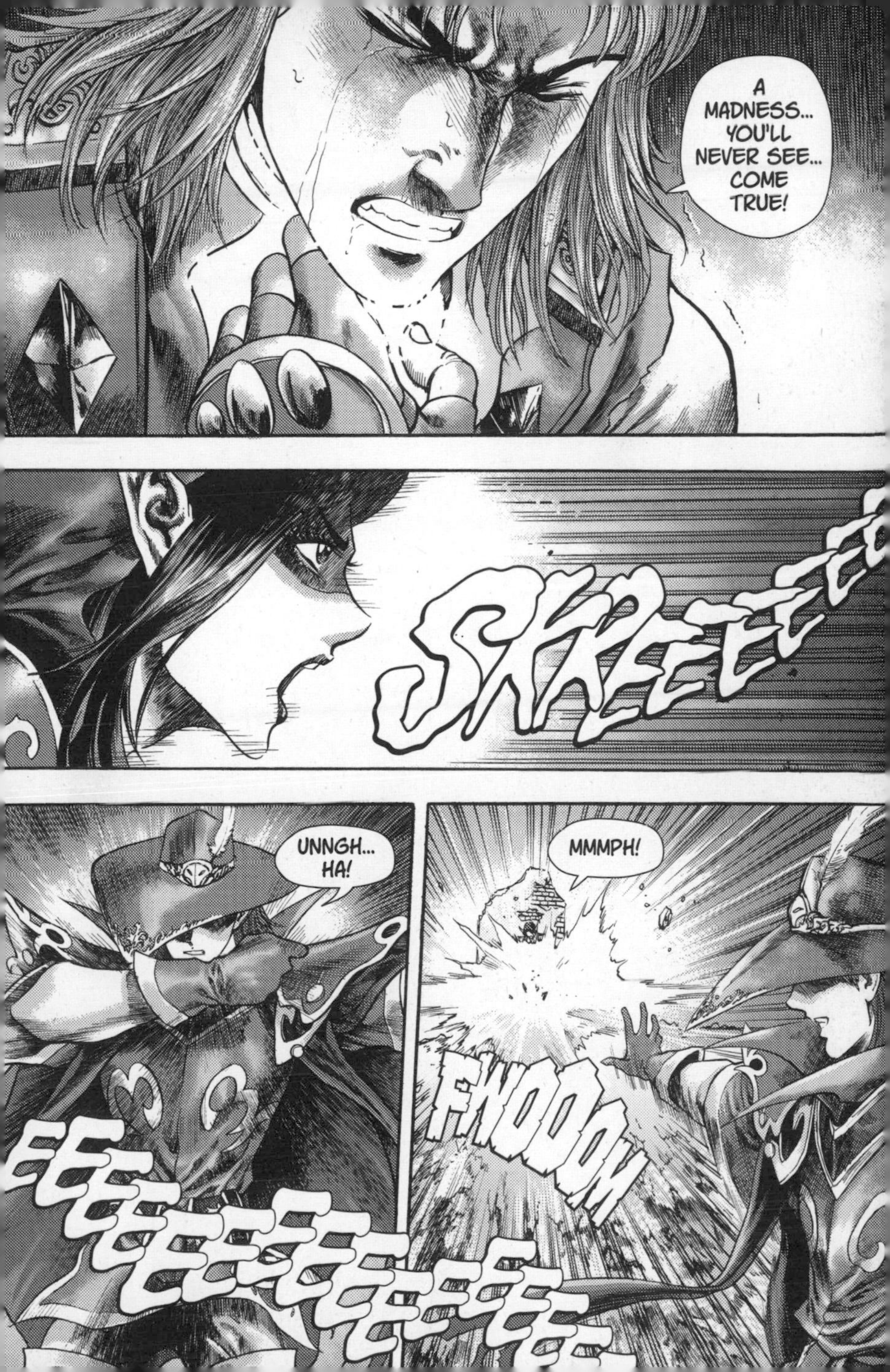
A MADNESS... YOU'LL NEVER SEE... COME TRUE!
SKREEEEEEEE
UNNGH... HA!
MMMPH!
FWOOOM

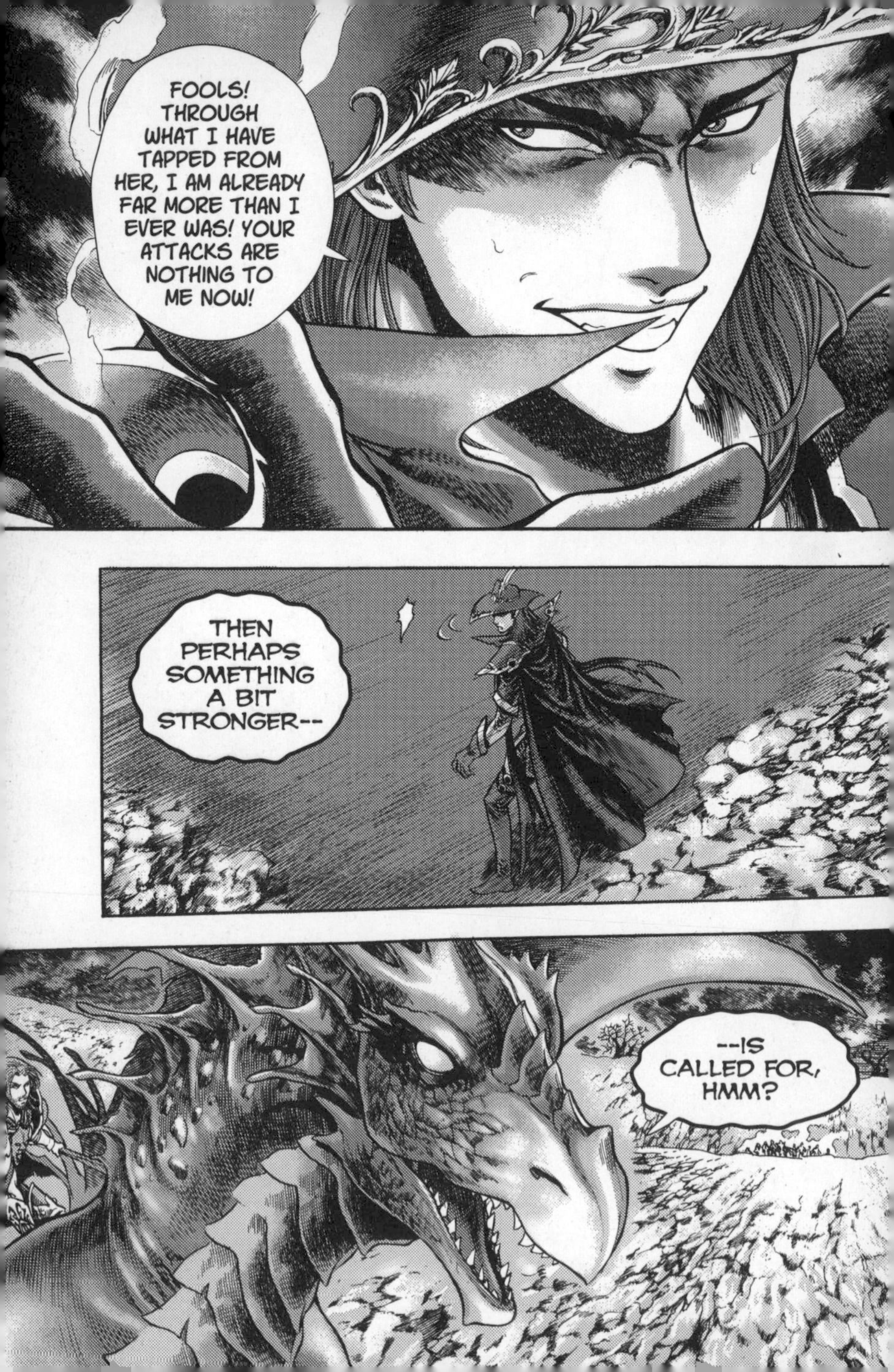
FOOLS! THROUGH WHAT I HAVE TAPPED FROM HER, I AM ALREADY FAR MORE THAN I EVER WAS! YOUR ATTACKS ARE NOTHING TO ME NOW!
THEN PERHAPS SOMETHING A BIT STRONGER--
--IS CALLED FOR, HMM?

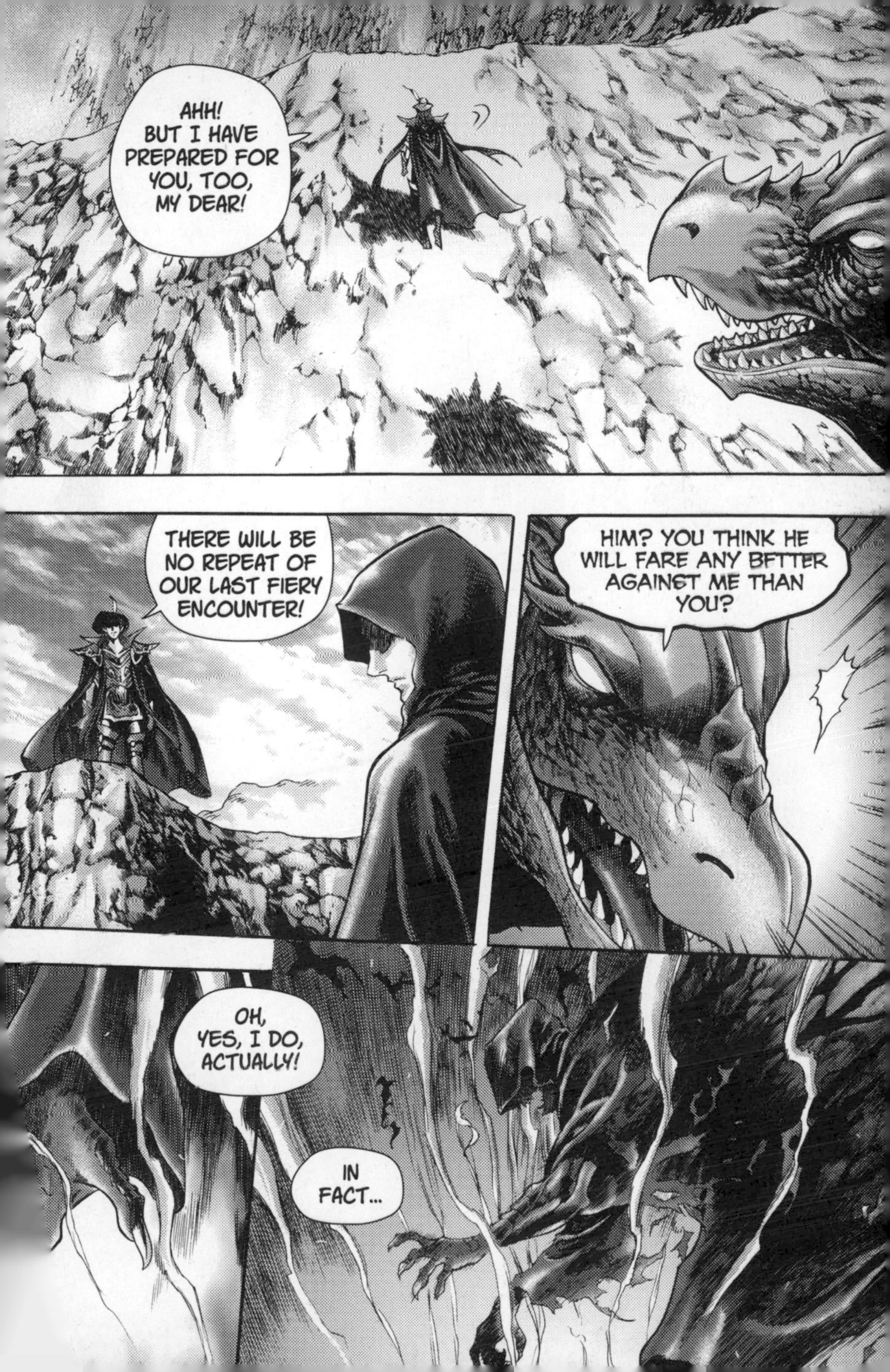
AHH! BUT I HAVE PREPARED FOR YOU, TOO, MY DEAR!
THERE WILL BE NO REPEAT OF OUR LAST FIERY ENCOUNTER!
HIM? YOU THINK HE WILL FARE ANY BETTER AGAINST ME THAN YOU?
OH, YES, I DO, ACTUALLY!
IN FACT...

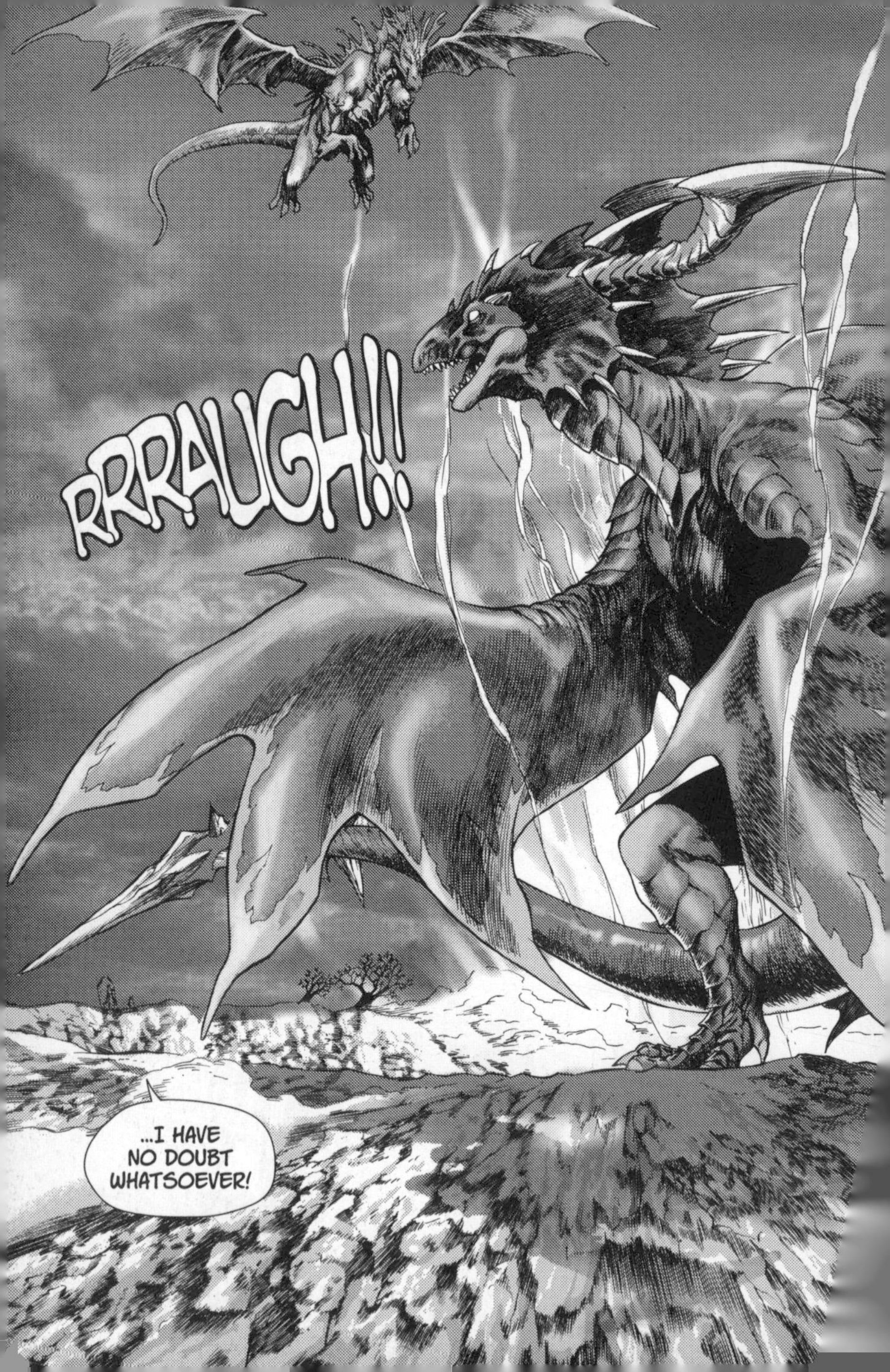
RRRAUGH!!
...I HAVE NO DOUBT WHATSOEVER!

CHAPTER SIX

FIRE AND FURY

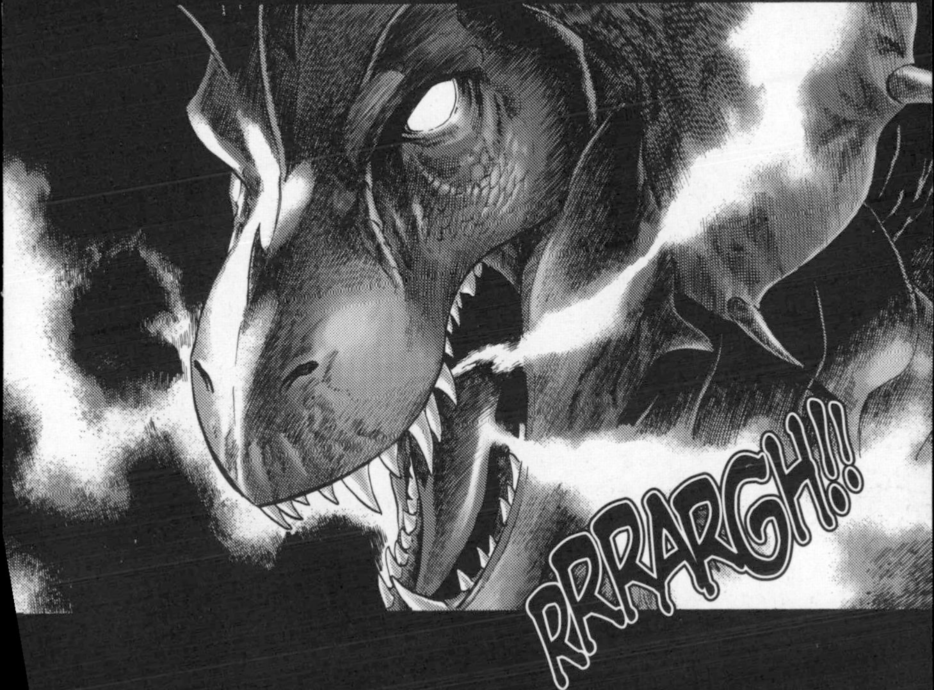
RRRARGH!!

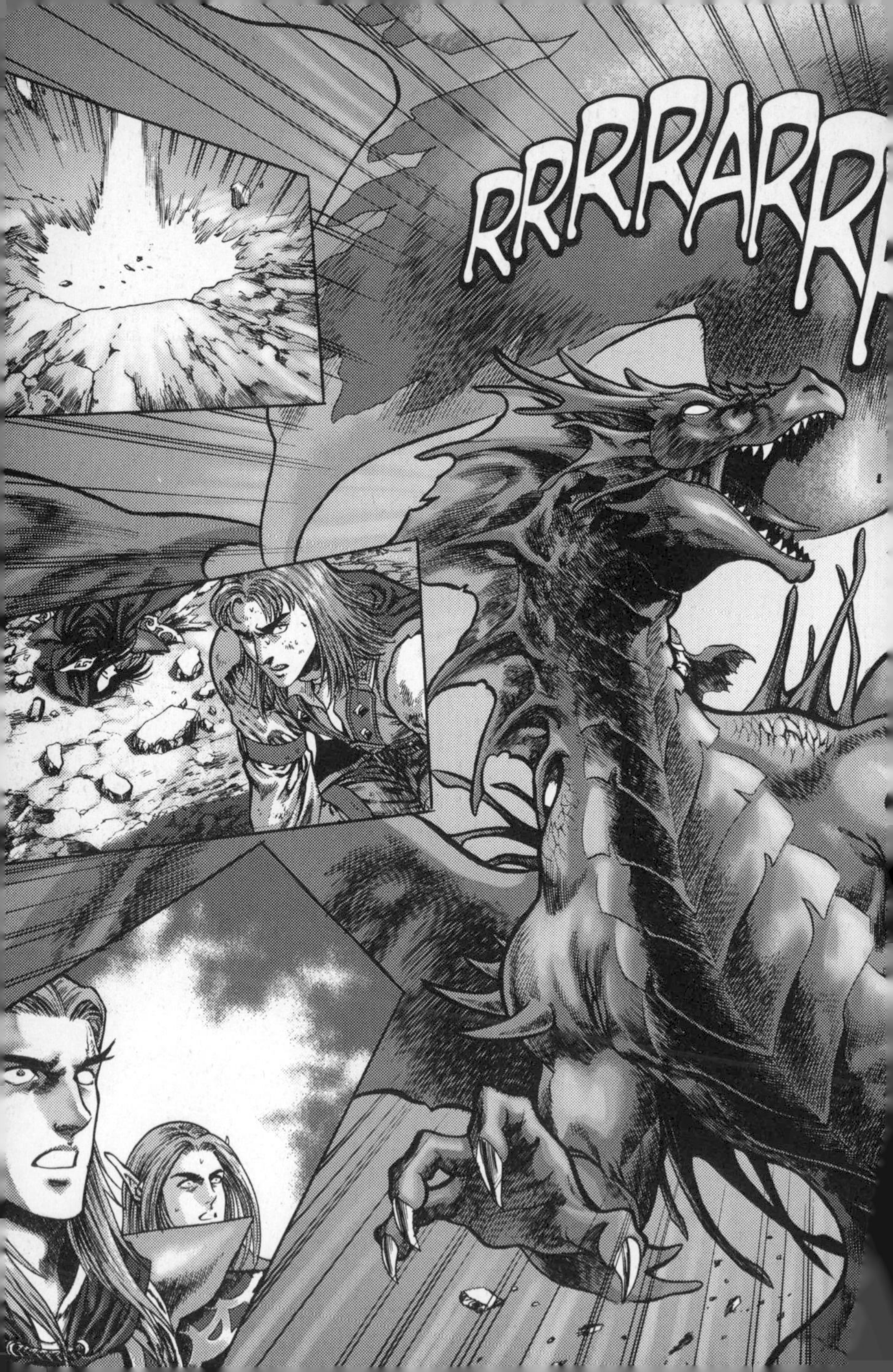
RRRRARRR

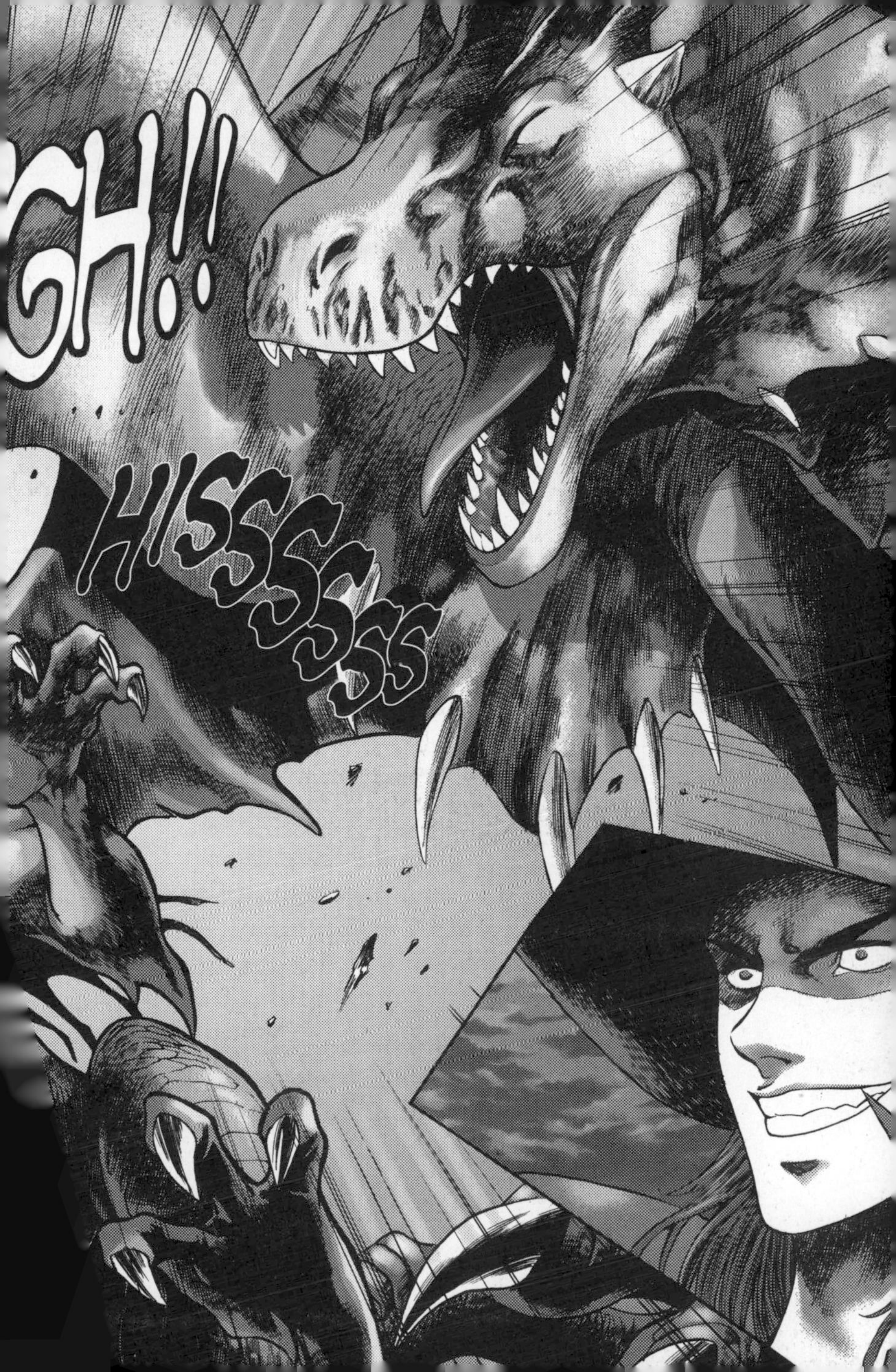
GH!!
HISSSSSSS

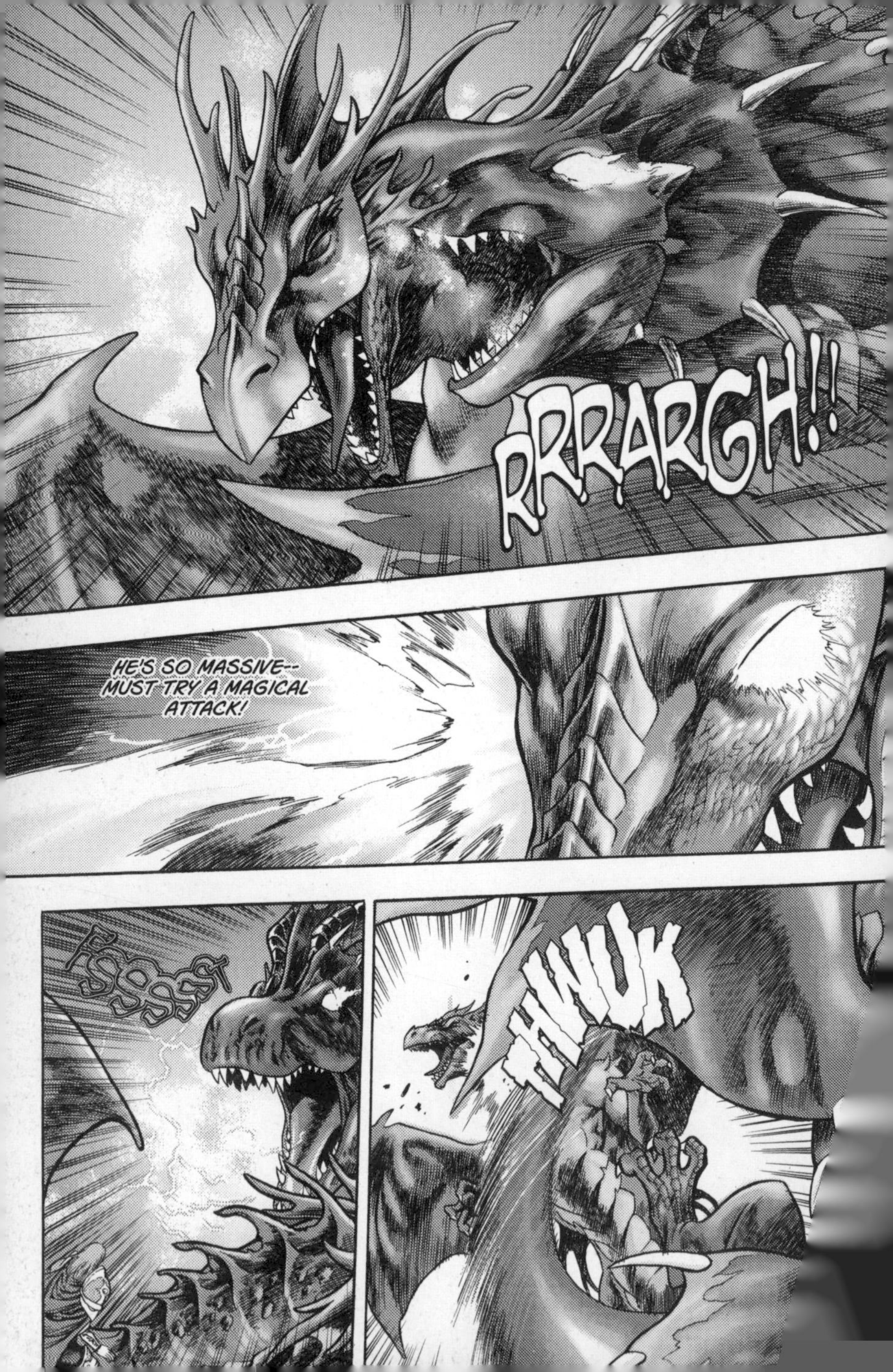
RRRARGH!!
HE'S SO MASSIVE-- MUST TRY A MAGICAL ATTACK!
FSSSSST
THWUK

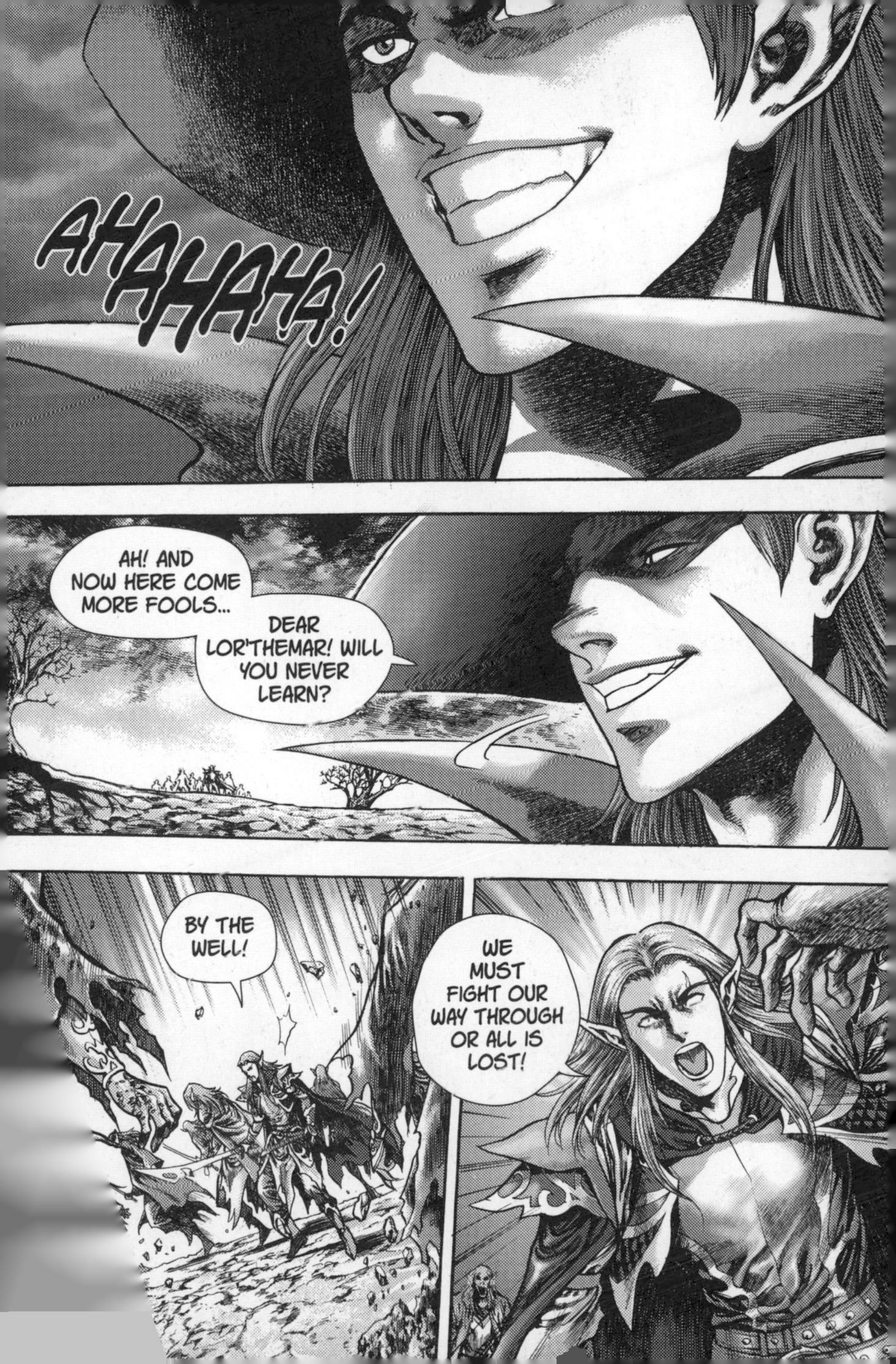
AHAHAHAHA!
AH! AND NOW HERE COME MORE FOOLS...
DEAR LOR'THEMAR! WILL YOU NEVER LEARN?
BY THE WELL!
WE MUST FIGHT OUR WAY THROUGH OR ALL IS LOST!

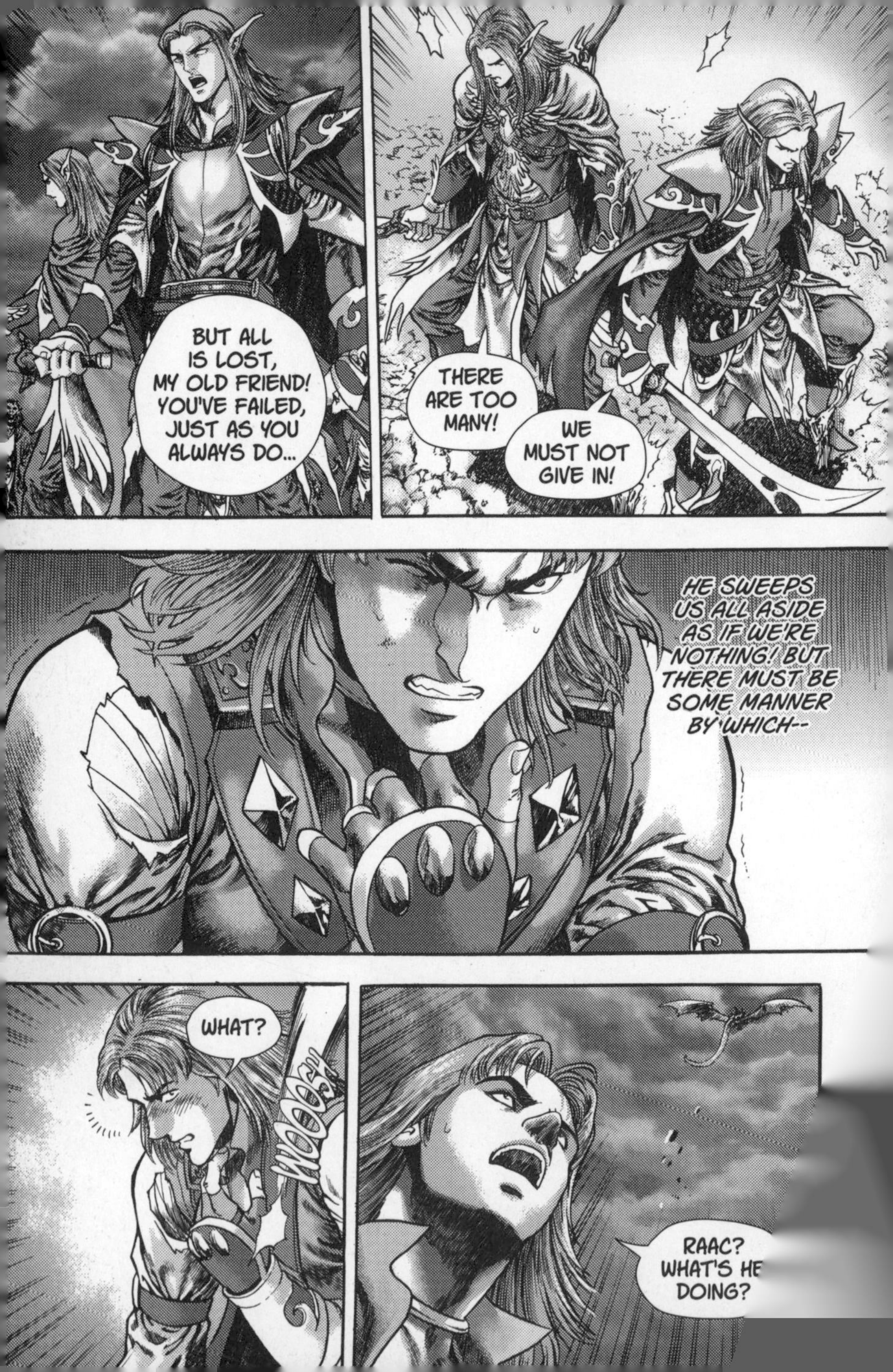
BUT ALL IS LOST, MY OLD FRIEND! YOU'VE FAILED, JUST AS YOU ALWAYS DO...
THERE ARE TOO MANY!
WE MUST NOT GIVE IN!
HE SWEEPS US ALL ASIDE AS IF WE'RE NOTHING! BUT THERE MUST BE SOME MANNER BY WHICH--
WHAT?
WOOOSH
RAAC? WHAT'S HE DOING?

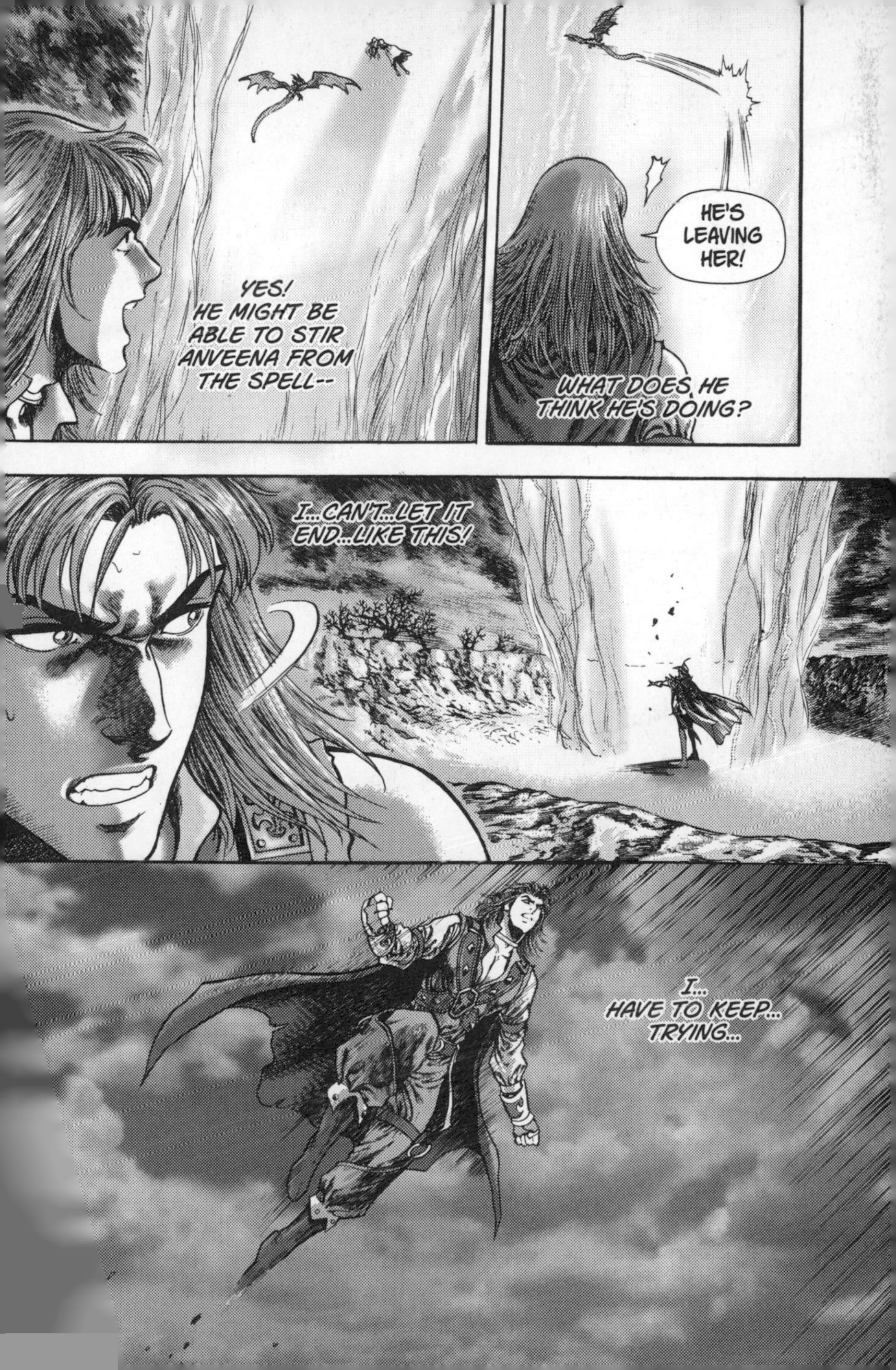
YES! HE MIGHT BE ABLE TO STIR ANVEENA FROM THE SPELL--
HE'S LEAVING HER!
WHAT DOES HE THINK HE'S DOING?
I...CAN'T...LET IT END...LIKE THIS!
I... HAVE TO KEEP... TRYING...

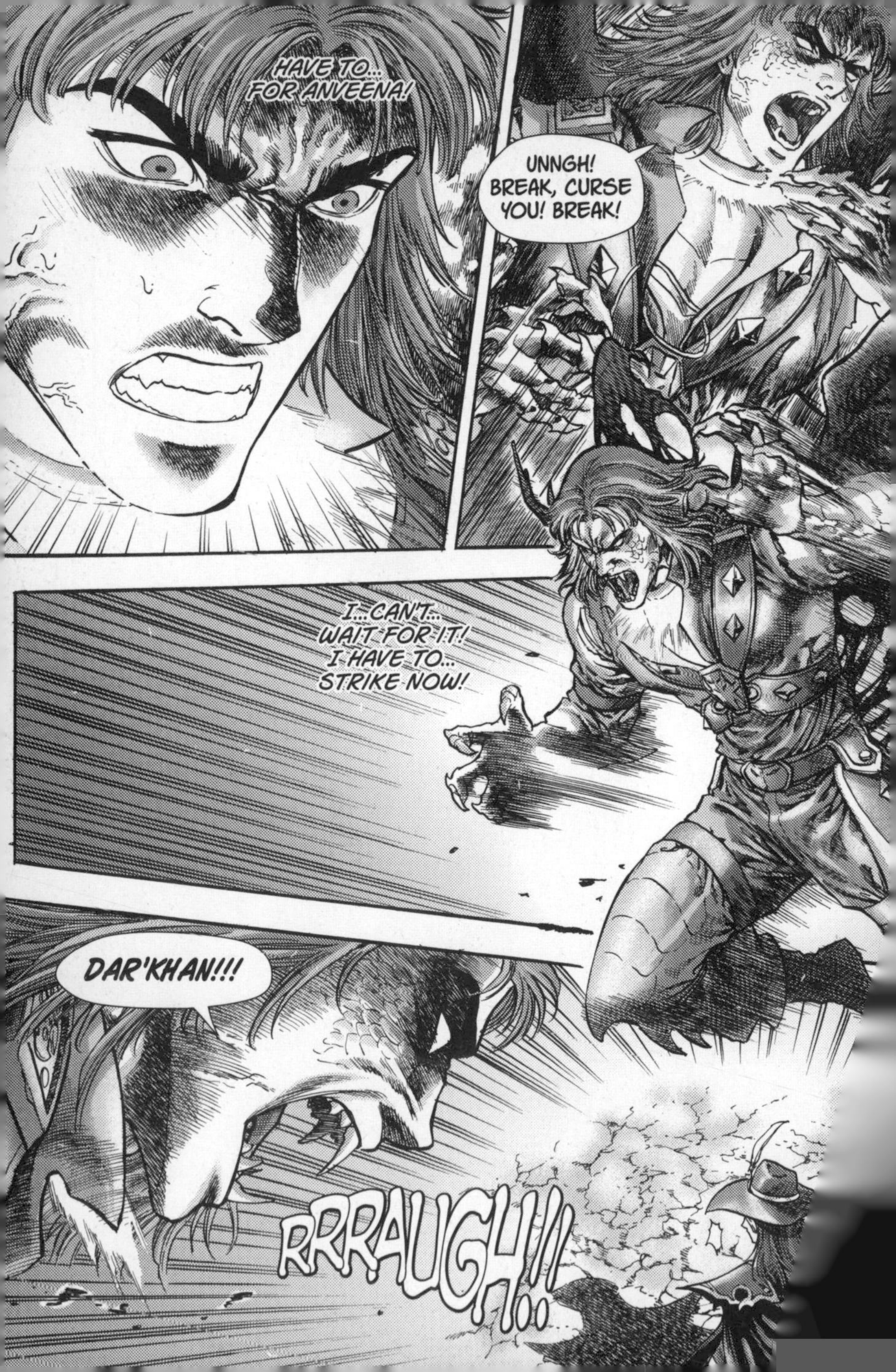
HAVE TO... FOR ANVEENA!
UNNGH! BREAK, CURSE YOU! BREAK!
I...CAN'T... WAIT FOR IT! I HAVE TO... STRIKE NOW!
DAR'KHAN!!!
RRRAUGH!!

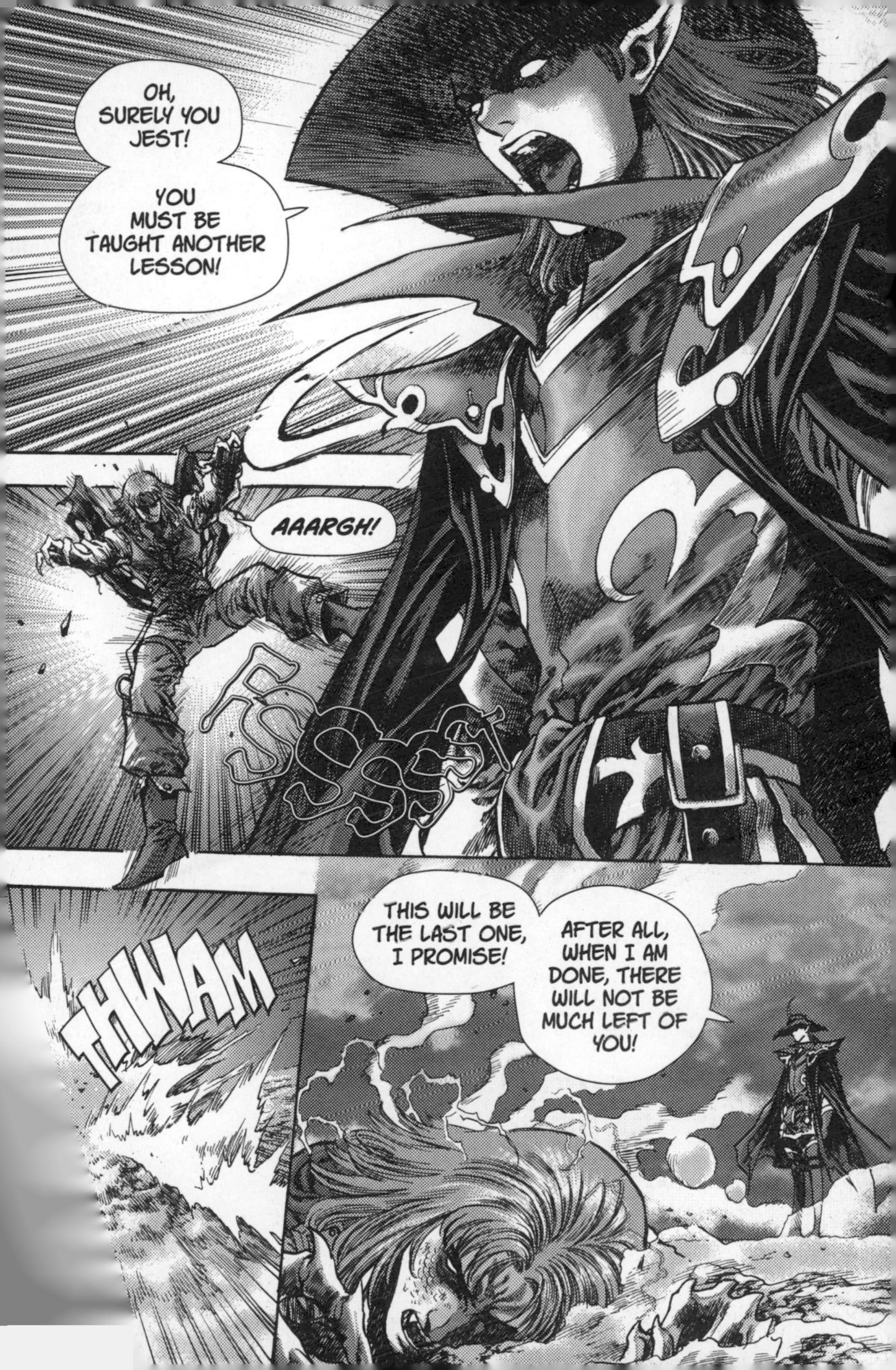
OH, SURELY YOU JEST!
YOU MUST BE TAUGHT ANOTHER LESSON!
AAARGH!
FSSSSST
THWAM
THIS WILL BE THE LAST ONE, I PROMISE!
AFTER ALL, WHEN I AM DONE, THERE WILL NOT BE MUCH LEFT OF YOU!

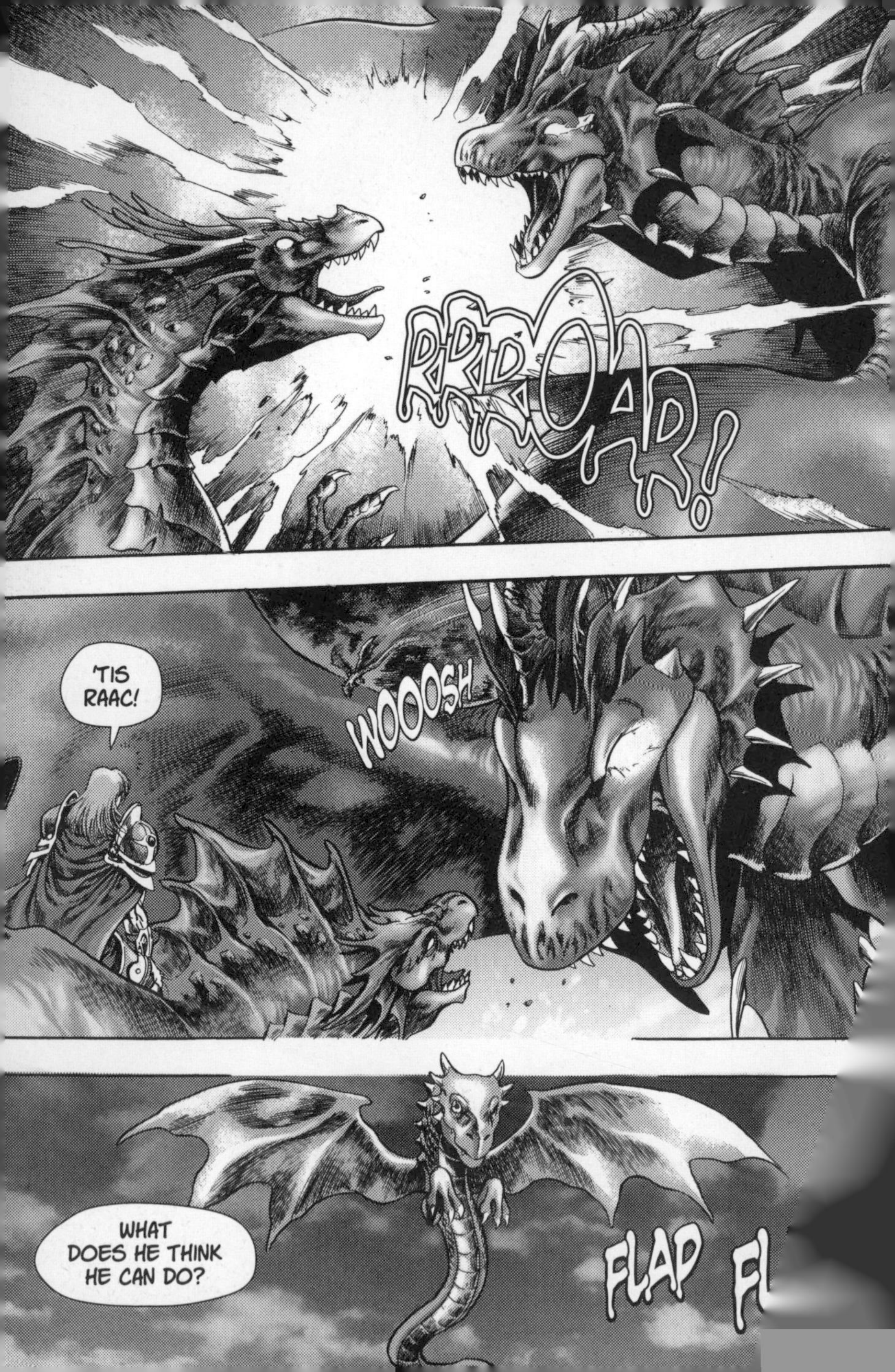
RRROAR!
'TIS RAAC!
WOOOSH
WHAT DOES HE THINK HE CAN DO?
FLAP
FL

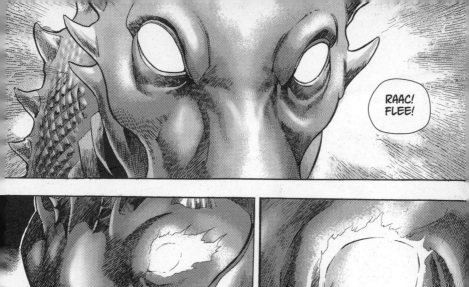

RAAC! FLEE!

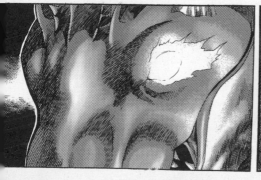

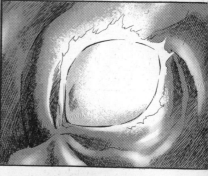

SO, LITTLE ONE...

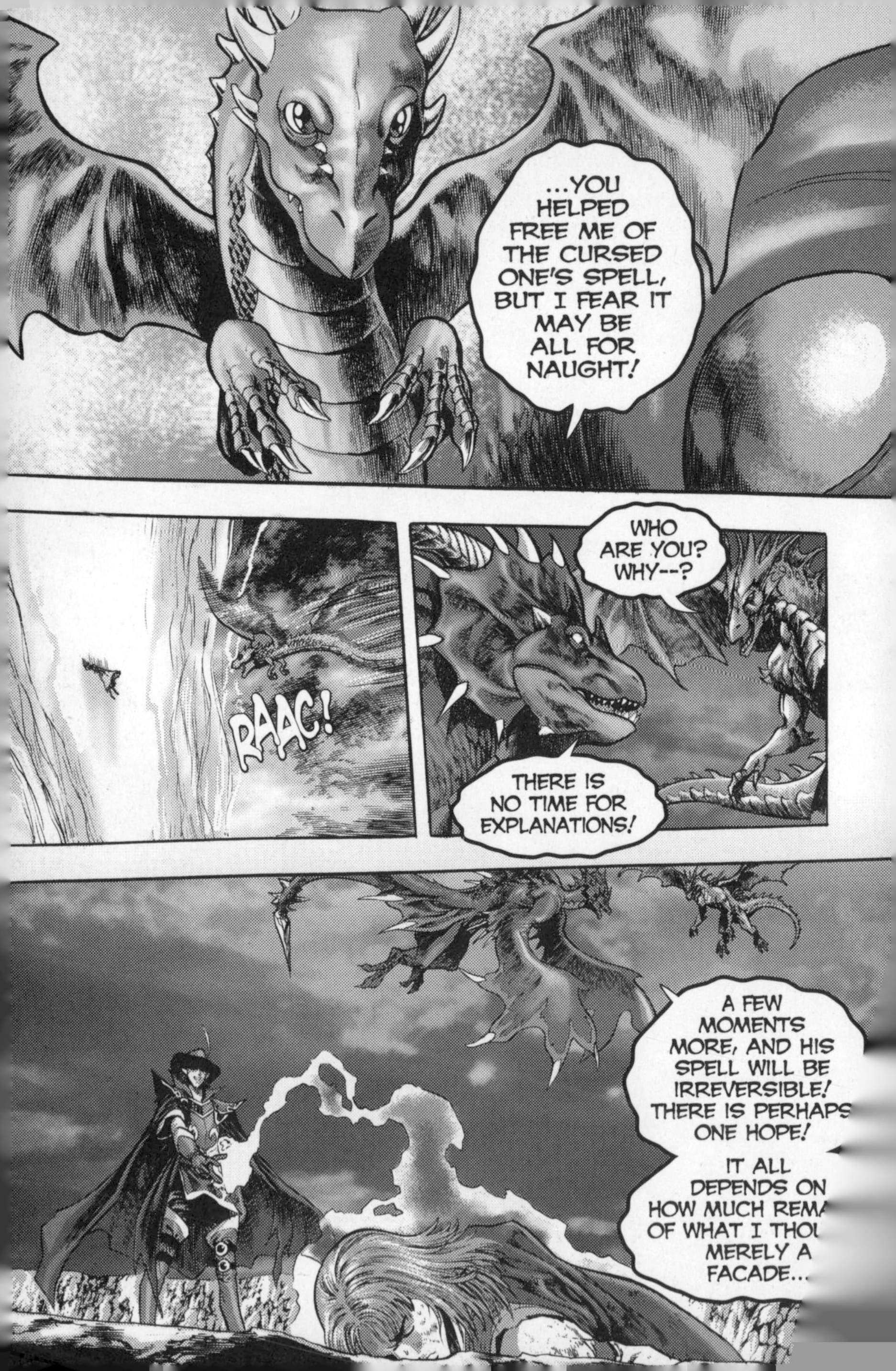
...YOU HELPED FREE ME OF THE CURSED ONE'S SPELL, BUT I FEAR IT MAY BE ALL FOR NAUGHT!
RAAC!
WHO ARE YOU? WHY--?
THERE IS NO TIME FOR EXPLANATIONS!
A FEW MOMENTS MORE, AND HIS SPELL WILL BE IRREVERSIBLE! THERE IS PERHAPS ONE HOPE!
IT ALL DEPENDS ON HOW MUCH REMA OF WHAT I THOU MERELY A FACADE...

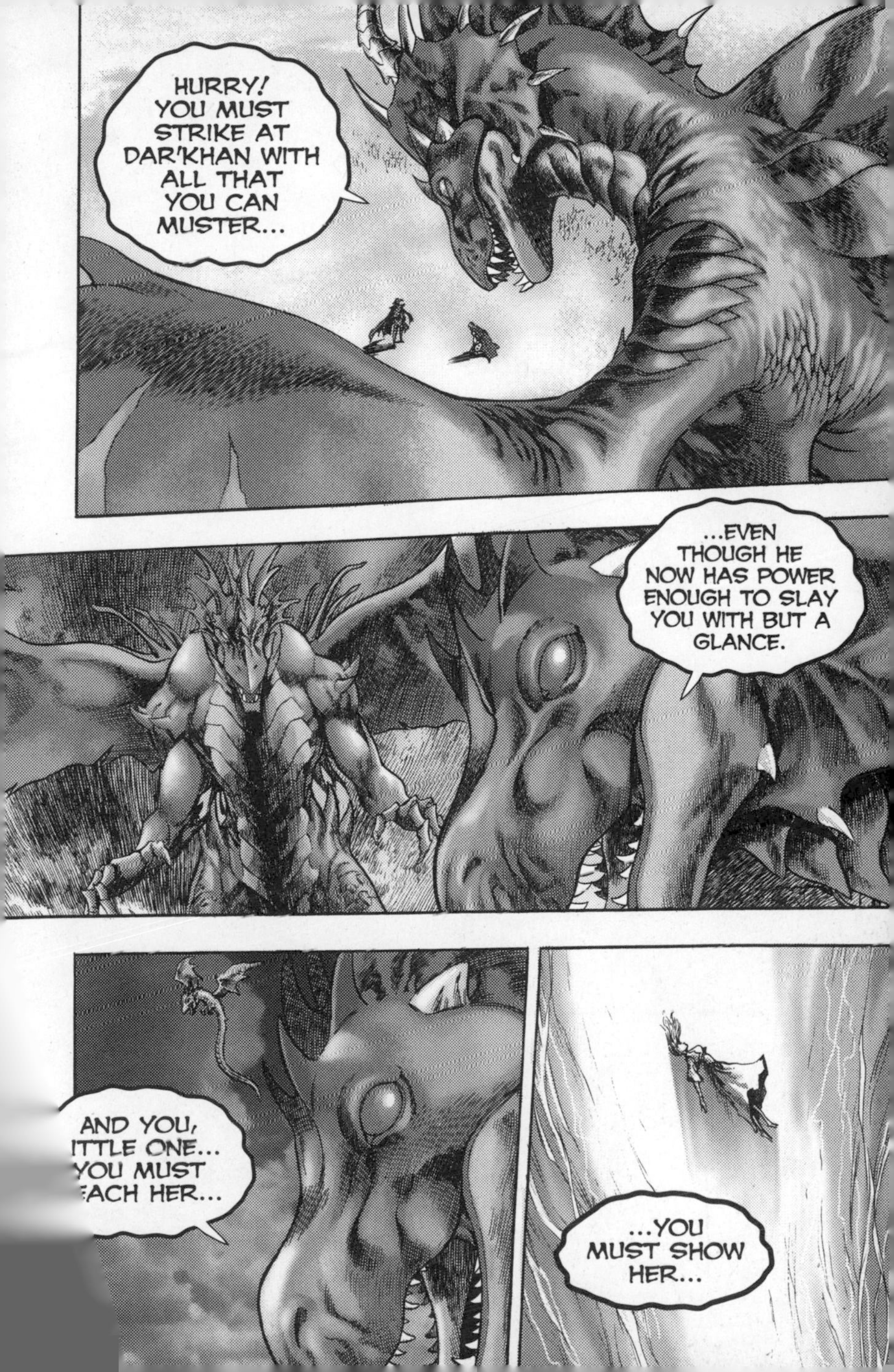
HURRY! YOU MUST STRIKE AT DAR'KHAN WITH ALL THAT YOU CAN MUSTER...
...EVEN THOUGH HE NOW HAS POWER ENOUGH TO SLAY YOU WITH BUT A GLANCE.
AND YOU, ITTLE ONE... YOU MUST EACH HER...
...YOU MUST SHOW HER...

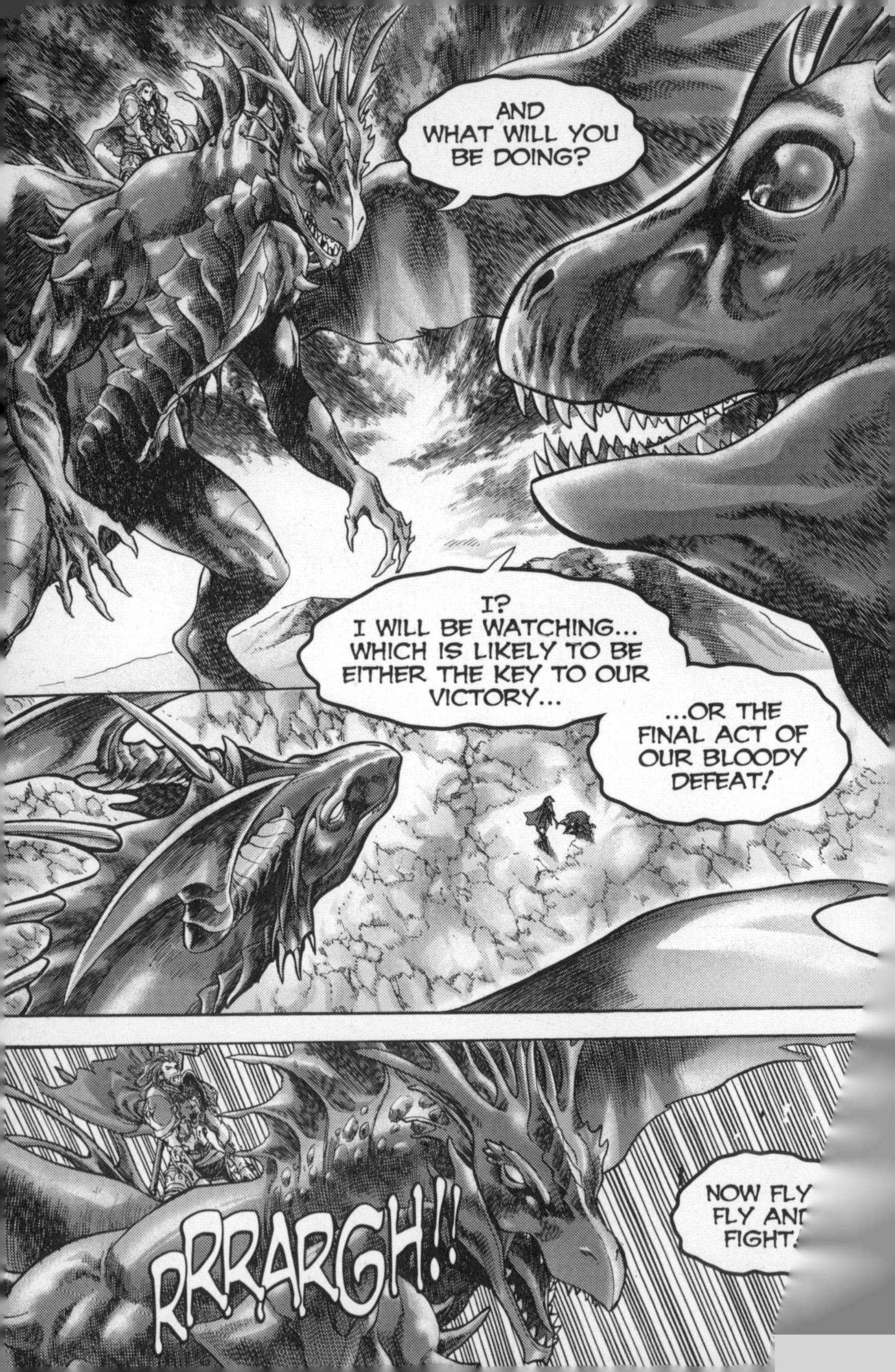
AND WHAT WILL YOU BE DOING?
I? I WILL BE WATCHING... WHICH IS LIKELY TO BE EITHER THE KEY TO OUR VICTORY...
...OR THE FINAL ACT OF OUR BLOODY DEFEAT!
RRRARGH!!
NOW FLY FLY AN FIGHT

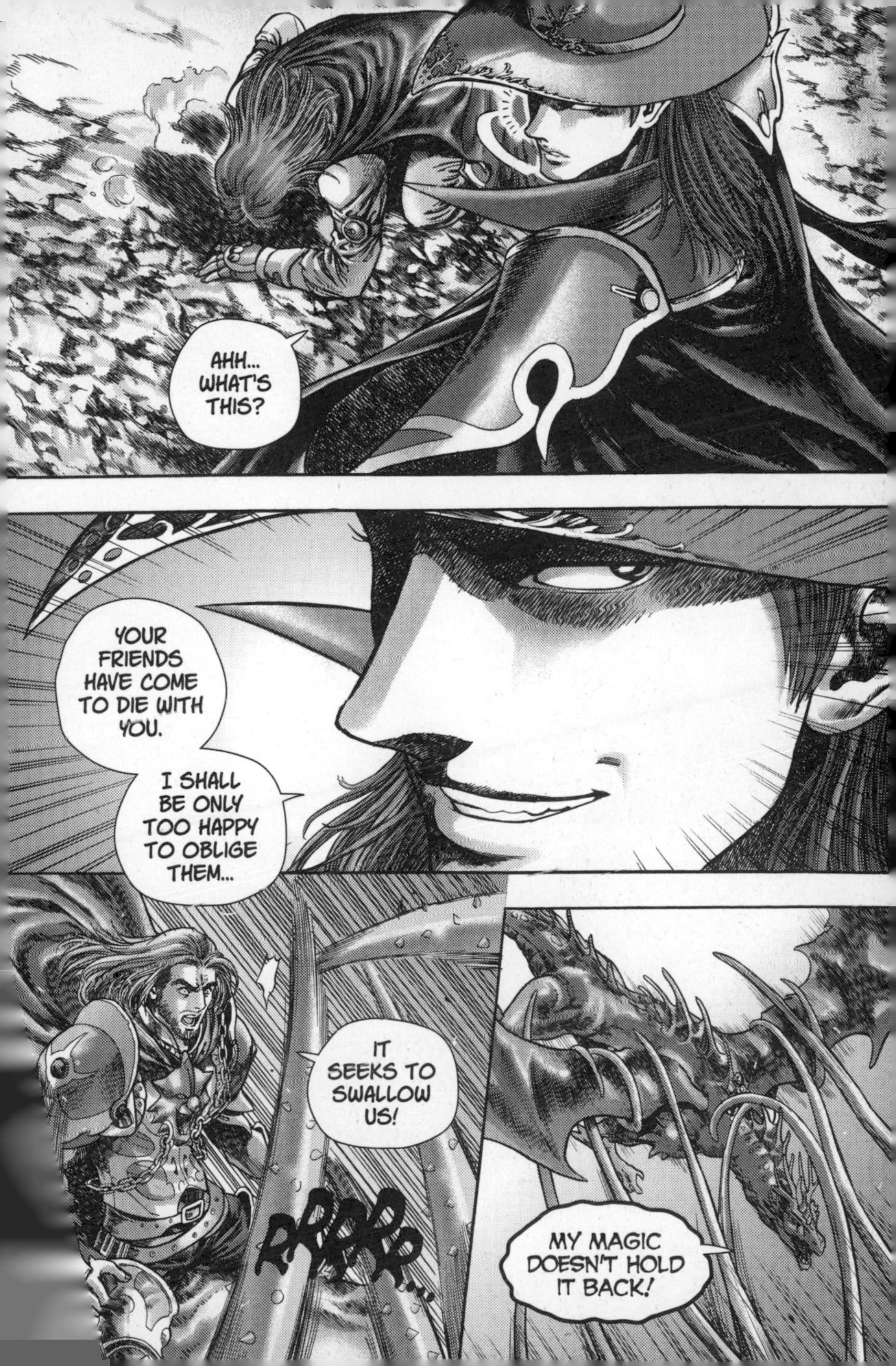
AHH... WHAT'S THIS?
YOUR FRIENDS HAVE COME TO DIE WITH YOU.
I SHALL BE ONLY TOO HAPPY TO OBLIGE THEM...
IT SEEKS TO SWALLOW US!
RRRR...
MY MAGIC DOESN'T HOLD IT BACK!

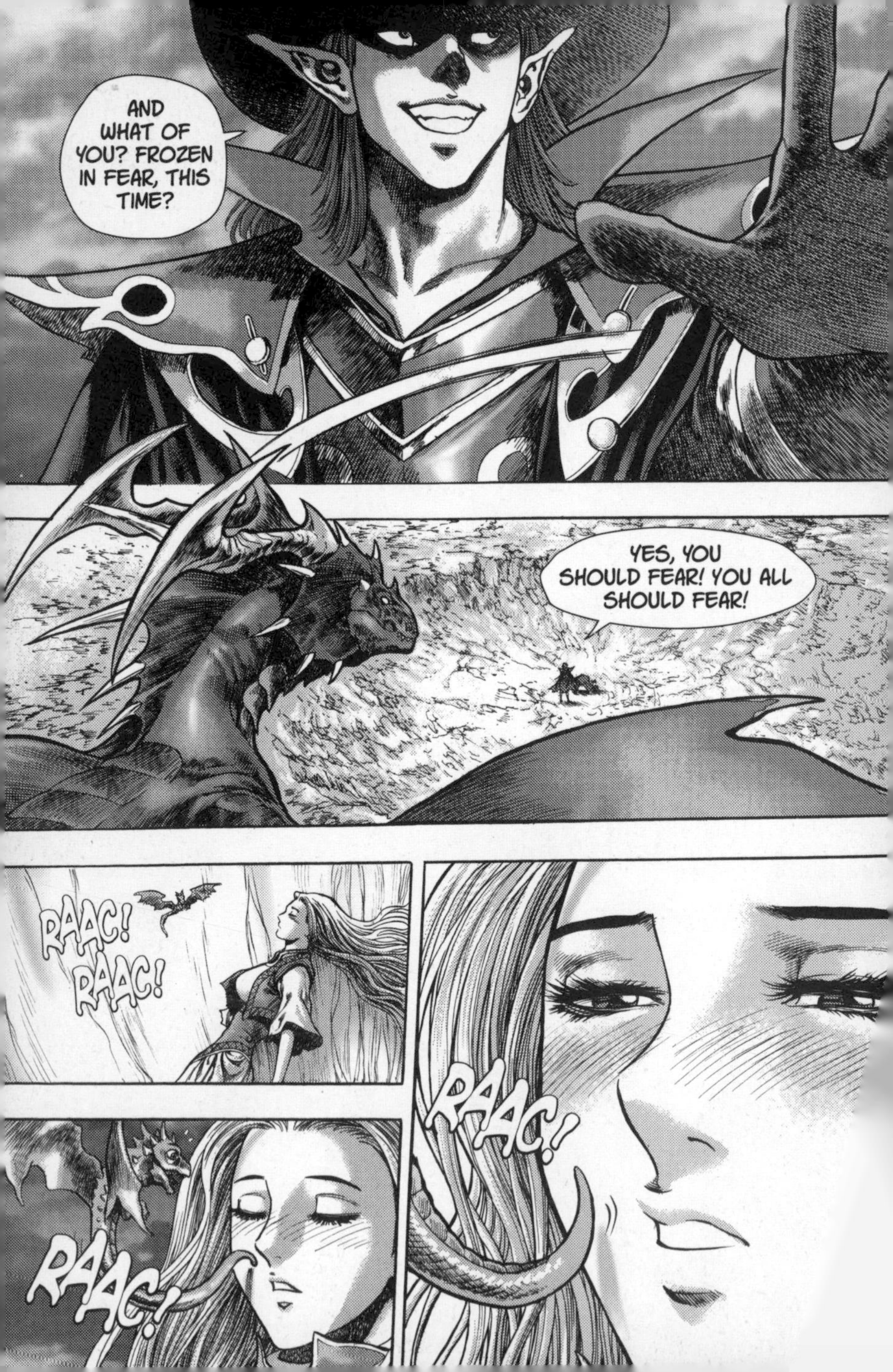
AND WHAT OF YOU? FROZEN IN FEAR, THIS TIME?
YES, YOU SHOULD FEAR! YOU ALL SHOULD FEAR!
RAAC! RAAC!
RAAC!
RAAC!

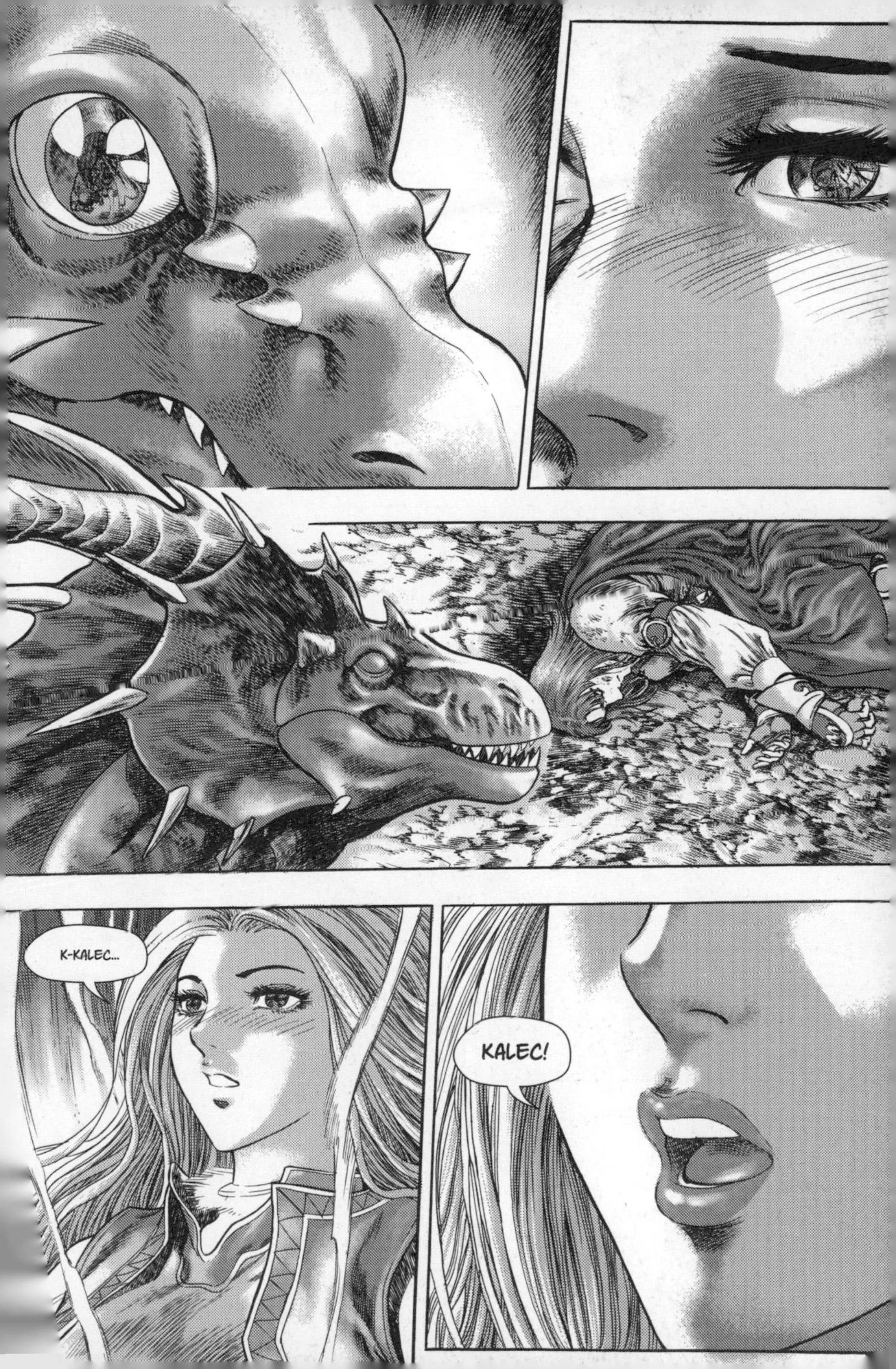
K-KALEC...
KALEC!

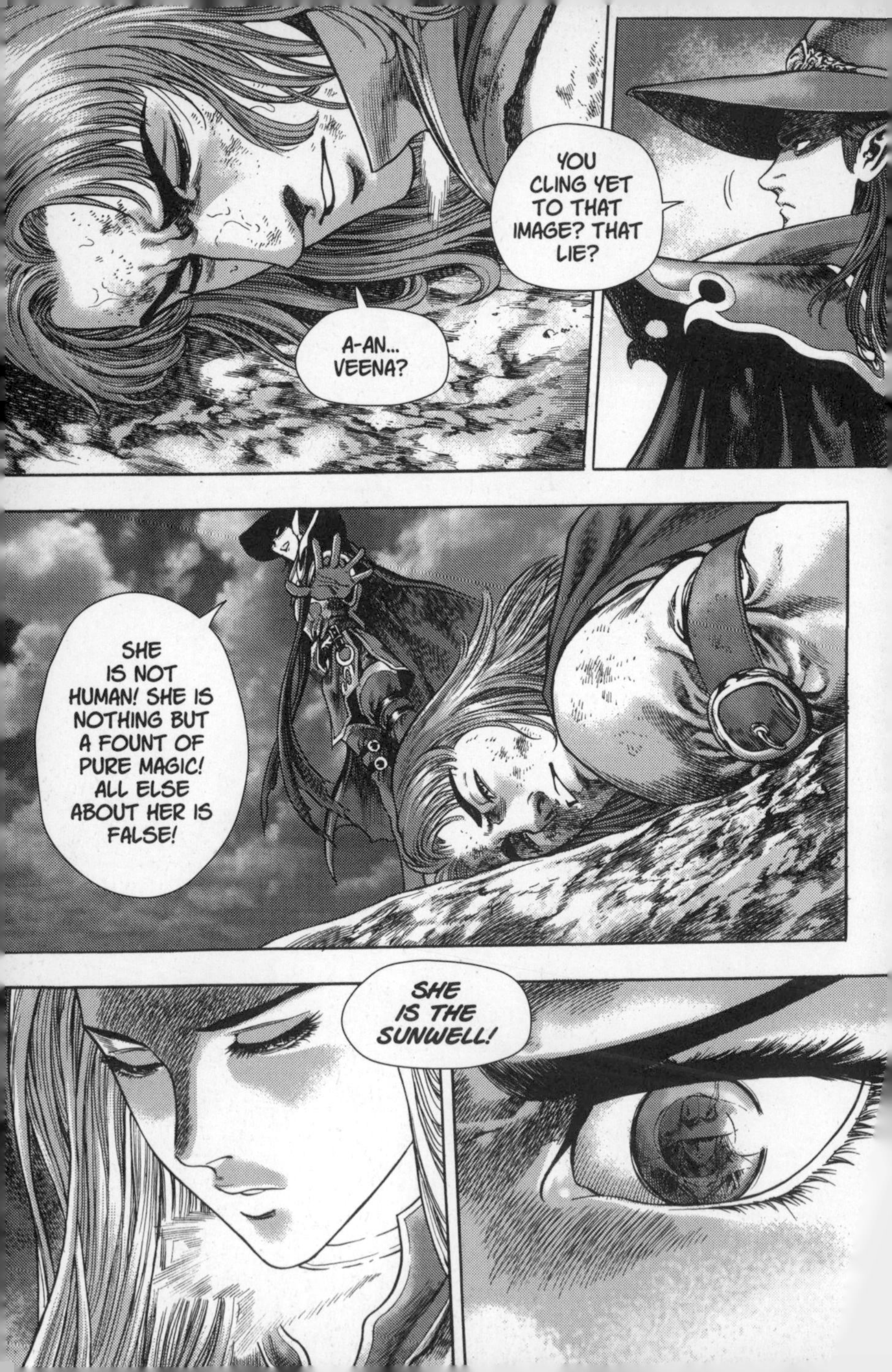
A-AN... VEENA?
YOU CLING YET TO THAT IMAGE? THAT LIE?
SHE IS NOT HUMAN! SHE IS NOTHING BUT A FOUNT OF PURE MAGIC! ALL ELSE ABOUT HER IS FALSE!
SHE IS THE SUNWELL!

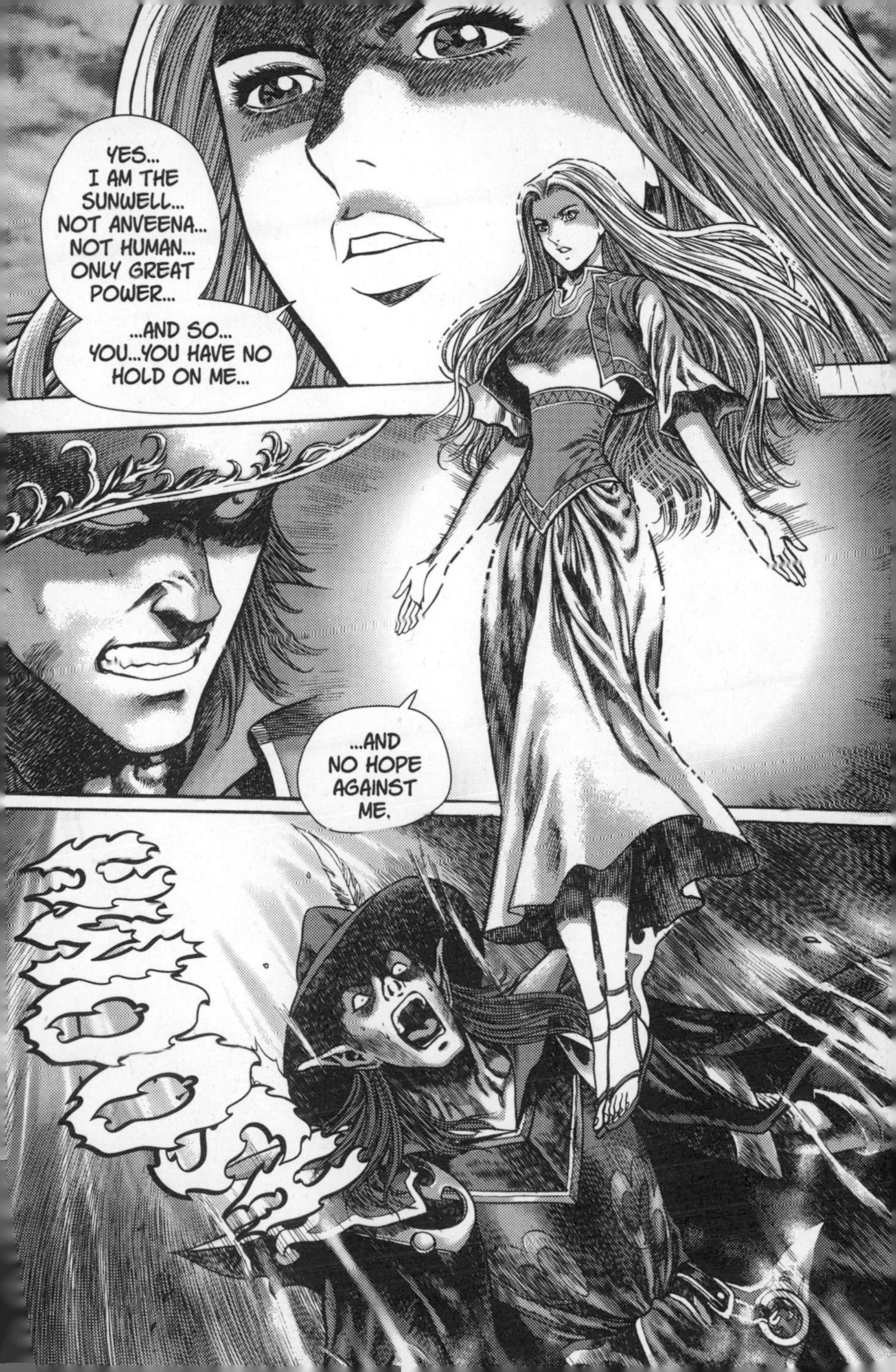
YES... I AM THE SUNWELL... NOT ANVEENA... NOT HUMAN... ONLY GREAT POWER...
...AND SO... YOU...YOU HAVE NO HOLD ON ME...
...AND NO HOPE AGAINST ME.

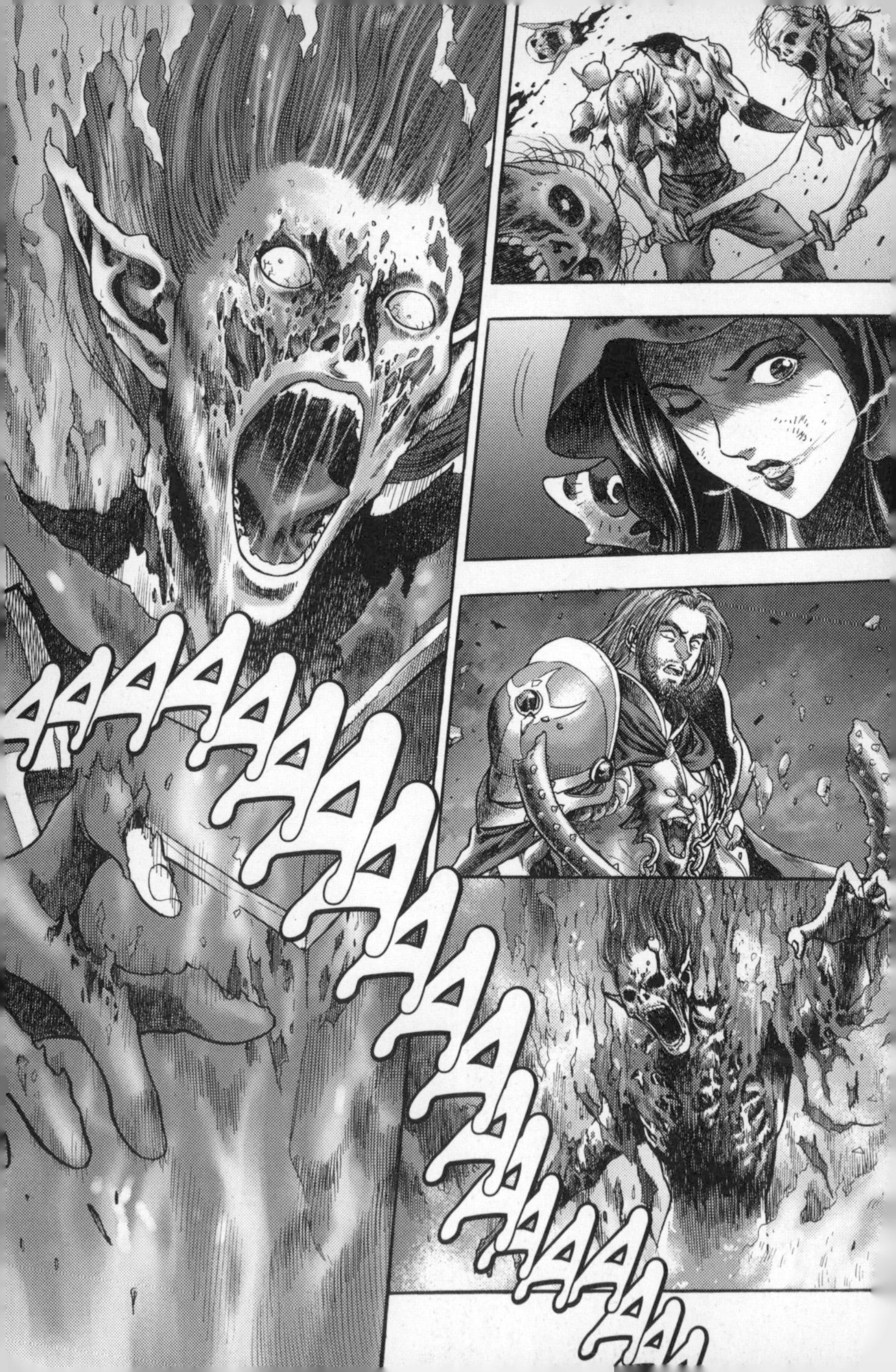
AAAAAAAAAAAAAAAAAAAAAAAAAAAAAAAAAAAAA

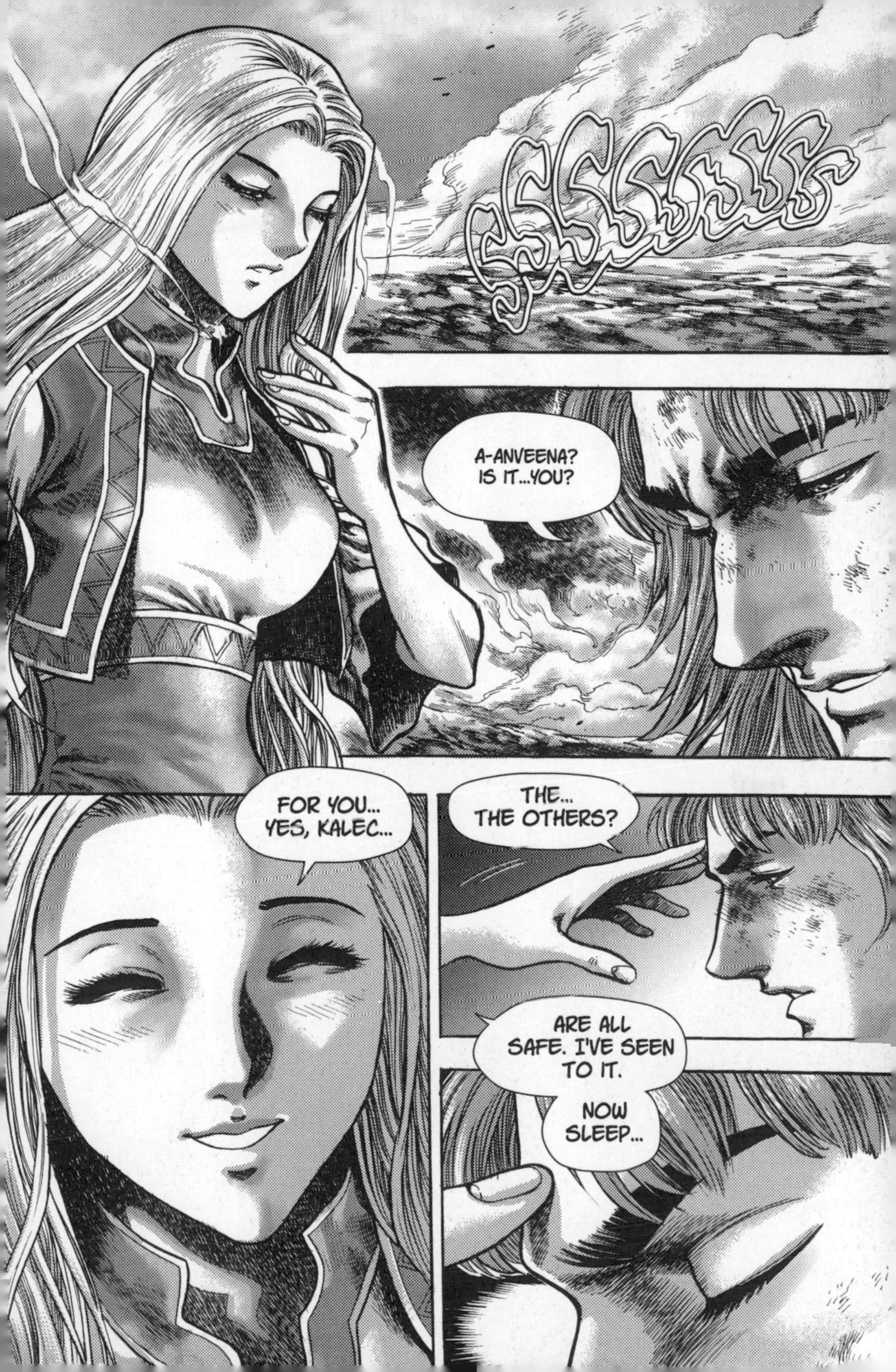
A-ANVEENA? IS IT...YOU?
FOR YOU... YES, KALEC...
THE... THE OTHERS?
ARE ALL SAFE. I'VE SEEN TO IT.
NOW SLEEP...

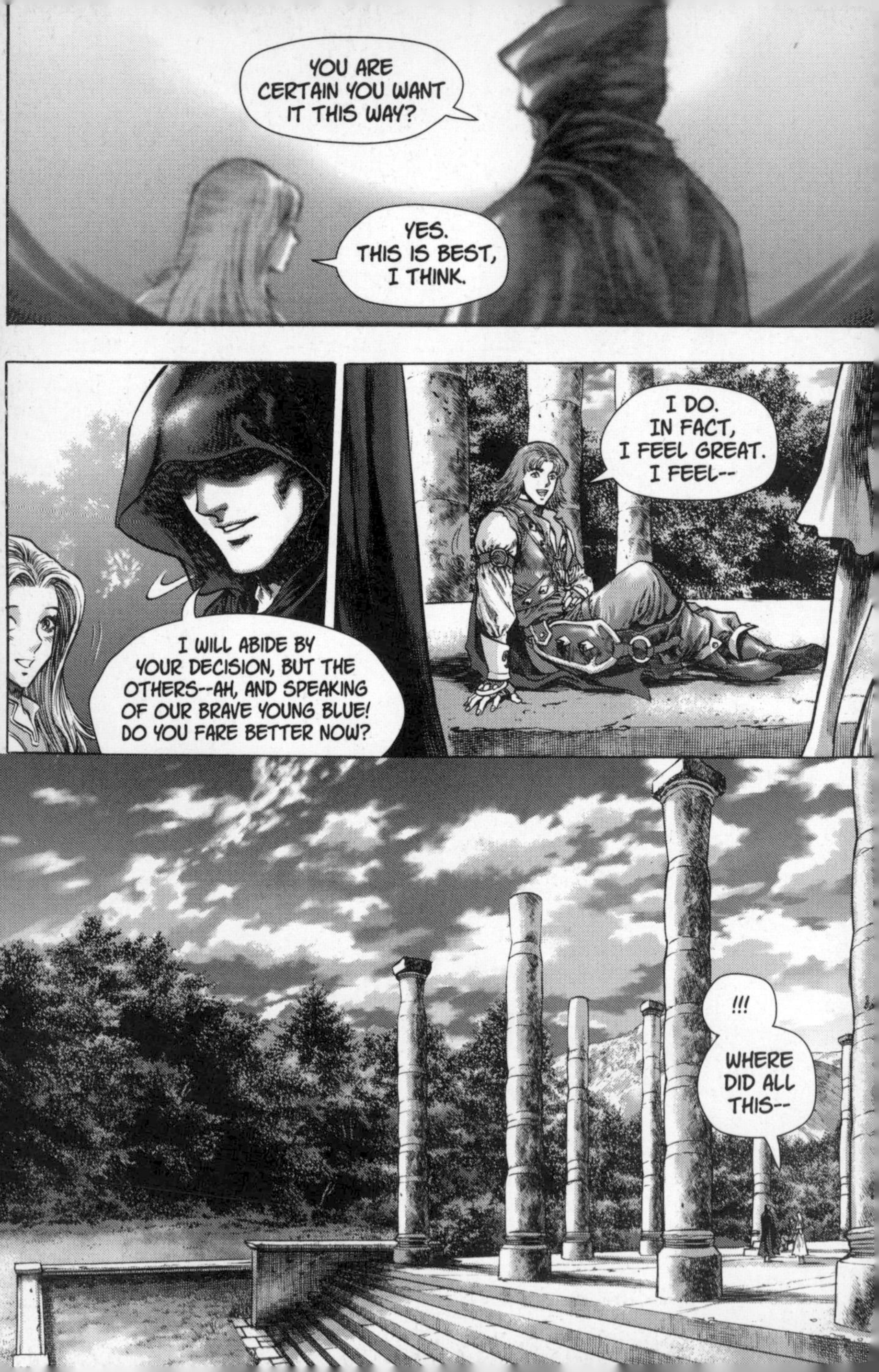
YOU ARE CERTAIN YOU WANT IT THIS WAY?
YES. THIS IS BEST, I THINK.
I WILL ABIDE BY YOUR DECISION, BUT THE OTHERS--AH, AND SPEAKING OF OUR BRAVE YOUNG BLUE! DO YOU FARE BETTER NOW?
I DO. IN FACT, I FEEL GREAT. I FEEL--
!!!
WHERE DID ALL THIS--

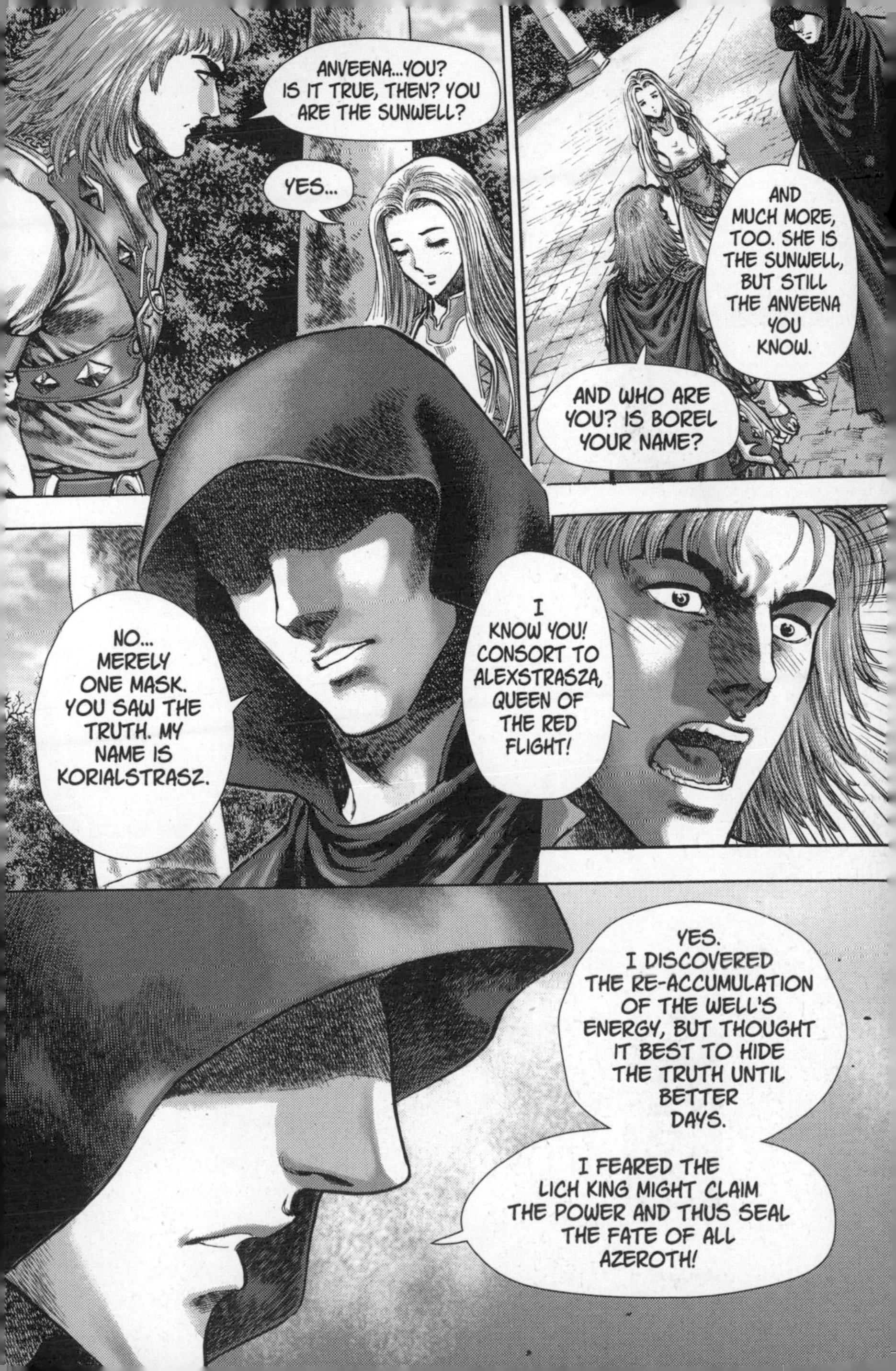
ANVEENA...YOU? IS IT TRUE, THEN? YOU ARE THE SUNWELL?
YES...
AND MUCH MORE, TOO. SHE IS THE SUNWELL, BUT STILL THE ANVEENA YOU KNOW.
AND WHO ARE YOU? IS BOREL YOUR NAME?
NO... MERELY ONE MASK. YOU SAW THE TRUTH. MY NAME IS KORIALSTRASZ.
I KNOW YOU! CONSORT TO ALEXSTRASZA, QUEEN OF THE RED FLIGHT!
YES. I DISCOVERED THE RE-ACCUMULATION OF THE WELL'S ENERGY, BUT THOUGHT IT BEST TO HIDE THE TRUTH UNTIL BETTER DAYS.
I FEARED THE LICH KING MIGHT CLAIM THE POWER AND THUS SEAL THE FATE OF ALL AZEROTH!

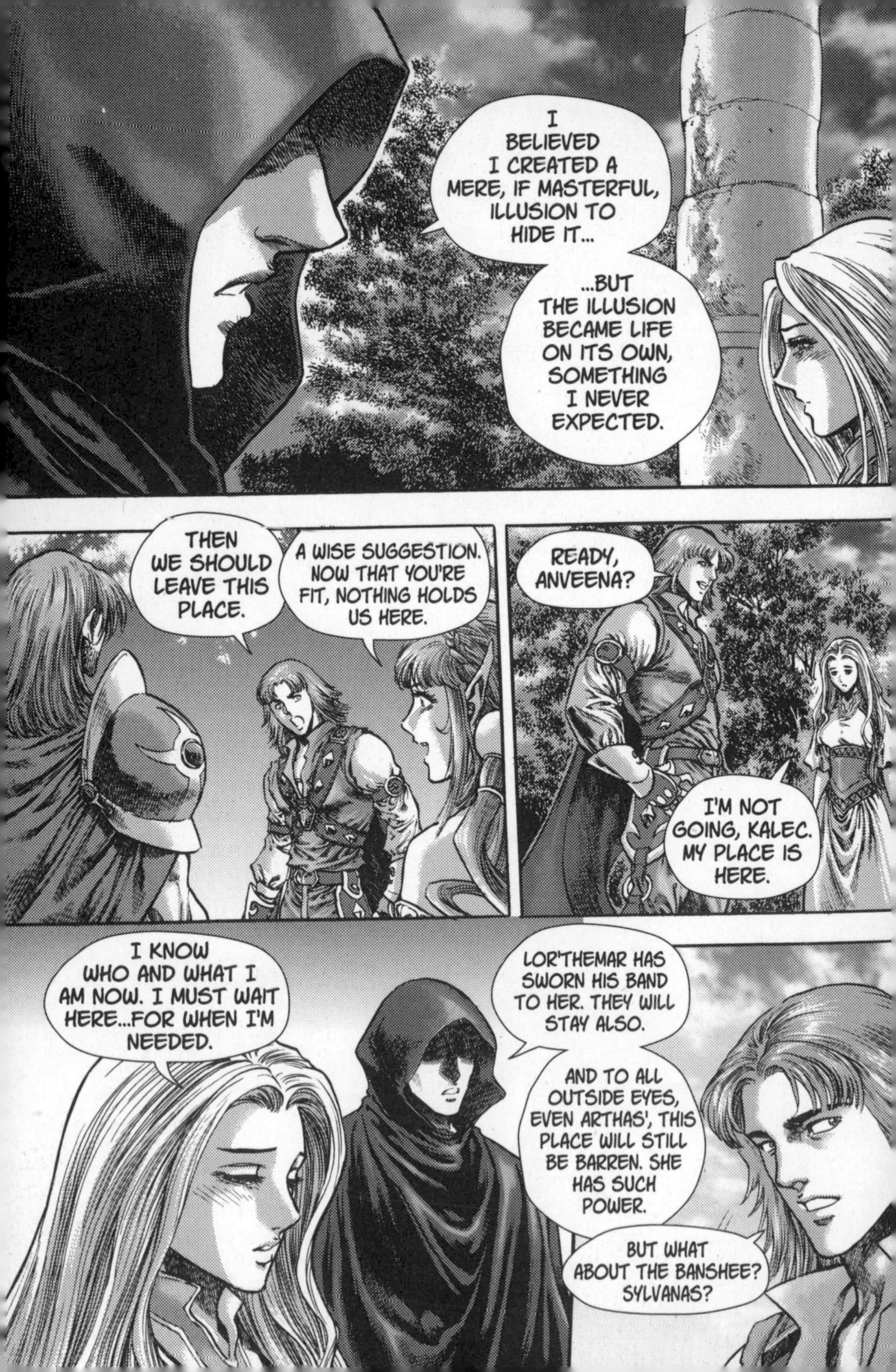
I BELIEVED I CREATED A MERE, IF MASTERFUL, ILLUSION TO HIDE IT...
...BUT THE ILLUSION BECAME LIFE ON ITS OWN, SOMETHING I NEVER EXPECTED.
THEN WE SHOULD LEAVE THIS PLACE.
A WISE SUGGESTION. NOW THAT YOU'RE FIT, NOTHING HOLDS US HERE.
READY, ANVEENA?
I'M NOT GOING, KALEC. MY PLACE IS HERE.
I KNOW WHO AND WHAT I AM NOW. I MUST WAIT HERE...FOR WHEN I'M NEEDED.
LOR'THEMAR HAS SWORN HIS BAND TO HER. THEY WILL STAY ALSO.
AND TO ALL OUTSIDE EYES, EVEN ARTHAS', THIS PLACE WILL STILL BE BARREN. SHE HAS SUCH POWER.
BUT WHAT ABOUT THE BANSHEE? SYLVANAS?

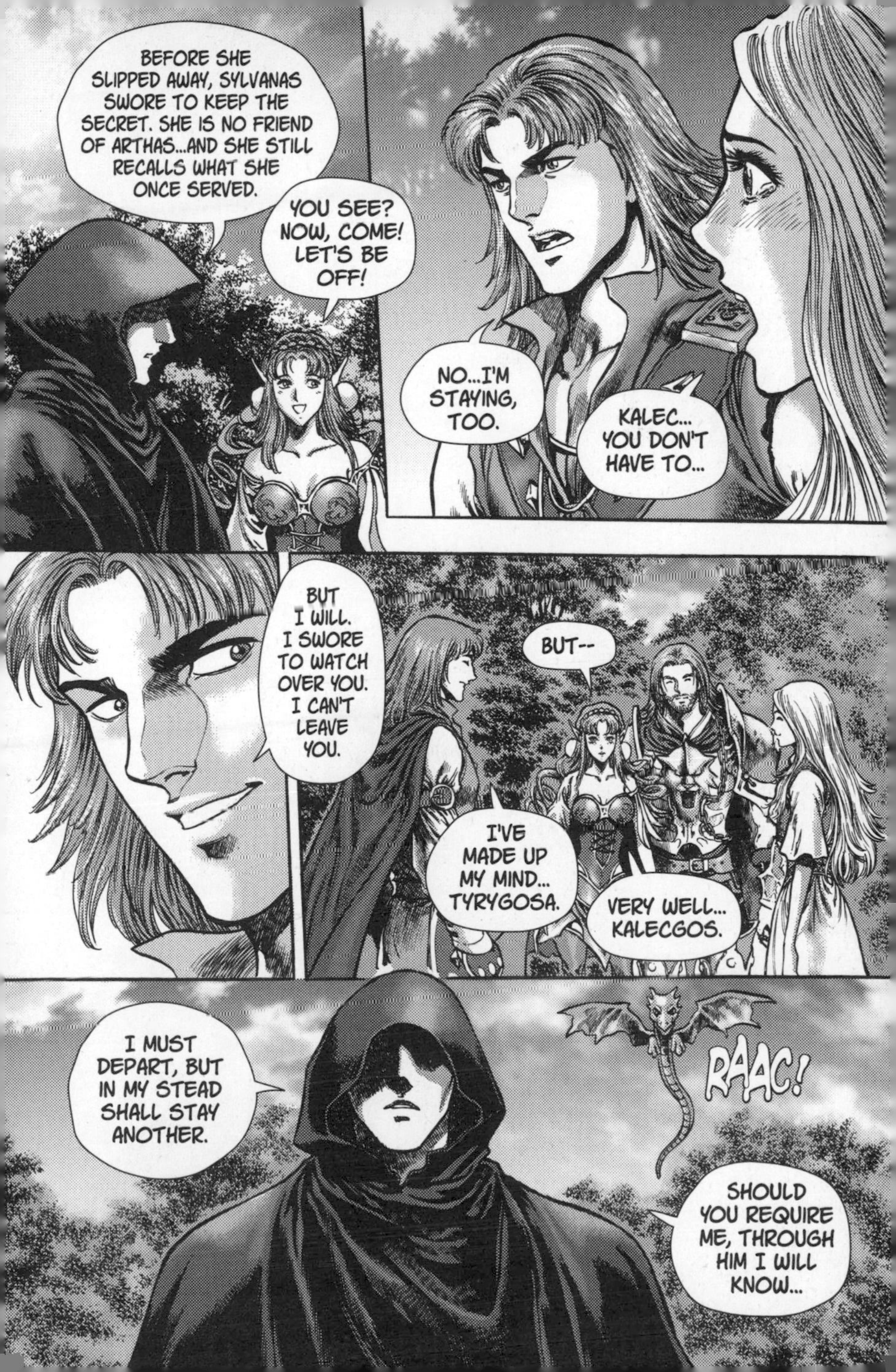
BEFORE SHE SLIPPED AWAY, SYLVANAS SWORE TO KEEP THE SECRET. SHE IS NO FRIEND OF ARTHAS...AND SHE STILL RECALLS WHAT SHE ONCE SERVED.
YOU SEE? NOW, COME! LET'S BE OFF!
NO...I'M STAYING, TOO.
KALEC... YOU DON'T HAVE TO...
BUT I WILL. I SWORE TO WATCH OVER YOU. I CAN'T LEAVE YOU.
BUT--
I'VE MADE UP MY MIND... TYRYGOSA.
VERY WELL... KALECGOS.
I MUST DEPART, BUT IN MY STEAD SHALL STAY ANOTHER.
RAAC!
SHOULD YOU REQUIRE ME, THROUGH HIM I WILL KNOW...

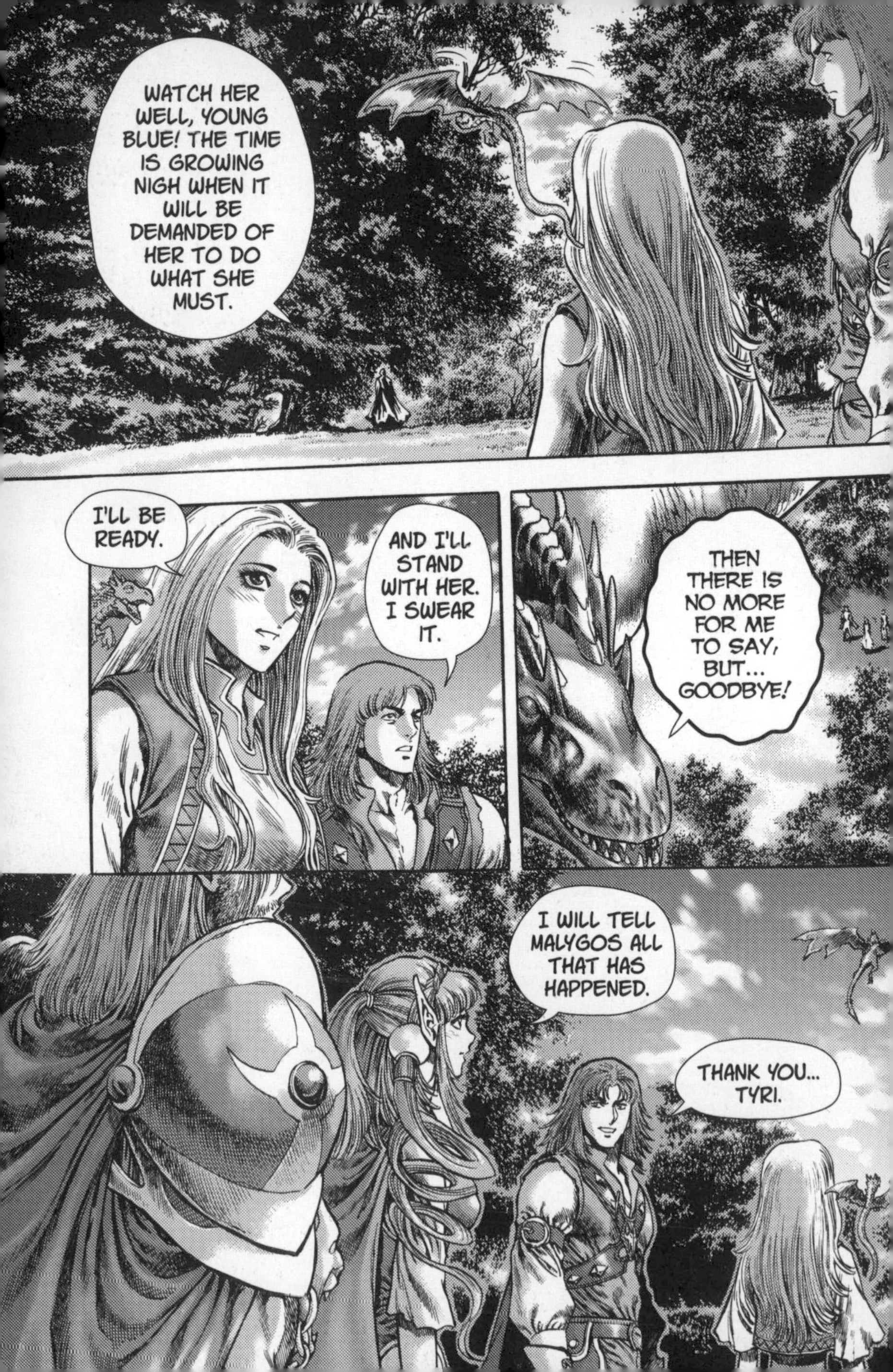
WATCH HER WELL, YOUNG BLUE! THE TIME IS GROWING NIGH WHEN IT WILL BE DEMANDED OF HER TO DO WHAT SHE MUST.
I'LL BE READY.
AND I'LL STAND WITH HER. I SWEAR IT.
THEN THERE IS NO MORE FOR ME TO SAY, BUT... GOODBYE!
I WILL TELL MALYGOS ALL THAT HAS HAPPENED.
THANK YOU... TYRI.

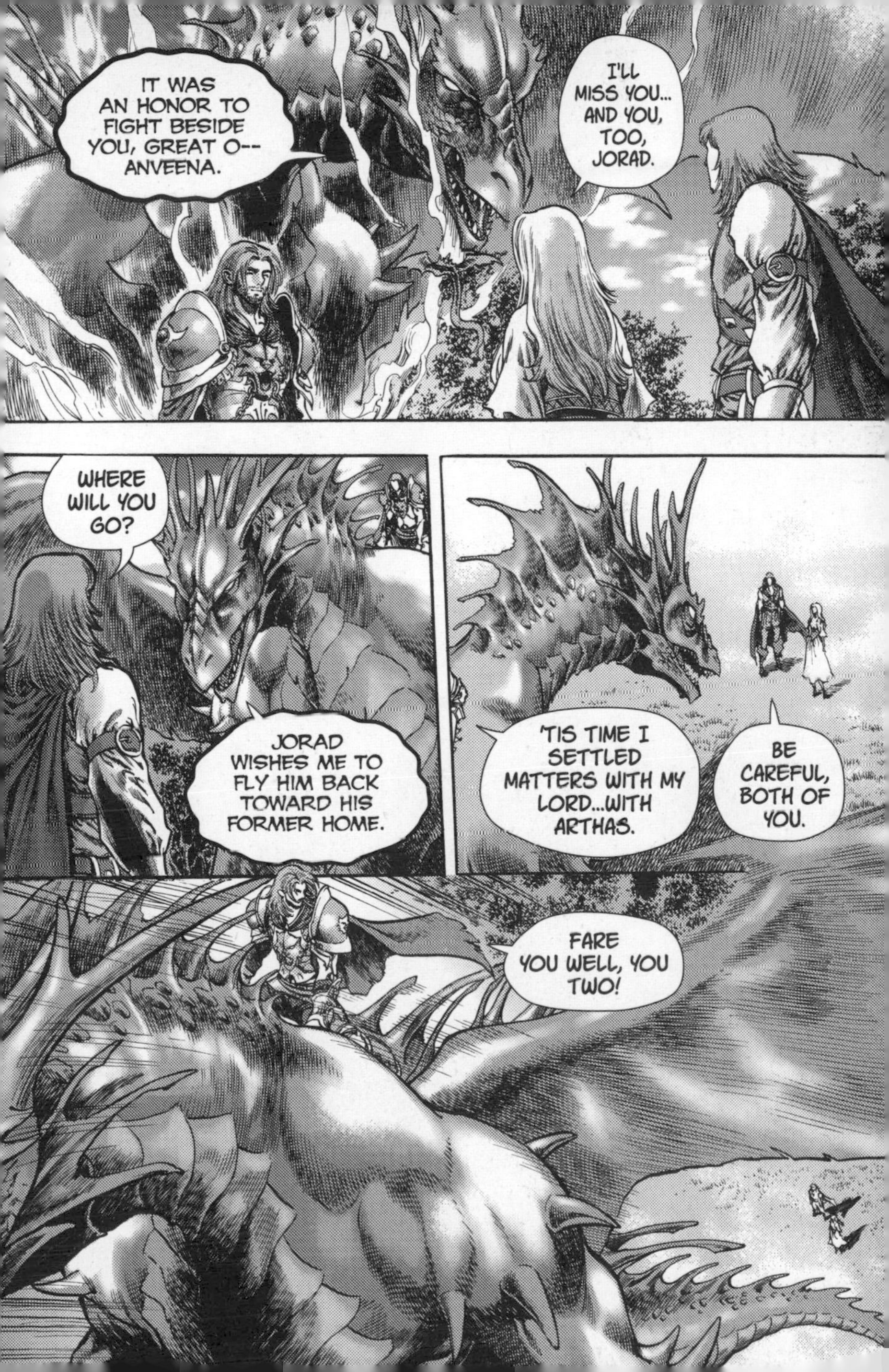
IT WAS AN HONOR TO FIGHT BESIDE YOU, GREAT O-- ANVEENA.
I'LL MISS YOU... AND YOU, TOO, JORAD.
WHERE WILL YOU GO?
JORAD WISHES ME TO FLY HIM BACK TOWARD HIS FORMER HOME.
'TIS TIME I SETTLED MATTERS WITH MY LORD...WITH ARTHAS.
BE CAREFUL, BOTH OF YOU.
FARE YOU WELL, YOU TWO!

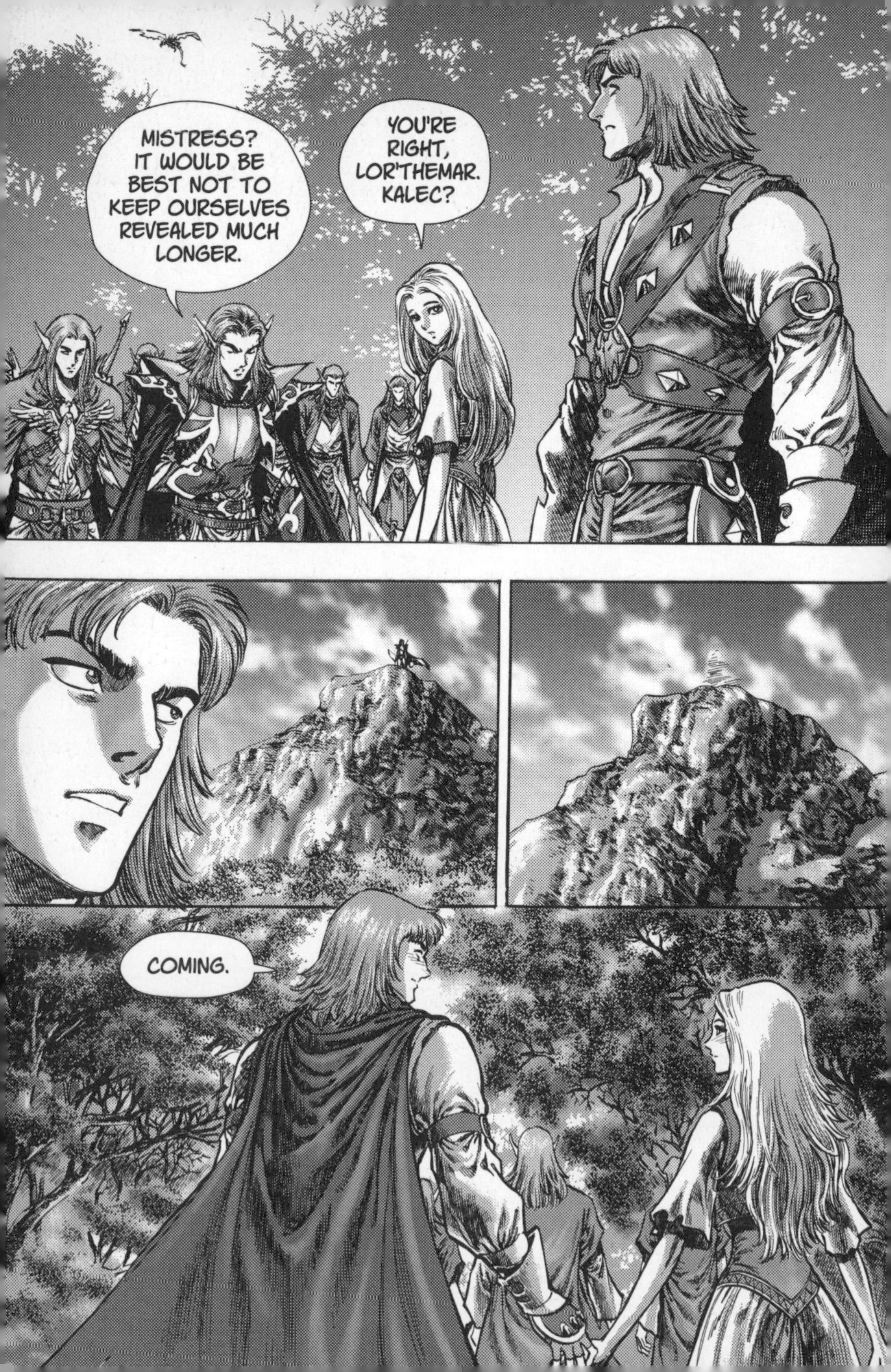
MISTRESS? IT WOULD BE BEST NOT TO KEEP OURSELVES REVEALED MUCH LONGER.
YOU'RE RIGHT, LOR'THEMAR. KALEC?
COMING.

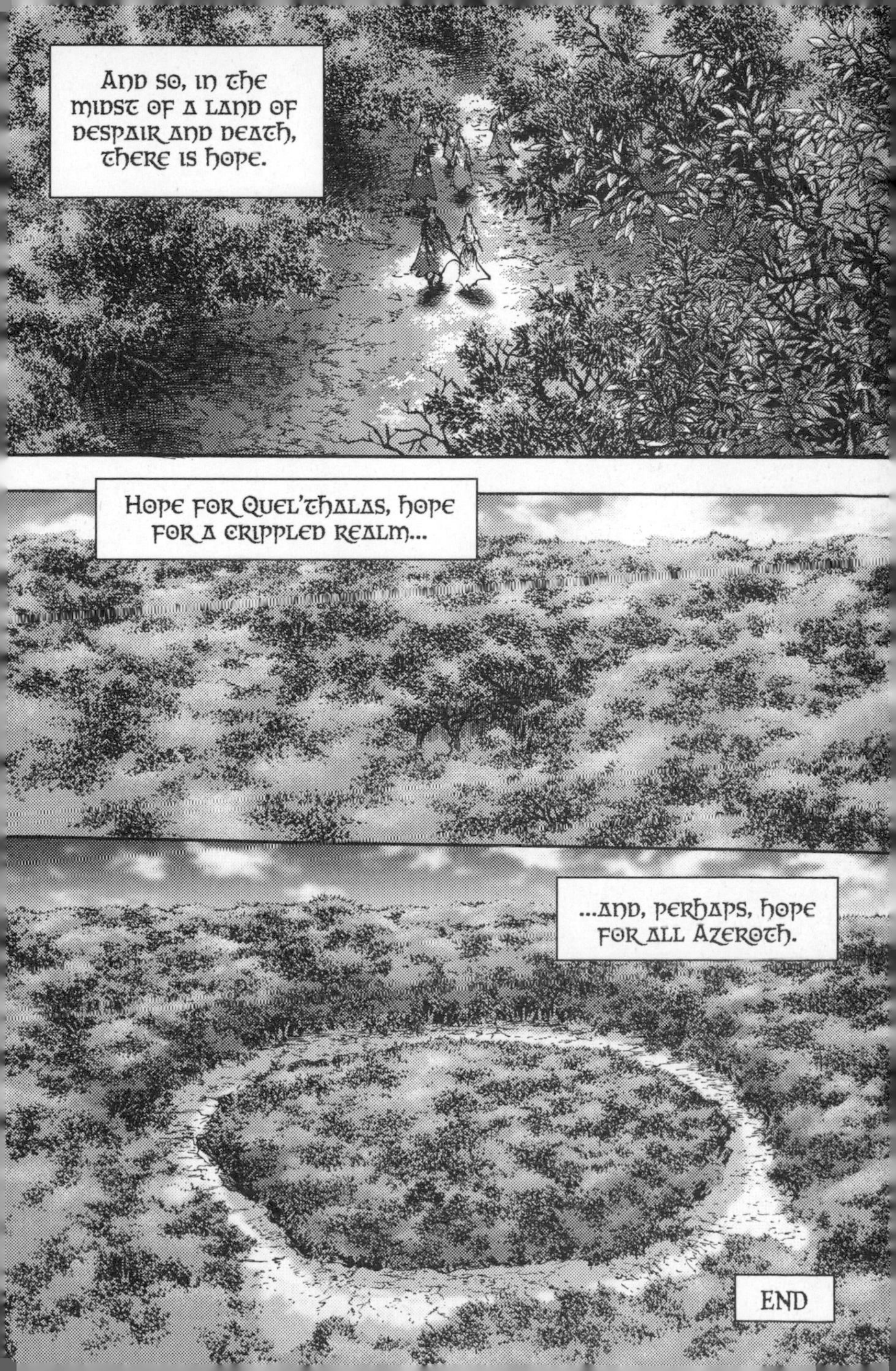
And so, in the midst of a land of despair and death, there is hope.
Hope for Quel'thalas, hope for a crippled realm...
...and, perhaps, hope for all Azeroth.
END

ABOUT THE

In addition to his work on *Warcraft: The Sunwell Trilogy* and *Ragnarok* (also by TOKYOPOP), Richard A. Knaak is the New York Times bestselling fantasy author of 27 novels and over a dozen short pieces, including *The Legend of Huma* and *Night of Blood* for Dragonlance and *The Demon Soul* for Warcraft. He has also written the popular Dragonrealm series and several independent pieces. His works have been published in several languages, most recently Russian, Turkish, Bulgarian, Chinese, Czech, German, and Spanish.

To find out more about Richard's projects or to join his e-mail list for announcements, visit his website at http://www.sff.net/people/knaak

CREATORS

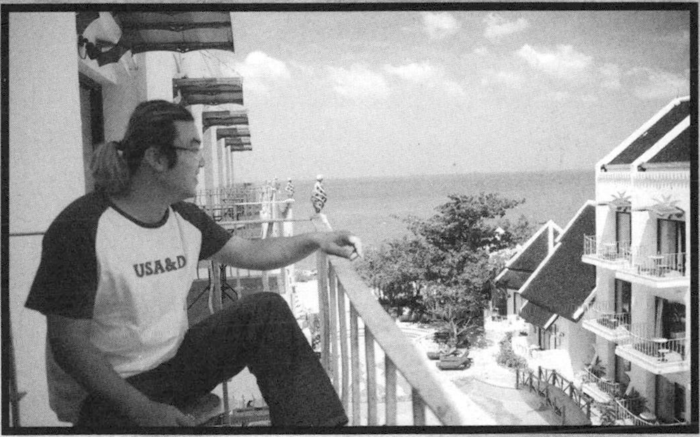
USA&D

Jae-Hwan Kim was born in 1971 in Korea. His credits include *Ducal*, *Combat Metal*, *Hae Mo Soo*, *Rainbow*, *Mech Destroyer*, *Green Tank Hae Mo Soo TV animation* (produced by KBS), and character designs for *Taengu and Oolashong*, *Max Man* and an Aerosmith music video.

In addition to *Warcraft: The Sunwell Trilogy*, Jae-Hwan is currently working on two additional series published by TOKYOPOP.

Those interested in more information about *Warcraft: The Sunwell Trilogy, or Jae-Hwan's other works should visit the* TOKYOPOP website: www.TOKYOPOP.com.

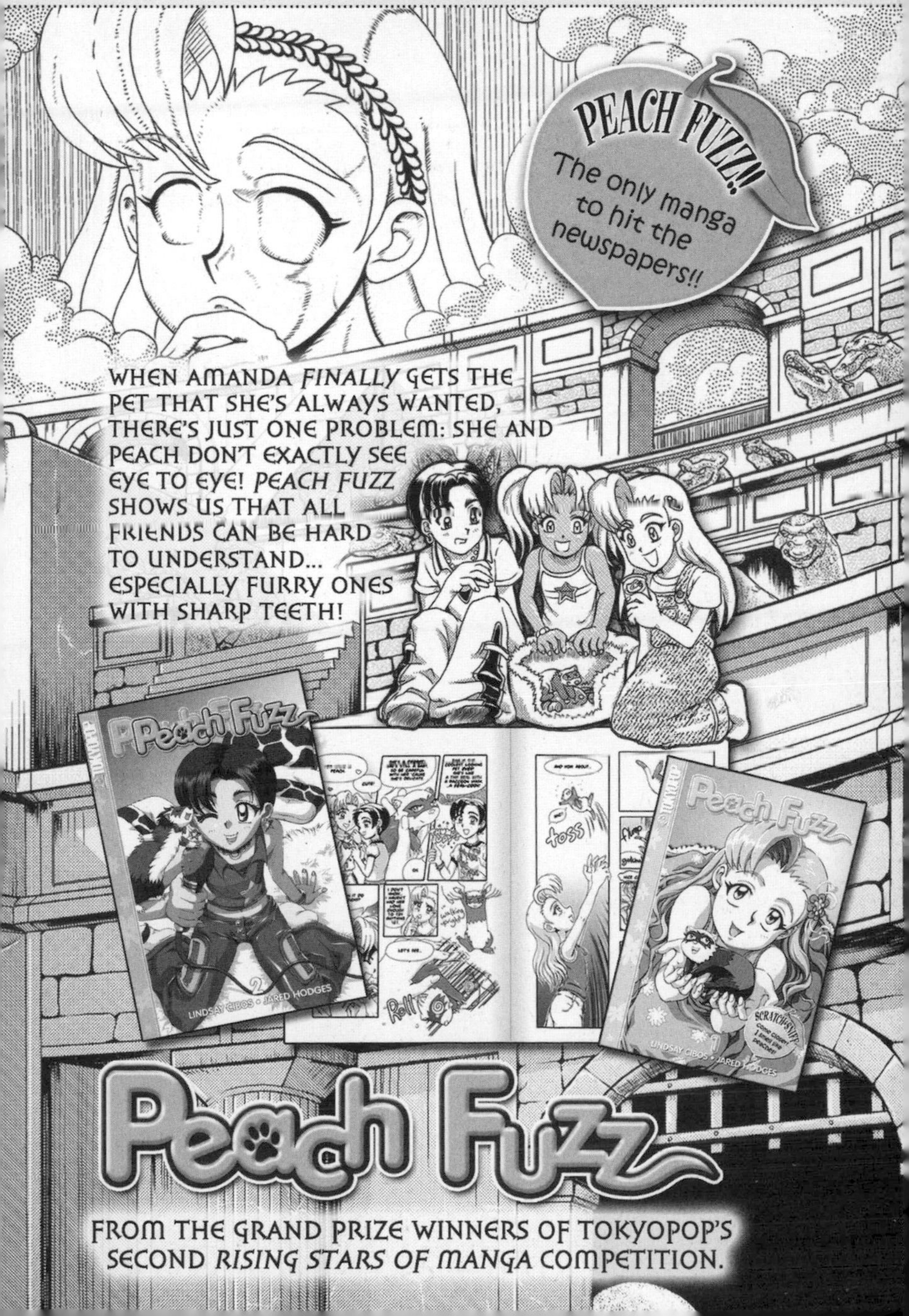
PEACH FUZZ!!
The only manga to hit the newspapers!!
WHEN AMANDA *FINALLY* GETS THE PET THAT SHE'S ALWAYS WANTED, THERE'S JUST ONE PROBLEM: SHE AND PEACH DON'T EXACTLY SEE EYE TO EYE! *PEACH FUZZ* SHOWS US THAT ALL FRIENDS CAN BE HARD TO UNDERSTAND... ESPECIALLY FURRY ONES WITH SHARP TEETH!
Peach Fuzz
LINDSAY CIBOS • JARED HODGES
Peach Fuzz
LINDSAY CIBOS • JARED HODGES
Peach Fuzz
FROM THE GRAND PRIZE WINNERS OF TOKYOPOP'S SECOND *RISING STARS OF MANGA* COMPETITION.

My name is Thrall. The word means "slave" in the human tongue, and the story behind the naming is a long one, best left for another time. By the grace of the spirits and the blood of heroes before me that runs in my veins, I have become Warchief of my people, the orcs, and the leader of a group of races known as the Horde. How this came to be, too, is another tale. The one I wish to set to parchment now, before those who lived it pass to dwell with the honorable ancestors, is the story of my father and those who believed in him; and of those who betrayed him and indeed, all our people.

What might have become of us had these events not unfolded, not even the wise shaman Drek'Thar can say. The paths of Fate are many and varied, and no sane being should ever venture down the deceptively pleasant one of "if only." What happened, happened; my people must shoulder both the shame and the glories of our choices.

This is the tale not of the Horde as it exists today, a loose organization of orc, tauren, forsaken, troll, and blood elf, but of the rise of the very first Horde. Its birth, like that of any infant, was marked by blood and pain, and its harsh cries for life meant death to its enemies.

For such a grim and violent tale, it begins peacefully enough, amid the rolling hills and valleys of a verdant land called Draenor. . . .

The heart-beat rhythm of the drums lulled the younger orcs to sleep, but Durotan of the Frostwolf clan was wide awake. He lay with the others on the hard-packed dirt floor of the sleeping tent. A generous padding of straw and a thick clefthoof pelt protected him from the chill of the bone-cold earth. Even so, he felt the vibrations of the drumming travel up through the earth and into his body, as his ears were caressed by the ancient sound. How he longed to go out and join them!

Durotan would have another summer before he would be able to participate in the *Om'riggor*, the rite of adulthood. Until that much-anticipated event, he would have to accept being shunted off with the children into this large group tent, while the adults sat around the fire and talked of things that were doubtless mysterious and significant.

He sighed and shifted on the pelt. It was not fair.

The orcs did not fight among themselves, but neither were they particularly sociable. Each clan kept to itself, with its own traditions, styles and manner of dress, stories, and shaman. There were even variations of dialect that differed so much that some orcs could not understand one another unless they spoke the common tongue. They almost seemed as different to one another as the other sentient race who shared the bounty of the field, forest, and streams, the blue-skinned, mysterious draenei. Only twice a year, spring and autumn, did all the orc clans come together as they were doing now, to honor that time when day and night were the same length.

The festival had officially started last night at moonrise, though orcs had been gathering at this spot for several days now. The Kosh'harg celebration had been held on this sacred spot in the land the orcs called Nagrand, "Land of Winds," which lay in the benevolent shadow of the "Mountain of Spirits," Oshu'gun, for as long as anyone could remember. While ritual challenges and combat were not unusual during the festival, true anger or violence had never erupted here. When tempers flared, as they sometimes did when so many were gathered together, the shaman encouraged the parties involved to work it out peaceably, or else they were to leave the holy area.

The land in this place was lush and fertile and calming. Durotan sometimes wondered if the land was tranquil because of the willingness of the orcs to bring peace to it, or if the orcs were peaceful because the land was so serene. He often wondered such things, and kept them to himself, for he heard no one else voicing such odd ideas.

Durotan sighed quietly, his thoughts racing, his heart thumping in answering rhythm to the voice of the drums outside. Last night had been wonderful, stirring Durotan's soul. When the Pale Lady cleared the dark line of trees, in Her waning phase but still bright enough to cast a powerful light that was reflected on the blankets of white snow, a cheer had gone up from the throat of every one of the thousands of orcs assembled—wise elders, warriors in their prime, even children held in their mother's strong arms. The wolves, both companions and mounts to the orcs, had joined in with exultant howls. The sound shivered along Durotan's veins as the drumming did now, a deep, primal cry of salutation to the white orb who commanded the night skies. Durotan had glanced around to behold a sea of powerful beings raising their brown hands, silvered in the light, to the Pale Lady, all with one focus. If any ogre had been foolish enough to attack, it would have fallen in a matter of heartbeats beneath the weapons of this vast sea of single-minded warriors.

Then had come feasting. Dozens of beasts had been slain earlier in the season, before the winter had set in, and dried and smoked in preparation for the event. Bonfires had been kindled, their warm light merging with the fey, white glow of the Lady, and the drumming had begun and had not stopped since.

He, like all the other children—lying on his clefthoof pelt, Durotan sniffed dismissively at the term—had been permitted to stay up until he had eaten his fill and the shaman had departed. The shaman of every clan left, once the opening feast had been consumed, to climb Oshu'gun, which stood careful watch over their festivities, enter its caverns, and be advised by the spirits and their ancestors.

Oshu'gun was impressive even from a distance. Unlike other mountains, which were irregular and rough in their shape, Oshu'-gun erupted from the ground with the precision and sharp point of a spearhead. It looked like a giant crystal set into the earth, so clean were its lines and so brightly did it glisten in the sun- and moonlight. Some legends told that it had fallen from the sky hundreds of years ago, and it was so unusual that Durotan thought those tales might be right.

Interesting though Oshu'gun might be, Durotan always thought it a bit unfair that the shaman had to stay there for the entire Kosh'harg festival. The poor shaman, he thought, missed all the fun. But then again, he suspected, so did the children.

During the day, there were hunts and game playing and retelling of the heroics of the ancestors. Each clan had its own stories, and so in addition to the familiar tales Durotan had heard as a youngling, there were new and exciting adventures to listen to.

Entertaining as these were, and as much as Durotan enjoyed them, he burned to know what the adults discussed after the children were drowsing in the sleeping tent, after their bellies were stretched full of good food and pipes had been smoked and various brews had been shared.

He could stand it no longer. Quietly, Durotan sat up, his ears straining for any sounds to indicate that anyone else was awake. He heard nothing, and after a long minute, he got to his feet and began to move slowly toward the entrance.

It was a long, slow progression in the darkened tent. Sleeping children of all ages and sizes were sprawled everywhere in the tent, and one wrong move could awaken them. His heart racing with excitement at his daring, Durotan stepped carefully between the only faintly glimpsed shapes, placing each large foot with the delicacy of the long-legged marsh birds.

It seemed to take an eternity before Durotan finally reached the flap. He stood, trying to calm his breathing, reached out—

And touched a large, smooth-skinned body standing right beside him. He jerked his hand back with a surprised hiss.

"What are you doing?" Durotan whispered.

"What are *you* doing?" the other orc shot back. Abruptly Durotan grinned at how foolish they sounded.

"Same thing you are," Durotan replied, his voice still soft. All about them, the others slept on. "We can either keep talking about it or do it."

Durotan could tell by the size of the faint shape in front of him that the orc was a large male, probably close to his own age. He couldn't place the scent or the voice, so it wasn't one of the Frostwolf clan. It was a daring thought—not only to do something so forbidden as to leave the sleeping tent without permission, but to do so in the company of an orc not of his own clan.

The other orc hesitated, the same thoughts no doubt running through his head. "Very well," he said at last. "Let's do it."

Durotan reached out again in the darkness, his fingers brushing the hide of the flap and curling around its edge. The two orc youths pulled back the flap and stepped out into the frosty night.

Durotan turned to look at his companion. The other orc was brawnier than he, and stood a bit taller. Durotan was the largest of his age in his clan, and unused to others being taller than he. It was a bit disquieting. His ally in mischief turned to look at him, and Durotan felt himself being assessed. The other nodded, apparently satisfied with what he saw.

They did not risk words. Durotan pointed to a large tree close to the tent, and silently the two headed for it. For a moment that was probably not as long as it felt, they were in the open, exposed to any adult who chose that instant to turn his head and see them, but they were not spotted. Durotan felt as exposed as if he were in bright sunlight, so powerful was the moon's glow reflected off the crystalline snow. And surely the sound of the snow squeaking beneath their feet was as loud as the bellow of an enraged ogre. At last they reached the tree and sank down behind it. Durotan's breath misted as he finally exhaled. The other orc turned to him and grinned.

"I am Orgrim, line of Telkar Doomhammer, of the Blackrock clan," the youth said in a proud whisper.

Durotan was impressed. While the Doomhammer line was not the line of a chieftain, it was well known and honored.

"I am Durotan, line of Garad, of the Frostwolf clan," Durotan replied. Now it was Orgrim's turn to react to the fact that he was sitting with the heir to another clan. He nodded approvingly.

For a moment they simply sat, reveling in the glory of their daring. Durotan began to feel the cold and wetness seep through his thick hide cape, and got to his feet. Again, he pointed at the gathering, and Orgrim nodded. They carefully peered around the tree, straining to listen. Surely now they would hear the mysteries for which they both hungered. Over the crackling sound of the huge bonfire and the deep, steady beating of the drums, voices floated to them.

"The shaman have been kept busy this winter with the fever," Durotan's father, Garad, said. He reached down and petted the huge white wolf who was drowsing by the fire. The beast, its white coat distinguishing it as a Frostwolf, made a soft crooning sound of pleasure. "Soon as one of the younglings gets cured, another falls ill."

"I am ready for spring, myself," another male said, standing and tossing another log on the fire. "It's been harsh with the animals, too. When we were preparing for the festival, we had a hard time finding clefthooves."

"Klaga makes a delicious soup from the bones, but she refuses to tell us what herbs she uses," a third said, glaring at a female who was nursing an infant. The female in question, presumably Klaga, chuckled.

"The only one who'll get that recipe is this little one when she comes of age," Klaga replied, and grinned.

Durotan's jaw dropped. He turned his head to stare at Orgrim, who wore a similar expression of stunned dismay. *This* was what was so important, so secret that the children were forbidden to leave the tent to listen to it? Discussions of fevers and soups?

In the bright light of the moon, Durotan had no trouble seeing Orgrim's face clearly. The other youth's brows drew together in a frown.

"You and I can come up with something more interesting than this, Durotan," he said in a low, gruff voice.

Durotan grinned and nodded. He was certain of it.

* * *

The festival lasted for two more days. During the daytime and at night, when the two would sneak out together, they challenged each other to different contests of skill. Racing, climbing, strength, sure-footedness—everything they could think of. And each defeated the other almost as if they had planned on taking turns. When, on the last day, Orgrim loudly called for a fifth challenge to break the stalemate, something inside Durotan made him speak.

"Let us not perform common, ordinary challenges," Durotan said, wondering where the words came from even as he uttered them. "Let us do something truly different in the history of our people."

Orgrim's bright gray eyes gleamed as he leaned forward. "What do you suggest?"

"Let us be friends, you and I."

Orgrim's heavily muscled jaw dropped. "But—we are not of the same clan!" he said, in a voice that indicated that Durotan might have proposed a friendship between the great black wolf and the mild talbuk.

Durotan waved a dismissive hand. "We are not enemies," he said. "Look around you. The clans come together twice a year and there is no harm in it."

"But . . . my father says it is precisely *because* we come together so seldom that the peace is kept," Orgrim continued. His brow knotted with concern.

Disappointment colored Durotan's words with bitterness. "Very well. I thought you braver than the others, Orgrim of the Doomhammer line, but you are no better than they—timid and shy and unwilling to see beyond what has always been done to what is possible."

The words had come from his heart, but had Durotan calculated them and honed them for weeks, he could not have chosen better. Orgrim's brown face flushed and his eyes snapped.

"I am no coward!" he snarled. "I back down from no challenge, you upstart Frostwolf!"

He sprang on Durotan then, knocking the smaller orc off his feet, and the two pummeled each other until the shaman needed to be brought in for healing and lecturing on the inappropriateness of fighting in a sacred space.

"Impetuous boy," scolded the head shaman of the Frostwolves, an ancient orc female they called "Mother" Kashur. "You are not too old to be beaten as a disobedient child, young Durotan!"

The shaman who tended Orgrim muttered similar displeased sounds. But even as blood streamed freely from his nose, and as he watched the shaman heal a wicked gash on Orgrim's brown torso, Durotan grinned. Orgrim caught his gaze and grinned back.

The challenge had begun, the final challenge, so much more important than races or lifting stones, and neither was willing to admit defeat . . . to say that a friendship between two youths of different clans was wrong. Durotan had a feeling that this particular challenge would end only when one of them was dead . . . and perhaps not even then.

SPOTLIGHT

TOKYOPOP MANGA SUPPLEMENT

THE DREAMING

BY QUEENIE CHAN

T
TEEN
AGE 13+

SU...
MAYBE IF I --
...AND WHAT'S BEHIND THAT DOOR ANYWAY?
!
WHAT THE--
TOKYOPOP
the dreaming
I
Queenie Chan
THE DORMS ARE ON THE SECOND FLOOR.
THIS WAY!
BATH-ROOM'S THAT WAY...
LIGHTS OUT AT TEN - BUT YOU CAN READ IN BED.
EVERY DORM ROOM HAS A NUMBER, AND 87--
IS YOUR ROOM NUMBER!

ALL OF THEM VANISHED...WITHOUT A TRACE.

When twin sisters Amber and Jeanie enroll in an Australian boarding school, they soon uncover a dark, unexplained secret: Students have been known to walk off into the surrounding bushlands, where they have vanished completely! Few know how the girls disappeared...fewer yet know why. Amber and Jeanie soon realize that the key to unlocking a secret that has been hidden for years may lie in the world of their dreams!

SUSPENSE-HORROR SHOJO FROM THE CREATOR OF THE HIT WEB COMIC *BLOCK 6.*

FOR MORE INFORMATION VISIT: WWW.TOKYOPOP.COM/THEDREAMING

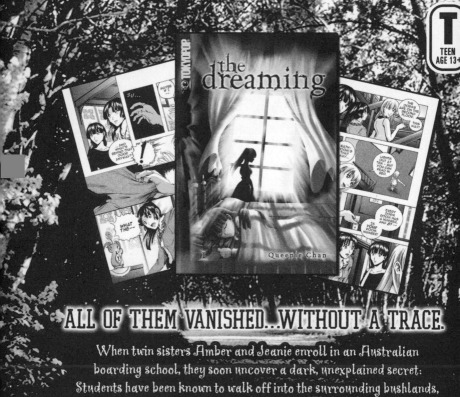

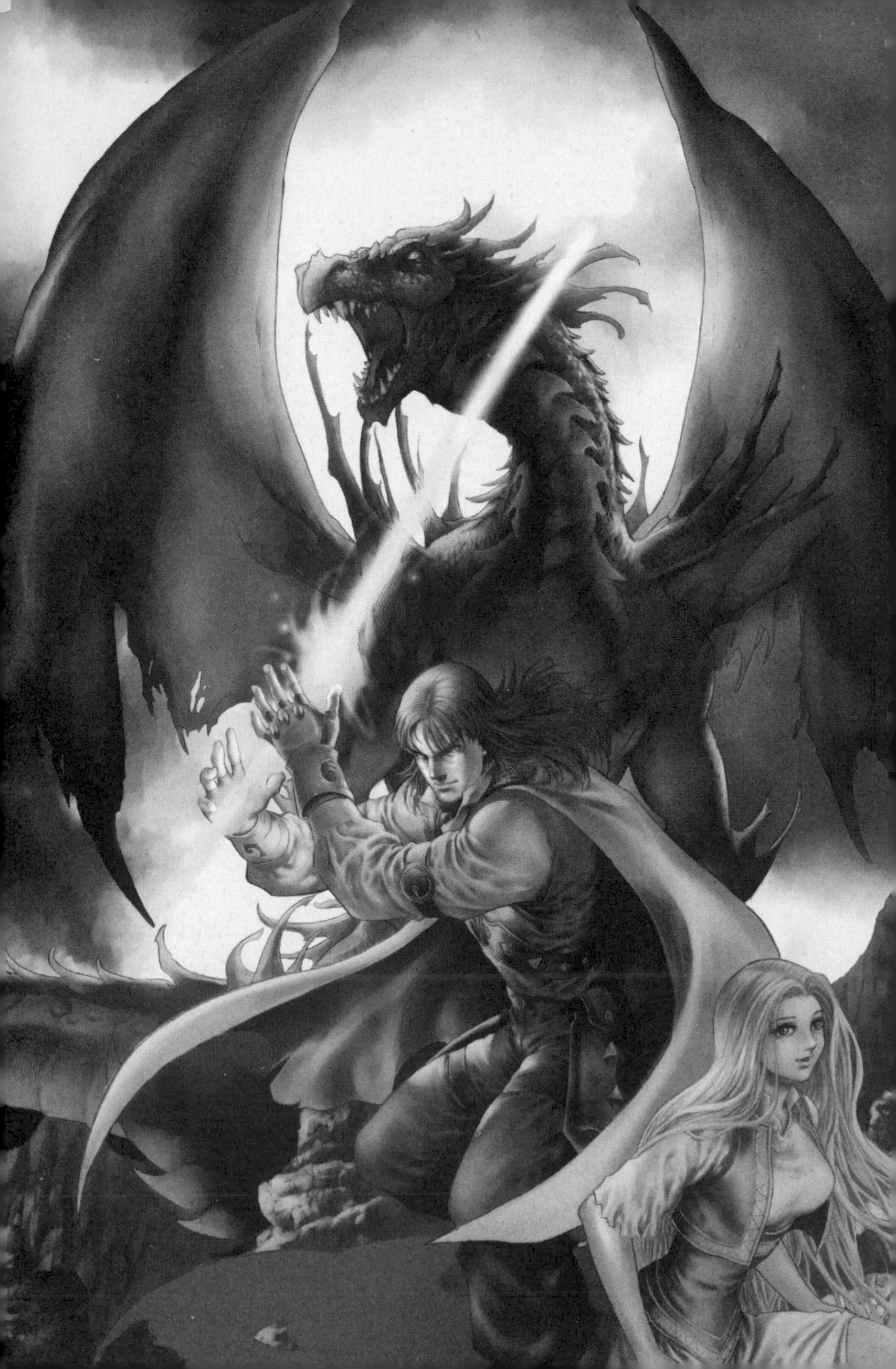

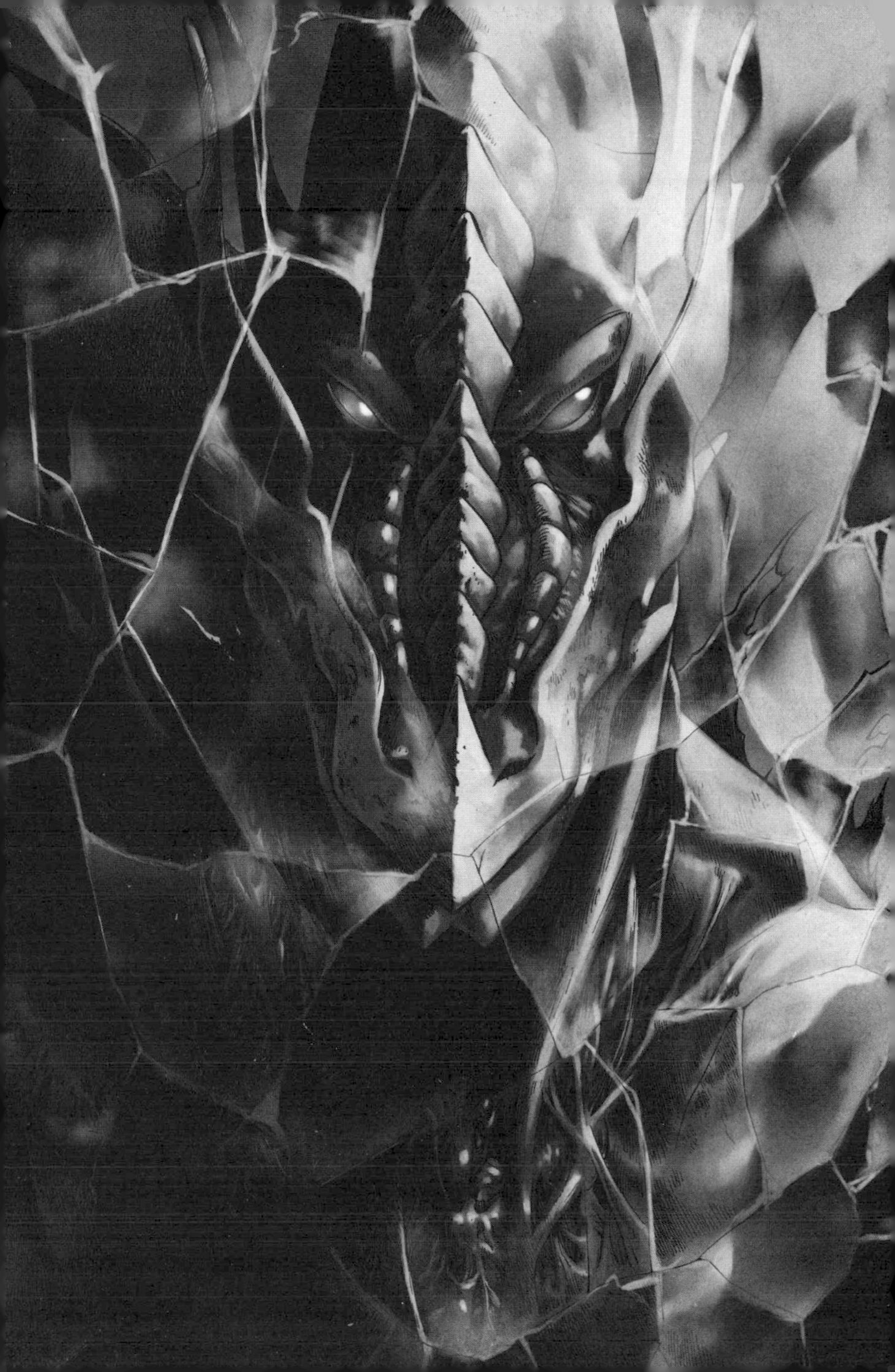

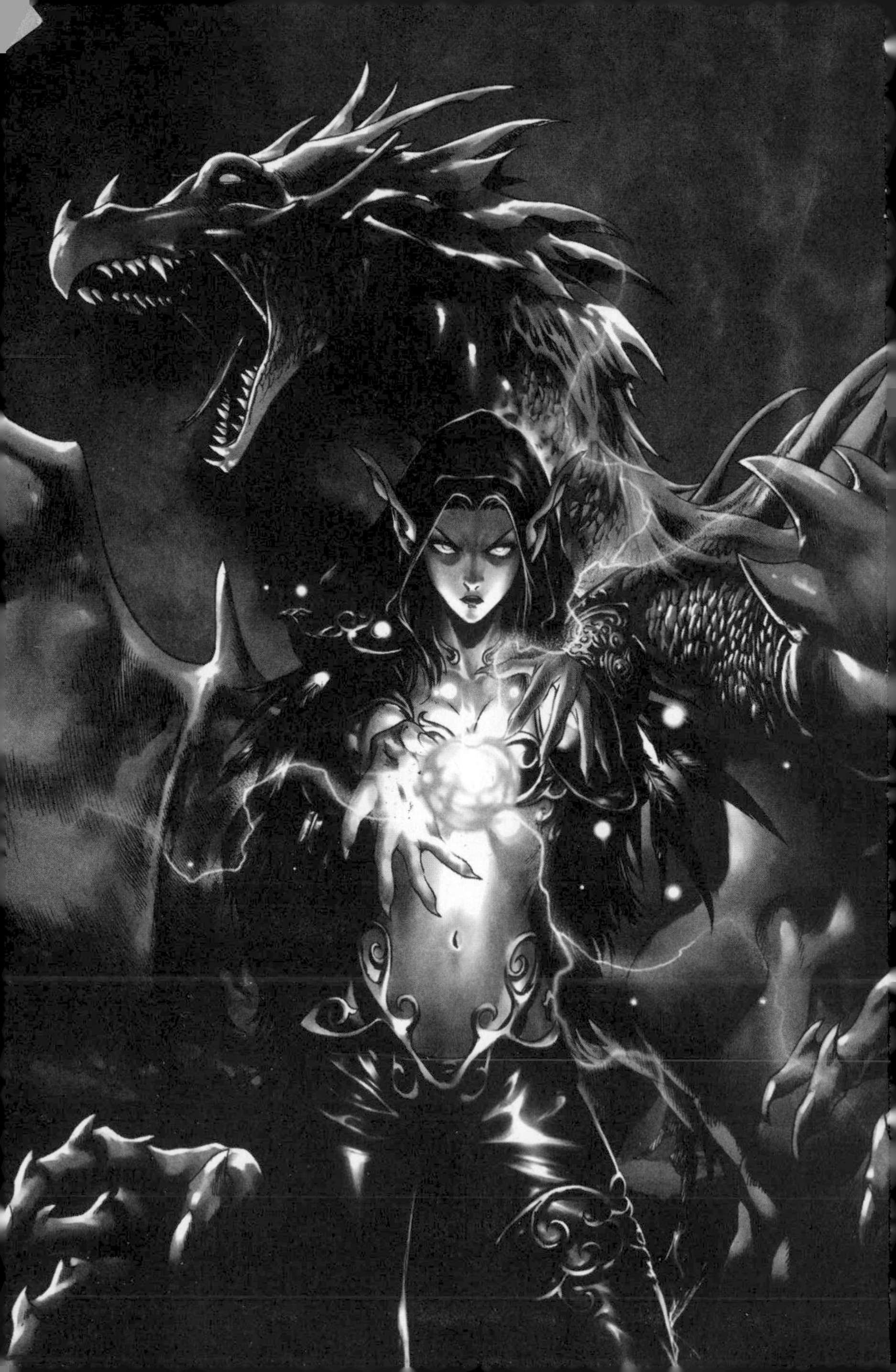